KU-401-612

THE GARDA SÍOCHÁNA

POLICING INDEPENDENT IRELAND
1922–82

Gregory Allen

GILL & MACMILLAN

Gill & Macmillan Ltd
Goldenbridge
Dublin 8
with associated companies throughout the world
www.gillmacmillan.ie
© Gregory Allen 1999

0 7171 2847 4

Index compiled by Helen Litton

Print origination by O'K Graphic Design, Dublin

Printed by MPG Books Limited, UK

This book is typeset in 10.5/13 pt Berkeley Book

All rights reserved. No part of this publication may be copied, reproduced or transmitted in any
form or by any means, without permission of the publishers.

1 3 5 4 2

CAVAN COUNTY LIBRARY
ACC No. C/181457
CLASS NO. 363.209417
INVOICE NO 6317HF
PRICE €19.99

For Mairéad,
who bore the heat of the day with me,
with abiding love and gratitude

Cavan County Library
Withdrawn Stock

CONTENTS

Acknowledgments   ix

Illustrations   xi

PART 1

  1. Constabulary, and Dutch Bobbies   3

  2. A Police Force for the New Ireland   7

  3. The Kildare Mutiny   31

  4. The New Police and the Civil War   49

  5. O'Duffy's Chivalrous Men of the World   73

  6. An Amiable and Attractive Man   97

  7. Making Room for Republicans   109

PART 2

  8. The Role of the Representative Body   121

  9. An Emphatic and Unequivocal Demand   131

  10. Interdepartmental Inquiry, 1950   140

  11. Straws in the Wind   155

  12. The Macushla Ballroom Affair   166

  13. The Inconsistency of Special Pay   179

  14. A Prophet Not Without Honour   191

  15. A Memorandum of Understanding   204

Appendix 1. Nominal Lists   218

Appendix 2. Barracks Attacked in the Civil War   226

Appendix 3. Selected Letters of Appreciation   228

Appendix 4. Roll of Honour, 1922–1996   231

Appendix 5. The Corrofin Hoax   234

Notes   236

Bibliography   287

Index   293

ACKNOWLEDGMENTS

T here is a kind of celebration in finishing my work on the history of the Garda Síochána fifty years after I discovered the National Library. As a young soldier interested in the national flag, I wrote my name in the readers' day-book for the first time. With that modest rite of passage I began a lifetime of abiding interest in scholarly inquiry, assisted by two generations of librarians and library assistants who were always painstaking in their advice and practical help to a neophyte. I recall especially the late Patrick O'Connor, senior library assistant, under whose guidance I took my first steps in historical research half a century ago.

The comrade of my army service, Séamas Ó Saothraí, FRSAI, in his gift of *A New Study of Police History* by Charles Reith (1956), was instrumental in revealing to me the philosophical dimension of my vocation as peace officer. In the providence of books, Reith's study of the roles of Charles Rowan and Richard Mayne in the creation of the New Police considerably widened my horizon and probably kindled my ambition to write the story of the Garda Síochána.

My employment as general secretary of the Representative Body for Inspectors and Sergeants (1965–67) exposed me to undercurrents of politics in negotiations on pay and conditions of service. The experience gave me unexpected insights into Garda history and was an invaluable preparation for my years of research that began in January 1980 in the old State Paper Office in Dublin Castle in the reign of Breandán Mac Giolla Choille. Using the splendid new facilities of the National Archives in Bishop Street, I found the same efficient and courteous service.

I acknowledge to the Director of the National Archives, the Archives Department, University College, Dublin, and the Mulcahy and O'Malley Trusts permission to use and make extracts from the various papers identified in my notes.

For support and encouragement in my work as Garda archivist I am indebted to Seán Sheehan, sometime assistant commissioner, research and planning, who assigned me to the archives project, and to the late Dr T. A. J. (Joe) Quigley, Garda Surgeon, who were never failing in their support as I pushed my horizons in a conservative milieu. I succeeded in gathering up substantial deposits of the surviving papers of the early decades of the force; working on my own, I was unable to undertake the classification of this valuable material.

My publisher, Fergal Tobin, knows that I might not have had the stamina to finish the course without his encouragement.

I am indebted to Inspector John Duffy, Garda archivist, who turned up many stones for me; and also to Séamus Helferty, archivist, University College, Dublin, and Commandant Peter Young, Military Archivist, Cathal Brugha Barracks. P. E. (Eamonn) Gunn, sometime chairman, and John Marrinan, general secretary, Representative Body for Guards, illuminated some mysteries. Tim O'Neill and Pádraic Ó Táilliúir offered valuable suggestions. Sister Mary Rose McCabe, Laurel Hill, Limerick, whose father, Sergeant Terence McCabe, bequeathed to his children an unbounded admiration for the Garda Síochána, was a source of friendly encouragement. Neighbours and former colleagues Tom Culhane and Pat O'Driscoll came to my rescue at different times when I was getting my lines crossed.

On my retirement in 1989, colleagues who gathered for my farewell party made me the gift of a word-processor, without which I doubt that I could have marshalled all the material in this book. My son Ultan, who was born into the electronic age, instructed me in the mysteries of my new keyboard.

I am especially grateful to Mairéad, who gave me her blessing as for lengthy periods I left her alone in her own retirement to pursue my research and to work at my desk at home.

LIST OF ILLUSTRATIONS

BETWEEN PAGES 84 AND 85

District Inspector Patrick Walsh, RIC, c. 1911

Sergeant Michael Duffy RIC and Mrs Duffy (Bridget McNamara, Cusheen, Co. Clare), c. 1906

Michael J. Staines, Quartermaster-General, Irish Volunteers, c. 1916

Assistant Commissioner Patrick Brennan, Civic Guard, showing the proposed Garda officer's uniform, modelled on the Army dress, Kildare, 1922.

John F. Maxwell, designer of the Garda badge

First printed version of the Garda badge, drawn by J. J. O'Reilly

Members of the Civic Guard at the funeral of Frank Lawless TD, Swords, Co. Dublin, April 1922

Michael J. Staines, Chief Superintendent Joe Ring and Superintendent D. J. Delaney, Kildare, summer 1922

Members of the Civic Guard Active Service Unit, Portarlington, August 1922

The occupation of Dublin Castle by the Civic Guard, August 1922

Mantel clock presented to Michael Staines, November 1922

Eoin O'Duffy, c. 1923, Garda Commissioner 1922–23

Civic Guard training staff on the evacuation of Kildare Depot, November 1922

The handing over of the Phoenix Park Depot to a national army contingent, December 1922

The first issue of Iris an Gharda, 26 February 1923

Sergeant John Beale, drill instructor, with recruits in the Phoenix Park Depot, January 1923

Training staff, Auxiliary Depot, McKee Barracks, Dublin, 1923

Phoenix Park Depot, 1923, including Chief Inspector John Tyrrell and Sergeant Patrick McAvinue

Garda cadet class, 1923, including Chief Superintendent J. J. Harrington and Senior Cadet P. J. Carroll

Garda James Mulroy, first recipient of the Walter Scott Medal for Valour, 1924

Members of the DMP armed with rifles in the wake of the 1916 Rising

Members of the DMP, c. 1922–25

Headquarters officers on amalgamation of the DMP and Garda Síochána, 1925

Kevin O'Higgins, Minister for Justice, unveiling a memorial plaque to murdered gardaí, 22 June 1927

Kevin O'Higgins, Minister for Justice, inspecting the Guard of Honour, DMP, Phoenix Park Depot, 1925.

James Fitzgerald Kenny, Minister for Justice, and Commissioner Eoin O'Duffy, Phoenix
    Park Depot, 1928
A parade of the Dublin Metropolitan Division, Dublin Castle, c. 1920
Illicit distillation equipment seized, c. 1930

BETWEEN PAGES 180 AND 181
Éamonn Broy, Garda Commissioner 1933–38
Garda motorcycle units, Dublin Castle, mid-1930s
Garda patrol cars, Dublin Castle, mid-1930s
M. J. Kinnane, Garda Commissioner 1938–51
Station party, Kanturk, Co. Cork, 1947
Recreation in a typical station day-room, 1940s
Chief Superintendent Patrick Carroll, Crime Branch, and Superintendent G. Lawlor,
    Technical Bureau, with a visiting Indian police officer, c. 1950
Superintendent Dan Stapleton and Detective-Garda F. P. McGrath, forensic laboratory,
    Technical Bureau, c. 1950
Daniel Costigan, Garda Commissioner 1952–65
Headquarters conference, 1954
Oscar Traynor, Minister for Justice, inspecting a guard of honour in Dublin Castle,
    c. 1959
Women gardaí: the first recruit class, 1959, with their instructor, Sergeant D. Prissick,
    Liverpool City Police
A group of visiting police officers at Garda Headquarters, c. 1960
Passing-out parade of recruits in the Phoenix Park Depot, c. 1960
The signing of the Garda Conciliation and Arbitration Scheme, 1959
The Representative Body for Guards, 1962
The Representative Body for Inspectors and Sergeants, 1965
The Garda badge, limestone medallion in granite by Michael Biggs, 1966, at Garda
    Headquarters
William P. Quinn, Garda Commissioner 1965–67
Patrick Carroll, Garda Commissioner 1967–68
Michael J. Wymes, Garda Commissioner 1968–73
Patrick Malone, Garda Commissioner 1973–75
The author as Garda archivist with P. J. Carroll and Assistant Commissioner Seán
    Sheehan, 1975
Edmund P. Garvey, Garda Commissioner 1975–78, with Assistant Commissioner J. M.
    McAleenan and Patrick Cooney, Minister for Justice, Templemore Training Centre,
    c. 1976
Patrick McLaughlin, Garda Commissioner 1978–83
Father Clarence Daly, C. P., Garda chaplain and peace-maker, 1956–83

PART 1

1

CONSTABULARY, AND DUTCH BOBBIES

The ramshackle system of unpaid parish constables and a night watch charged with keeping the peace in Dublin collapsed in the riots following the declaration of independence by the College Green parliament in 1782.[1] Under reforming legislation, in 1786 the city was provided with an organised police force. Membership was confined to Protestants; they wore uniform and were armed with muskets and bayonets.[2] Henry Grattan was unforgiving in his denunciation of a militia cast in the role of police: 'If ever a city entertained an odium capable of being ascertained by numerical calculation, the city of Dublin entertained such a hatred for this institution. No measure, no expense, no enormity of administration had ever excited discontent so strong or so general as this abominable establishment.'[3]

Rejected by the population, the 'abominable establishment' was replaced in 1795 with an unarmed Civic Guard under the supervision of the Lord Mayor and Corporation. Control by the local authority was short-lived, but the principle of unarmed police in the capital city survived as a benefit of Grattan's parliament to be enjoyed by the citizens of the modern Irish state. The unarmed Dublin Metropolitan Police, modelled on Robert Peel's New Police and the new philosophy of crime prevention, became the cornerstone of the formation of the Garda Síochána in 1922.[4]

British military patrols imposed a fragile peace in the provinces. As the Old Irish retreated, policemen as local petty officials appeared in the principal towns. The constabulary tradition began with the organisation of part-time police units in the baronies in the closing decades of the eighteenth century, who were paid an allowance of £20 a year. Selected from the least-qualified citizens, the barony police were untrained, and wore no uniform. According to one chief magistrate, Samuel Carter of Doneraile, the pioneer police constables were rendered helpless by 'feelings of partiality to their local connections and by a dread of becoming obnoxious to the disaffected.'[5]

The deployment of police in the baronies foreshadowed the formation in 1822 of a disciplined new force under county chief constables, with an inspector-general in each of the four provinces. As a more effective response to agrarian crime than Peel's Peace Preservation Force,[6] the County Constabulary inspired the last major reform fourteen years later when the provincial forces were centralised as the Irish Constabulary. The organising genius, Thomas Drummond, under-secretary in the Dublin Castle administration, made police reform his first priority. There is timeless wisdom, and a warning, in the political philosophy, especially apt in a police context, expressed in his letter to the magistrates of County Tipperary, who were demanding coercive measures to combat crime:

> Property has its duties as well as its rights; to the neglect of those duties in times past is mainly to be ascribed that diseased state of society in which … crimes take their rise, and it is not in the enactment or enforcement of statutes of extraordinary severity but chiefly in the better and more faithful performance of those duties, and the more enlightened and humane exercise of those rights, that a permanent remedy for such disorders is to be sought.[7]

Peel put his faith in an impartial police force as the key to peace in Ireland. From his desk at the Home Office he advised his successor in Ireland, Lord Francis Leveson Gower: 'I would certainly constitute that force in such a manner as to preclude all just objections to it on the score of partiality. I presume that at the present all party distinctions in the police are forbidden, all attendance at Orange lodges and so forth, and I think that the regulations in that respect … cannot be too scrupulously enforced …'[8]

Peel's advice was not followed; the regulations of the new police institutionalised what he sought to avoid. Constables were forbidden to join political or secret societies, but an exception was made of the oath-bound Society of Freemasons. This rule was written into the statutory oath taken by members of the RIC and DMP until the wording was changed as an indirect consequence of the 1916 Rising.[9] But within the ranks of the two police forces, Catholics—nationalist in political sentiment and Home Rulers to a man—and their Protestant and unionist colleagues worked contentedly in a common harness. Political debate was, of course, forbidden by regulation, strictly enforced.

Setting exemplary social and professional standards, the force exercised an extraordinary influence, contributing to the creation of an educated middle class in nineteenth-century Ireland. Springing from a people who were steeped in the folk memories of the penal days and the struggle for emancipation, the 75 per cent Catholic membership of the force set the education of their children as a first priority. Schooled by the teaching orders of the Catholic Church, notably the Christian Brothers, the children of RIC men became prominent in the professions and the public service.

In the close-knit organisation, the officers, representing the sophisticated Anglo-Irish ascendancy, influenced the rank and file in their ambition to climb the social ladder, with a consequential effect in Irish society. The officer class was burdened with some of the inherited defects of an aristocracy who had for generations regarded the native Irish as an inferior race. Joining the force as young cadets, they in turn were enlightened by the humility of their Catholic subordinates, to the benefit of society as a whole.

By the turn of the century, with the land question settled, the popular imagination was enlivened by the cultural renaissance, in literature, sport, the language revival, and the co-operative movement. The search for consensus on national identity found a sympathetic response among the officers of the RIC. In the eighteen-nineties, in a modest but significant gesture, dress uniform insignia indistinguishable from regimental patterns of the British army, dating from the formation of the County Constabulary, were discarded in favour of the cross and boss of Celtic art.

The policy of arming the police seemed to be justified by their rout of the Fenians in 1867, which won the 'Royal' accolade for the Irish Constabulary. In a period of peace up to the time of the Home Rule crisis in 1912, the RIC operated de facto as an unarmed force. But the ambiguity of their role determined their fate as casualties of peace, and in the War of Independence conservative policemen were thrown into the conflict alongside the British military. With the force ostracised by a decree of the First Dáil, the recruitment of undisciplined supernumeraries in England was the last straw, and morale was irretrievably broken.

The disarming of the Garda Síochána in 1922 enabled the government of the Irish Free State to proceed with the plan to amalgamate the two police forces long sought by the Irish Office in Whitehall, where the DMP as an unarmed force was perceived as an obstacle to the desired end.

The Dublin bobbies were cast in a different mould. A civil police force commanded by officers promoted, without exception, from the ranks, they had none of the paramilitary features that characterised the Constabulary.

The Garda Síochána, recruited as the Civic Guard, differed, it seemed, from the RIC only in titles and the colour of their uniform, the green giving way to 'a pleasing blue.' But the establishment of the Civic Guard under a native government brought about fundamental reform in an unarmed non-political force dedicated to the core principle of moral authority. The amalgamation of the two forces was accomplished in 1925.

The Police Organising Committee appointed by the Provisional Government in 1922 recommended the preservation of RIC records for use by the Civic Guard, unaware that the Inspector-General had ordered the destruction of papers other than Treasury records.[10] The RIC officers seconded by the Dublin Castle administration handed on ready-made structures that ensured the success of the new police. But the decision to destroy the old records copperfastened the Civic Guard as a new creation, already all but guaranteed by the recruitment of fresh young men from families that had traditionally given the RIC its best policemen.

Former members of the old police, out of proportion to their numbers—as few as 129 joined the Civic Guard—made a vital contribution to the reconstruction of the police service.[11] The overnight disappearance of the RIC from Irish life left a mistaken impression of the wholesale emigration of a disillusioned community. A mainly Protestant force regrouped in Northern Ireland as the Royal Ulster Constabulary; others felt they had to leave the country, younger men following the well-trodden trail of the Irish emigrant, out of a sense of adventure and to seek their fortunes abroad. Those who settled in the towns and villages where they had served were happy to advise their successors in the art of policing rural communities.[12]

I joined the Garda Síochána in the jubilee year of 1947. The anniversary passed without celebration. The founder-members who were still serving,[13] taciturn by nature, were reluctant to talk of their experience in securing the survival of the Irish Free State in the nineteen-twenties. It is sad to recall that the first generation in the force after years of neglect of their interests felt they had little to celebrate. Avid readers of the *Garda Review*, published monthly by the Joint Representative Body, were heartened by its trenchant criticism of conditions of service. Having read the leading article, they turned to the column 'Without Prejudice', contributed by Sergeant Patrick J. Gallagher, secretary of the JRB, and then to the Divisional Notes, contributed by local correspondents. In their company I absorbed a feeling for the history of the period they had helped to create. Within a few years they had all retired. When I was given the job of gathering up the history of the force for an archive and museum at Garda headquarters, most of my old comrades had gone to their reward.

2

A POLICE FORCE FOR THE NEW IRELAND

We do not want a casual Police Force without proper training. It is not necessary for me to illustrate this by pointing to the wretched Irish Republican Police System and to the awful personnel attracted to its ranks.

On Monday 16 January 1922, in the historic setting of Dublin Castle, the last of the English Viceroys, Lord FitzAlan, handed over the destiny of Ireland to Michael Collins, Chairman of the Provisional Government and Minister for Finance in both the government of transition and the cabinet of Dáil Éireann.

The Irish representatives included William T. Cosgrave, Minister for Local Government, distinguished by an air of gravity appropriate to the role of patriarch and prophet he was to play in the foundation of the Irish Free State, and the visionary Kevin O'Higgins, Minister for Economic Affairs, waiting in the wings to take over from Éamonn Duggan in Home Affairs. Duggan was already preoccupied with the increasingly urgent problem of raising a police force to replace the RIC, soon to be disbanded under the terms of the Anglo-Irish Treaty of 6 December 1921. The principals in the historic set-piece were accompanied by Patrick Hogan, Minister for Agriculture, Joe McGrath, Labour, Eoin MacNeill, Education, and Fionán Lynch, without portfolio. The founder of Sinn Féin and President of Dáil Éireann, Arthur Griffith, who was not a member of the Provisional Government, observed the culmination of his life's work from the sideline.[1]

The arrival of the Irish delegation was delayed, Collins having been held up by the mundane business of negotiating the settlement of a railway strike.[2] At one o'clock three taxis nosed their way through cheering crowds in Palace Street into the Castle. When the taxis drew up at the State Apartments in the Upper Castle Yard the unmistakable figure of the revolutionary leader, with a characteristic bound, was first to emerge, smiling and supremely self-confident.

Protocol was dispensed with; there were no guards of honour, no bands, no ceremonial lowering of the flag of the old enemy. The Viceroy was spared the indignity of hauling down the Union Jack by the simple expedient of an order to the guard commander not to hoist the flag at sunrise that morning, breaking a tradition of seven hundred years. The assembled pressmen duly noted the bare flagstaff on Bermingham Tower. Nor did the Irish leaders insist on the Tricolour being raised, if indeed the need for protocol crossed their minds. In the immediate aftermath of the Treaty debate, culminating in the tragic division in the Dáil on 7 January, the moment was hardly appropriate for national triumphalism.[3]

The Viceroy received Collins alone in the Privy Council chamber. The Irish leader announced to Lord FitzAlan the acceptance of the Treaty by the Dáil. When he passed the instrument of ratification across the table, the Viceroy formally surrendered to the Provisional Government the castle of Dublin, centre of foreign rule in Ireland since the reign of King John of England in the fourteenth century. Collins was unable to contain himself. The formalities over, he turned gleefully to Griffith: 'The Castle has fallen!'[4]

It was agreed that the State Apartments should be reserved for the temporary convenience of the old administration. A small garrison of the Royal Corps of Engineers remained on duty until 17 August, when the Castle was taken over by a contingent of a new unarmed police force. In the interval, and immediately after the transfer of power, headquarters for the Provisional Government were established in City Hall.

At 1:45 p.m. on the day of independence, Collins and his colleagues left the Castle in their taxis to renewed cheers from the crowds. Leaving quietly by the Cork Hill entrance, the former Viceroy was driven in a limousine through empty streets back to the Viceregal Lodge in the Phoenix Park.

The following day the Provisional Government reconvened in the Mansion House. The meeting was attended by Michael Staines, director of the Belfast Boycott in Robert Barton's Department of Economic Affairs in the Dáil cabinet.[5] The police crisis was on the agenda. Staines was present for the discussion, but only to report on his own brief. When Collins, with O'Higgins and Duggan, travelled to London at the weekend to settle details of the Treaty with officials of the Colonial Office he met the Unionist leader, Sir James Craig. In return for Craig's promise of protection for the Belfast Catholics who were under attack, Collins undertook to facilitate an end to the boycott; and this was done by decree of the Dáil on his return to Dublin on 24 January. Collins reported to his government colleagues that control of the unarmed DMP was to be transferred to the new Irish administration. The RIC was to be disbanded as soon as possible. With the Belfast Boycott called off, Staines gathered his papers and awaited assignment to an unexpected political role in the formation of a new police force.

A native of Newport, County Mayo, Michael Joseph Staines (1885–1955), a patriot and a born organiser, had committed himself wholly to the national cause, at first in the Gaelic League. In 1905, at the invitation of Arthur Griffith, he joined

Sinn Féin. He was in the Rotunda in November 1913 to hear MacNeill's call to arms; among the first to enlist in the Irish Volunteers, he was elected treasurer of the National Executive. As Quartermaster of the Dublin Brigade and staff officer to Patrick Pearse he fought in the GPO in the 1916 Rising.[6] His election as camp commandant of South Camp, Frongoch, admitted him to the councils of a wider circle of the revolutionaries; on release from internment he was elected to the Supreme Council of the IRB.[7] In the reorganisation of the Volunteers he was appointed Director of Equipment, then Quartermaster-General, both jobs bringing him into close contact with Michael Collins.[8]

Staines entered politics as an alderman of Dublin City Council. In the 1918 general election he won the seat in Dublin North-Central and was among the deputies not in prison who answered their names at the meeting of the First Dáil on 21 January 1919. He was involved in the organisation of the Dáil courts[9] and the national land arbitration courts, working closely with Kevin O'Sheil, a solicitor from Omagh, County Tyrone. He was to meet O'Sheil in less happy circumstances in the summer of 1922, when discipline in the nascent Civic Guard broke down and O'Sheil was appointed to head an inquiry.[10] On top of all his responsibilities as a member of the Dáil, Commissioner of the Civic Guard in a period of turmoil in the force, and an alderman, Staines somehow found time to act also as chairman of the joint committee of Grangegorman Mental Hospital.[11]

At the meeting of the Provisional Government on 17 January the director of the Belfast Boycott sat among the ministers as a figure of considerable stature and influence. Having made his report to the government on the progress of the boycott, he is not likely to have been drawn into the discussions on a long agenda, especially when Collins called item 12, on the police. Duggan reported that he had discussed the formation of a police force with General Richard Mulcahy, Minister for Defence in the Dáil cabinet.

THE IRISH REPUBLICAN POLICE

In June 1921 a general order confirmed the organisation of a police force called the Irish Republican Police, with Simon Donnelly as chief of police. In each brigade area a commandant was appointed to supervise local police officers attached to battalions and companies. Each company police officer selected four constables to serve the Dáil courts. Their duties included public order and the 'detection and punishment' of offenders. Arrests were made by warrant of a district or parish justice. Volunteers were required to co-operate closely with the Police 'in a spirit of true citizenship,'[12] not to 'interfere in civil matters' and to 'confine themselves rigidly to military duties.'[13]

Collins took a jaundiced view of the Republican Police. In August, in his role as commander-in-chief directing government forces in the Civil War, he considered a scheme for a 'popular organisation for the restoration of peace and security' submitted by Séamus Hughes, to operate in areas cleared by the national army. He had 'repeatedly asked for a … distribution of the Civic Guard in certain areas where in our judgement the Civic Guard could now operate,' Collins wrote impatiently to the acting chairman, W. T. Cosgrave.

> The nucleus must be the Civic Guard organisation … The matter is one on which we ought to hasten slowly. We do not want … a casual Police Force without proper training … It is not necessary for me to illustrate this by pointing to the wretched Irish Republican Police System and to the awful personnel … attracted to its ranks. The lack of construction and … control in this force have been responsible for many of the outrageous things which have occurred throughout Ireland.[14]

It seems that in early discussions the Provisional Government might have considered recruiting Simon Donnelly's men as regular police. The reorganisation of the IRP had already begun; an 'enthusiastic' Seán Lemass had accepted appointment as a training officer.[15] On 17 January, Duggan recommended that volunteers assigned to police duties should rejoin their units; pending the organisation of a regular police force, each Volunteer company was to assume responsibility for law and order in its own area. With these stop-gap measures in place he won approval for the employment of a trained police or military officer to organise a regular police force.

The matter was back on the agenda on 26 January, when, in an apparent contradiction, he was directed to submit draft proposals for 'a Volunteer Police Force'. In the Dáil on 28 February Duggan told Austin Stack, former Minister for Home Affairs in the Dáil cabinet, that the estimates for his department provided for payments to the Republican Police, which would continue to serve the people 'as in the past.'[16] Stack returned to the subject on 1 March. What steps were being taken, he asked, to give control of law and order to the Republican Police? Was there any truth in the rumour that the government was raising a police force other than the Republican Police? Duggan replied that the Volunteers in the Republican Police had returned to their units and that, as a temporary arrangement, the army was now responsible for police work.[17]

The 'rumour' was confirmed in a report in the *Irish Independent* on 7 March announcing the formation of the 'Garda Síochána or the Civic Guard.' It was understandable that the men Stack represented, who had been led to believe that they had made a valuable contribution as police in the national movement, should now feel let down. Later in the year, letters went out from the Dáil Police Department informing brigade police officers that their services were no longer required. An application form for the Civic Guard was enclosed, returnable to Captain P. Ennis, Chief of Police, based in Oriel House (33–34 Westland Row), Dublin.[18] It was expected that all useful IRP men would be absorbed into the Civic Guard.[19]

Some elements of the republican movement clung to an unreal ambition to supplant the Civic Guard. As late as 1932, in the euphoria of the Fianna Fáil victory in the general election, the IRA in Listowel marched to the local Garda station to celebrate the imminent arrival of the IRP.[20]

Duggan had been a popular Director of Intelligence. Having supervised the arrangements for the Truce, he had played a heroic part in the Treaty negotiations but was struggling with his brief in Home Affairs. On grounds of impracticability he may have felt himself unable to make the proposals for the 'Volunteer Police Force' called for by the Provisional Government. Considering the future of the Republican Police, on the one hand he was under pressure from the army and on the other harassed by the ambitions of Austin Stack. The no less urgent business of reconstituting the law courts must have been more attractive to the lawyer in Éamonn Duggan.

Behind the scenes Kevin O'Higgins met leaders of the national movement assembled in Dublin. He asked for the names of members of the RIC and DMP who were favourably disposed to the Provisional Government and would be willing to train a new police force. The dispensary medical officer at Letterkenny, Dr Joseph Patrick McGinley, a prominent Sinn Féin leader in County Donegal, named District Inspector Patrick Joseph Walsh of Letterkenny as a man of integrity and a pragmatic policeman who had succeeded in maintaining a delicate balance between his oath of office and his vocation as a guardian of the peace.

A PROFESSIONAL POLICE OFFICER

As the crowds were gathering in Dublin on 16 January for the formal inauguration of Irish self-government, District Inspector Walsh set off with an armed police detachment for the military base at Fort Dunree to provide an escort for explosives destined for the county council. The routine tour of duty occupied him until nightfall.[21] He was at his desk early the following morning, more from habit than necessity. By the spring of 1920 the RIC, under attack from local units of the Volunteers, had evacuated barracks in close on five hundred villages to regroup in the larger towns. In Walsh's Letterkenny command the barracks at Breenagh, Church Hill, Kilmacrenan and Manorcunningham had been abandoned; only the town of Letterkenny itself now had a garrison.[22] There was no correspondence of any significance in the locked leather-collared mail-bag delivered by his clerk. He attended to circulars from the County Inspector's office until the Dublin newspapers arrived.

A nationalist of the old school, Walsh had supported the moderate policies of the defeated Irish Party at Westminster. But, in common with many of his colleagues, he was not lacking in understanding of the breakdown in public order following the failure of constitutional politics, nor wanting in sympathy with the national aspirations of Dáil Éireann. He must have turned the pages of the *Irish Times* with quickening interest, reading of the 'tremendous event in Irish history' that had taken place in the capital the day before. As a professional policeman, he read with approval the agenda for the new administration urged by the paper. The Provisional Government had 'assumed great powers and great responsibilities ... Its first and most urgent duty is the restoration and maintenance of public order ...'

On the eve of the disbanding of the RIC, it was far from the thoughts of District Inspector Walsh that he was destined to play a major contribution in restoring peace. In the new Ireland, born in revolution, there seemed to be no future for a police officer who had sworn allegiance and given thirty years of loyal service to the Crown. At fifty years of age, with a young family, he did not welcome retirement on reduced pay, even though under the Treaty he was counting on enhanced pension rights.

The man who was to play a vital role in the reconstitution and reform of the RIC under a new name was born a farmer's son in 1871 at Carrickaduff, near Castleblayney, County Monaghan. On his first posting, in 1890, he was allocated to the command of the County Inspector at Tralee, who sent him to Lyracrumpane in the Stack Mountains. In that lonely outpost he spent his time well, studying for promotion. Making steady progress, in 1911 he was appointed district inspector, with all the professional and social status attaching to the rank.[23]

In Walsh's time the officers' mess was a preserve of the Anglo-Irish ascendancy class, to which a ranker of long service and exceptional ability might aspire. A career in the RIC, with the opportunity for appointment as a resident magistrate, settled the future of many of the younger sons of the landed gentry. They entered the service as young cadets to learn their trade under the tutelage of the utterly loyal and dependable head constables, who were father figures in the force. But one handicapped by age and length of service could not expect to advance beyond appointment as district inspector. 'If a constable by sheer worth became a district inspector, he was branded as a "ranker" ... Only by a miracle could a constable ever rise to the rank of County Inspector. By the time his elevation on seniority became due, he had reached the age of retirement ...'[24] But it was no mean achievement for the son of a small farmer in the Ireland of that period to have worked his way through the ranks to wear the officer's sword. Head Constable or 'Head' Walsh was now addressed in a familiar manner by the casual use of his surname and welcomed to table in the mess by the Inspector-General, Sir Neville Chamberlain.

As a newly promoted district inspector, his domestic life was disrupted by frequent transfer to any small town in Ireland where the presence of an experienced senior policeman was needed, and Walsh served in Killarney, Fermoy, Wicklow, Swanlinbar, Castlepollard, and Carrick-on-Shannon. He was posted to Letterkenny in 1919, the year of assembly of the First Dáil.

Walsh was an archetypal policeman in the rural Ireland of his day: in his family background, a farmer's son with a sound primary school education; in his standing in the conservative ranks of the RIC, highly respected by his peers as an ambitious man of steady, reliable character; and in his marriage at the mature age of thirty-seven to the daughter of a respectable burgher in a provincial town. In 1906 Sergeant Walsh had married Mary Frances Courtney, daughter of Cornelius Courtney, proprietor of Courtney's Hotel, College Street, Killarney. In 1922, as Walsh was preparing for the disbanding of the RIC, the ages of his six children ranged from fourteen to five.[25]

The remnants of the force, officers and men still serving, were informed in March that they were at liberty to join any other police force for which they had been accepted, including the Palestine gendarmerie.[26] Preliminary arrangements for formal disbanding on 31 March were notified by Deputy Inspector-General C. A. Walsh; all transfers were suspended, and leave was cancelled.[27]

On 15 March the office of the Chief Secretary informed the Cabinet in London that the disbanding of the RIC had been postponed, at the request of the Chairman of the Provisional Government.[28] Collins may have begun to regret the disbanding of the old police. If it had been politically possible he would have retained the RIC, shorn of its imperialist traditions and answerable to a native government, and concentrated on reform of the civil service;[29] instead the Constabulary was lost under the provisions of the Treaty, and the new state had to adapt as well it might to the colonial mentality of the remnants of the old administrators. The threat of anarchy increased, with murderous attacks by maverick Volunteers on the RIC still practically a daily occurrence.[30] Collins was probably already disillusioned at the failure of Duggan and Staines to make better progress in raising the new police force. But whatever his motive in calling for a delay in the disbanding, the die was cast for the RIC. The British government could not tamper with the Treaty, even if it had wished to throw Collins a lifeline.

The date on which Collins made his request to London was significant for another reason. A long-threatening split in the army, and moves by Austin Stack for recognition of the Republican Police, preoccupied the Provisional Government. A demand in January by Rory O'Connor and his supporters for an army convention was refused on 15 March. In defiance of the order, officers opposed to the Treaty met on 18 March and elected O'Connor to head an anti-Treaty Executive.[31] The mutinous officers demanded a stop to recruitment for the national army and the Civic Guard, describing the new police as a paramilitary force propping up the Provisional Government.

Collins may have contemplated some change in his plans for the Civic Guard. In any event, the obsequies for the RIC continued at demobilisation centres at Gormanston Camp and the military barracks in Mullingar. The force was formally disbanded on 31 March; District Inspector Walsh was discharged the following day. On 24 April, Major-General Emmet Dalton, Director of the Evacuation of British Forces, reported to the Department of Defence that the last RIC barracks in the provinces had been closed; Mullingar Barracks had been evacuated; and the stragglers were being discharged at Gormanston and at centres at Collinstown Aerodrome, Ship Street Barracks in Dublin, and the RIC depot in the Phoenix Park.[32]

In recommending Walsh to O'Higgins, Dr McGinley was motivated as much by personal considerations as by knowledge of a neighbour as police officer and family man. When a police patrol was ambushed and a young constable killed, Walsh saved Letterkenny from the fate that befell Balbriggan in similar circumstances. The Black and Tans quartered in Letterkenny Barracks were in a dangerous mood; Walsh refused to allow them out on the streets unless accompanied by disciplined regular police. In a biography of his father, Niall Mac Fhionnghaile gives an account of a raid on the McGinley home. Leading the raiding party, Walsh found Sinn Féin literature and some ammunition, not described but probably a handful of shotgun cartridges. He quickly put the damaging evidence out of sight, saving McGinley from arrest or a worse fate at the hands of the Black and Tans. In March 1968 Dr McGinley replied to Mother Joseph Magdalen (Una Walsh), Loreto Convent, Balbriggan, who had thanked him for a tribute to her father he had recently published in the *Irish Independent*. 'Your late father was one of the finest men I ever knew, and I owed him more than that letter in the *Independent*. Indeed, I have little doubt I owed him my life.'[33]

By 28 January 1922 Collins had taken the direction of police organisation into his own hands. On 3 February he wrote from his office in City Hall to P. Walsh Esq., D.I., RIC, Letterkenny:

> The Provisional Government are setting up a Committee for the purpose of drafting a scheme for the organisation of a new Police Force. Your name has been suggested to the Government for membership of this Committee and I shall be glad to learn whether you would be willing to serve. The first meeting of the Committee will be held at Room 85, Gresham Hotel, Dublin, on Thursday, 9th inst., at 7 o'clock p.m.
>
>   Micheál Ó Coileáin
>   Chairman of the Provisional Government.[34]

Duggan was directed to clear the attendance at committee meetings of the serving policemen who had agreed to work with the Provisional Government. On Tuesday 7 February, Walsh conscientiously made an appropriate record of duty in his office—the last entry in his official journal. The following day, with his clerk, Sergeant McCormack, he set out for Dublin. On 9 February, at six o'clock in the evening, Walsh and McCormack reported at RIC headquarters in Dublin Castle,[35] presumably to confirm the sanction for absence from their barracks arranged by Duggan, then made their way to the Gresham Hotel in O'Connell Street.

CONFERENCE IN THE GRESHAM HOTEL

On 28 January, Collins informed the Provisional Government that a Police Organising Committee was being formed; within a week Duggan announced that all the arrangements had been completed. When the committee assembled in the Gresham on the evening of 9 February, the attendance included the ubiquitous

Collins, accompanied by Duggan and Staines. The army Chief of Staff, General Eoin O'Duffy, who was to succeed Staines as Garda Commissioner, was also present, fired by a declared ambition to organise the new police. They were joined by a small group of Volunteer officers: Brigadier Michael J. Ring, West Mayo Active Service Unit; Colonel-Commandant Patrick Brennan TD, Meelick, County Clare, East Clare ASU; and Jeremiah Maher, a former sergeant in the RIC who had distinguished himself on active service in the War of Independence as intelligence officer with the First Eastern Division. A fourth Volunteer officer joined the committee later, Commandant Martin Lynch, brigade police officer, County Laois, whose name was put forward at the meeting of the Provisional Government on 10 February.[36]

The meeting was also attended by General Richard Mulcahy, Minister for Defence in the Dáil cabinet. Fully stretched as he was in the organisation of the national army, his presence among the policemen is surprising; but there was political sense in it.

On the nomination of Collins, Mulcahy and not Duggan took the chair. Mulcahy 'in general terms set out the lines which were to be followed in the formation of the new Force.'[37] There appears to be no record of what Mulcahy said in setting the guidelines, but his intentions may be gleaned from the organisation of the Civic Guard as it emerged in the early period, from February to May 1922: a lightly armed force on the lines of the RIC, distinguished from the old police by the colour of the uniform and by new insignia and new rank titles.

Having declared his preoccupation with army business, Mulcahy named Staines as acting chairman, which put the Westport man in place for elevation as Garda Commissioner, the 'obvious choice' for the job[38] and a disappointment for O'Duffy. The appointment of Staines was made over the heads of the professional policemen who were present, some of whom might have considered themselves better qualified. From among their number he was to select Walsh as his deputy, the 'trained police officer' anticipated in the minutes of the Provisional Government of 17 January. His neighbour from Westport, M. J. Ring, he named as depot commandant, with the rank of chief superintendent.

Ring perhaps was better placed than O'Duffy to have succeeded Staines as Commissioner in the aftermath of the Kildare Mutiny. Disgusted at squabbling in the Civic Guard, he resumed his military career and fought with government forces in the Civil War. On 14 September 1922, within days of O'Duffy's appointment, Ring was killed in an ambush at Bunnyconnellan near Ballina. The funeral was attended by a Civic Guard detachment, with Michael Staines among the mourners.

The policemen present at the meeting were all recommended as sympathetic to the Provisional Government. With Staines in charge, they worked into the small hours of 10 February. Later on the same day Duggan was able to report progress, with sub-committees already at work:

Organisation: District Inspector John Kearney, Boyle (chairman); Head Constable James Brennan, RIC Depot; Sergeant Michael McCormack, Letterkenny; Sergeant

John Galligan, Carrick-on-Shannon; Inspector Michael Kelly, DMP, Donnybrook.

Recruiting: Head Constable J. P. Foley, Musgrave Street, Belfast (chairman); ex-Sergeant Thomas J. McElligott; P. Shea, unidentified.

Training: Sergeant Edmund Prendeville, Clonmel (chairman); District Inspector Patrick Riordan, Cork; Sergeant Matthias McCarthy, Chichester Street, Belfast; Constable Thomas Neary, DMP, Kevin Street.

Conditions of service: District Inspector Thomas M'Gettrick, Howth (chairman); Sergeant Patrick Harte, County Inspector's office, Roscommon; ex-Sergeant Edward (Éamonn) Broy, DMP.

An additional sub-committee—McCormack, Harte, M'Gettrick, and Prendeville—was nominated to draft a finance code; there is no evidence that it produced a report. Riordan, M'Gettrick, Foley and Shea dropped out. The three high-ranking constabulary officers must have been professionally better qualified for advancement in the new police than the men of junior rank who were afterwards rapidly promoted; they may not have wished to count the Volunteer officers as colleagues or may have been unwilling to become embroiled in the political drama. In quitting the historical stage, Riordan and M'Gettrick and Head Constable Foley proved themselves wiser than their colleague District Inspector John Kearney, who was drummed out of the force in an unfortunate incident, as will be seen.

McElligott also resigned—according to his son, because he was disillusioned by manoeuvring in the committee for preferment in the new police.[39] Early in 1924 O'Duffy was informed by Home Affairs that an order excluding RIC men from membership of the Civic Guard would be relaxed in favour of those who had resigned or were dismissed because of nationalist sympathies. He was distinctly unhappy at the proposal because of the part 'men of this type' had taken in the Kildare Mutiny. In an accompanying list in January he identified former members of the Civic Guard who had been dismissed for misconduct, including a Michael McCormack, probably the Sergeant McCormack who accompanied Walsh from Letterkenny. McCormack was elected accounting officer on the proposal of McElligott and was afterwards appointed chief superintendent. O'Duffy also noted as undesirable Edward Tarpey, who was an associate of McElligott in the agitation for reform in the RIC and for recognition of the short-lived National Union of Police and Prison Officers, and 'especially T. J. McElligott.'[40]

A native of Duagh, Listowel, McElligott was an articulate propagandist for the rank and file in the RIC, protecting himself from official wrath behind the nom-de-guerre Pro Patria. Early in 1919, as chairman of the police union, he attended a conference in London. Proposing the disarming of the RIC, he succeeded in having a resolution adopted to that effect. Having lost his anonymity, he was forced to resign by the convenient stratagem of a transfer from Trim to the distant station of Belmullet, County Mayo.[41] In August the following year, as a free agent and still with influence among his former colleagues, he proposed an all-Ireland police conference to organise discontent in the RIC, supplying a list of sergeants and constables who were prepared to assist in the patriotic movement. He named Mathias McCarthy, J. P. Foley, Patrick Harte, John Galligan and Edmund Prendeville as members of an 'emergency committee', all of whom became McElligott's colleagues on the Police Organising Committee.[42] He resigned from the committee 'for reasons best known to himself,' O'Duffy informed Home Affairs.[43] McElligott afterwards took the anti-Treaty side in the Civil War. He was arrested following the discovery of letters outlining a plan for the disruption of the Civic Guard, and was interned.[44] Much respected by the rank and file in the RIC, he retained the lifelong friendship of Patrick Walsh.[45]

The members of the Police Organising Committee collectively have been described as agents of Michael Collins.[46] On the evidence, this was not true of Inspector Michael Kelly of the DMP. When Commissioner Sir Walter Edgeworth Johnstone, towards the end of 1922, recalled him to duty in his former station, O'Duffy eulogised Kelly's contribution in the formation and training of the Civic Guard and recommended him for 'a position of greater responsibility.'[47] Inspector Kelly retired from the DMP in his old rank early in 1924.

The role of the spy in the War of Independence is graphically described in the reminiscences of David Neligan, a detective-constable in G Division of the DMP with unrestricted access to Dublin Castle.[48] Éamonn Broy, as a clerk in the detective office in Brunswick Street,[49] Jeremiah Maher in the County Inspector's office in Naas and John Kearney in Boyle passed on to Collins information that was vital to the Volunteer war effort. As sergeant-clerk in Naas, Maher supplied Collins with an impression of the key to the safe in the County Inspector's office; a counterfeit key gave him access to the RIC cipher, which he copied and passed to Collins.[50]

District Inspector Kearney in Boyle supplied information to Patrick Delahunty, intelligence officer of the North Roscommon Brigade.[51] A cousin of Fionán Lynch, Matthias McCarthy 'became one of Collins's most useful agents.'[52] As delegate of the Munster sergeants on the RIC Representative Body, Edmund Prendeville was in London in 1921 for negotiations with Sir Hamar Greenwood on the future of the Irish police forces. There he made contact with 'Provisional Government representatives', which led to the invitation to join the Police Organising Committee.[53]

BLUEPRINT FOR A 'PEOPLE'S GUARD'

With the assistance of Walsh, Staines correlated the recommendations of the sub-committees and had a report ready for the meeting of the Provisional Government on 17 February.[54] He presented a blueprint for a 'People's Guard', 4,300 strong, organised in 21 divisions,[55] compared with about 7,000 RIC men who patrolled 29 divisions in the twenty-six counties, excluding the city of Dublin, based on deployments in 1914.[56] This optimistic estimate fell short of actual needs by about a thousand men. Station strengths were to be not less than five men, but it was expected that a system of village constables would evolve in peacetime. The uniform would be quite distinct from RIC dress, a cloth of Irish manufacture in a colour appealing to national sentiment. In recommending the preservation of RIC records for the use of the new police, the committee were obviously not aware that an order to destroy records was at that moment being carried out in every barracks abandoned by the departing RIC.[57]

The report recommended recruiting stations at each county headquarters, a Civic Guard officer in charge assisted by a local medical officer and a representative of the national army; and apparently for this purpose the committee immediately, on its own authority, employed a number of 'appointment officers' at £7 a week and 'assistant appointment officers' at £4 10s and travelling expenses.[58] In the selection of recruits, serving army personnel were to be preferred, then constables of the Republican Police, RIC men who had been dismissed or had resigned from conscientious or patriotic motives, the civilian population, and, lastly, members of the DMP and the RIC after disbanding. A report in the *Irish Independent* on 7 March put the national army and Republican Police in the first preferred category, followed as recommended by dismissed or resigned police constables, civilians, and the old police after disbanding. A central interview board of high-ranking Volunteer officers, two with police experience, and the Civic Guard surgeon would assist the depot commandant in making the final selections.

With more hope than economic sense, the committee recommended the very attractive rates of pay awarded in 1919 by a Viceregal commission on the Irish police forces headed by Lord Justice Ross.[59] These rates were immediately introduced but were cut back in the 1924 budget as the government came to grips with the disastrous state of the economy following the War of Independence and the recent Civil War.

The RIC representatives on the organising committee were all rank-and-file men whose service had been soured by a promotion system that had favoured the old aristocracy, perpetuating the class divisions in Irish society. It was predictable that they should recommend an end to privilege in the RIC officer cadet system; and they were supported by the Volunteer representatives. In the new police all promotions would come from the ranks, save that RIC men could expect promotion to 'ranks for which they were considered qualified, having regard to former career,' a recommendation that was to create difficulties immediately.

Critically, it was recommended that the force should be armed, a Webley revolver for each constable, to be carried on a leather waistbelt in the manner of the RIC. Brennan and other Volunteer officers were likely to have agreed. The reform of the police service in the most fundamental sense of its philosophy was to hinge on this recommendation.

The more urgent decisions were taken on 27 February. The recommendations on recruiting procedures and qualifications for recruits, and on conditions of service for sergeants and 'constables', were approved. The form of oath to be taken on attestation was also approved, based on the old formula but with the deletion of references to the Society of Freemasons.[60] The old police were forbidden to join or belong to political or secret societies, an exception being made for the Society of

Freemasons. This rule, with its waiver, was written into the oath taken by every member of the RIC and DMP until the wording was changed as an indirect consequence of the 1916 Rising. In practice the oath in its old form was not amended. As recommended by the Police Organising Committee, the text concluded with an undertaking not to join political or secret societies and specifically the Society of Freemasons.

If removal of the privilege hitherto enjoyed by the Freemasons satisfied the historical complaint of nationalists, the deletion of the ban on secret societies might have been helpful to Collins and the IRB. A form of the oath without the reference to secret societies was printed on the Civic Guard attestation form signed by each recruit in the period from February 1922 until the ban on secret societies was restored the following year; the attestation form was then amended.

The report of the Police Organising Committee in its entirety, including the recommendation on arming the force, was 'provisionally' approved on 3 March and put back for further consideration.

NAMING THE NEW POLICE

In the deliberations of a committee dominated by men of senior rank who represented the paramilitary tradition of the RIC, it is questionable whether Inspector Kelly, Neary and Broy adequately represented the DMP. They had a story to tell of a quite different tradition of community policing in Dublin. In the presence of a formidable team of self-confident district inspectors and head constables with their other tradition of a pretended social status above that of the humble Dublin bobby, it may be asked whether Kelly and his comrades demanded to be heard on their own professional experience, despite the tribute from O'Duffy that accompanied Inspector Kelly on his return to duty in Donnybrook.[61]

The recommended name for the new force lacked the felicity of phrase that the historic moment demanded; but if the prosaic title People's Guard was unlikely to appeal to popular imagination, the name decided by the Provisional Government, Civic Guard, was hardly an apt description of the role of a largely provincial police.[62] Duggan and O'Higgins, and notably the Minister for Education, Professor MacNeill, may have had thoughts of their own. The meeting of the Provisional Government on 27 February, at which the matter was decided, was attended by Arthur Griffith, journalist and historian, present to make representations for a constituent. His knowledge of the history of Ireland in the eighteenth century, especially the work of the College Green parliament, was unchallenged. In the naming of the new police it is probable that Griffith was inspired by Henry Grattan's passionate interest in police reform and the creation of the unarmed Civic Guard in Dublin in 1795.

In the search for a title for the new force, the Provisional Government seems to have been intent on grafting onto an organisation borrowed from the RIC the philosophy of the unarmed DMP. In the discussion of the report presented by Staines on 27 February, among all those present Griffith was uniquely informed to suggest for the new police a name redolent of history. The restoration of Grattan's parliament was the central aim of his life's work. He believed that the crucial goal of political independence transcended desirable cultural programmes; a title in Irish may have seemed less important than a symbolic link with the College Green parliament.[63]

To Collins and his ministers 'Civic Guard' must have seemed an inappropriate title for a mainly rural police force. The inspired title in Irish, meaning 'Guard of the Peace', by which the new police were destined to be known appeared for the first time in the *Irish Independent* of 7 March: an announcement of the formation of a police force to be called 'the Garda Síochána or Civic Guard'. The definitive title did not appear in the report of the Police Organising Committee. Considering the Government decision of 27 February, someone clearly was determined to force the issue of the name.

As a contribution of far-reaching significance to Irish police history, the name was suggested apparently by one of the constabulary representatives on the organising committee. According to Mathias McCarthy, writing in the *Garda Review* several years later, it was he who suggested the Irish title.[64] There is a ring of truth in McCarthy's claim, which was never contradicted. The vocational description 'peace officer' or 'guardian of the peace' was familiar to McCarthy as a benign definition of the role of the RIC. But the credit was given to McCarthy's colleague Michael Ring by J. J. Hughes, a founder-member of the force who worked throughout his service in various offices at Garda headquarters.[65]

As a member of the Gaelic League, Staines would have been attracted by the title in Irish. Whoever made the suggestion, it was Staines who ran with it, acting on his own initiative or having informally consulted Duggan and perhaps other ministers. Collins, O'Higgins and most of their colleagues were bound to have deferred to the founder of Sinn Féin, out of respect if not in sympathy with Griffith's obsession with history. There may have been agreement on the description *Garda Síochána na hÉireann* as a legend on the badge.

Staines would not have been slow to seek the advice of the Celtic scholar Eoin McNeill. He was out of office towards the end of 1922 when the need arose for an equivalent in Irish of *Hue and Cry*, the official publication of criminal activities circulated to police stations. At the suggestion of Deputy Commissioner Éamonn Coogan, Superintendent Jeremiah O'Shea turned for advice to the Minister for Education, who offered the perfect solution in *Fógra Tóra*.[66]

THE GARDA BADGE

There is no record of formal sanction for the Garda badge. The design was decided and settled before the civil servants in the Department of Home Affairs began to tighten their grip on the force.[67] The only recorded decision on police insignia affected the DMP, a recommendation in July 1922 in the name of Ernest Blythe and approved by the Provisional Government that features in the coat of arms of Dublin be substituted for the crown in the insignia of the force.[68]

A photograph of the new Garda badge appeared in the *Irish Independent* on 18 August, the caption stating that a competition had been held and that John Francis (Seán) Maxwell, an art teacher in Dún Laoghaire and Blackrock Technical Schools, had submitted the winning design. It appears, however, that Staines commissioned the design and ordered the badge on his own authority. Maxwell was a personal friend, both members of the Blackhall branch of the Gaelic League.[69] Presenting the report of the organising committee on 17 February, he expected delivery of 'some police uniforms ... in three weeks, and 1,000 ... in five weeks'[70]—an impressive demonstration of his organising ability. The blue uniforms may have been delivered on time but they were not issued until August, when a Civic Guard detachment was dressed for the funeral of Arthur Griffith.

By April 1923 the Garda badge had become a familiar symbol of government in the Irish Free State. The badge was criticised in the Department of Home Affairs when the Commissioner sought financial sanction for the casting of metal station plaques.[71] If the civil servants had had their way, a nondescript device would have been adopted, negating Staines's idealism, and, when O'Duffy took command of the force, would have made his unique appeal to esprit de corps less effective.

In the early months of independence Staines was given a free hand, and he made his own decisions within the framework of his committee's proposals. The policemen who drew up the report and who were now heading for high rank must have been intrigued by the unexpected freedom from civil service restraint, which quickly proved to be an illusion. When O'Duffy, straight from his army command under martial law, took over at Garda headquarters, he resented interference by the new civil servants, who were equally determined to assert their authority, soon to be confirmed by the Ministers and Secretaries Act.

In taking on the officers of the Civic Guard in the matter of the Garda badge, Home Affairs trespassed on the sensitive ground of an emerging tradition and self-respect and pride in the new police. Deputy Commissioner Coogan was told by the secretary of Home Affairs, Henry O'Friel, that the design would have to be changed and the monogram *GS* replaced with the monogram *SE*, for Saorstát Éireann; the force was inaccurately described in the badge as Garda Síothchána na hÉireann (in pre-standardised spelling): the official title was An Garda Síothchána, as in the Civic Guard Bill then before Dáil Éireann.

O'Duffy was out of the country, attending a meeting of the International Association of Chiefs of Police in New York. Looking into his own heart, Coogan correctly anticipated what O'Duffy would say in reply. The proposed changes in the badge would not be acceptable to the Commissioner, he told O'Friel. The name of the force in Irish was adopted on the formation of the Civic Guard.

> We are looking ahead; we look upon the Guard as the Civic Guard of Ireland ...
> To treat the Guard as a Guard for a portion of Ireland would be a great mistake

... Surely it is not seriously suggested that we must change our badges in order to make it clear that we are a police force for only 26 counties of Ireland?

Coogan's letter prompted a civil servant in O'Friel's office to dismiss the matter as 'not very important,' to be 'settled without heat or misunderstanding.' O'Friel added his own view: the insignia of the RIC had incorporated the Crown; the Garda badge had no device representing the state. He agreed to await the Commissioner's return from New York, but he was determined that the Saorstát monogram be included in the design: all uniformed officers of the state must be identified as such in a common badge. O'Duffy convened a meeting of his headquarters officers on Friday night, 25 January 1924. It was unanimously agreed that the badge was now the recognised symbol of the force. They had

weathered the storm, and some had died on duty. The Garda as a whole and especially the men who have suffered in defence of their uniform will not welcome any change ... The officers and men of the Garda put a high value on their badge and uniform. To destroy its distinctiveness would be to ignore this fine feeling ...

The army had a distinctive badge, incorporating the monogram FF (for Fianna Fáil, 'warriors of Ireland') and the legend Óglaigh na hÉireann. And, as O'Duffy pointed out—it may be assumed with no little satisfaction—the long title of the Garda Síothchána (Temporary Provisions) Act (1923) described the force in a new polyglot title as 'The Garda Síothchána'; to substitute the definite article in Irish would contravene the Act.

Enlarging on Coogan's initial response, O'Duffy made a political point. If there was any objection to the appropriation of the title Garda Síothchána na hÉireann, it was still more objectionable for the 'Six-County Police appropriating to themselves the title Royal Ulster Constabulary. A more appropriate title was "Royal Six-Counties of Ulster Constabulary".'

O'Friel gave an assurance that the existing badge and buttons could be retained, but O'Duffy refused to give way. He had no guarantee that the force would not be obliged to change its insignia at some future date to conform with the station badge. The case for retaining the original design was conceded to the Garda Commissioner.[72]

'EVERY POSSIBLE FACILITY' AT THE RDS

The need for a training depot with accommodation for four thousand men was mentioned at the meeting in the Gresham Hotel on 9 February. With an element of unreality, the committee expected that the police depot in the Phoenix Park would be vacated in a matter of weeks.[73] At the meeting of the Provisional Government the following day, Collins undertook to ask General Macready to arrange for the surrender of Wellington (Griffith) Barracks as a matter of urgency.[74] O'Friel raised the matter with the Assistant Under-Secretary in the Castle administration, Alfred Cope, who had played a crucial role behind the scenes in the Treaty negotiations and was now facilitating the orderly transfer of power. With an organiser's clearer view of the obstacles, Staines set about solving the problem for himself.

On 13 January soldiers of the nascent national army took over Beggar's Bush Barracks, recently vacated by the Auxiliary Police; the other military establishments in the city were crowded with British troops preparing for evacuation. Accompanied by Patrick Brennan and M. J. Ring, he inspected the Royal Dublin Society exhibition halls and showgrounds in Ballsbridge. 'Every possible facility' was offered by the director of the RDS, Edward Bohane.[75]

On 21 February, de Valera, Griffith and Collins shared a platform in a bid for unity at the crucial Sinn Féin ardfheis, while a special conference of the Labour Party heard Tom Johnson pledge support for the Treaty.[76] On the same day, against the background of intense political activity to avert civil war, recruiting for the Civic Guard began informally at the RDS. On the first day four young men looking for jobs presented themselves for enlistment; two were Volunteers, and one claimed previous service in the DMP. These three applicants failed to conform to the strict discipline imposed from the very inception of the Civic Guard and were dismissed, the former DMP constable for assaulting prisoners in military custody, following a sworn inquiry ordered by Staines.[77]

The fourth candidate was a former RIC constable with a record of distinguished service in the War of Independence. A Cavan man, Patrick McAvinia was stationed in Eglinton Street, Galway, where he met his future wife, Christina Allen, an active member of Cumann na mBan in the city. Resigning in 1918, he returned the County Inspector's Certificate of Service, which stated the cause of his leaving as voluntary resignation; he insisted on the endorsement 'on account of Sinn Féin sympathies,' and he had his way. He volunteered for the Republican Police and in the Sinn Féin courts came under the notice of Michael Staines, who invited him to join the new police.[78] The informal reception of recruits continued until the first contingents selected by the local recruiting officers began to arrive at the Ballsbridge depot. These early stragglers were immediately employed on fatigue duties.

The brigade recruiting officers became the first targets for the opponents of the new state.[79] 'They were arrested, kidnapped, held in custody and threatened; attempts were made to extort pledges of neutrality from them.' The recruits themselves 'were held up, turned back, arrested and threatened with the most severe penalties. The object was to strangle the infant Garda at its birth.'[80] In September, Assistant Commissioner Patrick Brennan, in charge of recruiting, applied for a supply of plain envelopes for use in areas controlled by Irregular forces, to protect the identity of candidates.[81]

The sub-committee on training recommended the use of RIC bedding, but this was hardly feasible, as the old police in the throes of disbanding had to be provided for at the demobilisation centres.[82] It is probable that the barrackmaster, Chief Superintendent McCarthy, organised deliveries of bedding and field kitchens, at first from nearby Beggar's Bush Barracks, now occupied by the army. In the event, the Civic Guard recruits were provided with the triple bedboards and trestles then in use in military establishments, core mattresses, and army blankets. The recruits were accommodated in the main exhibition hall; by the end of March, seven hundred men occupied the vast floor space.

On 24 February, Staines requisitioned furniture and thirty transport vehicles from the RIC, followed three days later by a requisition for a hundred rifles with bayonets, seventy Webley revolvers, another four vehicles, and office equipment, followed on succeeding days by further separate applications for stationery, waist-belts, and lanyards. Taken together, the several requisitions made in rapid succession give the impression that McCarthy had no clear idea of what was needed. Cope informed Home Affairs that he had supplied to the 'representatives of the Provisional Government at the Ballsbridge Police Depot' a hundred rifles with bayonets and a hundred revolvers with 10,000 rounds of ammunition, a three-ton lorry, six Crossley tenders, twelve Ford cars, and one touring car.[83]

'THE UTMOST LOYALTY, OBEDIENCE AND DEVOTION TO DUTY'

The report of the training sub-committee may have been written by District Inspector Riordan, who signed the recommendations ahead of the nominal chairman, Sergeant Prendeville. The document is stamped with the authority and confidence of professional policemen. Any slackness in the initial training of the recruit was likely 'to prove fatal to obedience and discipline during his whole career.' In the short term, an acceptable standard of discipline must have been difficult to achieve in an organisation destined to remain in plain clothes for the first six months of its existence, with armbands to distinguish rank.[84]

Prendeville's sub-committee anticipated the exemplary role the Garda Síochána was to play in the life of the nation. The selection of instructors was 'a matter of the utmost importance,' men capable of instilling in recruits 'a pride in their position.' Their 'courage, temper and patience' would be tested. Above all, the recruit had to be taught that he was the

> servant and not master of the people ... He must also be made fully to understand that he is now enforcing laws made by his own countrymen who have the welfare of their country at heart, and that the utmost loyalty, obedience and devotion to duty will be demanded.[85]

These excellent sentiments were undoubtedly included in classroom instructions from the very beginning but were not immediately available in any printed form. In August the urgent need for a Code was noted in an internal Home Affairs memorandum. In October, Deputy Commissioner Coogan conveyed his anxieties to O'Friel. By then a thousand men with no police experience were on duty in the country, 'the great majority' ill-prepared for the challenges facing them. In what seems like a reflection on the competence of the depot staff, Coogan described them as having no training in police duties. He submitted the proofs of a Garda Code for approval; and these were passed for legal revision to District Justice George P. Cussen.

O'Friel's critical eye fell on one paragraph recommending a 'bearing of … good fellowship' on the part of the new police in their dealings with elected public representatives, government and local authority officials, and the clergy of all denominations. He directed that the ideas in the offending paragraph, which read 'more like a manifesto,' should be based on the broad conception of normal conditions in the country, with parliament and the necessary machinery of government and the Civic Guard 'just stepping into their proper place'; there should be 'no reference to political history or partition,' and no fine points about their role as servants of the people, which would most probably lead to a lessening of central control and a flabbiness in dealing with the public. 'The importance of the Civic Guard in social and economic life cannot be exaggerated.' The government and people looked with 'deep concern' to the Guards, with great work to do 'restoring order from chaos, and securing life and property in a society in which moral and legal rights [had been] long in abeyance.' Too much emphasis could not be laid on the non-sectarian, non-political character of the force.[86]

From among 'the most intelligent recruits … men of intelligence and initiative,' Staines appointed temporary company orderlies and classroom and drill instructors.[87] The syllabus included police duties, squad and company drill, physical training, and firearms instruction. Sporting activities were organised by the enthusiast Mathias McCarthy. There were classes in Irish and also in English, presumably in report writing and the keeping of records.

As the depot routine was organised, the men were monotonously paraded for drill and fatigues. For the instruction of recruits in law enforcement the sub-committee recommended the use of the existing *Policeman's Manual,* a catechism of police duties first published in 1866 as *The Constabulary Manual of Law and Police Duties.* The Manual remained in use until 1942, when a *Garda Síochána Manual* was published, also in the form of a catechism.[88] The first edition of the *Garda Síochána Code,* published in 1928, was largely based on the old RIC Code.

One of the recruits, George Lawlor from Monasterevin, who was to make a name for himself as the distinguished head of the Garda Technical Bureau, described the conditions in the depot, not surprisingly, as less than ideal.

> The position of things did not make for the best form of police training and most of the time was taken up with drill, physical exercises and lectures on simple Acts of Parliament from the British Law Code. Thus the knowledge obtained by men in law and procedure and general police duties was poor. It can well be said that in the investigation of crime the members of the force were dependent on their

own resources, and as the Irish law reports of that period record, there was a total disregard for the Judges' Rules.[89]

In April, intending exhibitors at the RDS Spring Show were pressing Edward Bohane for access to the Ballsbridge halls. Staines renewed his appeal for the RIC Depot and for temporary use of the adjoining Marlborough (McKee) Barracks. In a verbal reply, Collins referred him to Cope, complaining that on previous occasions he had received from the Assistant Under-Secretary vague and unsatisfactory promises; he had no intention of approaching Cope again.

Staines was worried about his men 'herded' into the draughty exhibition hall; their health was causing serious concern, and a decent standard of discipline was impossible. 'I am reluctantly compelled to say, if I cannot have possession of the RIC Depot and ... Marlboro Barracks within a week, I shall have to hand control over to some other person as I cannot accept responsibility ... under existing conditions.' Having despatched this ultimatum to Duggan on 11 April, he sent an angry postscript the following day, apparently in reply to some message of reassurance from Duggan. 'The professed willingness [in Home Affairs] to facilitate us appears to be non-existent in practice ... something must now be done.'[90]

There was little Duggan or his civil servants could do to hurry the imperial army on its way. The request made by Collins personally to Macready for the early evacuation of Wellington Barracks had come to nothing. The Phoenix Park depot itself was now occupied by British forces and was not expected to be handed over before the end of November.

Staines was inspecting the military aerodrome at Baldonnel[91] when the government decided to act, prompted perhaps by the politics of the approaching general election in June. Accompanied by Duggan, Mulcahy, and the Adjutant-General, Gearóid Ó Súilleabháin, Collins received a deputation of residents from the Curragh and Newbridge (Droichead Nua) areas, where the evacuation of British troops had resulted in much unemployment. A member of Kildare County Council, J. J. Fitzgerald, reported that in Newbridge alone a thousand workers who had served the garrisons had lost their jobs; in north Kildare three thousand were out of work. Fitzgerald and his deputation were told that the Curragh was about to be reopened by the national army; meanwhile they were urged to form a committee to promote local industry.[92] At the government meeting on 10 April, Duggan suggested that the Artillery (McGee) Barracks in Kildare might be suitable as a depot.[93] It is not recorded whether Staines was consulted. The RDS premises were evacuated on 25 April, and Staines marched his motley corps of aspirant policemen across the city to Kingsbridge (Heuston) Station, where a special train was waiting to shuttle them to Kildare.

STAFF APPOINTMENTS
At the height of the Anglo-Irish war, Brigadier-General E. F. Crozier, commander of

the Auxiliary Division of the RIC, resigned in protest at the indiscipline of the men under his command. After the Treaty he was 'not at all anxious to be a mere spectator at this critical time in the history of the country.' Out on a limb, he applied to the Provisional Government for a job, pleading 'past loyalty to Ireland.' Offering his services 'in the maintenance of law and order in any capacity,' he requested an interview; he was informed that the Minister was 'exceedingly busy' and unable to see him.[94] A place in the new police could hardly have been made for a former officer of the Auxiliaries, irrespective of his credentials.

Early in its deliberations the Police Organising Committee purported to elect Patrick Brennan as depot commandant. There were at least two other such appointments: Sergeant McCormack as accounting officer, and ex-Sergeant Galligan as assistant storekeeper. A mess committee was also elected: Staines (president), Kearney (vice-president), Prendeville, Ring, and Lynch.[95]

Staines was appointed Commissioner of Police on 10 March but regarded his appointment as temporary.[96] He had undertaken the organisation of the Civic Guard for a period of three months, he told the Kildare Mutiny inquiry. 'When the government made me Commissioner … I said it must be distinctly understood that it is temporary until the Free State parliament is elected.'[97] Accepting the will of the organising committee, he confirmed Brennan as depot commandant. On 27 March he notified Brennan, Ring and the depot adjutant, P. J. Haugh, that he had received the approval of the government for the promotion of Brennan as assistant commissioner, with responsibility for recruiting, discipline, and finance, and for the appointment of Ring as depot commandant. The memorandum also stated the guidelines for the administration of the depot.[98] The following appointments were made in the period up to 1 May:[99]

Michael J. Staines TD (Volunteers), Commissioner; Patrick Walsh (RIC, Letterkenny), Deputy Commissioner; Patrick Brennan TD (East Clare ASU), assistant commissioner; Chief Superintendent Michael J. Ring (West Mayo ASU), depot commandant; Chief Superintendent Mathias McCarthy (RIC, Letterkenny), barrackmaster; Chief Superintendent Michael McCormack (RIC, Letterkenny), accounting officer; Superintendent Jeremiah Maher (RIC, Naas, and Volunteer intelligence officer), private secretary; Superintendent P. J. Haugh (Volunteers, West Clare), adjutant; Superintendent James Brennan (RIC Depot), assistant barrackmaster; Superintendent Patrick Harte (RIC, Roscommon), assistant accounting officer; Superintendent Bernard O'Connor (RIC, Dingle), receiving and measuring officer; Chief Inspector Robert McCrudden (RIC, Belfast), already appointed, 1 March.

Company officers: Superintendent Martin Lynch (brigade police officer, County Laois); Superintendent Seán Liddy TD (Volunteers, West Clare); Superintendent John Keane (Volunteers); Superintendent Francis Burke (Volunteers); Superintendent Daniel Hallinan (Volunteers, County Cork); Superintendent P. Kelleher (Volunteers); Superintendent Edmund Prendeville (RIC, Clonmel); Superintendent John Galligan

(RIC, Roscommon); Superintendent Thomas Neary (DMP, Kevin Street); Superintendent John J. Byrne (Volunteers).

The dominant figure in the organising committee, Patrick Walsh, was appointed Deputy Commissioner on 6 April, probably on the recommendation of Staines, supported by Walsh's principal sponsors, O'Higgins and Collins. It was a logical appointment, the government having decided on 17 January to place the organisation of a regular police force in the hands of 'a trained police or military officer.'[100] In the earliest definition of the role of the new police, Staines stated that the Civic Guard would 'not be required as soldiers.'[101]

'THE KERRY LADS'

The probable effect of the promotion of Walsh over the heads of Volunteers of the calibre of Brennan and Ring, who had borne the brunt of battle in the War of Independence, must have been calculated by the government. Anticipating the problem, Staines in his memorandum of 27 March appealed for co-operation between all ranks. The Civic Guard would have 'much to contend with from various sources'; the force could not afford 'internal dissensions.'[102] The employment of the RIC men was bound to cause trouble, but Collins was determined to follow the sensible course in retaining the services of professional policemen. As O'Higgins recalled in the Dáil on 20 October, Collins had been Director of Intelligence during the War of Independence.

> We accepted his information implicitly. We acted on it to the advantage of the country ... It is to be regretted that when certain members of the RIC were admitted into the Civic Guard with his endorsement there was not the same implicit acceptance of his endorsement. It is to be regretted that there was trouble in the Civic Guard over this question.

By 25 March the recruited strength was 400; of these, 370 had served in the Volunteers. Of the thirty former RIC men,[103] ten were destined to remain in the ranks. They could reasonably complain at finding themselves in the same category as inexperienced recruits and on the lowest rate of pay. These men, and others who joined later, who had been unemployed, some for up to three years, were supported by Inspector Patrick Meehan, County Clare. It was 'a poor recompense to men who had made such sacrifices for the common good and to whom so many glowing promises had been made.' Collins had promised T. J. McElligott that they would be treated 'not less generously' than their former colleagues who had continued to serve in the RIC.[104] Staines was sympathetic. He could 'not regard with any feeling other than dismay the idea of sending units of the Civic Guard to police country districts ... without the presence in each party of at least some RIC men.'[105]

When Staines set out from the RDS for Kildare, he travelled without one of his best officers. District Inspector John Kearney became a prime victim of the early tensions in Ballsbridge. Complaints about the appointment of Kearney and his former colleagues in the RIC were considered by the Dáil cabinet on 21 March. Duggan, Staines and Desmond Fitzgerald were directed to prepare a statement for publication.[106] 'False statements are being assiduously circulated with regard to the Civic Guard ... There are no Black and Tans in the Civic Guard.'[107]

Early in March, when two hundred recruits had been received and measured at Ballsbridge, Staines instructed Chief Inspector McCrudden to form an armed depot defence unit from among the more experienced Volunteers.[108] Within this elite group Thomas P. Daly emerged as leader. Described by Brennan as 'a great commander of Tom Barry's, the famous south-west Cork column commander,'[109] he was named by the inquiry into the Kildare Mutiny as an agent of the Executive forces under Rory O'Connor. As depot commandant, Brennan sent word that he would meet the committee, and on 14 March he received a deputation, which also included Sergeant J. J. Byrne, Sergeant J. J. Branigan, Sergeant P. Coy, Sergeant M. Hennessy, and a man named O'Halloran. Brennan told the deputation that the appointment of the RIC 'advisers' was temporary, and the men were satisfied.[110] At the inquiry, Sergeant Patrick McNamara testified that at 'about that time, a Black and Tan named Lillis, and D.I. Kearney left the depot.'[111]

It is not clear how Kearney was employed at Ballsbridge—probably as a company officer. He was at once recognised as the Head Constable in Tralee when Roger Casement was arrested near Ardfert on 21 April 1916. In colourful reminiscences, ex-Chief Superintendent Seán Liddy described the reaction of a faction among the handful of Volunteers who then constituted the membership of the Civic Guard. 'The Kerry lads denounced Kearney as Casement's betrayer and executioner to all and sundry ... He confined himself to his office and quarters by day and became a noctambulist after dark ... His physical condition began to deteriorate and one evening he quietly disappeared from the camp, driven in a State car to catch the mail boat.'[112]

Kearney was promoted in the RIC, Liddy alleged, 'for his exceptional zeal in the Casement case.' Kearney's son, Thomas Moran Kearney of New Barnet, Hertfordshire, protested at Liddy's garbled account of Casement's imprisonment in Tralee. His father had 'the greatest respect' for Casement. Accusing Liddy of 'false witness', he referred to René MacColl's biography for evidence of Casement's own respect for Kearney, who was due for promotion on seniority before the drama at Banna Strand in the early hours of 21 April 1916.[113] Casement was questioned in Tralee Barracks by District Inspector Frederick Britton. Britton was friendly and sympathetic: 'I think I know who you are, and I pray to God it won't end the way of Wolfe Tone.'

Many years later Dr Michael Shanaghan, who was called to attend the prisoner, recalled 'a clean-shaven man ... of distinguished appearance sitting over a smoky fire in the policemen's billiards room. He looked jittery and exhausted. When I went to examine him two policemen remained in the room. I ordered them outside and closed the door after them. The man then whispered to me that he was Casement and expressed the hope that I was in sympathy with the Irish cause.' He wanted the people outside told that he was in the barracks and hoped to be released. 'The barrack door was wide open and half-a-dozen men with revolvers could have walked in there and taken Sir Roger away.'[114] Shanaghan alerted the local Volunteers, who refused to act, for fear of revealing the plans for the rising.

Casement was befriended by Kearney, who entertained the prisoner in his own quarters.[115] 'The Chief Constable at Tralee was v. friendly to me,' he wrote in notes for counsel at his trial, A. M. Sullivan QC.[116] 'We became close friends.'[117] Kearney persuaded Britton to spare Casement the indignity of handcuffs on the way to the railway station on Easter Saturday morning. As they parted company, Casement wished to reward Head Constable and Mrs Kearney for their hospitality and kindness. The Kearneys protested. They found afterwards that Casement had left his pocket watch behind him as a token of gratitude.[118] On the entire journey to Dublin he was accompanied by a single policeman. The arrangements for the safe custody of the prisoner were almost an invitation to the Volunteers to rescue him.

In Dáil Éireann on 22 February 1922 Austin Stack, the local Volunteer commander in 1916, described Kearney as 'one of the most vigilant servants the enemy had in this country.'[119] During all the time Casement was in custody, Stack was also imprisoned in Tralee Barracks, on a charge of conspiracy to import arms. Stack must have known that his denunciation of Kearney was false, but he was prepared to make the charge in furtherance of his case for the employment of the IRP as a regular police force.[120]

Set against the inactivity of the Volunteers in Tralee in 1916, Stack's attack and the treatment meted out by 'the Kerry lads' in Ballsbridge were extraordinary. The young civic guards had been too deeply involved in the recent warfare and too easily swayed by Daly's propaganda to avoid the kind of hasty judgment that made a scapegoat of Kearney for a perceived betrayal of the Republic. To conciliate a minority of protesting Volunteers, Kearney was pushed out. 'He was not appointed by me,' Staines told the inquiry. 'He was appointed by the Provisional Government. When it came to the question of appointing officers, I sacked Kearney.'[121] His departure in disgrace encouraged the malcontents, who were now determined to consolidate their victory.

Staines took over his new depot in Kildare on 25 April, his authority weakened by the unresolved command problem posed by the RIC men: Walsh; Jeremiah Maher, his private secretary; McCormack and Harte in accounts; McCarthy and James Brennan in stores; O'Connor in recruiting; the company officers Prendeville and Galligan; and Sergeant McAvinue, mess caterer—men of mature years committed to the national cause, accustomed to discipline and, with their police experience, all deemed indispensable by the Provisional Government.

3

THE KILDARE MUTINY

All those RIC men walking around smoking pipes with their hands in their pockets.

I f time had allowed the planning of an ideal police force, it might have been possible for the Volunteers to undertake the organisation themselves, the men's advocate, John Aloysius O'Connell, passionately argued at the Kildare Mutiny inquiry.

The 26-year-old solicitor from Derry, forsaking a pin-striped career, joined the Civic Guard at Ballsbridge in March. With Volunteer service dating from 1915 and highly recommended, O'Connell began with good prospects of high rank, but having succumbed to the temptation to represent the disaffected faction in Kildare, his career ended in personal tragedy.[1] In a conservative organisation, his superiors may not have appreciated the contribution he made in giving a voice to his less qualified colleagues in their hour of need. Brennan scorned O'Connell as 'a professional gentleman ... a gramophone ... his master's voice.'[2]

O'Connell dissected the animosity of republican Ireland towards the RIC, largely fanned by the propaganda of the War of Independence, exaggerating as 'detestation' the cautious attitude to the force in Irish community life, at least before the relationship began to break down after 1916.

> The majority of the men were actuated by patriotic motives and keenly interested in sending the Garda Síochána to the country free from the stigma of having been ... established, governed and trained ... by resigned and disbanded members of the detested body which had policed the country for England ... We have in Ireland, organising and administrative ability sufficient to build up and administer a civilian police force on a model different from the weapon invested by English and anglicised Irish brains ... We have ideas of our own and we wish to develop and apply them ... unfettered by R.I.C. Rules and Codes and Regulations.

Trouble was inevitable when the Civic Guard began to reflect the organisation of the RIC. It was bad enough that the former RIC officers were 'ruling the roost' as civilians; giving them high rank in the Civic Guard had provoked the men. It would have been 'more honest and less costly' to have recruited the old police as a body. The civic guards had 'an intense and undying objection to modelling their organisation structurally or mentally' on the RIC.[3]

Sergeant Patrick Coy, another witness at the inquiry, complained that the RIC officers had all the keys. They controlled the depot, holding sway over the soldiers of the IRA who had given seven years' voluntary service to their country. As Brennan colourfully testified, they resented 'all those RIC men walking around smoking pipes with their hands in their pockets.' The young Volunteers down from the hills saw erstwhile enemies disporting themselves at the officers' mess, 'up on the balcony smoking after dinner.'

Brennan articulated the social dimension in the tensions between the confident, ambitious and well-paid membership of the RIC and the struggling mass of the people.[4] In his view, there was no hope of a reconciliation: in the conflict with the RIC, the men of the active service units were 'representative of a type' and the former RIC district inspector, Deputy Commissioner Walsh, was representative of another type. 'If this thing goes on in the Civic Guard, even though it is fixed up, you will have the same bloody row in ten years.'

Sergeant Patrick McNamara, who headed the Republican Police in Kilmallock, told of his arrest and imprisonment by the RIC and Black and Tans, who had beaten him with their rifle butts. Sergeant Thomas Kilroy of Galway, a former Volunteer officer, had also been assaulted while in custody. He found it hard to absolve even those RIC men who had served the national cause. Putting RIC officers in command of Irish soldiers who had fought in the War of Independence was 'very hard on ordinary men to understand.' The government had many other ways of rewarding such men. The recruits gave the RIC men a hard time, obeying them but not showing 'very much respect,' Staines told the inquiry.

A CABAL FROM COUNTY CLARE

The spoils of revolution was clearly an issue of immediate concern, as Guard John Hamrogue admitted. The Clare faction had an intense loyalty to Brennan, 'who fought heart and soul for the cause all along and sacrificed his life' and had been 'ousted by a D.I. [Walsh] who fought against us.' The assistant commissioner had a just grievance because of 'the way he was treated in the matter of promotion.'

A cabal from County Clare—Brennan, Seán Liddy, Seán Scanlon, and Patrick Haugh—succeeded in packing a third of the membership of the Civic Guard with recruits from their own county. Walsh in cross-examination put it to Brennan that 'the Brennan sphere of influence' gave the force 'more a County Clare complexion than an R.I.C. one.' Staines was told of a rumour that Brennan would be dismissed unless the 'Black and Tans' were expelled.

There was another straw in the wind. The Commissioner defended his Dáil seat as a 'panel' candidate in the June elections. Early in May an election poster denouncing 'Staines and his satellites' appeared in one of the squad rooms.[5] The poster, printed by the *Wicklow People* and brought to Kildare by an unnamed civic guard, came into his possession on the eve of the election. Overnight, on 15 June, they were put up in his own constituency of St Michan's and from one end of the city to the other. The posters were intended to damage his prospects, he reported to Home Affairs. They were not the work of the 'comparatively ignorant men', who were being used by the malcontents.[6]

Despite the warnings, Staines was taken off guard when Daly's committee threw down the gauntlet. The appointment of Walsh as Deputy Commissioner on 6 April was followed two days later by the promotion of Sergeants Harte, McCormack and Prendeville. The announcement in Routine Orders was delayed until 1 May. Daly had been waiting for such an opportunity to challenge the Commissioner's authority; but he held his hand.

Approaching the June elections, Collins persuaded the opposing factions in the Volunteers to make a stand for national unity. Because it was based on the assumption that a majority of the people would vote for the Treaty, the agreement reached in the 'Army Document' was rejected by Rory O'Connor. Within days, on Monday 15 May, Daly served on Staines an ultimatum in writing demanding the expulsion of five officers: ex-District Inspectors Walsh and O'Connor, Head Constable Brennan, and Sergeants Maher and Prendeville. Daly overlooked or ignored the others—McCormack, Harte, Galligan, and McCarthy.[7]

Faced with the open challenge to his leadership, Staines ordered a general parade for two o'clock. Under command of the adjutant, Superintendent Haugh, the entire depot complement, numbering 1,500 young men, formed up in a hollow square and were then stood at ease for half an hour 'awaiting the Commissioner's pleasure.'[8] Staines read out the ultimatum and called on the eight signatories, one by one, to step forward. It is not clear who among the committee put their names to the document; the president, Thomas P. Daly, and secretary, Patrick (Sonny) Sellars, were the first names called.[9]

The Commissioner's voice did not carry to the back of the parade, and the role of the eight men who stepped out was misunderstood by one witness. In reminiscences published twenty-five years later, James Donohue described Staines calling on 'all who favoured his views to fall in behind him.' A voice answered: 'We are willing to stand by you, but not by the Black and Tans.' The reply seemed to electrify almost the entire assembly. There was a pause, a slight shuffling movement, and about half a dozen members lined up behind the Commissioner. A tense moment followed when the Commissioner vehemently called out, 'Are you going to stand by me?' An uneasy silence followed. Staines turned on his heel and marched off.[10]

Other witnesses who gave evidence at the inquiry described the shambles on the square. Holding up the document, Staines 'became very heated.'[11] Four of the former RIC men listed had done good work for Ireland, more than those who were now demanding their expulsion. The organisers had challenged the Commissioner's authority because, he shouted, 'they had been refused promotion.'[12] The scene became farcical as Staines and various members of the committee competed for the ear of the recruits, who were now breaking ranks.

From Sergeant Joseph Rochford, a Volunteer in Brennan's own East Clare ASU, there was a shout of support for the man from Meelick: 'We will stand by Paddy Brennan!'[13] The assistant commissioner was absent from the parade. On 15 May, with Inspector Seán Scanlon, he attended a meeting of Clare County Council in Ennis, Superintendent Martin Lynch, taking the weekend off, travelling with them. Brennan took the opportunity to visit his family in Meelick, where his mother was unwell, he told the inquiry.

Surrounded by wildly excited men, Staines took the only course open to him. Denouncing the committee as 'a pack of hooligans', he turned his back on the chaotic scene and left the commandant to restore order. Ring, soon to rejoin the army, where his true vocation lay, fell back on his authority as a Volunteer officer and his reputation as the tough leader of a flying column in the War of Independence. 'I am commandant of the camp. Who is going to stand by me?' (A quarter of a century later, James Donohue attributed these words to Staines.) 'I can't take a demand from you … Send it in the form of a request.'

The commandant 'adopted a bullying attitude,'[14] making things worse 'boasting of his exploits';[15] he gave 'a glowing account of himself.'[16] Ring was defiant. 'If you throw these men out you will have to put me out along with them, and there is no man fit to put me out.'[17] He was drowned out by the men, 'shouting and roaring';[18] he was 'furious', and left the square, accompanied by some of his followers from County Mayo.[19]

In an address to the inquiry, probably personally damaging to himself, the men's advocate, Guard J. A. O'Connell, blamed the Commissioner for the disorder on the parade ground.

> That the trouble eventually developed into insubordination and might have had tragic consequences [was] solely due … to Commissioner Staines … whose high and responsible position called for the exercise of great tact and fine judgement … Rather did he, by his method, behaviour and language, rouse to hasty actions the passion of men many of whom during the recent fight with England faced death and had dealt out death.[20]

In his reminiscences, Seán Liddy described Staines as 'powerless to navigate … no longer the skipper. A perfectly honest man, a fine soldier … innocent of intrigue,' betrayed by 'his loyalty to Michael Collins.'[21] Liddy was closely questioned on his part in the overthrow of the Commissioner. He had collaborated in the mutiny 'to hold the men together,' he told Walsh, who pursued him on the question of obedience to the government. Did he consider the Civic Guard the servants of the people, or their masters? As an officer of the Civic Guard—forgetting for a moment that he was a member of the Dáil—did he think a servant should dictate whom his master should or should not employ?

'We are at a very, very serious crisis in our history,' Liddy replied. On the evening of the mutiny 'men were rushing here and there. It was all excitement. We just did our best to ... restore order.' The inquiry chairman, Kevin O'Sheil, was not satisfied. The witness had been quick to respond to anonymous authority. 'Someone rushed up ... and said the "committee" passed this and told you to act as adjutant.' Liddy was defensive: he was trying to get the men back on duty.

Michael McAuliffe intervened with a more searching question. 'On the fatal day ... the Commissioner stood on one side, and the "committee" stood on the other ... Ring was standing between the two ... Was it right on that day for Commandant Ring to stand by the Commissioner, or to stand by the "committee"?' In a cleft stick, Liddy dithered. 'I suppose he was right in standing by the Commissioner.' But he had discussed the circumstances with Collins and Duggan, and they appeared satisfied that he had acted correctly. Brennan on the same point in his evidence tended to support Liddy. 'Mr. Collins and Mr. Duggan asked myself to go back [to Kildare] and try to fix up this blessed row.'

The die was cast on 15 May, when Michael Staines, with conspicuous moral courage, faced the phalanx on the depot square. From the Commissioner down they were all in plain clothes, or garbed in a variety of quasi-military dress. The new police uniform, promised for March, had not yet been delivered; there was neither formal dress nor insignia to create the psychological barriers of rank for young men who had hardly begun to discover that the democratic structures and ad hoc discipline of the Volunteers had no place in a professional police force.

'I THOUGHT IT BETTER NOT TO INTERFERE'

In the period before the mutiny the training programmes included the care and use of firearms, rifle drill, and revolver practice. For a force that by July did not exceed 1,500 members there was an arsenal of two hundred rifles and a thousand revolvers with ammunition, delivered at Ballsbridge and transferred to Kildare.[22] The existence of this arsenal changed the course of police history in Ireland, paradoxically contributing to the evolution of a stable Irish Free State.

On the morning of the mutiny, the barrackmaster, Mathias McCarthy, accounted for 'ammunition not counted, and 5 revolvers missing.' He was at work in his office in the afternoon when he heard 'the commotion ... a lot of shouting and all that ... They all seemed to be shouting ... I met one of the guards. I asked him what was the matter. He said the parade had turned against the Commissioner ... The men ... were all cheering and booing and all that. I saw about a hundred or more going to the armoury ... I thought it better not to interfere.'

Immediately after the parade, Staines detailed Sergeant Patrick Coy to protect the armoury. When Coy and a party of guards arrived at his post, he counted 33 rifles and 757 revolvers, as noted by McCarthy in a further entry in the armoury record.

On the morning of Tuesday 16 May the nearby Curragh military camp was taken over by Lieutenant-General J. J. O'Connell, Deputy Chief of Staff. Simultaneously, at 10:30 a.m., the military barracks in Newbridge was evacuated.[23] Ring detailed Superintendent Patrick Kelleher to parade 350 men of 6 Company at the transport office, where a convoy of cars was drawn up. Amid shouts of defiance from Daly's supporters, the men were persuaded to board the vehicles, and the convoy moved off for Newbridge. Having supervised the occupation of the barracks in Newbridge, Staines returned to Kildare, where he was told that Daly was planning to seize the armoury. Deciding to transfer the arms and ammunition to military custody, he telephoned the new national army post at the Curragh to requisition a lorry and an armoured car escort; after lunch he sent Superintendent John J. Byrne to the Curragh to seek the personal assistance of Lieutenant-General O'Connell.[24] He then retired to his office to write his resignation.

> Yesterday a document was forwarded to me designated a petition, but which was really an ultimatum. It ... demanded the immediate expulsion from the Training Depot of ... Deputy Commissioner Walsh, Private Secretary Maher, Supts. Prindiville [sic], Brennan and O'Connor. All are ex-members of the RIC and the reason assigned for the demand was that they had continued to serve contrary to the wishes etc. of the Irish people ... The document concluded with the threat that if immediate compliance with the demand was not given, drastic action would be taken ...
>
> I at once ordered a General Parade of the men in the Depot and addressed them pointing out the serious nature of the course they were about to follow, and warning them of the consequences.
>
> From the demeanour of those assembled ... it was at once apparent that some secret agitation had been fomented and that what should have been a disciplined force was in process of being converted into an unruly mob. There were shouts of 'We will follow Paddy Brennan' referring presumably to the Assistant Commissioner who was not present. Why this should be the catch-cry it is difficult to say, for nothing said had any reference to him, but it was quite clear the observations were understood by the Parade.
>
> Seeing ... that the discipline of the men had been undermined to a serious extent, and that it was hopeless to appeal to their reason, I dismissed the Parade.
>
> No developments have since taken place, except that I have, on this morning, with a party of the Guard, taken over Newbridge Barracks from British Military ...
>
> Michael Staines
> Commissioner, Garda Síochána.[25]

In reporting to Duggan that there had been no developments since he dismissed the parade the day before, Staines gave the clearest signal that the Commissioner did not know what was happening in the depot. He failed to disclose the fact that the armoury had been raided and 167 rifles and 243 revolvers taken. The inquiry found that the 'intrigues were not communicated to [Staines] by his officers.'[26] Walsh and the other RIC officers were presumably also left in the dark by the conspiracy of silence.

At the Curragh, Superintendent Byrne discovered that the Commissioner's telephone call requesting a military escort for the arms had been relayed to Beggar's Bush Barracks in Dublin. Daly was now in complete control of the depot. The next day, Wednesday 17 May, he published at the guardroom a typewritten document purporting to be routine orders for that day, announcing the appointment of his own nominees in important posts, including Brennan as Commissioner, Patrick Haugh as assistant commissioner, Martin Lynch as commandant, and Seán Liddy as adjutant.[27]

Before the day was out, the mutineers had taken over the armoury, with its depleted arsenal; the weapons removed on Monday by the excited recruits were gathered up, and the rifles in the guardroom were also seized. With the armoury secured, Daly waited for a signal from Rory O'Connor before making his next move.

When Daly's ultimatum arrived on his desk, Staines was bound to have consulted his deputy. With instinctive loyalty, Walsh also resigned, a move that Eoin O'Duffy was to regret when he realised the extent of his dependence on the career policeman, whom he found relegated to the role of civilian adviser.

With his own resignation in his pocket, Staines left for Dublin, accompanied by Walsh, Chief Superintendents McCarthy and McCormack, and Superintendents James Brennan, Francis Burke, John J. Byrne, John Galligan, Patrick Harte, Jeremiah Maher, Thomas Neary, Bernard O'Connor, and Edmund Prendeville.[28]

With the camp 'in the hands of a lot of wild men,'[29] and considering his life in danger, Joe Ring had barricaded himself in his room with members of the Mayo faction. When armed men approached his quarters he drew his revolver. 'I told them that if they didn't get back, I would shoot.'[30] His neighbour from County Mayo, Superintendent Keane, told the inquiry: 'I had a bomb in my hand.'[31] On Wednesday they were able to leave the camp with the assistance of Guard Jim Staines, who 'held up' the sentries.[32] Following the Commissioner and the other officers, they made their way to the Clarence Hotel, where they met Staines.[33]

The retreat from Kildare was severely criticised by the inquiry. Whatever the motive, the decision by practically the entire headquarters staff to follow Staines made it possible for the Civic Guard almost immediately to make a fresh start in the less dignified but calmer surroundings of a warehouse in Little Denmark Street in the city.

Late on Tuesday evening Staines reported to Collins, who ordered him to return to Kildare. It was after dark, on Tuesday or in the early hours of Wednesday, when he drove into the silent town. He found the gate of the barracks barred, the sentries refusing to admit him. Standing on the wrong side of the depot gate, the Commissioner had no means of assessing the conditions in the camp for himself, and he returned to the city. It was unlikely that Assistant Commissioner Brennan, who was either in his office or in the officers' mess, was not informed of the Commissioner's visit.

During his absence, late in the afternoon of 16 May, an armoured car and an armoured Lancia arrived to collect the arms, almost precipitating an early battle in the Civil War, before making a tactical retreat. The warlike presence at the barred gate sparked a panic reaction. Liddy 'rushed down at the double,' followed by scores of civic guards armed with rifles and revolvers. Ring was first at the gate, in conversation with the army officer in charge, a Captain Corry. Liddy identified himself as a member of Dáil Éireann; purporting to speak for the Provisional Government, he stoutly denied that a mutiny had taken place and disputed Ring's authority. Ring stood his ground, negotiating with more heat than common sense. 'I am the Commandant ... There's a mutiny here. You have your orders. Take them out, I will see them blown to hell out of here, the pack of hooligans.'[34]

The news that 'Ring was urging Dáil soldiers to turn the machine gun of an armoured car on the men spread like wildfire,' J. A. O'Connell told the inquiry. Losing his patience, Corry threatened to force the gate. He would force his way in, Liddy answered, 'over my dead body.'[35] The men ran for cover as Corry cruised the armoured car up and down the road outside, heightening the tension. Ring tried to contact Staines on the telephone. Liddy also left the scene to telephone the military, and he succeeded in getting an order for Corry to withdraw. It was all a misunderstanding, O'Connell told the inquiry: the transfer of 6 Company to Newbridge was interpreted by the men as a ploy to 'divide and conquer,' and the arrival of the military was misjudged as the start of an attack on the Civic Guard, which had been prevented by Seán Liddy.

During the confrontation at the depot gate, Staines was at Government Buildings in conference with Collins and Duggan when Daly and Sellars arrived from Kildare to put their case directly to Collins. The following Monday, 22 May, Brennan and Liddy were summoned to appear before a departmental committee: Collins and Duggan, with a senior civil servant, the future Mr Justice Black, Kevin O'Sheil, and Michael McAuliffe, Department of Labour, who sat on the inquiry in July.

Brennan was called in first, and he remained in the room when Liddy entered. In Liddy's account of the meeting, Collins

> looked angry ... He said: 'Liddy, what is your explanation for your conduct down in Kildare?' I said: 'It's quite simple, sir. The 1,500 men down there, the vast majority of whom are veteran I.R.A. men, strongly object to disbanded R.I.C. men being promoted to commissioned rank.' I was about to continue when he

interrupted me ... 'Liddy, you should know as well as I do what the country owe these men.' I replied: 'I am sorry, sir, I do not.' Then he said: 'It would be interesting to hear what your solution would be.' I replied: 'I should hand them their thirty pieces of silver and call it a deal.'

To my surprise ... he sprang to his feet in a towering rage, banged the table with his clenched fist, and shouted: 'By —, if I smashed the country by it, these men will remain in the Force.' He grabbed his file of papers and with a bound was out of the room ... Mr. Duggan was the first to recover, and realising he should do something ... said: 'Gentlemen, that appears to terminate the meeting.' The Colonel [Brennan] and I left the room together, and when we got outside he said to me: 'Let us get out of here and back to Kildare ... or we shall find ourselves in Mountjoy.' I replied: 'No, sir, we are both T.D.s, they need our support.'[36]

On Thursday 25 May, Griffith, Duggan and O'Higgins left for London to explain the de Valera-Collins pact to Churchill and his colleagues in the British cabinet. Collins, who followed at the weekend, remained at home to attend personally to the crisis in the Civic Guard. The next day he went down to Kildare to seek a settlement. The crisis was so serious, he told the men, that as leader of the government he considered it necessary to visit the depot himself. They had hoped for great things from the Civic Guard.

A higher standard of discipline is required in a police force than in any other body. It is your duty to enforce discipline on others, and to show by your example that you are fit persons to do so. When you leave the Depot, you will be scattered over the country in small bodies, removed from the immediate control of your higher officers ... The honour of the force is in the keeping of each one of you ... It is up to you so to train and discipline yourselves that when you go out amongst the people your conduct will contrast favourably in every way with that of the force whose place you are filling. You will have one great advantage over any previous regular police force in Ireland ... You will start off with the good will of the people, and their moral support in carrying out your duties. You will be their guardians, not their oppressors; your authority will be derived from the people, not from their enemies ...[37]

Lobbying Collins and Staines at Earlsfort Terrace on 7 June, Daly and Sellars attempted to impose terms for a settlement. They agreed only to rephrase their ultimatum as a 'request' for the removal of the named RIC officers. At the inquiry, Deputy Commissioner Walsh, with more than a trace of irony, challenged Sellars to explain the difference. 'Is it not pretty much the same as saying, I won't shoot you through the heart, but I will blow your brains out?'

The following day, Collins and Duggan and their fellow-deputies Staines, Brennan and Liddy attended at Earlsfort Terrace for a meeting of the Dáil. In further discussion on the crisis in Kildare, Brennan protested that he was helpless in the situation; he had urged Staines 'ten times' to resume his command. Staines had resisted, saying he had resigned and would have nothing more to do with the Civic Guard.[38]

'I HEARD THE SINGING AND THE HUMMING OF THE BULLET'

On his visit to the depot, Collins had promised an inquiry, proposing that in the meantime the Commissioner and his staff should return to their posts in Kildare. Daly agreed, on condition that a party of not more than five officers attend. On 9 June, bowing to pressure, Staines once again presented himself at the depot gate, accompanied by practically his entire staff. Excited sentries ordered them away, and they returned immediately to Dublin. Later in the day, Superintendent Byrne and Sergeant McAvinue, who were based at Clonskeagh Castle in the south Dublin suburbs, arrived by train. Their appearance rekindled the mutineers' earlier anger. The two officers retreated, followed by armed civic guards and 'hundreds' of townspeople shouting insults after them; in the melee Sergeant McNamara 'pulled a gun, and I pulled mine.' McNamara shouted: 'Close in, fellows, don't be afraid,' and fired a shot. 'I heard the singing and the humming of the bullet,' Byrne testified. McAvinue saw the 'smoking gun' in McNamara's hand and drew his own revolver. McNamara claimed that Byrne had made the first move: 'I drew my revolver and fired a shot in the air.' In the stampede that followed there was uproar, and a section of the mob sang 'The Bold Black and Tans'.[39]

Stones rained down on Byrne and McAvinue as they ran from the scene. At the Railway Hotel, McAvinue was attempting to make a telephone call when the crowd outside threatened to set fire to the building. Pushed out the back door by the excited manager, they took refuge in the attic of a house. When the crowd began to disperse they fled through back yards to a cottage, where an old man befriended them. At the approach of armed men wearing bandoliers, the fugitives escaped across the fields. It was now raining hard. Leaving their pursuers behind, they found their way to the Carmelite church at Whiteabbey. In the tradition of sanctuary, they were given shelter by 'Father Brady'[40], and they returned to Dublin on the morning train.

Brennan was present in the depot during all the time the drama was being played out. 'I heard there was some kind of "fan-dango" up the street,' he told the inquiry.

The rout of the Commissioner and his officers strengthened Daly's hand. On 18 June he informed the 'commandant', Superintendent Lynch, that he had received a message by telephone to go to Dublin to collect a party of guards. A guard named Delahunty who was on duty in the transport lines saw nothing irregular in Daly's requisition for vehicles. Suspicious of Daly's intentions, Lynch conferred with Superintendent Haugh, and the two officers decided to take charge of the detail. Armed with rifles, Daly and his accomplices left the depot, Daly leading the way in a car, followed by two tenders.

At Kildare Cross, three miles on the Dublin side of the town, they were held up and disarmed by a band of Irregulars, who were on a mission important enough for the personal attention of Rory O'Connor, accompanied by the guerrilla commanders Ernie O'Malley and Tom Barry, all three travelling together in an armoured car.[41] Lynch and Haugh were misled by the armoured car; Haugh 'never dreamed the Irregulars had one.'[42] O'Connor called on the civic guards to join him, promising to pay their overdue wages. Lynch and Haugh refused and were taken prisoner and held with captured national army soldiers in a roadside cottage guarded by O'Malley.[43]

Daly now became a prominent actor in the drama, returning to the depot in a convoy led by O'Connor in the armoured car. The password, betrayed by Daly, admitted the raiders to the depot. Making their way unchallenged to the armoury, they tied up Guard Michael Fallon and the other guards on duty, loaded the arms, and left immediately for Dublin. At Kildare Cross they released their prisoners, leaving Lynch and Haugh to return to the depot on foot. The defiance of the Provisional Government in this enterprise, carried out a full week before the bombardment of the Four Courts in the early hours of 28 June, signalled the start of the Civil War.

On Saturday 24 June, President Arthur Griffith and his wife and family and the Minister for Home Affairs, Éamonn Duggan, and his wife were guests at luncheon in the officers' mess. The Griffiths were driven down by Staines, followed by the Duggans travelling in Brennan's car. For the battle-weary politicians the drive to Kildare in the troubled summer of 1922 held out the prospect of some relaxation after the turmoil of the recent elections. The outcome in Dublin North-Central was a personal triumph for Staines, who overcame the poster campaign to retain his seat.

The distinguished visitors were received by Surgeon Madden, who alone was available to meet them. Ring was at a football match in Dublin, and Lynch was also on leave. Liddy had already dined. Brennan did not appear, under the mistaken impression that the RIC men were at table with the guests: not being commissioned officers of the Civic Guard they were not entitled to be there, he told the inquiry. He alleged that the Volunteer officers, Brigadier Ring, Commandant Lynch, and Commandant Liddy, had not been invited; these men, with Commandant Staines and Colonel-Commandant Brennan himself, could alone claim the status of commissioned rank. On this point the inquiry was sympathetic to Brennan: he was within his rights in refusing to sit with non-commissioned men.

THE COMMISSIONER BACK AT HIS DESK

In post-prandial discussions in Brennan's absence it was decided that the time was ripe to put the Civic Guard back on an even keel. The following Wednesday, 28 June, at 4:07 a.m., national army troops began the bombardment of the Four

Courts. Later in the day, in a highly symbolic move, Staines 'resumed charge' in Kildare, accompanied by McCarthy and McCormack and others. Staines met Assistant Commissioner Brennan in what must have been a frosty encounter. He also interviewed the other officers, including Patrick Haugh, who had resumed duty as depot adjutant. Liddy, with two subordinates, Seán Scanlan and P. Kierse, was absent in County Clare for the county council elections.[44] Reporting to Home Affairs on the visit, Staines was 'glad to say' that the general impression conveyed was much more favourable than on previous visits. He did not recover substantive command until 12 July, when the remnants of Daly's committee surrendered control of the depot on the eve of the inquiry.

As accounting officer, McCormack checked the available pay-sheets for May and June. The recruits and staff members who remained on duty in Kildare and Newbridge had received no wages since the money due to them for April was paid early in May. According to Sellars, the Commissioner had 'bluntly refused' to pay the men pending a 'complete stocktaking'.[45] Liddy accused Staines of conducting 'a cold war … between Kildare and Dublin.'[46] The men were not paid simply because the pay-sheets had not been presented to the Commissioner, for the obvious reason that his officers had been prevented from carrying out their duties. Giving his evidence at the inquiry, Staines reasoned with the other witnesses: 'I got the pay sheets two days before you were paid, men.'

In later years Liddy recalled the esprit de corps in the cash-starved camp. In adversity they had discovered 'a sort of Foreign Legion loyalty … of share and share alike.' Mess debts running into thousands of pounds were incurred with local traders; all these bills, including the slate in the public houses of Kildare and Newbridge, were 'fully paid up.'[47] Canteen funds amounting to some £246 were seized to pay public debts. The canteen committee was afterwards reimbursed by Home Affairs, O'Friel deeming it 'imprudent to stir up again the trouble.'[48]

On 12 June a guard was accidentally shot dead in Newbridge. Brennan reported that his comrades had no money to pay the funeral expenses. The incident was grist to the mill in Little Denmark Street, where Staines wrote of a 'tragic occurrence' illustrating 'the state of indiscipline which exists in the Guard since the members encouraged by those who might have known better went into open revolt and repudiated all authority.'[49]

A strange story of money in a shoebox was recounted by a Garda widow half a century later. On the afternoon of 15 May Brigadier George O'Dwyer, a Kilkenny Volunteer officer, presented himself in Kildare to take up an offer of employment in the new police. Travelling on to Newbridge, he took command from Superintendent Kelleher, who was leaving the force. O'Dwyer had begun an adventurous career in 1907 as a constable in the DMP. Resigning to join an uncle prospecting for gold in Australia, he was soon back in uniform in the Sydney City Police, followed by a spell in the New Zealand Mounted Police. Hearing of the 1916

Rising a year after the event, he returned home to form a company of the Volunteers in Castlecomer.

Recently married, O'Dwyer took up residence in the officers' quarters in Newbridge Barracks. On a warm midsummer afternoon in 1922, Angela O'Dwyer was in the garden gathering strawberries left behind by the previous British army tenant when she was startled by a volley of shots. Guard William Meskill, from Kilfinan, County Kerry, who was on duty in the cookhouse, shouted to her to take cover. The brigadier may have considered the volley as providential in solving the problem of morale in the company lines; the following morning, at all events, acting on his own initiative, he left for Dublin to report the explosive situation to Collins, taking with him his young wife, a former captain in the Dunbell (County Kilkenny) company of Cumann na mBan.

Collins listened with good humour to O'Dwyer's report, and then produced a cardboard shoebox packed with banknotes and tied with string. Mrs O'Dwyer expressed fears for the journey in carrying so much money; she hoped they would not be held up on the way back to Newbridge. Collins laughed: 'If you're stopped and asked what's in the box, tell them ladies' unmentionables, and if they're gentlemen they won't want to look.' At Rathcoole they were stopped by a man named Kennedy, who warned that the road was mined. Taking to the back roads, Kennedy in his own car led the O'Dwyers safely into Newbridge, where they were greeted with delight by the penniless guards.[50]

In justification of a delayed claim for car hire, O'Dwyer took the opportunity to impress General O'Duffy, who replaced Staines in September. He had arrived in Kildare on 15 May to find that the Civic Guard had mutinied, 'weaned from their allegiance ... I set to work to instil discipline into them and show them the errors of their ways ... My actions largely contributed to holding together the Civic Guard.'[51] The new Commissioner made no comment on O'Dwyer's report.

On another file, O'Duffy acknowledged the part played by a former Volunteer officer in County Cork, Superintendent Daniel Hallinan, in stabilising the force in the aftermath of the mutiny. Towards the end of 1922 Hallinan was accused by army personnel of 'partiality and disloyalty' in the enforcement of the licensing laws in Naas. O'Duffy defended his officer as 'one of the men who stood out fearlessly at the time of the Kildare split ... He took a strong stand against the self-appointed committee [and] stood his ground in Kildare ... and bad as the position was, it would have been much more disgraceful were it not for the steadying effect of Supt. Hallinan.'[52]

'DISBANDED BUT NOT DISPERSED'

The warrant of the Provisional Government appointing a commission of inquiry was signed by Collins on 12 July, perhaps his last act as chairman before taking up duty as commander-in-chief of the government forces in the Civil War.[53] The inquiry convened at Kildare the following day and sat on Friday, Saturday and

Monday to hear the evidence of witnesses. The only shot fired in anger from beginning to end in the affair was admitted by Sergeant McNamara, the Volunteer of the East Limerick ASU who had been beaten with police rifle butts. He was called on the third day. Lumping the RIC together with the Black and Tans, he vented his resentment on the Deputy Commissioner. When Walsh moved to question the witness, McNamara refused to be cross-examined by 'a disbanded District Inspector ... I do not recognise him as an officer and never did and never will ... My conscience would not allow me to answer a man of his type.' McNamara's outburst brought the proceedings to a sudden close, before Brennan was called. It seems that O'Sheil and McAuliffe were prepared to make their report on the basis of the evidence already given. Brennan insisted on being heard and appealed directly to Collins.[54] On instructions from Collins, the commissioners reconvened the inquiry at Government Buildings the following Friday and Saturday to facilitate Brennan.

The report, presented on 7 August, found that the infiltration of the Civic Guard and the seizure of its arms by anti-Treaty forces was planned from the day the recruits began to arrive at Ballsbridge.[55] Thomas Daly and his fellow-conspirators identified District Inspector John Kearney as the most vulnerable among the RIC men.

Practically all the evidence tendered on behalf of the disaffected parties hinged on the question of the former RIC men and their influence in the Civic Guard. In the circumstances 'the extensive use made of the R.I.C. ... may have been unwise ... Considering that the main body were ex-I.R.A. men ... the presence and power of the ex-R.I.C. lent itself to give a certain amount of justice to the view point of the men.' But Commissioner Staines had appointed policemen who were naturally specially qualified, and more especially 'whose credentials were satisfactory to the Provisional Government.'

Jeremiah Maher resigned from the RIC in September 1920 to join the Volunteers as a divisional intelligence officer. The other former RIC men either had similar histories or were ordered to remain in the force 'for special purposes.' The expulsion of these officers 'was undoubtedly looked upon with favour—if not actually connived at—by a number of [Civic Guard] officers and men, some from honest if misguided motives, and some from a purely selfish standpoint'; but 'the main cause of the disaffection was undoubtedly ... propaganda from outside the force, aided to a small extent from within [aimed at] smashing the Civic Guard completely.'

The force was also gravely compromised by the presence within its ranks of active politicians, principally Staines, Brennan, and Liddy; and the conspirators had not hesitated to exploit their advantage. 'Defamatory posters were put up in Dublin with the evident intention of defeating the election of Michael Staines, T.D.' It was self-evident that the presence of civic guards on duty at an election contested by a member of the force would provoke trouble, and the commissioners could not contemplate 'what serious developments' might have resulted from the divided loyalties of public representatives wearing policemen's uniforms. The force had been so compromised that disbanding seemed unavoidable. McAuliffe turned for advice to Superintendent Bernard O'Connor.[56]

O'Connor impressed McAuliffe, who put him 'a serious question': if the charges before the inquiry were proved, was it possible for the Civic Guard to survive? Thinking aloud, O'Connor carefully framed his answer. 'As a disciplined, well-trained force to protect the Irish people?' he mused. If the instigators of the trouble were removed, no doubt the men, seeing their folly, would make good policemen. O'Sheil asked him if that could be achieved without disbanding the force. O'Connor demurred; it was too serious a question for him to answer. McAuliffe encouraged him, 'as a man with previous experience in a disciplined force … I put the question to you, before I would put it to anybody else.' O'Connor considered his reply and offered sound advice, which also brought some light relief to the proceedings. 'Youth is youth. I was recommended for dismissal myself … I had two years' service in the R.I.C., and turned out a good boy afterwards.'

The report was considered by the government on 18 August, Collins making his last appearance at a meeting before setting off on his tour of the southern battlefields. In view of the 'extraordinary situation' in the country, but also clearly influenced by O'Connor's optimistic assessment of the potential for a new start, the report stopped short of the drastic step of sending the men home. Adopting the formula suggested by O'Sheil and McAuliffe, it agreed to technically 'disband but not disperse' the Civic Guard and immediately, by selective enrolment, to reconstitute the force, with temporary officers and every man on probation. It was also decided that Staines should resign, on the obvious grounds that, with his politician's hat, he was compromised in his role as commissioner of police.[57]

On the fateful 22 August, as Collins was touring the west Cork countryside he knew so well, his colleagues in government, with W. T. Cosgrave as acting chairman, accepted the resignation of Michael Staines 'with regret.' The Deputy Commissioner's principled resignation in the immediate aftermath of the mutiny was refused;[58] but the tragedy at Bealnablagh was soon to overtake that wise decision, leaving Walsh on the sideline until, at O'Duffy's urging, he was reappointed as assistant commissioner.

In a significant recommendation, O'Sheil and McAuliffe echoed the views of the recruits put by their articulate representative, J. A. O'Connell, who had argued for an international solution. 'If experts had been required to establish a new police force for Ireland, the Government should have very easily procured the services of retired officers of the American, French or German police forces … of any police force in the world, except the R.I.C.' The report urged the government to retain the services of 'highly experienced officers or ex-officers of a foreign police body to act as high superintending officers of the Civic Guard … for preference American, French or German police officers.' It also recommended an advisory council, significantly under Patrick Walsh as chairman, assisted by 'one or two others,' not former members of the RIC or DMP. Former policemen with a good national record would have a part to play, but only in subsidiary roles: command posts in the Civic Guard were reserved for Volunteer officers and others who had fought in the War of Independence.

Crucially, the O'Sheil-McAuliffe inquiry recommended disarming the new police, to the extent that not even a privately owned firearm was to be held by any member of the force.

To copperfasten this radical departure and bring the police service into a new close relationship with the people, the report recommended the use of the Civic Guard in a wide range of local government activities: the collection of census returns and agricultural statistics, weights and measures duties, the supervision of standards and prices of food and drugs, and local transport facilities, fire brigade and ambulance duties; and it envisaged the employment of civic guards even as sanitary inspectors.

The report idealised 'a police body that shall be the servants of the people ... neither militaristic nor coercive, above party and class, serving the Government of the people, no matter what form of Government the people may elect at any time, and responsible to that Government alone.' This definition of the role and character of the new police, adumbrated by O'Sheil and McAuliffe, provided the basis for the message of a new Minister for Home Affairs, Kevin O'Higgins, to the officers and men of the Civic Guard that appeared in the first issue of a new magazine, *Iris an Gharda*.[59]

> The internal politics and political controversies of the country are not your concern. You will serve, with the same imperturbable discipline and with increasing efficiency any Executive which has the support of the majority of the people's elected representatives. Party will, no doubt, succeed party in the ebb and flow of the political tide. New issues will arise to convulse the Nation. The landmarks of today will disappear. You will remain steadfast and devoted in the service of the people and of any executive which it may please the people to return to power. That is the real meaning of Democracy—Government of the people by the people through their elected representatives. It is the only barrier between mankind and anarchy.

CASUALTIES OF PEACE
In the confused aftermath of the mutiny, some of the principal actors—those who threw in their lot with the anti-Treaty faction, and perhaps 350 young men who were disillusioned by the events of May and June—quietly left Kildare and did not return. A strength of 1,500 early in May fell to 1,150 in mid-June; by mid-July the strength was 1,170, and thereafter it increased progressively week by week.[60]

Brigadier M. J. Ring, victor of the battle of Carrowkennedy, whose compassion for the Black and Tan casualties was legendary, was only twenty-nine when he died in the Bunnyconnellan ambush. His obituary was written by Staines.

> Though [he] worked with the greatest energy (very often late into the night) it was apparent to me that his métier was not at the desk, but in the field … He chafed under routine and rigid rules … Had he acted from selfish motives and embraced the opportunity of comfort and ease, he would have retained the post [in the Civic Guard] he was so competent to fill. The lure of Army life was irresistible.[61]

Superintendent P. J. Haugh, who was saddled by the mutineers with dubious honour as 'assistant commissioner', having served briefly as district officer in Wexford, resigned from the force. 'Commandant' Martin Lynch and 'adjutant' Seán Liddy and others directly involved in the upheaval survived in the service and attained high rank, Lynch and Liddy as chief superintendents. Liddy at first was given the task of opening new stations, which involved the discovery of suitable— or any available—premises. He was obviously happy at his work, as he reported to O'Duffy in October. 'I am extremely pleased by the manner and enthusiasm of the various towns and villages in Leix/Offaly taken over by our men … We were received with the greatest courtesy and kindness … far beyond what I had anticipated … They look upon the Guards as their future protectors.'[62] Having so strongly opposed the appointment of disbanded RIC officers to high rank in the Garda Síochána, Liddy served as district officer in Longford-Westmeath under a former RIC man, Chief Superintendent Bernard O'Connor.

Chief Inspector Robert McCrudden, the short-lived 'chief superintendent', was also rehabilitated and was transferred as district officer to Boyle. He retired soon afterwards, leaving no record of his service.

While Sergeant Patrick McNamara was not spared by O'Sheil for his personal attack on Deputy Commissioner Walsh, neither his involvement in the mutiny nor a stern rebuke in the inquiry report interrupted his career. Promoted inspector in 1929, he had the misfortune to be sent to Waterford, where he was caught up in the case of the missing Stradbally postman Laurence Griffin, who disappeared on Christmas Day that year. McNamara was held to have been negligent in the investigation and was called upon to resign. He was back in the force a year later, and he recovered his former rank in 1934; in 1940 he was promoted superintendent and sent to Carrick-on-Shannon, under Liddy, now chief superintendent in Sligo. He retired with an exemplary record in 1954.[63]

Sergeant Patrick Coy, the witness who joined Daly's committee in Ballsbridge, was sent as sergeant-in-charge to Cootehill, County Cavan, where he resigned to return home. O'Duffy accepted his resignation 'with regret … As he is urgently needed at home, I suppose it is useless asking him to reconsider his intention.'[64] Daly's right-hand man, Patrick Sellars, without reference to his Civic Guard superiors, joined the national army at Loughrea as an adjutant in the First Western Division. O'Duffy held open for months a file on Sellars's absence from duty. He had held his hand, wishing to give Sellars what chance he could, 'as no member of the Guard was punished or discriminated against for any action he had taken' in the mutiny.[65]

4

THE NEW POLICE AND THE CIVIL WAR

I hope you will not think that I do not appreciate the sacrifice that I am asking
of the Army ... I know that I am asking for its right arm.

A s Brennan was protesting his vision of the Republic in the mistaken belief
that he was being asked to dine with RIC men in the officers' mess, Rory
O'Connor was barricading the Four Courts. The murder of Field-Marshal
Sir Henry Wilson in London on 22 June hardened the attitude of the British
government. In the House of Commons on 26 June, Churchill warned that they
would seize the initiative if the Irish ministers did not move against the Irregulars.

That evening Leo Henderson, director of the Belfast Boycott in the Dáil
cabinet, was arrested in the act of raiding a garage for transport. In retaliation,
O'Connor's men captured the Assistant Chief of Staff, Major-General J. J. O'Connell,
and held him as a hostage for the release of Henderson. The Provisional
Government the following day served notice on 'the armed men in the Four
Courts.'[1]

On Wednesday 28 June, at 4:07 in the morning, Dublin awoke to the fury of
renewed fighting. The Irregulars surrendered on Friday, and O'Connor and Liam
Mellows were taken prisoner. Over the weekend there was scattered fighting in the
city, the two armies occupying buildings on opposite sides of O'Connell Street.
Austin Stack, Chief of Staff, and de Valera, now a private soldier in the army of the
Republic, evaded the cordon of national army troops to carry the fight to the
provinces.

The Provisional Government on 12 July, having decided unanimously to
confront the Irregulars in their strongholds in the provinces, appointed General
Michael Collins as commander-in-chief to head a council of war,[2] with General
Richard Mulcahy, Chief of Staff, and General Eoin O'Duffy, GOC South-Western
Command, Assistant Chief of Staff. In the absence of Collins on active service, W.
T. Cosgrave took the reins of government as acting chairman.

In Kildare and Newbridge the guards, in good spirits with their pay restored, awaited the outcome of the inquiry promised by Collins. There were good grounds for optimism. The gathering storm, which might otherwise have compromised the new police as armed participants in the Civil War, left the guardians of the peace standing on the neutral sidelines when the shooting started. There was a brief diversion when Brennan, reverting to his role as military commander, led a company of guards onto the battlefield.[3]

In his address to the Kildare Mutiny inquiry, J. A. O'Connell read into the record a declaration of loyalty on behalf of the men, repudiating 'T. P. Daly, Seán O'Brien, E. J. Ryan, Malachy Collison, Seán Doyle' and their comrades who had deserted to the Executive forces. 'Our loyalty is to Ireland, and we shall serve her through whatever Government she may lawfully elect.' No more than forty-one civic guards may have absconded.[4] O'Connell also read a letter dated 7 July sent by Brennan to Collins: 'Lest there should be any misapprehension ... it is my duty to convey to you the assurance that the officers and men of the Civic Guard in Kildare and Newbridge are holding themselves in readiness for any call (regardless of its nature) which the Government may make upon them.' Intervening, Staines stated that Brennan had been told by the Department of Defence that the men of the Civic Guard would render the best service by becoming efficient policemen.[5] But Staines himself felt obliged to depart from this advice when the needs of the commander-in-chief were presented to him as paramount.

Collins assumed control of an army of six thousand untrained soldiers; before the end of the war sixty thousand men were in uniform. In an apparent response to Brennan's pledge of support, he immediately sought the employment of the Civic Guard in military duties. Summoned urgently to attend a meeting of the Provisional Government, Staines reported resistance to the proposal among the men; but, ever loyal to Collins, he believed there would be no difficulty in getting enough men to volunteer.[6] Within twenty-four hours Staines had assembled in Kildare a full company ready to take up arms for Collins.[7]

The inquiry into the mutiny having collapsed when Sergeant McNamara refused to be cross-examined by Deputy Commissioner Walsh, O'Sheil returned to Dublin to describe to the cabinet 'a state of grave insubordination and lack of discipline.' Not alone was it impossible to employ the force as suggested by Collins but 'as constituted the Civic Guard could not be organised as a competent police force ... the only solution was to disband the men and organise a new force.'[8] The Minister for Agriculture, Patrick Hogan, rowed in with Collins. From O'Sheil's statement it was 'fairly clear' that 95 per cent of the men were 'loyal and first-class material.' The trouble appeared to have begun among the officers and to have influenced only a very small proportion of the men. Hogan proposed that a senior Volunteer officer be sent to Kildare to recruit eight hundred volunteers for active service. They were 'very anxious to re-establish themselves.'[9]

Collins had to be satisfied with the hundred men who had already volunteered. He wanted them organised as 'a sort of flying column' to keep in touch with the military in Newbridge and the Curragh and to patrol the railways in County Kildare day and night.[10] He demanded a daily report of activities, 'an exact statement'. It would not be enough to say nothing had happened: without details, the reports would not show whether or not the work was being done.[11]

Colonel-Commandant Brennan re-entered the fray in command of policemen armed with rifles, who became identified as the Civic Guard Active Service Unit. On Sunday 16 July posts were established at the railway stations in Newbridge and Monasterevin, in the towns of Kildare and Monasterevin, and later at Cloney, Duneany, Portarlington, and Athy.[12]

There was some early friction when soldiers taunted the policemen as 'green Black and Tans'.[13] At the head of an armed band in civilian clothes, Brennan was soon running into trouble; he asked for uniforms, caps at least, to avoid 'a collision with National Troops.' The people were suspicious: 'they take us to be Irregulars.'[14] He had to argue with the Quartermaster-General to have his bills paid. 'The ASU should not be asked to pay for billets or rations on active service.'[15] An official of the Great Southern and Western Railway complained that a gang repairing a bridge were surrounded by armed men not in uniform, who ordered the workmen to put up their hands, threatening them: 'We only shoot the bosses.' In the circumstances, the workmen were hardly reassured.[16]

There were other complaints. Early in August a letter to Collins from Ernest Blythe on behalf of the Minister for Home Affairs recorded an interview with Brennan at which Staines was present. Brennan admitted that on two occasions he had rounded up parties of civilians to assist in bridge repairs; he promised it would not happen again. At this meeting, Staines undertook to supply the new police uniform for men on railway patrols. 'With a view to checking the tendency ... to develop Flying Column activity,' the Civic Guard in future would be armed with revolvers and not rifles.[17] Brennan had seventy rifles, in addition to side-arms, but he was adamant that to cope on the battlefield he 'absolutely' required a hundred rifles.[18] Lieutenant-Commandant Seán Kavanagh, Naas military barracks, complained to the Adjutant-General that Brennan's men 'were not supposed to carry rifles while wearing Civic Guard uniform.' If the rifles were necessary they should wear military caps and greatcoats.[19] Collins was impatient. He had repeatedly stated that patrols out of uniform were 'a danger rather than a help' and created 'an extremely bad impression.'[20]

The rifles had been surrendered when, towards the end of August, a night patrol armed with revolvers was caught in the crossfire in an attack on the military barracks in Athy. As a result, Brennan was informed by telephone that Civic Guard patrols should carry rifles, 'for the present.'[21]

Preoccupied with the problems of the Civil War, Collins fretted at the setback in the Civic Guard and delays in the machinery of government that were denying the people the full enjoyment of national independence. In a familiar phrase, he had 'repeatedly asked' for the organisation of a voluntary local security force to respond to acts of vandalism, and he listed road-cutting, demolition of bridges, and attacks on the railways. 'The Civic Guard with the help of the population would discover the perpetrators and call in the military if necessary,' he wrote to Cosgrave.[22] To the end of his life he desperately sought to restore civil order, planning for a future he would not live to see. 'I have scarcely a moment for any business other than the urgent business of restoring peace and settled conditions to the country,' he wrote to Churchill on 25 July.[23] Reading Brennan's reports, Collins was increasingly troubled by the contradictions in the employment of civic guards in military operations. But the men had volunteered to protect the property of the railway company, and that was 'a civic duty' and properly police work.[24]

THE SIEGE OF LIMERICK

The real fighting was taking place in Munster, where O'Duffy had a pivotal role. The strategic city of Limerick was occupied in strength by anti-Treaty forces. When the British garrison moved out in February the city was taken by Liam Lynch, through a miscalculation by O'Duffy. The Assistant Chief of Staff was sent to Limerick to defuse a dispute over precedence between Commandant-General Michael Brennan, First Western Division—brother of Patrick Brennan of the Civic Guard—and Brigadier-General Liam Forde, Mid-Limerick Brigade. In a compromise, Brennan and Forde both retired, leaving Lynch and a band of anti-Treaty supporters in possession of the city.

To prevent the Irregulars in the 'Munster Republic' from advancing on Dublin, it was vital for the government to take the initiative in the south. General Emmet Dalton, with overall command of operations in the Cork area, planned a surprise attack by sea on Cork. He was well qualified for the task; as Major Dalton he had fought with distinction on the western front in the Great War, winning the Military Cross for bravery in battle. But in the view of General Brennan, 'the whole Civil War really turned on Limerick.'[25]

The assault on Limerick fell to O'Duffy. He had the good fortune to have assigned to him as command adjutant another experienced former British army officer, Brigadier-General William R. E. Murphy DSO MC. But the tactics of a professional soldier who had taken part in campaigns on the French and Italian fronts in the Great War were not always understood by officers conditioned by the guerrilla warfare of the War of Independence. His elaborate plans for the attack on Kilmallock, including an order to dig trenches, baffled the erstwhile Volunteers.[26]

National army troops laid siege to the city on 4 July, manning a line of barricades from Sarsfield Bridge, through William Street, Broad Street, and Mungret Street, to Athlunkard Bridge.[27] The new GOC, with fresh troops and badly needed weapons, including a solitary siege gun, reached Nenagh on Monday 17 July.[28] Directing operations from his headquarters at Killaloe, O'Duffy deployed his forces for the final assault on Limerick. The battle flared in street fighting the next day. On

Wednesday, with his artillery in position on Arthur's Quay, O'Duffy shelled enemy strongholds across the river, and resistance collapsed.

The retreating Irregulars set fire to buildings in the city. A newspaper reporter described

> the beginning of the end ... The weird and terrifying spectacle appals me ... Everywhere is lighted up with the dull red glare of many fires ... The people flock into the streets ... shocked and pained and bewildered. Friday morning 7.30 a.m.: Limerick has fallen ... The streets are still thronged with people. Provisions are eagerly sought and bought. Limerick today sorrows over her piles of blackened and smouldering ruins.[29]

On Sunday, in euphoric mood, O'Duffy signalled Collins: 'The civil population are jubilant, and at all the Masses today thanksgivings were said for the success of the National troops ... The 3rd Siege of Limerick has been a success ... I do not think that Sarsfield and his troops were as popular as the present victors.'[30] By the end of July he had taken Bruree and, advancing into north Kerry, had occupied Listowel and Tralee. In his drive into County Cork he suffered a setback when Commandant Cronin and a detachment of forty-seven soldiers were captured by enemy forces. O'Duffy was furious. 'This is the first reverse since I took command here, and it is a serious one. I gave express instructions, verbally and in writing that on no account were our troops to move south of Kilmallock until the Irregulars were driven out.'[31] Fanning out from Cork, Dalton raced O'Duffy to take Macroom. The Civil War ended in effect when Liam Lynch, Chief of Staff of the anti-Treaty forces, was killed by a stray bullet in a skirmish with national army troops in the Knockmealdown Mountains the following April.

In organising the old Volunteers and the new army recruits into a disciplined fighting force, O'Duffy had to grapple mainly with the problems of rivalry between officers who had been the unchallenged warlords in command of their own flying columns in the War of Independence. Reporting on the opposition of some of his officers to reorganisation of the South-Western Command, he described a Gilbertian competition for the possession of warlike stores between his commanders. Immediately on delivery, officers succeeded in 'collaring' supplies for themselves. He was determined 'to make Officers do their work ... and if they fail to remove them.'[32]

On Sunday 20 August, beginning a tour of the Munster battlefields, Collins called at Field General Headquarters in Limerick to congratulate O'Duffy personally on the capture of the city. He arrived in Cork towards nightfall and booked in at the Imperial Hotel. The following afternoon he wrote his last letter, expressing to Cosgrave his burning desire to see the new police on duty among the people. 'It would be a big thing to get the Civic Guards both here and in Limerick. Civil administration urgent everywhere in the South. The people are splendid.'[33]

On Tuesday 22 August, Collins resumed his tour of inspection. Late in the evening, travelling the narrow roads of west Cork, his little convoy of military vehicles drove into the ambush at Bealnablagh. As if every great movement of people in history requires a sacrificial offering, the death of Collins galvanised the Provisional Government into action to get the half-trained Civic Guard into the country.

As the relieved population of Limerick resumed normal life under martial law, Commandant-General McManus, Provost-Marshal, 'after a great deal of preparatory spade work,' enlisted twenty-four unarmed army reservists for service in a civil police force under the command of Lieutenant Kelly.[34] A decision having been taken that the new police would reoccupy the abandoned RIC barracks in the city, the Department of Home Affairs was informed that, the quartermaster in Limerick being fully stretched, the Civic Guard would have to provide for the needs of its own men.[35]

ASKING THE ARMY FOR ITS RIGHT ARM

When, in January 1922, O'Duffy was made Chief of Staff he expressed a preference for a police career. The following month he was present at the inaugural meeting of the Police Organising Committee, with an unconcealed ambition for the job of Commissioner. A civil engineer by profession, with a genius for organisation, he had learnt whatever he knew of military strategy and tactics as commander of a flying column in his native County Monaghan. The officer commanding Cork Command, Major-General Dalton, directed operations in the Civil War with the confidence of a professional soldier. In his own South-Western Command, O'Duffy counted on the advice and practical assistance of his adjutant, Commandant-General W. R. E. Murphy. It was not in his nature to be intimidated by the qualifications of professional soldiers; but clearly he had misgivings in his role as commander of a regular army in the field.

When Mulcahy on the death of Collins took over as Commander-in-Chief, in addition to his burdens as Minister for Defence, he wished to separate these responsibilities by making O'Duffy head of the army. Writing to Mulcahy on 6 September, O'Duffy recalled misgivings he had voiced earlier in the year.

> When it was first suggested that I should accept the position of Chief of Staff, I told you my objections—a fair conception of my shortcomings for a position of such responsibility involving sound military knowledge. I felt I had not this and suggested to you that I would be better suited for the position now offered. I would have accepted this position willingly then as I had an idea that I could organise a proper Police Force and that I would be of more service to the nation in such a capacity.[36]

In a government reshuffle on 30 August, approved by the postponed Third

Dáil on 9 September, O'Higgins was moved from Economic Affairs to replace Duggan in Home Affairs. He addressed himself immediately to the paramount problem of law enforcement. He was personally determined to appoint O'Duffy as Commissioner. Possibly to make way for O'Duffy, Mulcahy on 26 August undertook to speak to Commandant Seán Ó Muirthile, who had been nominated to replace Staines; within a week he reported that Ó Muirthile had declined the position.[37] O'Higgins barely gave himself time to sit at his desk before he wrote to Mulcahy.

The foundations of civil government were crumbling. Decrees of the courts were not being executed. Debts could not be collected; credit was no longer available; commercial life was at a standstill. With unemployment rising, O'Higgins feared a social crisis in the winter that would 'shatter all hope of founding a democratically governed Irish Free State.'[38] Extolling O'Duffy's unique fitness for office as chief of police, he reposed confidence to an extraordinary degree in the ability of one individual to restore peace. His man was 'by general agreement ... the only one capable of retrieving the Civic Guard ... and on the doing of that depends whether we shall succeed or fail in laying the foundations of a State.'

O'Higgins had studied the O'Sheil-McAuliffe report on the Kildare Mutiny. The condition in which he found the Civic Guard compelled him to ask the army to release O'Duffy, a request that he felt Mulcahy at first sight would consider 'astonishing'. The strength of the force was then 1,200 young men, 'fine fellows physically and drawn from the class which in the past supplied recruits for the R.I.C. ... the nucleus of a magnificent force which would rapidly restore security and respect for property in the country.' Discipline in the force had been undermined by the Four Courts conspirators, who had played on 'the ignorance of the men and the vanity of some officers ... about the worst possible experience for men who were to be peace officers.' O'Higgins was deeply impressed by his candidate's reputation as the army strong man par excellence. He left nothing unsaid in a job specification to match O'Duffy's prowess as a leader of men. The Civic Guard needed

> firm handling by some outstanding personality ... The new Commissioner's military service must be such as to dwarf that of any man or officer in the force ... a disciplinarian and himself a model to the men of efficiency and self-restraint. I am convinced that General O'Duffy could, in spite of all that has happened, mould these men ... I hope you will not think that I do not appreciate the sacrifice that I am asking of the Army ... I know that I am asking for its right arm.[39]

Mulcahy hardly had to urge O'Duffy to accept the challenge. 'I appreciate very much the fact that your taking up the police question would be a very important gesture ... would be looked upon as showing that the Government was effectively turning its mind to the constructive work of society.'[40]

Having written to Mulcahy on 1 September, O'Higgins three days later sent an impatient reminder. Tension in the Civic Guard was increasing; there was general dissatisfaction at the delay in implementing the report of the Kildare inquiry; but the leadership of the force had to be settled first. He wanted a decision by telephone, 'yes or no'; and would O'Duffy 'come to town with the minimum of delay.'[41]

O'Duffy 'from a sense of duty' signalled his acceptance. 'I appreciate the difficulties of the Government.' And he added: 'The Command staff and other senior officers are very much upset over my leaving.'[42] In the South-Western Command it is not unlikely that there was also a sigh of relief at the departure of a general who was 'rather given to making pompous little homilies to meetings of army officers.'[43]

THE GENTLEST OF MEN

On 13 August the civil servant Alfred Cope notified the government of the arrangements for the evacuation two days later of Dublin Castle and the adjoining Ship Street military barracks. The stragglers of the RIC having withdrawn, the responsibility of the British government for the safety of the Castle and barracks would cease.[44] In a separate letter to Mulcahy, Cope expressed anxiety for security: the Castle was 'very vulnerable,' which would have been good news for generations of Irish revolutionaries. The RIC sentries had been armed with rifles; machine-gun posts were manned by soldiers. As it was likely that the Provisional Government would not be arming the Civic Guard 'in a military fashion,' he recommended that a detachment of troops take charge of the machine-gun posts.[45]

On 17 August, Staines led a contingent of the new police into the Lower Castle Yard. Under the command of Chief Superintendent McCarthy, the policemen, dressed in the unfamiliar new uniform, paraded for inspection under the gaping windows of the Revenue building—a proud experience for the young men taking part. For Staines personally, in his last weeks in office, his own role in the highly symbolic occupation of Dublin Castle by unarmed servants of the new state compensated in no small measure for the disappointments of previous months.[46] He was again a candidate in the August 1923 elections; losing his seat in the re-drawn constituency of Dublin North, he was appointed to the Senate of the Irish Free State and later established himself in business as a manufacturer's agent.

The revolutionary years had called for 'ruthless leadership', the secretary of the Joint Representative Body, Sergeant P. J. Gallagher, recalled on the death in 1955 of the first Garda Commissioner. 'Michael Staines … was the gentlest of men, and his whole life was characterised by a complete absence of bitterness.'[47] His one act of ruthlessness, the unjust 'sacking' of District Inspector Kearney in the highly charged atmosphere in the Ballsbridge depot, was out of character. The idealist of non-violent Sinn Féin, friend of Arthur Griffith, the organising genius identified by Collins and confirmed by Mulcahy as the 'obvious choice' for the top job in the new police, by a single misjudged decision gave himself as a hostage to history. His assistant commissioner, Patrick Brennan, made greater mistakes; with Staines, he left the force to take up a job as 'officer in charge of communications' in the Dáil.[48]

With Eoin O'Duffy in office as chief of police, President Cosgrave appointed Éamonn Coogan to the post of Deputy Commissioner vacated by Patrick Walsh. In preferring the neutral figure of his former civil service official in the Department of Local Government, Cosgrave avoided controversy over the appointment of former RIC officers to high rank and the conflicting ambitions of Volunteer officers in the new police. Coogan was to assume the duties of Commissioner for lengthy periods during the critical early years of the state, when O'Duffy was out of the country attending meetings of the International Association of Chiefs of Police in 1923 and 1925 and in 1924 during his absence as Inspector-General of the Defence Forces in the aftermath of the army mutiny. O'Duffy, Coogan and Walsh together steered the unarmed force through the crisis of the Civil War.[49]

GETTING THE CIVIC GUARD OUT ON DUTY
Early in September, Mulcahy informed Home Affairs that General O'Duffy, who was still at Limerick, and General Dalton in Cork were pressing for the deployment of the Civic Guard; to concentrate its forces, the army was evacuating outposts, exposing to attack by Irregular forces scarce accommodation needed for the police.[50] O'Duffy, hardly a week in his new job, notified his intention of beginning the deployment immediately; he had already detailed officers to supervise the preparations.[51] Barrack accommodation had to be evacuated by the army and made ready for the police, and furniture and culinary equipment provided. Where a barracks had been destroyed, alternative accommodation had to be found.

The desperate need to re-establish a police service created a logistical nightmare for Sir Philip Hanson, chairman of the Commissioners of Public Works. Apart from the insuperable problem of finding adequate barracks in rural areas, the Office of Public Works overnight had to provide bedding and basic furniture for a force of four thousand men leaving for the country at an accelerating rate. The barrackmaster, Superintendent James Brennan, complained that supplies were 'entirely insufficient'.[52] On top of all his difficulties, O'Duffy was chided by O'Friel for dealing directly with the OPW; in future all communications were to be directed in the first instance to his department.[53]

Station parties of a sergeant and four or five guards with rudimentary furniture and equipment, including a standard parcel of stationery, travelled by train and bus to the nearest town. They were met by the Civic Guard liaison officers; those destined for more remote stations were conveyed by hackney car on the last leg of the journey. Their luggage followed usually in farm carts.

There was no honeymoon for the new police. As winter closed in, a proclamation by the Irregulars over the name of Brigadier A. Murphy was posted in Munster:

The Civic Guard has been organised by the Provisional Government as a police force of semi-military character … a continuance of the old R.I.C. … After January 1st, 1923, such measures as are deemed necessary will be taken to prevent the Civic Guard functioning … Before taking drastic action, an opportunity will be afforded to all members of the Civic Guard to return to their homes and civil employment.

O'Duffy reported that 'similar warnings in identical terms' had been delivered by 'nocturnal visitors' in various parts of the country, to 'force the Government to arm the force.'[54] A long, troubled winter lay ahead. Under cover of darkness, bands of armed Irregulars attacked isolated police units and burned or bombed the improvised barracks, the flames engulfing furniture and bedding, station records, and the bicycles and other private property of the men. As it would have taken days for new stores to arrive from Dublin, general sanction was given to purchase bedding locally to replace that destroyed in raids.[55]

In a characteristic response, O'Duffy addressed a rallying cry to the force. In its naked appeal to patriotism, it is a remarkable document, wholly authentic for its time and place. He was addressing personally every individual member of the force, for he felt 'very much one of the Civic Guard' himself. Their barracks had been raided. Were they obliged to open their doors

> … to give over the public property and equipment which was given in charge to them, and to strip themselves of their clothing and hand them over to the first low corner-boy who comes in and makes such a demand? I think I can answer for them … The Civic Guard are unarmed … Therein lies their strength, and the place they have obtained in the hearts of the people.
>
> The Civic Guard is largely composed of Column men whose name for bravery and resource has become household words. If they were nothing more, they are Irishmen, and the Gael is not by nature a coward or a poltroon. Have the men whom I have described lost the bravery and daring which was theirs, or have they forgotten the attributes of their race since they became members of the Civic Guard?
>
> The Civic Guard is a strong man unarmed. What should he do when the armed loafer comes along to humiliate a man he would not dare speak to at other times?
>
> Men of the Guard, you are not bound to open your doors—they will be broken in—let them … There will be shots fired—probably—but you have heard firearms speaking before. You are not alarmed at the sound surely …
>
> Your clothes are wanted—will you hand them over? I think not—let the man who wants them take them—unless I am mistaken he will not have an easy task …
>
> The enemies of the Guard are the enemies of Ireland, and this is in itself the strongest reason why there should be no weakening in the resistance to the

intolerable demands of those scoundrels ... Poor men throughout the country have resisted, and women have resisted, and successfully resisted, such invasions, and shall it be said the Civic Guard tamely surrendered ...?[56]

The refusal of the station party at Wolfhill, County Kilkenny, to open the barrack door foiled an attack. Their success was lauded by O'Friel. 'Such courageous adherence to orders by unarmed Guards against armed attackers augurs well for the future of the force.'[57] Following an attack on Feakle, County Roscommon, Coogan decided that a general assault was being mounted on the Civic Guard.[58] The more experienced O'Duffy, sitting at his desk on Christmas Day, was more optimistic. It could be said that a general attack was in progress. There were a few men in each area not well disposed to the police who might succeed in enrolling a few others for an adventure in which there was 'so little risk.' No-one was more likely to organise a raid than dismissed guards, and it was known that on some occasions they had been among the raiders—a more probable explanation of the incidents than part of a settled policy.[59]

He circulated his optimistic analysis of the situation to his officers in the field. Acknowledging the Commissioner's reassurance, the district officer at Bandon, Superintendent Éamonn O'Duffy, described his men as 'somewhat restive' since the Irregulars posted their proclamation. He drew an angry rebuff from O'Duffy. The thing was a lie, and every member of the Civic Guard knew it to be so, and the public knew it also.

> There is nothing of a militaristic character about the Civic Guard. They are absolutely unarmed, and they have absolutely nothing to do with the Army. There are no persons in the country more alive to these facts than the authors of [these] 'Proclamations' ... They know there are some people ready to swallow anything, and amongst the gullible ones, so far as I can gather, are some of the Civic Guard themselves ... There is no place in the Guard for men who are uneasy or restive or discontented ... I am prepared to accept at short notice the resignations of all such men ... irrespective of rank ... The last thing the people require ... is the retention of faint-hearted or faithless public servants.[60]

Early reports of attacks on stations in County Clare caused him 'some misgivings', but he did not think there was any reason for despondency.[61] At Kilkee, towards the end of 1922, 'resolute determination' by the sergeant and station party was 'deserving of all praise and impressed even the cowardly crew who fired into a house occupied by unarmed men.'[62] Commenting on an attack on Ennis early in January, he wrote: 'There are few more curious things ... than the relapse of Clare. For a county free from Irregular opposition not long since, armed robbers appear to move with singular freedom and impunity and safe victims are selected in the unarmed Guard while of fighting proper there is none.'[63] In Kilkenny a 'rowdy class' had become more aggressive and needed 'to be firmly dealt with.' The 'better elements' were 'rallying slowly to the side of order.'[64]

The superintendent at Elphin reported a rumour in circulation that an order had been given to the Irregulars 'to harass and drive out the Civic Guard.'[65] When the barracks was destroyed on 13 January, emergency accommodation was provided in the local grammar school.[66] The station party presumably were still in occupation on the night of 19 February when the town was again attacked. In a typical report, Sergeant Patrick Allen described what happened. A knock was answered by the barrack orderly, Guard Michael McGowan, who refused to open the door.

> The door was then forced in and a number of armed men entered, all carrying rifles with the exception of the leader who carried a revolver. On coming towards me he said, 'Were you not ordered to leave this district before?' I replied ... the only orders we could accept was orders from our own officers. He then orders his men to collect all public property ... The raiders collected all the bed clothes, mattresses, bed springs, and carried them out towards the road.

Sergeant Allen instructed his men to put on their greatcoats and to hold on to their uniforms. The raiders,

> having loaded their loot on a commandeered lorry ... seized the station diary and patrol book. The leader came to me and said, 'Which way will you go, to Boyle or Strokestown?' I replied, 'We're not leaving town.' He said, 'You will have to.' I said, 'If we do we will go dead ...' Two men then appeared carrying petrol and started to sprinkle the floor ... The town was patrolled by about 60 men carrying rifles.[67]

In a bout of pessimism uncharacteristic in O'Duffy at that period but casting a long shadow, he was so concerned at 'numerous attacks on premises occupied by the Civic Guard' that he felt constrained to serve notice on Home Affairs that he would not occupy any barracks 'at any time in the future' unless a military unit was also stationed in the neighbourhood.[68] In a postscript, Coogan stressed that the Commissioner was not seeking evacuation of stations by the army for use by the Civic Guard, if evacuation meant that the soldiers would be withdrawn.[69]

The campaign intensified in the new year. Up to 31 March, sixty-six barracks were attacked, and in nineteen instances civic guards on patrol were assaulted.[70] In an attack on Rathowen barracks, a sledgehammer was used to break open the door; the floors were sprinkled with kerosene and the building set alight. 'The people of Rathowen treated the Guards with the utmost possible kindness and consideration.'[71] In the late autumn of 1923, following an isolated attack on Monivea, County Galway, Inspector Edmund Tobin found the station party 'serene'.[72]

There are few records of personal injuries to guards during the Civil War. In May 1923 Guard James Mulroy and Guard John Donlon, stationed at Broadford, County Clare, on patrol at O'Callaghan's Mills, were attacked by two armed men. Mulroy tackled one of the criminals and in the struggle was clubbed with a shotgun and left for dead. Mulroy became the first recipient of the Walter Scott Medal for Valour, the Garda decoration for bravery.[73] At Toornafulla, County Limerick, Sergeant Francis McCague was wounded in a 'cowardly and murderous attack.'[74] An unnamed guard serving a summons near Shannon Harbour was set upon by two armed men and beaten with revolvers. He lay unconscious where he fell until found by a military patrol.[75]

In another case reported by Superintendent O'Duffy of Bandon, the intended victim was more fortunate. In November, close on seven months after the ceasefire, at Berrings, near Coachford, County Cork, Sergeant John Mulvey was jeered by a crowd of bystanders. 'Come on, the Civic Guards, we'll give it to you. We don't give a damn about Civic Guards or Free Staters. We have guns tonight.' A shot was fired in Mulvey's direction. A government marine officer appeared on the scene, firing his revolver in the air, and the crowd fell back. Mulvey arrested the two culprits and, with his rescuer, retreated into the post office. As the crowd smashed the windows, the sergeant telephoned the army post in Macroom for assistance.[76]

COMMISSIONER'S MONTHLY CONFIDENTIAL REPORT

In February 1923 O'Duffy submitted to the Department of Home Affairs an objective analysis of conditions in the country at the height of the Civil War.[77] In Dublin the greatest problems were caused by gangs, 'city scum … always alive for any chance to plunder and loot, ready to espouse any cause which undermines order and government.' The situation in east Wicklow was 'practically normal'; on 'the western slopes of the county the Irregulars had complete freedom and the people were intimidated.' The reports from the stations spoke of coldness and a want of support, but the Wicklow people were not 'at any time a demonstrative people.' County Kildare was scourged by 'an orgy of crime which inevitably follows on decay of ordered government.' County Wexford was 'thoroughly unsatisfactory and unsafe'; the military situation was 'deplorable'. The people were well disposed but were fearful; 'the shadow of the anarchist' loomed over the county.

O'Duffy was hearing 'golden opinions' about the Civic Guard in County Donegal, the best-policed county, with 'none of the wild and insane orgies of crime common in other counties'; but the poitín trade was a serious problem. In December 1922 an attack on Gaoth Dobhair and destruction of the barracks, 'burned to the ground,' was the work of poitín-makers and of people who did not wish to pay rates, who saw in the Civic Guard 'a menace to their schemes.' Vested interests in Gaoth Dobhair were 'taking steps to secure their industry.' In County Mayo 'wholesale activity' in illicit distillation was 'the greatest evil'; in County Longford over twenty people 'in a demented state' from drinking poitín had been committed to the mental hospital. County Kerry was 'spared the curse of illicit distillation' but otherwise was 'unsatisfactory in the extreme. This county baffles description.' The people were well disposed but inarticulate; the 'noisy and cowardly ruled the many with gun and torch.'[78]

The monthly *Iris an Gharda* featured the campaign against the poitín trade with photographs of stills and other equipment seized in raids.[79] The magazine quoted the *Spectator* on an 'appalling' situation; the bishops in their Lenten pastoral letters had expressed their views 'in tones almost of despair.'[80] The poitín trade was endemic in rural Ireland; in the short term the Civic Guard could do little more than contain the traffic. But the crime problem in general was being tackled with considerable success. Criminal activity continued into 1924 but on a decreasing scale.[81]

The Commissioner's monthly confidential report to the Minister for Justice, based on local assessments furnished by divisional officers, became part of the routine business of the Garda Síochána. Summing up the first report, for January and February 1923, O'Duffy took a jaundiced view of a supine community. It was 'not creditable to a people to sit and look on at the robbery and destruction of their all and raise no hand in defence ... The people must be saved, almost in spite of themselves.'

THE ATTACK ON BALTINGLASS

In an attack on Baltinglass, County Wicklow, on 13 January 1923 the station party of four unarmed civic guards defied a company of fifty Irregulars. How the raiders were faced down by a handful of guards was described by a proud Commissioner in a bombastic report to Home Affairs.[82] O'Duffy's style may strike the reader in another age as theatrical, but there is no gainsaying his sincerity. Taken together, General Order No. 9, 'Raids and Attacks on Civic Guard Barracks' (already quoted), and his report on the Baltinglass incident stand on the record as evidence of the moral response by the state to the Civil War.

Only two members of the station party were named in the Baltinglass report, Patrick Joseph O'Halloran and a Guard O'Sullivan; the sergeant was absent on leave. In the early hours of 13 January there was loud knocking on the door and a peremptory order to 'open the door at once ... IRA.' The station orderly shouted back, 'There are no IRA in Wicklow. There never was an IRA colonel in Wicklow while there was fighting on ... There are some IRA [here in the barracks] so go away and don't make so much noise.' The raiders returned with sledgehammers and crowbars; breaking in the door, they made their way upstairs, where the four policemen were nonchalantly lying on their beds dressed in uniform. Guard O'Sullivan challenged the intruders to single combat. Guard O'Halloran produced a photograph of the erstwhile depot commandant at Kildare, Brigadier-General M. J. Ring. 'I fought with that man in the west for three years, and some curs like you murdered him. What do we care for you, a lot of contemptible robbers. I often looked down a rifle barrel.' He had been wounded in a fight with the enemies of their country, and so had his comrades. O'Halloran showed his scars: 'Where are your wounds?'

Ordered to open the sergeant's box, O'Sullivan held up the key and defied the intruders to take it. The box was broken open with a crowbar and its contents looted. The raiders started a fire and ran off, to the jeers of the quartet of civic guards.

> This is the story of the raid on Baltinglass, one of the many which the Guards have suffered in their isolated outposts, and the full story of the indignities they suffer, and the heroism they show will probably never be known ... I think some degree of publicity should be given ... It would hearten the Guards everywhere and would open the eyes of the public.

O'Higgins authorised the publication of O'Duffy's report, without disclosure of the names of the men or of place-names, and the *Irish Independent* carried the story.[83] O'Duffy circulated a detailed account to the force, taking advantage of the opportunity to give vent to his personal feelings. The interests of the men on duty in the country were his own interests, as they well understood.

> The wrongs they suffer, and the injuries and indignities unjustly inflicted on them, affect me no less than if the cruelties were practised personally on myself ... I feel elated as they do, and have the same pride and confidence in the Guard and in their future when I receive the modest reports which cover heroism of the highest kind. This is why on occasion, as now, I feel impelled to address the Guard as a whole, and to say how much I appreciate their courageous stand and firm attitude ...[84]

A year later, on 25 January 1924, Guard O'Halloran, aged twenty-eight, a former railway signalman from County Galway, was passing the National Bank in Baltinglass when he heard sounds of a struggle. Immediately two armed and masked men emerged and ran off, leaving the manager wounded. O'Halloran, in hot pursuit, was gaining ground; one of the criminals turned and fired point blank at the policeman, who fell mortally wounded.[85]

Behind the bravery of the Mulroys and the O'Hallorans and the countless unsung heroes of the Civic Guard, it was not humanly possible that there were no failures to live up to O'Duffy's uncompromising standards. Many conscientious young men in isolated barracks with no telephones or alone on country roads at night, calculating personal risk, did not treat with the enemy but rather with cold logic decided to suffer loss of face when challenged by armed marauders. Under pressure of the confused loyalties dividing the country, some guards may have been compromised in fraternising with other young men in raiding-parties, their persuasive innocence contributing perhaps more to the cause of peace than the provocative resistance of braver hearts.

In his determination to make heroes, O'Duffy could be ruthless. In the incident in May 1923 at O'Callaghan's Mills, where Guard James Mulroy won his Scott Medal, his companion on patrol, Guard John Donlon, believing Mulroy was dying, ran from the scene to summon assistance. At the presentation ceremony on the depot square, O'Duffy intemperately accused Donlon of cowardice.[86] It was only on the eve of his retirement and on his own appeal, having lived with the stigma for many years, that the injustice to Donlon was acknowledged by the Commissioner.

THE 'SHEER MADNESS OF UNARMED POLICE'

In December 1921, within days of the signing of the Treaty, Sir Mark Beresford Sturgis, one of the triumvirate of English civil servants sent from London earlier in the year to take over the Irish administration (the others were Sir John Anderson and Alfred Cope), contacted C. F. Dalton, acting chief liaison officer on the Irish side, to convey British concern on the state of law and order in Dublin. In view of an 'epidemic of robberies and attempted robberies with violence by armed men,' Sturgis wished to arm the DMP, claiming he had the authority to act on his own judgment. The city was 'infested with armed robbers,' Dalton agreed, passing the suggestion on to Mulcahy. But the threat to the status of the DMP as a civil police force was of little real concern, because, as Dalton stated, 'arming the DMP only concerns us in as much as the provisions of the Truce do not permit the force to be armed.'[87]

Neither were the ethics of the proposal an abiding concern for the British authorities. An attempt to arm the Dublin police was made in the aftermath of the 1916 Rising. Rifles were distributed to all stations in the metropolitan area, and the constables paraded on Dollymount Strand for training in the use of firearms. The move coincided with agitation for more pay, and the Ancient Order of Hibernians stepped in to organise the campaign for the men. Amid rumours of an impending police strike, the rifles were withdrawn.[88] When O'Duffy was trying to have his men relieved of armed protection duties in the city, Gearóid Ó Súilleabháin proposed the employment of the DMP, presumably by breaking with tradition and arming the force.[89]

The wisdom of sending unarmed police into the battlefield was questioned by community leaders, but within the Civic Guard attitudes were muted. If O'Duffy had misgivings he kept his views to himself, but he was later to betray ambivalence. Within weeks of his appointment he personally inspected protection posts manned by the new police and was impatient at the sight of guards, 'rifles at the ready ... Considering the decision that the Civic Guard is to be an entirely unarmed force, it looks somewhat ridiculous ... that they should be carrying out military duties armed with rifles.'[90] An armed defence unit protected the Phoenix Park depot and McKee Barracks, but outside the city not a single lethal public or privately owned weapon was in the possession of the Civic Guard.[91]

In Clonmel a committee of prominent citizens urged the rearming of the Civic Guard 'as a temporary measure' while the spate of robberies and violence lasted.[92] The manager of the Bank of Ireland in Bagenalstown (Muine Bheag) gave a graphic description of lawlessness in County Carlow.

> We have no protection except a few unarmed Civic Guards who are helpless when faced by men with revolvers … Bands of armed ruffians are roaming the district who hold up travellers and traders' vans and loot them. They quarter themselves on farmers in lonely districts who dare not resist them. They drive off cattle and sheep and take by threats of force money and other valuables … There is nothing to prevent armed men driving up in a motor and raiding the three banks [in the town].

The manager would have been less than reassured to have learnt that civil servants in Dublin considered him to be 'unduly alarmed'.[93] Similar complaints were received from threatened communities in many parts of the country. The Garda Representative Body was ambivalent. While opposing 'the use of arms as a general principle,' it urged the supply of arms to stations, the local sergeant deciding when the weapons were to be carried, and that the barrack orderly be armed at stations where firearms were held.[94]

GENERAL ORDER NO. 1

In a curious way, it seems that when O'Duffy took up office in September 1922 he acted as though the Civic Guard was to remain an armed force. He immediately issued General Order No. 1, fixing responsibility for proficiency in the use and safe custody of arms: 'owing to the causing of deaths from the accidental discharge of firearms … arms will only be carried by men going on duty.'[95]

When his orders on various operational matters were reissued in 1923, General Order No. 1 was shown as cancelled.[96] It seems unlikely that in the interval he was not shown the O'Sheil-McAuliffe report. But in a proposal to rearm the force that he made to the government in 1926, O'Duffy claimed personal credit for the original decision to base the organisation on moral authority. 'I am as convinced now as I was when I first recommended it after my appointment as Commissioner, that it was sound policy and a magnificent experiment to send out the Garda unarmed.'[97]

The Civic Guard evolved as an unarmed force without an express decision by the Provisional Government on the core recommendation in the O'Sheil-McAuliffe report, O'Friel revealed to the Department of Finance in 1925. 'It may be taken as having been tacitly accepted as the proper thing … It was not until October 1922 that the necessity for deciding [the matter] really arose, as it was only then [that] distribution to the country seriously began … Up to October … it would be difficult to say that the Civic Guard was an unarmed force.'[98] This suggests that O'Higgins, having studied the O'Sheil-McAuliffe report, took a personal initiative and conveyed his decision to O'Duffy.

Towards the end of September the new Commissioner addressed the first detachment of fifty civic guards who were preparing to leave the Ship Street depot for Limerick. As unarmed police they were the advance guard in a historic 'experiment'. O'Duffy hardly spared their feelings with his assurance that if any one of them was murdered, they would be 'armed to the teeth.'[99]

With his right-hand man, Assistant Commissioner Walsh, O'Duffy attended the convention of the International Association of Chiefs of Police in New York in the early summer of 1925. A reference by O'Duffy to the unarmed Garda force in Ireland was greeted with a standing ovation. 'We consider that it is not necessary for the uniformed policemen to carry guns. They rule by moral suasion rather than by force, and the people have taken kindly to them.'[100] He recalled in 1929 that the policy of sending the men out on duty without a means of defending themselves had been 'denounced as sheer madness' but that the Minister for Justice and the Commissioner were determined not to launch another armed body on a country 'groaning under the weight of armed wrong.'[101] Only two years earlier he had been urging the government to rearm the force.

On the night of 14 November 1926 two unarmed policemen were murdered in concerted attacks on twelve barracks in various parts of the country, Sergeant James Fitzsimmons, a County Down man, at St Luke's, Cork, and Guard Hugh Ward, from Nobber, County Meath, at Hollyford, County Tipperary. Sergeant Fitzsimmons, aged twenty-three, confronted armed and masked raiders in the hallway of his station and was shot dead; Hugh Ward, aged twenty-nine, the station orderly, was shot dead when he answered the door in Hollywood.

These murders had a traumatic affect on O'Duffy, whose affection for the force and loyalty to the rank and file knew no bounds. His emotion on this occasion led him into bad judgment. He immediately summoned divisional officers to a headquarters conference. Having listened to their views, he submitted to the government on 6 December proposals for arming the Garda Síochána.[102] In continental Europe the concept of 'an unarmed and, at the same time, effective police force' was not understood. On recent visits abroad he had 'tried to explain' the Irish policy to police officers and others,

> but they were incredulous … In order to [assure] the community that their lives
> and property will be protected adequately, to put it out of the power of any group
> to cut across all sense of security in the State, to remove once and for all the threat
> of the gun, to harass and wear down the will and endurance of those engaged in
> organising such armed association, and to save the morale of the Garda, I have
> come to the conclusion, after full consideration and consultation with the senior
> officers, that the time has now arrived when I, with a full sense of my

responsibility in the matter, should request authority to arm the force. I am of opinion that short [point] 45 revolvers should be the official weapon and would be sufficient. It may not be practicable or desirable to arm the entire force just now, but I submit that I should have the authority to do so.

Members of the detective force were, of course, already armed. A suggestion from the conference of chief superintendents that their number should be increased by as many as a thousand men was rejected by O'Duffy. It is not clear what overt support the Commissioner received from his officers for the radical proposal to put guns back on the belts of the men in uniform; but at least two of the officers present at the conference did oppose the idea outright, one of them threatening to resign if the force was armed. 'He evidently would not, in certain eventualities be prepared to carry out any orders involving personal risk,' O'Duffy told the government, adding, in a harsh judgment on conscientious dissent, 'I have no sympathy for the officer or the guard who threatens to resign rather than carry out his orders.'[103]

The views of the Department of Justice were conveyed to the government in a definitive memorandum early in 1927. The Garda Síochána had functioned successfully as an unarmed force for five years when the risk of armed attacks was greater than it was likely to be in the years ahead. Would it have functioned more successfully as an armed force? Its success to a considerable extent had been due to the moral support of the community. The RIC had created the impression that an armed force was a symbol of oppression. Not alone would arming the Garda Síochána not deter armed attacks but it would probably guarantee that patrols would be fired on and barracks raided for arms. O'Friel recalled the recommendation in the O'Sheil-McAuliffe report for disarming the Civic Guard and concluded with a warning of the harmful effect on the reputation of the state abroad if the government decided to rearm the police.

The wisdom and far-sightedness of Kevin O'Sheil and Michael McAuliffe was now confirmed at another turning-point in modern Irish history. At the government meeting on 24 January, O'Duffy's proposal to arm all members of the Garda Síochána was not approved.[104]

That the danger of losing that inheritance is always present was dramatically demonstrated in 1934. Faced with the Blueshirt crisis, 'the ideal of the unarmed policeman had been unofficially declared dead by the Fianna Fáil government.'[105] In January, citizens passing the Phoenix Park depot were startled to see through the railings a company of uniformed guards drilling on the square with Lee-Enfield rifles.[106] At the government meeting on 5 September approval was given for 'the steps taken by the Department of Justice to obtain from the Department of Defence supplies of arms, ammunition and equipment, together with one Lancia and 2 Rolls Royce armoured cars [with equipment] for the use of the Special Armed Unit of the Garda Síochána.'[107]

In the aftermath of O'Duffy's initiative in 1926, O'Higgins in a personal letter explained in detail why the government had turned him down. 'Arming the Garda Síochána would be misunderstood in Ireland and abroad'; the Executive Council had been 'largely influenced by this consideration.' The possession of a revolver by a guard on patrol might prove too strong a temptation for local Irregulars. 'The revolver would always be a bait … It is just possible that many of the public who would condemn and resent any attack on a Garda barrack … would be inclined simply to "keep the ring" if the Gardaí were armed.'[108]

EXAMPLE BETTER THAN PRECEPT

O'Duffy based his case for rearming the Garda Síochána on the political situation in the country as he saw it, barely three years after the Civil War. He doubted the commitment to constitutional politics by republicans who had recently broken away from Sinn Féin to regroup in Fianna Fáil. There were two groups, not named, one led by extremists, including ordinary criminals, masquerading as patriots; lashing out, he described the second group as lacking the moral courage to join de Valera's new party: they were having nothing to do with the fanatics but were 'actively inclined towards the use of arms in furtherance of their alleged patriotic ideals.' For centuries it had been preached in Ireland

> that beyond all doubt we are the most intellectual, the most capable, and the most abused people on the face of the earth … the one thing standing between us and our proper place in the sun … control of our affairs by an inefficient, unenlightened and grasping foreign power … Succeeding generations, seeing in everything that represented authority the symbols of the system that was responsible for all their miseries—real and imaginary—have directed their main attention towards the destruction of the normal institutions of civilised Government …
>
> Natural initiative, creative ability, even character, was permitted to lie dormant … the net result being that today we possess a carefully-trained and well-developed destructive outlook and ability, whilst our constructive faculties are numbed and undeveloped … Many of our people were so utterly misguided as to believe honestly that we had inflicted a military defeat on the foreigner, and became more convinced than ever in the belief that authority—whether enforced by the head of a family or by a government constituted by the people … can always be met and defeated by force …

Having demolished the misguided patriots in physical-force politics, O'Duffy turned his attention to the Irish people as a whole. They had no appreciation of the rights and responsibilities of citizenship. Civics was not taught in the schools and rarely if ever mentioned in the pulpit, or by statesmen. The clergy, teachers and statesmen had the primary responsibility as educators. The police had no more than a secondary role: 'the enforcement of principles already learned, rather than teaching them to the unenlightened.'[109]

Coming from the Garda Commissioner, this was a remarkable statement in what it revealed of O'Duffy's apparent rejection of, or perhaps his failure to grasp, the principle in the evolving role of police as exemplars in society: ideal citizens, setting in their public and private lives objective standards of obedience to those in the service of authority and to the law and of deference to the rights of others.[110] And yet he was applying the principle, and his own instinctive philosophy, in his direction of the Garda Síochána as a primary force in re-establishing self-respect in Irish society. He was certainly emphasising the exemplary role when four years later he wrote: 'The Garda ... is expected to give example to the citizens by the conduct of their daily lives, and this is particularly so in small towns and villages where [they] enter intimately into the lives of the inhabitants ... as guides and counsellors of the people.'[111] In other words, he was simply restating the age-old wisdom that example is better than precept.

But at this point he was going off the rails, asserting that national stability depended on the police,

> teaching those who either will not learn, or will not practise the duties of citizenship, that a violation of its principles will not pay ... The lesson taught by the police must be thorough and effective ... A service that will not be attacked with impunity ... capable not alone of its own defence, but of aggression, real aggression ... To this body could be entrusted the task of demanding and insisting on respect for the law of the land, and the extermination of the type that is incapable or unwilling to assume the responsibilities of citizenship.[112]

O'Duffy was largely instrumental in fashioning the Garda Síochána as the moral force it became in the great decade of reconstruction; under his charismatic leadership it had outgrown its swaddling-clothes. But in 1926, overcome by his emotions, he put forward extremist views on ending once and for all the violence endemic in Irish society. 'If the Garda in the course of his ordinary duty encounters a criminal—armed or unarmed—in the act of committing a crime, he will be in a position to deal effectively with him as becomes a policeman.' The shock to the government of the prospect of armed guards dealing 'effectively' with criminals can only be imagined. And against all the fine feeling O'Duffy had put into the moulding of the force, he added pessimistically: 'I cannot find any reason for thinking that a sense of loyalty is so highly developed in the force that its members will be prepared to face unequal odds at the imminent risk to their lives.'[113]

He had clearly overplayed his hand. O'Higgins, who 'always had reservations about him,'[114] now made up his mind to remove him from office. On the night of the November raids, prisoners captured in Waterford were assaulted by guards. O'Higgins sent for the Commissioner and in an angry confrontation demanded the dismissal of the culprits. O'Duffy said he would resign before he would act against the men responsible. 'White with indignation,' O'Higgins challenged him to carry out his threat.[115]

O'Duffy's imminent departure from office was discussed among senior officers. It was one of the great tragedies of the period that O'Duffy, who was yet only thirty-four years of age, was not then prevailed on to take up other work. His replacement as Commissioner, already identified by O'Higgins, was apparently to be Chief Superintendent Michael Francis Leahy, a former clerk in the Admiralty in London.[116] O'Duffy's removal from office by his own political friends might have been less painful than it proved to be when he was unceremoniously pushed out by de Valera's second administration in 1933. If the government had been entertaining an early change in the management of the Garda Síochána, its intention was tragically overtaken by the assassination of the Minister for Justice on 10 July 1927.[117]

A NATIONAL FORCE OF ARMED DETECTIVES

For a period after the Civil War, the army was employed as the first line of defence against armed criminals. Responsibility for major crime and violent political movements was incompatible with the role of the Defence Forces in peacetime, O'Higgins submitted in a memorandum to the government in 1924. He recommended a national force of armed detectives, drawing on the tradition and experience of the Criminal Investigation Department of the Dublin police, then under the command of Chief Superintendent David Neligan. To accomplish his 'pivotal idea' he proposed the absorption of the DMP as a division of the Garda Síochána. 'No reasonable man will cavil at their carrying small arms and nobody can honestly pretend the police are an armed force just because a limited number specialising in serious crime carry with them arms when apprehending armed criminals.'[118]

Strongly objecting to the proposed amalgamation, the Dublin police commissioner, Major-General W. R. E. Murphy, reported 'deep discontent and resentment in the force at large.' Passionately dedicated to the rehabilitation of his demoralised force, he disliked 'intensely the thought of being back into the melting pot … without the means of arousing esprit de corps.'[119] He complained that the work of the DMP was not appreciated, to which O'Friel replied that the minister had always gone out of his way to reassure the Dublin police that he did not regard them as different from the Garda Síochána. Amalgamation would 'not be nearly as difficult as the merger of Oriel House in the DMP,'[120] a reference to the cadre of Republican Police raised in 1922 'for the purpose of protecting the lives and property of persons who supported the established government [and who were] in danger of attack by Irregulars.'[121]

The amalgamation of the two police forces proceeded in 1925, Murphy taking command of the new Dublin Metropolitan Division of the Garda Síochána with the personal rank of deputy commissioner, the head of the new Detective Branch, Chief

Superintendent Neligan, moving his office from Dublin Castle to the Phoenix Park depot.

THE CIVIL WAR AND THE McAULIFFE CHAPLAINCY

In July 1922 the Bishop of Kildare and Leighlin, Dr Patrick Foley, wrote to Kevin O'Higgins expressing concern for the spiritual welfare of the recruits languishing in Kildare.

> I believe that there should be special provision for the instruction of these young men, and a special priest appointed to keep in touch with them. I need hardly add that I do not expect that much can be done in the present deplorable state of affairs ... These young men are very good as a rule and very religious, but I dread the influence of segregation in barracks on their moral fibre.[122]

In Dublin the Jesuits of Gardiner Street had been caring for the DMP since the eighteen-forties[123] and the Passionists at Mount Argus in Harold's Cross since 1893.[124] The parish priest of Aughrim Street was officially designated chaplain to the majority Catholic membership of the RIC stationed at the Phoenix Park depot.[125] The widely scattered constabulary garrisons in the provinces had looked to local parish clergy for their spiritual needs. The parish priest in Kildare, Father Campion, was consulted, and he agreed that a chaplain was not needed.[126]

In December, O'Duffy waited on Archbishop Edward Byrne, who wished to appoint a resident chaplain in the Phoenix Park depot. O'Duffy recommended Father Patrick Dunlea of Glasnevin, who was acting as spiritual director to recruits residing at Collinstown Aerodrome.[127] A former British army chaplain, Father Dunlea was considered 'right from the national point of view ... during the Trouble his mother's home at Dungarvan was burned by the Black and Tans.'[128]

The archdiocese appointed instead Father Patrick McAuliffe of Kilcullen, County Kildare, who quickly established himself as a 'second Father Mathew', devoting himself to the enrolment of recruits in the Pioneer Total Abstinence Association.[129]

Hardly noticed in the closing months of the Civil War, and overlooked in every history of the period, the brief Phoenix Park chaplaincy had an important influence in stabilising the force far beyond the confines of the depot.[130] McAuliffe himself became a central figure in the restoration of peace. In an age of slow communications, reports on the police grapevine of a mixed welcome for the new unarmed Civic Guard hardly lost any lurid detail in stories of the countryside held up to ransom by marauding groups of armed bandits. The true situation was bad enough; but so far there had been only one fatal casualty. On 28 October 1922 Guard Henry Phelan, in the company of Guards Tom Irwin and Tom Flood, all stationed at Callan, was visiting Mullinahone to buy hurleys for a team they were starting in Callan. Mistaken for his brother, a former RIC man, Phelan was followed into a shop and shot dead. His body was returned to Callan in a coffin tied to the roof of a car; at the burial service in his native Mountrath, 'no oration was delivered ... not a drum was heard, not a funeral note.'[131]

In the early spring of 1923 the war showed no sign of abating. The attitude of the rank and file to the government's policy on arms was muted, but it seems certain that morale was being undermined, especially among the recruits. To revive the spirits of his young parishioners, Father McAuliffe took an initiative that had a profound impact throughout the force. Devotion to the cult of the Sacred Heart characterised the strong faith of the generation of the independence movement; the familiar image and red votive lamp adorned every Catholic home. Appealing to that tradition, McAuliffe on Easter Sunday morning, 1 April 1923, arranged a service of consecration of the Civic Guard to the Sacred Heart, 1,500 recruits with their instructors forming up on the square to take part in the ceremony. Led by O'Duffy, the greatest parade of policemen in Irish history made no headlines in the national press. *Iris an Gharda* reported the ceremony with photographs in a centre-page spread.[132] In a spontaneous movement, the men already on duty in the country invited local clergy to consecrate their work and bless the Sacred Heart pictures that were still to be seen in some Garda stations up to recent times.[133]

The question arises: if the religious ceremony on the depot square in the spring of 1923 had not taken place, would the politics of the Irish Free State have taken a different course? Under pressure in the country to rearm the Civic Guard, and with growing unrest in the force itself, would the Provisional Government have been able to hold the line on its policy of creating a police service armed with moral authority as the only sure way to peace? The Civil War was drawing to a close. On 27 April, Frank Aiken, Chief of Staff of the Irregular forces, ordered the suspension of all offensive operations, followed on 24 May by the order to dump arms. Would guerrilla warfare have ended if the Civic Guard, like the paramilitary RIC, individually armed with revolvers, backed by rifle-bearing mobile support groups, was not winning the struggle for moral authority?

In the tradition of the country, the people would not have given their support to an armed police force. This was clearly understood by the first Garda Commissioner. On 9 September 1922, on the eve of his departure from office, Michael Staines circulated hurriedly prepared instructions for units about to go out on duty. He defined the future role of the police in Irish society: 'The Garda Síochána will succeed not by force of arms or numbers but on their moral authority as servants of the people.'[134]

5

O'DUFFY'S CHIVALROUS MEN OF THE WORLD

Orders, orders, orders, and strident objurgations … to obey, obey and nothing but obey.

In the move to Dublin Castle on 17 August 1922, Staines remade his headquarters for the fourth time in a little under six months.[1] The euphoria of the ceremonial occupation was quickly replaced by dismay at the squalid conditions in the barracks recently evacuated by the British military and the last of the RIC to pack their bags. The barrackmaster, Superintendent James Brennan, protested to the local official of the Office of Public Works; the ensuing correspondence set the pattern for decades of endless wrangling with the OPW over the atrocious standards of barrack accommodation endured by the first generation in the force. The barrack-rooms had been left in a filthy state, 'not fit for habitation.' Without lighting in the rooms, the men were obliged to retire at night in the dark. The kitchen ranges were not working.

Brennan's report drew coals of fire on his head, and he had to defend himself to Staines. 'Ship street was in a most awful state when the Civic Guard went into residence.' Staines mildly observed that no great efforts had been made to clean up the barracks; and the Civic Guard was not 'a fastidious body': men were prepared to 'rough it' to a very considerable extent.[2] In a threatening turn of phrase, Chief Superintendent Seán MacManus reported 'rumblings of revolution … in Ship street barracks.'[3]

In all the circumstances, discipline was lax, and a strong hand was needed. When O'Duffy took over in September the cacophony of police whistles sounding reveille offended his sense of military decorum, and he requisitioned an army bugle.[4] Ship Street was used as a receiving centre; from there, recruits were divided for training between Kildare and the former military aerodrome at Collinstown (now Dublin Airport), whence they were drafted back to Ship Street for allocation to stations.

O'Duffy made urgent representations to O'Higgins for access to both the RIC depot, soon to be evacuated by the British military, and the adjoining Marlborough (McKee) Barracks. The arrangements for handing over the remaining military posts were notified by General Macready for Sunday 17 December. At noon the Phoenix Park depot was taken over by a detachment of the national army under Captain Augustine Gormley, he in his turn, 'with the usual formalities,' handing over the key to representatives of the Civic Guard.

During the morning a column of British soldiers half a mile long marched by the city quays to the North Wall to board waiting troopships; another large convoy, with armoured cars, left Marlborough Barracks bound for Newry. Macready sent a personal message to Cosgrave:

> Before leaving Ireland, I ask you to accept my thanks for the manner in which your officials have met our wishes during the handing over of the barracks, stores etc. in Dublin. The utmost courtesy and good feeling has existed on both sides. It is, I hope, unnecessary for me to say that you and your Government have my best wishes for success in the difficult task before you, and my three years' sojourn here enables me to estimate, at all events to some extent, the difficulties that are before you. It would be hypocritical of me to say that my command in Ireland has been a pleasant task …

But Macready was optimistic enough to hope that he might yet live to see 'a united and prosperous Ireland devoid of bitterness and recrimination.'[5]

The constabulary depot was soon functioning again as a police training centre, for which it was built in the eighteen-forties. Writing in *Garda Review* at the end of the decade, O'Duffy revealed contemporary attitudes in Garda personnel management. He had the highest regard for the quality of the young men attracted to a career in the police service. They came 'from all classes in the community, from the College and University, from commercial life and from the professions, but in greater measure from the farming community where the standards of health, physical excellence and morals are the highest. In the plainest terms I state that the son of the peasant is the backbone of the Force.'[6]

The depot was organised on military lines. The commandant had the duties of 'an officer commanding a battalion,' with an adjutant responsible for drill and discipline; the depot chief inspector was cast in the role of 'regimental sergeant-major'. The chief instructor in police duties, with the rank of superintendent, supervised a staff of seasoned former soldiers and former RIC men who inculcated in the raw recruits 'habits of implicit obedience and discipline.' For young men who had left home in remote parishes, some for the first time in their lives, the depot regime as O'Duffy described it had to be an unnerving experience: 'Orders, orders, orders, and strident objurgations … to obey, obey and nothing but obey.'[7] For a minority of more exuberant spirits an impression of a penal regime may have been well founded; but it is doubtful that in practice the recruits were required to endure more than the rigours of tough military-style training. Reveille at half six, wash and shave at a cold-water tap, and tidy and dry-scrub the squad rooms; first parade at seven, followed by an hour on the square before breakfast.

The recruit was permitted to leave the depot on recreation from six to ten in the evening, followed by the ever-vigilant instructors. 'If he smokes in public, if he walks with a hand in his pocket, if he wears his greatcoat partly buttoned, if he lounges at a street corner or walks aimlessly along a footpath ... and is seen by a member of the provost staff, he will find himself ordered back to the Depot as a preliminary to any other action that may be taken.' The recruit 'learned to keep his head up and shoulders back ... The unsophisticated youth', O'Duffy proudly recorded, was now 'a man of the world ... chivalrous.'⁸

A regime resembling the spit-and-polish of nineteenth-century army life was in part justified by the need for keeping a tight rein on 1,500 healthy young men in training at the peak of the early recruiting campaigns. It was also necessary to copperfasten command and control in a new police force scattered in isolated units in a country recovering from the recent warfare. In 1930, writing to the Representative Body, O'Duffy stated his philosophy, all the more revealing in a confidential letter. 'The one characteristic above all others which I have sought consistently to develop from the earliest days is the characteristic of manliness. On every possible occasion I have tried to impress upon the force the difference between authority and servility.'⁹

The Garda Síochána had the primary role as catalysts in the work of reconstruction. By the autumn of 1923 the results were 'already seen in the peaceful and well-ordered countrysides.' The licensing laws were enforced; the moral discipline of observance of the law had brought about 'a very valuable asset to the people.' Motor vehicles were licensed and traffic better regulated. There was 'a refreshing air of tranquillity' in a country stricken in recent years with crime and disorder. 'The Guards go forward.'¹⁰

The Civic Guard had hardly settled in to its new headquarters when the recruits discovered that they were to be employed on fatigue duties, including the cleaning of toilets. The appropriateness of this work for police trainees was questioned by Chief Superintendent Brennan, supported by the commandant, Chief Superintendent McCarthy. The employment of civilian labour was recommended by Deputy Commissioner Coogan, influenced by McCarthy and Brennan, both of whom, having risen from the ranks in the RIC, had soiled their hands in similar duties and were now seizing the opportunity to upgrade the service. The assistant secretary in the Department of Home Affairs, Patrick Sheehan, helpfully observed that 'a very large number of country people have no knowledge of the working of a flush toilet, and this would apply to the average Garda recruit'—

a comment on contemporary social conditions that may have been close enough to reality in some rural areas. Every opportunity was to be availed of to give instruction in sanitation and hygiene, which had been 'notoriously neglected' in the country at large; the duties in contention were likely 'to promote the men's efficiency and general usefulness.' It had never occurred to the commandant that the duties 'might be imposed as punishment for minor offences ... unpunctuality and slovenliness.'[11]

O'Duffy himself was certain that the work of cleaning toilets was conducive to both discipline and moral uplift. The new police force had undertaken heavy manual labour moving into a succession of premises, all left in very bad condition by the previous occupants. As a result there was 'pardonable discontent and a growing feeling that the guards were not being allowed to pursue their studies.' That much said, in a separate private letter to the assistant secretary O'Duffy first excused himself: it was 'impossible to deal with all things personally. The Commandant should not have made such an application.' The fatigue duties afforded 'a splendid opportunity of giving guards practical knowledge of sanitation, hygiene and cleanliness.'[12]

Fatigues were still a feature of depot life when the author joined the Garda Síochána in 1947; for minor breaches of the regulations, weeding cobblestones was added for good measure.

TOWARDS A NEW ESTABLISHMENT

O'Duffy took command of a force of 1,689 men, with recruiting virtually at a standstill.[13] Working long hours with great urgency to make up for lost time, the new Commissioner and his small headquarters staff presented to the Department of Home Affairs a tentative establishment scheme providing for a complement of 5,520.[14] By February 1924, with the Civic Guard close to its established strength, there were on file six thousand applications from hopeful candidates; altogether, thirty thousand applications had been examined in the period since O'Duffy took over.[15] The legislation in 1925 bringing about the amalgamation of the Garda Síochána and the DMP provided for a maximum establishment nationally of 7,646.[16]

During the hiatus in the autumn of 1922, Superintendent Bernard O'Connor, pending directions, continued to receive and measure a slow intake of recruits. In early clear-cut minutes in O'Duffy's hand he was instructed that his responsibilities ended on handing over recruits to the commandant for training. On his own responsibility he was to call up candidates with pre-Truce service in the Volunteers, certified by the local Volunteer officer;[17] this certificate, with a character reference from the candidate's minister of religion and a medical report from a local doctor, were essential requirements.

'Numerous irregularities' occurred in local records. One candidate who was found to be medically unfit and paid off succeeded in rejoining; he was promoted sergeant, and retired in 1963 with a certificate of exemplary service.[18] Before regulations were promulgated, O'Connor was authorised to ignore half an inch under the required height and to allow up to three months over the upper age limit, then twenty-seven. This was too high, and O'Duffy wanted it reduced to twenty-two: a man who had not made up his mind to join the force until he was twenty-seven was 'not likely to succeed.'[19]

Candidates sat an examination in arithmetic and dictation and in their ability to write a 'sensible letter.'[20] O'Duffy welcomed a Home Affairs proposal to give responsibility for the entrance examination to the Civil Service Commission.[21] He criticised a standard pegged at third class in primary school, which may have been adequate in the nineteenth century but unrealistic in the nineteen-thirties. Contrasting the work of the old Courts of Petty Sessions, serviced by unqualified magistrates, and the new District Courts with lawyers as justices, O'Duffy stressed the need for higher educational standards. 'The day of the dull, unintelligent policeman is gone.'[22]

In an imaginative initiative, he introduced an efficiency and fitness test for all ranks and presented well-designed certificates, each signed personally by the Commissioner. These certificates greatly appealed to many of the recipients, coming from a culture unused to such acknowledgments of personal achievement. O'Duffy had to defend his initiative from the ambitions of the Civil Service Commission. The tests conducted by his own officers were 'entirely a matter of internal administration … it would be manifestly unfair to bring in an outside body to determine the fitness of members of the Garda Síochána for the ranks now held by them.'[23]

In the haste to organise the new police, Commissioner M. J. Kinnane in 1944 recalled that 'hundreds of men' had been admitted who would not normally be accepted for a police force, because they had served in the army and had to be 'provided for.' The standard of education of many of these men was so low that the state engaged teachers to give them elementary instruction in writing and simple arithmetic. After the change of government in 1932, several hundred men were admitted 'who were not fit for a police force.' Kinnane noticed that public representatives sometimes urged greater preference for 'an ordinary national school education'; but the real test was the capacity of a candidate to appreciate and absorb and afterwards to perform his duties efficiently.[24]

During the war years, when jobs were scarce, the force attracted some of the best-educated young men ever to have presented themselves for a police career in Ireland. Tested in a recruiting campaign in 1942, new appointment regulations worked against the interest of the force.[25] No less than 3,305 candidates offered themselves for a hundred vacancies. Kinnane selected 329 for interview by a board appointed by the Civil Service Commission. A headquarters officer who attended as an observer, Chief Superintendent Hugh Duffy, was 'struck by the confident bearing of practically all the candidates, and by the well-cut clothes and taste in dress of even those who came from the most backward parts of the country.' He was also impressed 'by the average physique.' Believing that all those who appeared before the board had already given evidence of satisfactory standards in their all-round education, on the strength of the interviews he would have had no hesitation in recommending them all for acceptance as recruits, subject to the medical test.[26] To Kinnane's 'great disappointment', the commissioners listed only sixty-one candidates as qualified. Kinnane was satisfied that a board of Garda officers could 'impartially, efficiently and expeditiously assess the educational requirements of Garda recruits.' The assessment of other qualifications was 'largely based in any case on the utilisation of Garda machinery.'[27]

RECRUITING REOPENED

O'Duffy enjoyed a short-lived honeymoon in his relations with the Department of Home Affairs. On his arrival in office he found that more than half the recruits in training hailed from the Clare, Limerick and Galway region. These men were 'largely responsible for the Kildare Mutiny … led astray by one or two individuals who were formerly their old Volunteer officers.' As recruits from these counties continued to pour in, he found it necessary to suspend recruiting. This was the first time that it came to notice in Home Affairs that recruiting had been practically confined to a few counties before O'Duffy's appointment. 'As usual he seems to have acted very wisely.'[28]

Recruiting in all counties was reopened in March 1923. The force was still two thousand under strength; a weekly intake of 100, found to be too slow, was increased to 150 a week. O'Connor was instructed to reject candidates from the cities of Dublin and Belfast who did not fulfil the conditions 'in every particular.'[29] Members of the DMP wishing to join the Civic Guard were also turned away.[30]

Early in November 1922 O'Higgins backed representations from the army for the recruitment of a thousand former soldiers. O'Duffy was unhappy at the prospect. Discipline was enforced differently in a police force. He was 'jealously' guarding the reputation the Civic Guard had earned for itself, but agreed to take five hundred of 'the best of the disbanded troops' at the rate of fifty a week. More than four hundred had been recruited by August 1923, when O'Duffy had to resist renewed pressure to accept a further 680 former soldiers; to do so 'to the exclusion of the old type that had made the Garda what it is, I fear the standard at which I aimed will be impossible to maintain.'[31]

An order excluding former members of the RIC was relaxed in 1924 in favour of sergeants and constables who had been dismissed or had resigned on account of nationalist sympathies. O'Duffy objected; 'men of this type' had taken part in past activities that had undermined the Civic Guard. He was strongly against admitting them en masse.[32]

Searching for defects in the organisation at every level, he was slow to make appointments to the officer ranks, among whom were men 'no better qualified than an ordinary Garda.' He found it necessary to dispense with the services of a number of them, and had others reduced in rank.[33]

As an encouragement to RIC families to foster police vocations, preference had been given to the sons of serving policemen, who were accepted at eighteen, a year earlier than the age for open recruitment. In 1927 the Garda Síochána was still a young force, made up mostly of single men who were slow to marry. Conceding that it was unlikely that applications from the sons of guards would be received for years to come, O'Duffy laid out a policy for the future. In his experience, the sons of members of the RIC 'brought up in an atmosphere of discipline made very good guards and in pre-Truce days made very good Volunteers.'[34] There was no response from the Department of Justice, and there the matter rested until Commissioner Éamonn Broy a decade later reopened the debate, pleading that the son of an efficient, well-conducted policeman, being familiar with the routine and the hardships and compensations of police life, was more likely to follow confidently in his father's footsteps.[35] The proposal was rejected out of hand by the Minister for Finance, Seán MacEntee, as being against civic justice and smacking of nepotism.[36]

OUTCRY FOR DEPLOYMENT

The outcry for deployment of the new police was rising in September 1922 when the Minister for Defence, Richard Mulcahy, desperately appealed to Kevin O'Higgins for 'the presence of some authoritative police body' in areas cleared by the army. He had not heard anything further of the Civic Guard 'taking up positions in Dundrum, County Dublin, Lucan, Swords, Howth,'[37] stations in the outer suburbs adjoining the city boundary. As early as 19 September, on the basis of reports from liaison officers on the prospects of providing barrack accommodation, O'Duffy was able to state that deployment would begin on the twenty-fifth in Limerick and at scattered locations throughout the country.[38]

Nothing so much illustrates the dire straits of the impoverished Irish nation setting out from a standing start on the long road to political and economic independence, nor epitomises so graphically the patriotic commitment of ordinary people, than the bleak conditions that awaited the young civic guards in many of the towns and villages. A quarter of a century later the founder-members, now married with growing families, were counting the years to retirement; a new generation of young men was coming into the force; and still the atrocious conditions in many stations were largely unchanged. Down through the years the Representative Body adopted a consistently responsible attitude in pressing the case for urgent improvements. Its views were presented in generally restrained language in the columns of the *Garda Review*, typically in editorials in the nineteen-fifties.

> The type of accommodation our men were forced to occupy in the early years of the Force can be appreciated and forgiven because of the conditions which then prevailed coupled with the fact that the State itself was in swaddling clothes. The country had to be policed and policed quickly to fill the vacuum created by the disbandment of the R.I.C. ... [In 1951] many of the buildings occupied as Garda

Stations remain a disgrace to the nation.[39]

> If rural electrification comes to a village more often than not the one building to remain unconnected is the Garda station. The smoking paraffin lamp and the humble candle must continue to suffice … Where a County Council decides to give a village a water supply … the Garda station again more often than not will be excluded. The resident Guards and the Sergeant and his wife and their children must still trudge to the village pump for their buckets of water.[40]

The critics were not unmindful of the priorities in reconstruction. On top of the ravages of the War of Independence the young state was handicapped by the legacy of the Civil War. That so much had been achieved reflected 'extraordinary credit on our Irish Governments, but the State had failed the Garda Síochána'; conditions at certain stations 'beggared description.'[41] Guided by whatever instructions they may have been given, taking a pragmatic view of conditions as they found them, the liaison officers reported in one instance that the building would 'suit temporarily'—in other words, provide a roof. In other cases, conditions were 'not in a good state of repair but habitable'; 'not habitable but could be made so if properly taken in hand'; in a 'bad state of repairs, would be injurious to men; no cooking facilities'; 'very dilapidated'; 'windows and doors broken'; and over and over again, 'no sanitary accommodation.' O'Duffy himself inspected barracks on offer in County Dublin and found most of the buildings in the same state of disrepair.[42]

Based on an establishment scheme of 807 stations, 270 had been occupied by the end of April 1923. O'Duffy was then passing out a hundred recruits a week. O'Friel informed the OPW that barracks had been found with difficulty in the larger towns; he felt it might be impossible to acquire quarters in the villages.[43]

In an immediate personal reply the chairman of the OPW, Sir Philip Hanson, held out no hope for barrack accommodation at over five hundred centres still to be provided with a police service. Owners were willing enough to sell, but the Department of Finance was opposed to the purchase of premises. Regarding temporary accommodation, compulsory powers had to be used with 'great discretion' to avoid hardship to property owners, who feared destruction of their property.[44] In IRA arson attacks, eighty government-owned barracks and upwards of four hundred privately owned premises had been destroyed, and therein lay the problem.[45]

In spite of all the difficulties, stations were opened, some in the wings of destroyed houses, even in partial occupation of premises. Morale and discipline were being put at risk. But the people were clamouring for police protection; the rapid distribution of the force would play a big part in restoring normal conditions, O'Higgins told the Dáil.[46] The cost of restoring government property alone was put at £300,000, not to be contemplated in prevailing financial circumstances; but partial restoration could be undertaken for a small fraction of the estimated cost.[47] The OPW needed the power to offer compensation, and the staff and funds to rebuild quickly.[48]

At the onset of winter and faced with inevitable deterioration in already 'wretched housing conditions,' Deputy Commissioner Coogan threatened to withdraw the force from at least half the established stations, 'a very grave prospect,' unless repairs were carried out or alternative accommodation provided.[49] In an internal minute to O'Friel, M. J. Kinnane dismissed Coogan's report on conditions as 'a palpable gross exaggeration.' Backing up Coogan's note of alarm, the district officer at Longford, Inspector James Hunt, reported that landlords had declined to carry out repairs; he listed broken doors and windows, leaking roofs, no fireplace in one house, and no closet in any of the premises occupied as barracks.[50]

The former RIC barracks at Ballinabrackey, County Meath, destroyed at the beginning of the Troubles in 1920, was hurriedly reoccupied after repairs when, as reported by Sergeant C. G. Severs, the inside walls were 'still soft and continually weeping ... the white residue from the plaster ... coming off in wet paste.' Bedclothes folded in the morning were wet before nightfall. They had no cooking facilities; under the one roof there were twelve people, including the station party and Sergeant Severs's family, all sharing a small parlour grate. It was impossible 'to cook a square meal of any kind.'[51] The local medical officer certified the house as 'highly dangerous to human life.'[52]

In 1929 O'Duffy assured the Representative Body that the question of sub-standard barrack accommodation was 'never lost'; he was personally aware of the 'untiring efforts' of O'Friel and the assistant secretary, Kinnane, to improve matters.[53] The *Garda Review* published a long list of resolutions passed at recent Representative Body meetings, together with O'Duffy's observations, including an adverse comment on the performance of the OPW.[54] Hanson bridled at the public criticism: it was 'an elementary rule in Government service that one Department of Government is not to publish an attack upon another.'[55]

THE CORROFIN HOAX

In the winter of 1925 Deputy Commissioner Coogan inspected the divisions of Clare and Galway.[56] The inspection was 'generally satisfactory', but he found that the men had no more than a 'rudimentary knowledge' of their duties. On parade they lacked 'military click'; uniforms were 'baggy ... They do not fold them properly nor press them, nor do they know how to keep them free from dirt and grease, with the result that in some cases the men presented a horribly dirty appearance.' The report did not acknowledge that the men had left the depot in Dublin three years earlier with one makeshift uniform. The uniform cloth weathered badly, the blue fading to a nondescript blue-grey, and soon became soiled and rumpled. When the new navy-blue uniforms arrived they were immediately taken into everyday use. Efficiency was 'as good as could be expected' from officers and men who had very little training and whose educational standard was inadequate. The report did concede that the men were 'hardly to blame' for their appearance.

It seems doubtful that the force in Counties Clare and Galway in 1925 was 'on the whole well housed,' as Coogan reported, allowing for some stations that were 'utterly unsuitable,' with more than 'a few frightfully bad hovels.' The men were overcrowded in cold and damp makeshift accommodation, with no water supply: in some stations water had to be carted from distant wells. Sanitary facilities were primitive or non-existent. In the County Clare village of Maurice's Mills the guards were suffering from the cold and damp; 'in such a ... hopeless shambles' it was impossible to have either discipline or order. The conditions at Milltown in the Tuam district, not described, were so bad that Coogan ordered an immediate evacuation.

Coogan reserved his strongest criticism for the very poor domestic arrangements in the stations. The housekeeping was left in the hands of inexperienced barrack servants, resulting in 'waste and extravagance ... Never do you see a white apron or anything that would suggest neatness, cleanliness or economy.' The domestic servants who worked in Civic Guard barracks contrasted 'very badly with the barrack servants employed by the R.I.C.,' Coogan complained. His harsh criticism overlooked the political realities under the old regime. The disbanded RIC owed its century-old traditions to the pervading influence of an aristocracy, whose sons dominated the officer class. Under O'Duffy's watchful eye, untidiness amounting in some cases to slovenliness was soon corrected in a sometimes harsh disciplinary school.

Coogan's report was circulated to various headquarters officers for appropriate executive action. In an unfortunate sequel, the report, written in the author's colourful style, attracted the attention of a prankster, who forged a bogus document purporting to be the minute of an inspection of Corrofin (Tuam) Garda station carried out, it was alleged, by the Deputy Commissioner on 11 May 1923 (a station at Corrofin was not opened until 4 October 1923). The 'inspection minute' described a situation of incredible indiscipline, including acts of indecency by a fictitious sergeant and three guards.

To lend verisimilitude to a tall yarn, the characters were named as 'Sergeant M. Lennon 231 and Guards O'Neill, O'Toole and Burke.' It is clear from evidence in nominal rolls and old station deployment registers, to which the prankster had access, that 'Sergeant M. Lennon 231' and his merry men existed only in his imagination. Conveniently, guard 231, who joined at Ballsbridge in the spring of 1922 (and whose name was not Lennon), had left the force before the hoax was concocted. In 1925, the year Coogan did inspect the Tuam district, the sergeant then stationed at Corrofin, James O'Neill, attended a general parade at district headquarters. Sergeant O'Neill described for the Deputy Commissioner the sub-standard conditions in Corrofin. Before anyone else, Sergeant O'Neill would have seen the joke of the 'w.c.' described in the 'inspection minute': water had to be carted two miles to the station.

It is probable that the barrack-room yarn owed its inspiration to apocrypha of the old police, including stories of a larger-than-life barrack servant, retold by former RIC officers in post-prandial banter. The joke was intended for the eyes only of a closely knit circle of kindred spirits in the officers' mess. Their laughter was to echo in the corridors of Garda headquarters at the Royal Hospital and beyond.

Among Richard Mulcahy's papers in the archives at UCD there is a file cover marked 'Copy of Inspection Minute by Deputy Commissioner Coogan, Corofin Garda Station, 11th May 1923.' The cover contains a carbon typescript on thin typing-paper showing the creases of a document that was originally folded.⁵⁷ The hoax came into the public domain for the first time in 1966. When Tim Pat Coogan was researching his book *Ireland since the Rising,* he discovered one of these typescripts among his father's papers. After decades of decent oblivion, the 'inspection minute' was quoted as historical fact in Coogan's book. 'The restoration of civil order was the greatest single problem of the new state. A new unarmed Civil [sic] Guard was founded. Initiated under circumstances of extreme difficulty, it was to become one of the finest police forces in Europe. The difficulties its founders had to cope with ... are in part illustrated by this report of my father's.'⁵⁸

In correspondence in the *Garda Review* half a century after the event, the hoax was exposed by the former Commissioner Patrick Carroll, who served with Coogan at headquarters during the entire period.⁵⁹ The author heard from Carroll's namesake, ex-Deputy Commissioner Patrick Joseph Carroll, the story of a joke that misfired.⁶⁰ Who was the culprit? P. J. Carroll was circumspect in revealing his identity. The evidence, pointing to one named individual, is far from conclusive.

Morals in the Garda Síochána

It cannot be pretended that there were no black sheep in the ranks of the Civic Guard. The force was well established in October 1929 when a letter on the irregular life-style of some rank-and-file members was published in the *Garda Review.* The recruits who joined in the early years had not all been models of virtue; not all the bad apples had been rooted out. Some married men were showing a poor example; there were single men whose conduct was not above reproach.

> Perhaps if we heard less often that we are a model Force ... we should be much better off and would conduct ourselves better. The blush of shame is coming to the cheeks of decent members ... because of the acts of a few ... Do we not feel small when ... respectable citizens ... tell us casually how a Garda or perhaps a Sergeant misconducted himself ... and what the clergy said, and what decent people said ... If we had drunkards amongst us it would not be so bad ... anything but this loathsome vice which all rational men are expected to combat.⁶¹

The writer was probably too sweeping in his comments; but allowing for that, the editor was prepared to publish the letter. It was saying something about the errant human nature of the individual guards concerned, but much less and more credibly than the Corrofin concoction.

There was obviously a problem for O'Duffy and his officers in establishing discipline among thousands of young, inexperienced recruits scattered in small units under youthful sergeants, depending on their bicycles as the only means of transport for maintaining contact with colleagues in neighbouring stations. In many instances in the early twenties there were no telephones. Except in team sports in their home parishes, almost to a man they had little or no tradition in organising their spare-time activities. They had regular money in their pockets, many of them for the first time in their lives. Beset by boredom, and suffering real privation in appalling living conditions, it was not surprising that some of the young guards resorted to the public houses that dotted the countryside in unconscionable numbers at that period. It would have been astonishing if in all the circumstances O'Duffy had not to contend with a drink problem among his men.

The *Garda Review* in 1926 made the point in an editorial on 'Brightening barrack life'. 'The reproach of Irish country towns is their deadly dullness, and who cannot name a score, at least, of promising young men who have taken to drinking in dismal surroundings simply because it seemed to them that there was no other way of escape from their misery.'[62] It is reasonable to suppose that the Representative Body was exaggerating the problem for its own ends. Cases of drunkenness in the social sense were rare and attracted the ultimate penalty; the disciplinary regulations outlawed offences involving 'the slightest departure from strict sobriety.'[63]

A SOBER POLICE FORCE

As the Provisional Government set about the task of restoring peace, the national psyche was agitated by memories of the Famine; though recalled only by a handful of survivors in old age, many more could recount almost as felt experience the stories imbibed from the lips of their grandparents. The older people who could recall Father Theobald Mathew's temperance crusade were dismayed at the rising tide of drunkenness and disregard for the licensing laws that had crept in during the War of Independence.

A Belfast citizen wrote to Mulcahy that 'the whiskey trade' had been the cause of 'most if not all of our national failures.' The enforcement of the liquor licensing laws was 'the first and most pressing social problem knocking loudly at the door of our new National Parliament. Everyone connected with the late Volunteer movement for our freedom knows that Teetotalism was alike its escutcheon and armour.'[64] The letter was passed to the Department of Home Affairs, where the matter was taken very seriously. O'Friel pointedly asked O'Duffy if the civic guards themselves were being warned that they 'must be extremely careful to set a good

Patrick Walsh, District Inspector, RIC, Letterkenny (*c.* 1911), appointed Deputy Commissioner, Civic Guard, 1922, Assistant Commissioner, Garda Síochána, 1923.

The Royal Irish Constabulary at home. Sergeant Michael Duffy RIC and Mrs Duffy (Bridget McNamara, Cusheen, Co. Clare), *c.* 1906.

Michael J. Staines, Quartermaster-General, Irish Volunteers (*c.* 1916), first Garda Commissioner.

Assistant Commissioner Patrick Brennan, Civic Guard, showing the proposed Garda officer's uniform, modelled on the design of the Army dress. (Note the absence of insignia, black buttons.) Kildare, 1922.

The artist John F. Maxwell, designer of the Garda badge (August 1922).

First printed version of the Garda badge, drawn by J. J. O'Reilly, one of the artists employed to design the new postage stamps. (From the heading of *Iris an Gharda*, February 1923.)

First public appearance of members of the Civic Guard, before the issue of the new police uniform, at the funeral of Frank Lawless TD, Swords, Co. Dublin, 19 April 1922.

A rare photograph of Michael Staines (*front, second from right*), with Chief Superintendent M. J. Ring (*with walking-stick*) and Superintendent D. J. Delaney, bandmaster (*front, extreme right*), Kildare, summer 1922.

Members of the Civic Guard Active Service Unit, Portarlington, August 1922.

The occupation of Dublin Castle by the Civic
Guard, led by Commissioner Michael Staines
and Chief Superintendent M. McCarthy,
August 1922.

Mantel clock presented to Michael Staines
on his marriage, November 1922, by the
officers and men of the Civic Guard.
(Garda Museum)

Eoin O'Duffy (*c*. 1923), Garda Commissioner 1922–33.

Civic Guard training staff on the evacuation of Kildare Depot, November 1922. *Front row (from left)*: Sergeant J. J. Brannigan, Inspector J. Feore, Inspector R. Creagh, Chief Inspector J. J. Tyrrell, Superintendent Liam Stack, Inspector C. O'Halloran, Inspector J. G. Kelly, Sergeant J. McAuliffe, Sergeant J. Leddane.

The handing over of the Phoenix Park Depot to a National Army contingent, December 1922.

Iris an Sárda

Uimir 1.   Feabra 26, 1923.   Vol. I.

Officers and Men of the Civic Guard

I take the opportunity afforded by the first issue of your journal to congratulate you must heartily, on behalf of the Executive Council, on the progress you have made in discipline and efficiency within the past few months, and on the splendid morale which has enabled you, despite adverse circumstances, to bear yourselves as worthy servants of the people. Drawn from the people, it is your proud duty to see that the laws and regulations which, through their elected representatives, they enact for the better ordering of their lives, are obeyed by all. There is no law in operation in Ireland now that has not been either sanctioned and adopted or actually initiated and passed by the elected representatives of the people. If the people require the amendment or repeal of a particular law, the machinery is at their disposal. No law prevails or can prevail which lacks the great seal of their endorsement. No Government can hold power, no policy can be pursued, which has not the sanction and approval of the majority of the people of Ireland. You are, therefore, in the fullest and truest sense, the people's servants, guardians of the people's peace. It should be your care to continue to fit yourselves for that service and to aim at becoming, as you bid fair to become, the finest police force in the world.

The internal politics and political controversies of the country are not your concern. You will serve, with the same imperturbable discipline and with increasing efficiency any Executive which has the support of the majority of the people's elected representatives. Party will, no doubt, succeed party in the ebb and flow of the political tide. New issues will arise to convulse the Nation. The landmarks of to-day will disappear. You will remain steadfast and devoted in the service of the people and of any executive which it may please the people to return to power. That is the real meaning of Democracy—Government of the people by the people through their elected representatives. It is the only barrier between mankind and anarchy.

As the political head for the time being of the Department which answers to the People's Parliament for your discipline and efficiency, I am glad to be able to express intense satisfaction with your progress and development. Continue that progress, Guards of the people, proud in the service of your fellow citizens. You have the good-will of all decent men and women in our country. You have the unqualified approval of the Executive of the day.

(Signed), C. Ó h-UIGIN,
Minister for Home Affairs.

The first issue of *Iris an Gharda*, 26 February 1923. It carried an address by the Minister for Home Affairs, Kevin O'Higgins, to every Garda station in the country.

Sergeant John Beale, drill instructor, with recruits in the Phoenix Park Depot, January 1923.

Training staff, Auxiliary Depot, McKee Barracks, Dublin, 1923. Some of the group (all unidentified) appear to be dressed in the first (blue) cloth.

Phoenix Park Depot, 1923, including (*seated, second from left*) Chief Inspector John Tyrrell and (*seated, extreme right*) Sergeant Patrick McAvinue.

The Garda cadet class, 1923, including (*front row, centre*) Chief Superintendent J. J. Harrington, instructor (former district inspector, RIC), and (*second row, centre, behind Harrington*) Senior Cadet (later Deputy Commissioner) P. J. Carroll, who broke new ground in researching Irish police history.

Garda James Mulroy, first recipient of the Walter Scott Medal for Valour, 1924.

Members of the DMP armed with rifles in the wake of the 1916 Rising.

Members of the DMP, before amalgamation with the Garda Síochána, with Station Sergeant F.
Carruthers, Mountjoy Division, *c.* 1922–25.

Headquarters officers on amalgamation of the DMP and Garda Síochána, 1925. *Seated:* Assistant Commissioner P. Walsh, Commissioner Eoin O'Duffy, Deputy Commissioner Éamonn Coogan; *standing:* Assistant Commissioner E. Cullen, Deputy Commissioner W. R. E. Murphy.

Kevin O'Higgins, Minister for Justice, unveiling a memorial plaque to murdered gardaí, Garda Headquarters, 22 June 1927.

Kevin O'Higgins, Minister for Justice, inspecting the Guard of Honour, DMP, Phoenix Park Depot, on the occasion of the amalgamation of the Dublin police with the Garda Síochána, 1925.

James Fitzgerald Kenny, Minister for Justice, with Commissioner Eoin O'Duffy at Aonach an Gharda and the presentation of Scott Medals, Phoenix Park Depot, 1928.

A parade of the Dublin Metropolitan Division, Dublin Castle, *c.* 1930.

Illicit distillation equipment seized, *c.* 1930.

example ... in order to preserve their independence as custodians of the law.' The minister was keenly aware of the temptations for young incompletely trained guards. Drinking on duty or after hours 'would deprive the Guards of all their public usefulness in the enforcement of the Licensing Laws, apart from the breach of discipline.'[65]

O'Duffy had inherited the unresolved problems of the Kildare Mutiny. Under the ad hoc command of confused officers, and without motivation, it was not surprising that some of the young men slipped into bad habits. In December 1922 he issued a general order on 'Intemperance in the Civic Guard'. Something more than half the estimated strength of the Civic Guard had been enrolled in the temperance movement, and it was a matter for satisfaction that the men recruited were, on the whole,

> free from this insidious vice. It has, however, been borne in upon me, and on evidence the accuracy of which there is no gainsaying, that a certain proportion ... of the Guard is developing or has developed a certain notoriety for drinking, and for frequenting the company of tipplers. The Guard must not forget that they are on trial, that the people are prepared, and have in fact already given many evidences of their willingness—even anxiety—to take them on trust, and that any little shortcomings they may have as regards the performance of their professional duties will be looked at in an indulgent way ... But there are certain things which the public will not readily pardon, and amongst them is a corrupt police force.[66]

O'Duffy addressed his men with missionary zeal in the columns of *Iris an Gharda*:

> Young men of the Civic Guard—ray of hope in those dark and dreary days—ask yourselves the question: When the time of trial comes, shall I stand or fall? Can I do anything to help myself? Certainly you can. You can provide yourself with an impenetrable shield against any such attack. Become Pioneers of the Sacred Heart [Total Abstinence] League ... Wear your badge proudly and publicly. It is a decoration of real merit—the outward sign of a sterling straight man—it will prevent even the attempt to undermine your character as a public servant, or your manhood as one of Ireland's sons.[67]

The weight of the law was soon felt in the land, to the chagrin of a client in one drinking-shop. On conviction in Kilkenny District Court for after-hours drinking, the defendant protested that he had been frequenting his local public house for forty years and was 'never interfered with by the old RIC.'[68] The Scott medallist James Mulroy and his companion, John Donlon, had been on public house duty when they were attacked.[69] On 28 December 1925 Guard Thomas Dowling, aged twenty-nine, of Fanore, County Clare, was ambushed and shot dead passing the graveyard at Craggagh, Fanore, in reprisal for his enforcement of the illicit distillation laws.[70]

The Mulroys and Dowlings, who had physical confrontation forced on them, made the headlines, but there are few records of the moral courage of untried young men who presented themselves in public houses after closing time to carry out their duty, of the petty resentment and taunts they accepted, and sometimes the humiliation of challenges to fight that in their good discipline were ignored. Years afterwards, in the reminiscences of modest men grown old in the service, there was never a word of their courage in young manhood facing down bullies in remote places.

CADETS AND PROMOTION FROM THE RANKS

When O'Duffy established his headquarters in the Phoenix Park he was only thirty, with the energy and drive of his years to carry a mounting work-load. He was tested to the limit of his endurance in a war of attrition with the officials of the Department of Justice, who asserted the primacy of their role, confirmed in the Ministers and Secretaries Act (1924) the following year. The Act conferred on O'Friel and his successors the responsibility for the accounts of the Garda Síochána, with the Commissioner in a subsidiary role. The conflict left deep wounds in O'Duffy's pride.

Despite difficulty in selecting confident men for promotion to officer rank, O'Duffy opposed a proposal initiated by Senator Benjamin Haughton for the recruitment of cadets.[71] 'I cannot see my way clearly yet,' he informed O'Friel in February 1923.[72] He was influenced by the strong views of Walsh, McCarthy and others who had fought this battle in the RIC and by the attitude of the recently formed Joint Representative Body for Sergeants and Guards, protesting at blighted hopes of promotion and the 'unwarranted recruiting of men with rank,' a reference to recent appointments of additional former RIC officers as senior instructors. The number of men ready for advancement was 'wholly inadequate'.[73] He had been slow to fill vacancies for chief superintendents. 'Carefully going over the ground and considering the material available, I am not satisfied I could fill more than a very limited number of vacancies from among the superintendents—appointments once made are not readily undone.'[74]

He welcomed representations from Mulcahy on behalf of army officers 'with a good Volunteer record' who were facing demobilisation. An open examination to fill vacancies for thirty cadets had produced a list of suitable candidates, none of whom had been called; he invited the first fifteen immediately and proposed a second competition confined to army officers, twelve of whom were accepted, which resulted in a call-up of eighteen candidates from the first list.[75]

O'Friel rejected a draft general order on promotion from the ranks, described by O'Duffy as a 'principle not laid down without serious consideration nor without perfect confidence in its wisdom.'[76] The response from Garda headquarters was signed by O'Duffy, but it is not difficult to detect the hand of the old warrior,

Assistant Commissioner Walsh, who had progressed through the ranks himself.

In Dublin the police force had been administered by commissioners appointed by the Lord Lieutenant, assisted by a bureau of civil servants. But the DMP held out to ambitious young men the prospect of promotion from the ranks to the highest post. The principle of promotion from the ranks dated from the inception of the force in 1836. Advancement was on merit: knowledge of duties and the criminal law, tact in the enforcement of the law, courage in the face of the dangers to personal safety that abounded in nineteenth-century Dublin; transcending all else, proven ability to command men.

In the provinces the RIC was commanded by officers who had entered the force as cadets at the age of twenty-one or, in the case of the sons of officers, nineteen. Candidates nominated by the Lord Lieutenant were selected by competitive examination both in literary subjects and in 'elementary principles of law as treated in Stephen's *Commentaries on the Laws of England* ... [and Stephen's] *Digest of the Laws of Evidence.'* They arrived at the depot in the Phoenix Park with a rudimentary knowledge of the law but none at all of police duties. When the cadet was a mere six weeks in training, the commandant reported to the Inspector-General on 'whether he [had] made sufficient progress in the knowledge of his duties and conducted himself in such a manner as would entitle him to promotion to the rank of District Inspector.'[77]

A quarter of the vacancies for district inspectors were reserved for head constables;[78] but in practice the vacancies were not all taken up, because of social and economic burdens involved in crossing the class barrier.[79] With very few exceptions, the head constables who did move up were handicapped by age and seniority factors and could not hope to advance beyond the rank of district inspector.

The highly experienced head constables, by their example in senior command rank, gave rise to misgivings about the cadet system. The Inspector-General, Sir Neville Chamberlain, in evidence to a committee of inquiry in 1914 acknowledged that 'some excellent young officers' had entered the service in recent times. But the quality of many of the 'gentlemen' who had come before him did not impress him as being 'quite fitted to command men.'[80]

'It was impossible not to recognise the ability of the head constables.'[81] Touring the country, the Chief Secretary for Ireland in Gladstone's administration, John Morley, had been 'impressed by the ability and comprehensive knowledge of ... the Head Constables and Sergeants and [the] comparative worthlessness of the cadet officers ... He personally interviewed the police officers and sergeants when he could ... and he saw that when it came to practical work and details, the cadet officer had invariably to turn to the Head Constable to help him out.'[82] Morley had pressed for the abolition of the cadet system, but the opportunity was lost when the Liberal government went out of office.

Representing the views of Garda officers, Chief Superintendent McManus objected to the cadet system as 'undemocratic ... tending to create class distinctions.'[83] Vacancies in the higher ranks in the years ahead would be few and far between; for that reason alone it would be a 'calamitous error' to deprive ambitious, energetic and capable young men of this incentive.[84] O'Duffy was passionately concerned for the future of serving men who knew their business and understood practical police work, men of superior calibre who had joined the force hoping for promotion from the ranks. In later years many of these men were employed as sergeant-clerks, in Garda headquarters as indispensable executive officers, or running divisions on behalf of chief superintendents—men of action who had served their country well, excellent commanders in the field but with no taste for administration. In the event, O'Friel conceded ground. 'As vacancies in officer ranks will not be numerous for some time to come,' and also taking into account the 'considerable number of men with high educational qualifications in the lower ranks,' the minister was prepared to recommend to the Executive Council the adoption of the principle of appointing members of the Garda Síochána to the rank of superintendent.[85]

In 1940 the Department of Justice submitted to the Government a memorandum on cadets for appointment to 'a proportion of the officer posts in the Garda Síochána.'[86] It was admitted that some of the best serving officers had been recruited as cadets, but it was 'equally true that a number proved unsatisfactory and their services were dispensed with'; but in any event the small number of vacancies—three a year in the decade ahead—did not make it feasible at the time to recruit and train cadets. It was expected that in the nineteen-fifties as many as a hundred officers would retire on grounds of age alone, a prospect that was already causing concern. It was 'quite clear' that it would 'not be practicable to secure in the force itself sufficient suitable material to fill the gaps in the officer class.' They would have to devise some new system to obtain enough men with the necessary education and other qualities for the officer rank.

It was decided to defer the matter until there were enough vacancies. A plan to resurrect the idea in 1948 was not taken up, and the force continued to select its own officers.[87]

The specialist needs of the service were modest indeed; the gifted amateur flourished in a variety of jobs. But the Government was concerned only with vacancies in command posts. The 1940 memorandum conceded simply that 'a proportion of the vacancies in the higher ranks must be reserved for men entering the force as guards.' The recently appointed Commissioner, the civil servant Michael Kinnane, urged that 'some experience of the duties of the ordinary garda would be of great advantage to all officers of the force.'[88] If Kinnane's solution represented a compromise between the views of the Department of Justice and those of the Representative Body, the proposal for a cadet system must have died a rapid death. It is unlikely that young men with higher educational qualifications would have been willing to serve before the mast for anything like the length of time necessary to make the experience effective.

LAUNCHING A POLICE FORCE ON BORROWED MONEY

The administration of the public service was transferred to the Provisional Government in March 1922. Towards the expenses of running the 'Ballsbridge Police Department', Staines had already received £500 in February; there were further subventions in March and April, bringing his total receipts to £13,500. The money was thought to have been paid out of funds available to the Dáil cabinet; it took an interdepartmental inquiry to discover that the British authorities, having withheld money from the local taxation account, had transferred precisely that amount to the Provisional Government for miscellaneous services, including the Civic Guard, 'a most unlikely source to look for payment for a police force.'[89] O'Friel decided that these payments need not be repaid from the Civic Guard vote.[90]

From his office in Kildare, Assistant Commissioner Brennan queried the June estimates, amounting to £16,767, which included payments by Staines to the Civic Guard in Denmark Street and Clonskeagh Castle and wages for the troubled month of May not paid to the men in Kildare and Newbridge.[91] The accounting officer, Chief Superintendent McCormack, as sergeant-clerk in the district inspector's office in Letterkenny had never been confronted with the responsibility of accounting for sums of money in five figures; putting in an estimate of £47,011 for expenditure in July and August, he went to some trouble explaining the details, 'to account for the seeming magnitude of the [total] amount demanded.'[92] The cost of running the Civic Guard for the first full financial year of its existence, 1922/23, amounted to £702,650.[93]

Every guard leaving the depot for the country was required to provide himself with a bicycle, for which he was paid a small maintenance allowance. In August, in a strange transaction on his own authority, Staines ordered four thousand Lucania bicycles for resale to members of the force. When the recruits refused to co-operate, McCarthy directed that the purchase of one of the unsold bicycles should be made a condition of service, which was one way to dispose of the problem; but the sales resistance continued. At the end of the year, when the barracks at Ship Street was evacuated, a hundred guards spent most of a day joy-riding three hundred unsold bicycles along the quays to new stores in the Phoenix Park depot. The army having been persuaded to accept half the bicycles ordered, Deputy Commissioner Coogan, in charge of administration, asked for authority to pay outstanding bills for the remainder. In the absence of any record of the transaction in the Department of Home Affairs, a civil servant minuted annoyance at 'another of those unsatisfactory cases.' The Commissioner had ordered bicycles costing £44,000 to equip a force with an establishment of 4,300 and a current strength of something over 2,000. The unhappy episode was wrapped up two years later when authority was given to sell the remaining bicycles at knock-down prices.[94]

The Dáil Committee on Public Accounts, in an interim report on the first year of independent government, described the difficulty of investigating the accounts of an administration in the process of reconstruction under a new parliament, new government departments springing up, existing departments under pressure, a new army and a new police force coming into existence, and a scarcity of experts in accounts offices.[95] On the Auditor-General's discovery of deficiencies in Garda store accounts, Coogan complained that the report was 'actually misleading.' Hundreds of new stations had been opened. 'Neither officers nor men had the slightest knowledge of store accounting or of the importance of furnishing returns.' The force was constantly on the move from depot to depot, company to company. It would have been 'utterly impossible' for company officers with years of experience to keep track of each man's property. The officers who had been obliged to leave Kildare in difficult circumstances could not be held responsible for public property left behind. 'Some of them carried documents and vouchers in their pockets for weeks and when permitted to do so returned to Kildare and took possession of every scrap of paper to build up proper records.' They deserved the Auditor-General's commendation, not his implied censure.[96]

LIMITATIONS TO THE COMMISSIONER'S AUTHORITY

Having discovered for himself the poor quality of some of the rankers on the Police Organising Committee who had been catapulted into senior positions, O'Duffy looked outside the force for officers of character with practical experience in high rank to stiffen the cadre of instructors in police duties. The names of two such men were strongly recommended to him: John H. Harrington, who had been district inspector in Mullingar, and Francis J. Maguire, in Raphoe. In December 1922 Coogan notified the Department of Home Affairs of Harrington's appointment as civilian adviser on crime—a courtesy not appreciated in Home Affairs. 'The whole procedure at Civic Guard Headquarters is wrong. They have presented the appointment of Mr. Harrington as a fait accompli, and this is their general attitude towards appointments.' The Commissioner should have consulted the department before making the appointments.[97]

O'Friel reminded O'Duffy that as accounting officer for the Civic Guard vote he himself was responsible for all transactions. Directing the Commissioner to report on the nature of Harrington's duties, he also required a statement of the circumstances that made it impossible or undesirable for the duties to be performed by an officer of the force; and he also inquired whether Harrington had a pension.[98]

Seething with anger, O'Duffy replied immediately.[99]

> I did not expect to receive from you ... a letter in this tone, and I hope it will be the last. When I reflect ... how hard I have worked to make a success of the task I have undertaken it is very discouraging to receive a document of this nature ... If this is an indication of what I might expect in future, it is not my intention to

seek a permanent appointment. I regret that you should be the medium of the Treasury for conveying to me these reminders of the limitations of my authority …

Getting into his stride, O'Duffy sought his real enemy, voicing the indignation of generations of ordinary people who had passed the iron gates of the Big House, reflecting on the disparity between their lot and the leisurely life of members of a privileged establishment.

It would appear that the Treasury are on my track. I am at a loss to know if they exercise the same vigilance over other Departments where hundreds of Civil Servants are employed at handsome remunerations who come in, in the morning, at 11 o'clock, take an hour or two for lunch and leave sharp at 5 o'clock, with a half-day on Saturday and not one of whom perhaps ever did a day's work or lost an hour's sleep for Ireland. My staff work an average of 12 or 13 hours a day— Saturday, Sunday and Monday. They do not grumble because they feel they are doing useful work for the Government and the Nation. This is the type that has made the Civic Guard the success, I am proud to say, it is, and this is the type that will secure confidence for the Government … I am being treated as if I had no sense of public economy and as if I were a squanderer of public funds, and I require to know where I have transgressed …

His superintendents practically to a man had already been appointed when he arrived; he had not appointed a single chief superintendent. He knew the ability of all his officers. In transport they were carrying on with a few broken-down lorries 'cast [off] by the Army and towed in here.' There was not a decent car in the service. He had travelled a thousand miles on inspection in a car borrowed from the army and had not claimed 'one penny either for travelling or subsistence allowance.' The Treasury had refused to refund £100 he had paid for uniforms. He was not behind the Treasury in his concern for the future of the country. He would 'not let Ireland down.'[100]

O'Duffy demonstrated his patriotism in total dedication to the responsibilities of his office. In his daily routine he accounted for every quarter-hour: reading the newspapers, attending to correspondence, visits to classrooms. He interviewed his officers at set times: 'Heads of departments desiring to see the Commissioner shall do so at hour in timetable.' Back at his desk after dinner in the evening, he worked until ten or later.[101] Correspondence from Home Affairs was delivered by an army despatch rider close to midnight; O'Duffy asked for an earlier delivery, to give him an opportunity to study personally the more important papers before retiring and more time in the morning to deal with the post from divisions.[102] He required his typists to live in, 'to be available for urgent work at any time … even on Sundays'; they did not look for overtime, and worked 'cheerfully whenever required.'[103] He took holidays no more than a week on average annually.[104] As a good manager, he delegated work to subordinates with confidence. 'Go into the matter fully and deal with it to a conclusion; a favourite expression, meaning you were not to trouble him further, asking for instructions.'[105]

In his angry reply to O'Friel's stricture on the employment of Harrington and Maguire, O'Duffy referred to a direction from the Department of Finance,[106] which he had interpreted to mean that the Commissioner could not make a single appointment to any rank in the Civic Guard without Treasury sanction. He was in the best position to make the decisions. 'I am absolutely opposed to jobbery, and the job-hunters who stormed the Castle a few months ago realise this pretty clearly now … Harrington and Maguire are the only skilled Police Instructors I have for the training of the entire Civic Guard.'

Harrington had not applied for employment. Having been told of his ability, O'Duffy had left 'no stone unturned' until he got him. There had been one small difficulty. As District Inspector Harrington he had been the arresting officer in the capture of Commandant Seán Mac Eoin, the County Longford guerrilla leader, in February 1921. O'Duffy asked Mac Eoin to come to Dublin to meet the former RIC officer. 'The General who fully understood all the circumstances of his arrest attached no blame whatsoever to Harrington, who [had] acted as a gentleman … The General further expressed his satisfaction that the man who probably saved his life when the Black and Tans were maltreating him should be recognised.'[107]

The appointments of Maguire and Harrington as chief superintendents were sanctioned by the Department of Finance, on O'Friel's recommendation.

When his anger had subsided, O'Duffy proposed the recruitment to the depot staff of additional former RIC officers 'approved by IRA officers of high standing and reputation.'[108] All his nominees were duly appointed,[109] but not without disapproval in Home Affairs, as Kinnane minuted. The Commissioner had strongly opposed the cadet system, on the grounds that the Garda had within itself a sufficient number of able men to fill the higher posts; it seemed strange that he was finding it necessary 'to fall back on ex-RIC men.'[110] It was stranger still that Kinnane did not appreciate O'Duffy's immediate need for experienced police officers for a very narrow range of administrative jobs, which no cadet system could have met; and anyway, in opposing the cadets, O'Duffy relied on his vision of intelligent young men, potential officers, maturing in the service.

'WHEN I ASSUMED COMMAND I WAS PROMISED FULL CONTROL'

The report of the Police Organising Committee recommended the appointment of a Garda accounting officer directly responsible to the Paymaster-General, with an inspector as finance officer in each divisional headquarters, along the lines of procedures that operated in the RIC. Wholly unaware of the impact the Ministers and Secretaries Act was to have on sectional ambitions in the public service, O'Duffy attempted to run his office as if he had financial autonomy; and, despite setbacks, he stood his ground. In October 1923, in a fourteen-page closely typed memorandum, he formally proposed the adoption of the RIC system of accounts, with the Commissioner as accounting officer for the Garda vote.[111] He was 'no slavish admirer of British means and methods,' but he would not deny 'the excellence of many of their institutions.' He was intimately acquainted with the strength and disposition of forces under his command; he was better placed than any other individual could be to control expenditure. No other officer in the country had 'a greater interest in securing the most rigid economy.'

He complained that the force had been 'badly treated.' When he assumed command he was promised 'full control' but was 'deprived of authority in the important matter of finance from the outset.' He did not consider the task of training capable paying officers and building up a financial control system more difficult than what had already been accomplished—the formation of the Civic Guard itself, 'not a promising nucleus for a police force' when he was appointed Commissioner.

Finding evidence abroad to bolster his case, he quoted Raymond Fosdick, former Commissioner of Accounts for the City of New York. In the London Metropolitan Police, Fosdick had written,

> the utter lack of control by the Commissioner over the acts and functions of his Receiver is a source of weakness which has led in the past as it will inevitably lead in the future to friction and irritation. The work of the two officers is too inextricably related to admit of each being independent of the other and there appears to be no reason why the Accounting Officer should not be made responsible to the Commissioner rather than to the Home Secretary.[112]

O'Duffy's submission was circulated to President Cosgrave, and to the Ministers for Finance and Home Affairs. In a covering note, O'Higgins confirmed to Ernest Blythe in Finance that, unlike the Inspector-General, the Garda Commissioner had not been appointed accounting officer for the police service, and this had led to friction. But essentially it was 'a technical matter', in which the minister should not interfere.[113] In the matter of the proposed divisional paying officers, O'Friel had 'failed with Finance,' where there was resistance to the concept of 'clerical police'. There was no derogation in the status of the Commissioner, who had 'primary responsibility on the technical police side'; the accounts side was 'merely subsidiary'. It was wrong 'to pay a man as a technical officer and employ him on ordinary Civil Service work.' The Inspector-General of the RUC, Colonel Wickham, had fought bitterly with his own minister over the same question. 'He was beaten in the end although he had a stronger case ... The R.U.C. is simply the R.I.C. in Northern Ireland and all district inspectors are trained in the accountancy system of the R.I.C.'[114] The battle lost, O'Duffy had to accept O'Friel in the role of accounting officer.

Out of all the wrangling there emerged the Accounts Branch of the Department of Justice, based in Molesworth Street, Dublin. A civil servant was seconded to the Commissioner's office to deal with financial matters. Chief superintendents were relieved of responsibility for certifying pay-sheets and claims; these procedures were transferred down the line to district officers, apparently without consultation with O'Duffy or any consideration of the effect of the change on the work of superintendents as operational officers. O'Duffy anticipated difficulties for inexperienced clerks, 'capable and efficient men who see that their time can be much more profitably employed in studying for promotion.'[115]

What emerged in the encounter between the policeman and the civil servant at the very formation of the modern Irish state was in essence the dichotomy in the public service described by the Tavistock Institute of Human Relations in its report of a seminar in Bray, County Wicklow, in February 1966. More than forty years later, the institute detected 'two groups ... the administrators representing the only role which is formally recognised in the traditional system, and the technicians [the very word used by O'Friel] whose skill and knowledge had been recognised as necessary but for whom only makeshift roles have developed as attachments to the original organisation.' This had led 'to the development of stresses between the people involved; on the one hand the administrators inside the system, and on the other the technicians claiming entry.'[116]

The conflicts at the top were felt in petty oppression of the men in the stations. In the interpretation of loosely worded allowance orders, the accounting officer co-operated with the Department of Finance, 'with complete indifference to ... welfare [and] a total disregard for efficiency in the service,' the Representative Body complained in 1937. A lack of understanding was 'evinced every day in the senseless querying of Garda claims ... in want of confidence in the certificates and statements of even the [high] ranks of the Service, in delay in paying claims.'[117]

FIGHTING ON A SECOND FRONT

When the Civic Guard towards the end of 1922 moved out of their grim billets in Ship Street Barracks, O'Duffy accompanied the recruits to the Phoenix Park depot. It would be difficult for managers in the modern age of upholstered, draughtproof office suites to visualise the added pressures on O'Duffy, without a headquarters, fighting his corner from a desk in the overcrowded depot, and the effect on the morale of his staff toiling in barrack-rooms, attics, and basements. The less than ideal working conditions in their new quarters were accepted in a spirit of patriotism; conscious of the parlous state of the national economy, O'Duffy hesitated to complain. The offices and squad rooms were lit by antiquated gas lamps, but he was reluctant in the prevailing circumstances to make a case for electric light.[118] Following a strike at the gas works in 1924 and a blackout in the classrooms and billets, the OPW was pressed to wire the depot, and this was done in 1926 in a general scheme that included the former Viceregal Lodge, then the residence of the Governor-General.[119]

The organisation and initial distribution of the force having been accomplished, O'Duffy began a frustrating search for a separate police headquarters, arguing that discipline was compromised by the exposure of recruits to the relaxed attitudes of established personnel.[120] In a personal appeal to O'Higgins, he described nineteenth-century working conditions in makeshift offices for a staff of 130 squatting in dark corners.[121] The Commissioner and his headquarters staff were eventually accommodated in the Royal Hospital, Kilmainham, until decay in the roof timbers forced their evacuation and return to the cramped offices in the depot.

THE GARDA SÍOCHÁNA AND THE IRISH LANGUAGE

One of the more mature candidates to join the Civic Guard, John Mackin of Cullyhanna, County Armagh, brought to his new career the experience of years of service as a Gaelic League organiser at home and among the expatriate Irish community in New York. He was immediately put in charge of the Irish classes for recruits, and he became one of O'Duffy's allies in the cultural life of the force.[122]

As in all his enthusiasms, O'Duffy put heart and soul into the Irish revival movement, though with an overriding anxiety for the capacity of the force to respond to the cultural revolution he was convinced was around the corner. The progress made by schoolchildren was such that 'within five years probably and within ten years certainly the vast majority of the young men and women of the entire State will know Irish, or will at any rate possess sufficient Irish and will be disposed to use [it] to make performance of his duty ... extremely difficult, if not impossible, for the non-Irish-speaking Guard.'[123]

In a report on proposals for new promotion regulations, two years before the Commission on the Gaeltacht published its own radical proposals, O'Duffy urged that no consideration should be given to a candidate who had no Irish or was not willing to learn it.[124] The *Garda Review*, in its first issue the following year,[125] published a programme of simple lessons for private study: 'What can I do for Irish?'[126] To structure the movement in the force, O'Duffy proposed a scheme of formal study based on a two-year course on gramophone records. The government made a contribution of £500 towards the cost of the gramophones, records, and textbooks; individual members of the force 'almost to a man' contributing the balance of £1,200.[127]

The *Review* backed the enterprise. There was 'no need to appeal to the patriotic instincts of the Force which had already shown a splendid example to the rest of the country without any material inducement or promise of reward.' The study of Irish was not alone a patriotic duty but 'a matter of prudence, supported even by the dictates of bread and butter.'[128] In later years, as a young guard, the author discovered the forgotten equipment gathering dust on top shelves in station offices and learnt of O'Duffy's ambitions from older colleagues, who scoffed at the notion that their contributions to the language fund had been voluntary.

The Report of the Commission on the Gaeltacht, published in 1926, recommended 'that systematic steps be taken to replace all non-Irish speaking officials in the Gaeltachts by competent Irish-speaking officials.' The operational needs of the force were the Commissioner's first priority. Very often the best Irish-speakers were the most efficient guards. It was 'impossible' to allocate such a guard to a backward district where his police efficiency and effectiveness were lost. Members of the force with a good knowledge of Irish felt that if they revealed their knowledge they would inevitably be sent to an Irish-speaking district. They associated the Gaeltacht with 'backwardness.'[129] It was 'manifestly unfair' to guards who had responded to exhortations to learn the language to be transferred to the Gaeltacht, where their chances of promotion were remote.[130]

In 1944 Comhdháil Náisiúnta na Gaeilge complained to the Taoiseach, Éamon de Valera, that in the Gaeltacht the Garda Síochána was actually obstructing the revival of Irish, carrying on the work of the RIC as 'a demoralising influence.' The Comhdháil demanded the immediate Gaelicising of the force, recruiting only candidates who were very proficient in the spoken and written word, with Irish the language of the depot.[131] Kinnane made the obvious point that unless the people wanted to speak Irish in their work and play, the first step had not been taken. It was 'too much to ask' the ordinary guard or teacher to persist in talking Irish to people who were indifferent to the language. The existing staff of highly experienced depot instructors, all 1922 men, had little or no Irish, and he was not prepared to replace them. He questioned the ability of recruits to come to terms with legal definitions in Irish.

De Valera telephoned Kinnane; he understood the difficulties but asked that the drill book, at least, be translated into Irish.[132] The recruits continued to drill on the depot square to commands in English; but every day for an hour, during the six months of their training, they were to sit in class learning by rote passages from a new Irish translation of the police duty manual. In a circular letter to the force in November 1946 Kinnane paraphrased the exhortations of his predecessors, adding: 'In view of the facilities provided in all our schools during the past twenty years ... the young garda who is unable to speak the language fluently cannot reasonably expect his superiors to regard him as having any real ambition either to become efficient as a policeman or to earn promotion for himself.'[133] No more was heard on the subject afterwards from the Commissioner's office.[134]

6

An Amiable and Attractive Man

I made two great mistakes. I did not marry, and I entered politics.

O'Duffy's reaction to the murder in 1926 of Sergeant Fitzsimmons and Guard Ward, followed by the assassination the following year of his patron, Kevin O'Higgins, left him emotionally drained. It was a personal tragedy that, not yet forty, he had already accomplished his life's work. 'His command and influence ... established for the Civic Guard a fine standard of discipline, efficiency and a notable esprit de corps.'[1] The pride of rank-and-file guards in their membership of an elite organisation in the new Ireland owed much to a sincere commitment to welfare in the force by a confident leader who signed his circulars with the additional title of 'Taoiseach'. Guards in all ranks who had worked under him at headquarters and were still in the service when the author joined their ranks held his memory in affection.

In an age of much social deprivation, the casualties of the Garda Síochána, penniless young men invalided out of the force, were left in dire straits. O'Duffy personally worried about their fate. Impoverished families of guards who died in the service often could not afford to bring their sons home for burial. A solution to this problem was sponsored by the Passionists at Mount Argus, who emerged as spiritual directors to the DMP in the eighteen-nineties. Recalling past neglect 'with pain and sorrow,' Assistant Commissioner John Mallon proposed the formation of an Obsequies Association to ensure dignified Christian burial for deceased constables, members contributing a penny a week to a burial fund.[2] In the RIC a burial fund was maintained from the profits of the depot 'wet' canteen, but this was rejected by O'Duffy as objectionable. He was also opposed to the practice of passing the hat as taxing the generosity of individual guards. Proposing to sponsor a benevolent fund, he urged that the state should 'encourage its servants to efforts of this kind by providing a nucleus on investment.'[3] But when the Garda Benevolent Society was established, the state only provided a facility on the pay-sheets for collecting the modest subscription.

Early in 1928, concerned at the incidence of tuberculosis in the force—arising in some cases from conditions in the stations—O'Duffy invited the Representative Body to discuss the problem with him.[4] In the particular case of a young guard who had contracted the disease in the course of duty, the Department of Finance refused to contribute either to the hospital or to the travelling expenses for treatment on the Continent recommended by the Garda surgeon. This sad case motivated the Representative Body to move for the establishment of a medical aid society, to be financed at first by a grant of £5,000 from the Reward Fund,[5] with an annual income of 20 per cent from the same source.[6] O'Duffy enthusiastically supported the proposal. The resources of the Reward Fund being 'far in excess of any reasonable or probable demands,' he had 'no hesitation in strongly urging the grant of money to form the nucleus of the Medical Aid Fund.' He proposed to augment the fund 'from other sources,' probably from the profits of the depot canteen.

O'Duffy was 'well aware of the heavy financial strain involved in prolonged even casual hospital treatment.' When this was followed by a recommendation for treatment abroad, 'or a sea voyage to a distant land,' it was about 'as practicable for the person with resources exhausted to be recommended a tour of the globe in a palatial liner.'[7]

The Reward Fund at the time stood at £19,000. Supporting the Commissioner, Kinnane in the Department of Justice could see no reason why the money should not be employed as proposed.[8] On the refusal of the Department of Finance to co-operate, the Representative Body responded more in baffled disbelief than in anger. 'We do not ask the State to do anything; we merely ask for permission to put useless moneys that already belong to us to use to a blessed purpose.'[9] It took four years and a change in government to overcome the opposition in Finance. On a visit to Garda headquarters in the summer of 1933 the Minister for Justice, P. J. Ruttledge, announced the transfer of £10,000 to the account of the medical aid fund, and the 'blessed purpose' was accomplished.[10]

The Representative Body appointed sub-committees to run the benevolent and medical aid societies, and a third sub-committee managed the depot canteen, with P. J. Gallagher as secretary to all three groups. Wearing yet another hat, Sergeant Gallagher administered St Joseph's Young Priests' Society, an old RIC charity for the education of impecunious students for the priesthood, revived under O'Duffy's patronage.[11]

IN A WORLD OF PLEASANT DIVERSION

With his inexhaustible energy, O'Duffy provided for sporting and cultural activities in an organisation he called Coiste Siamsa. The aim of the committee was not 'the production of champion athletes.' Participation in athletics had 'a moral value'; the Garda sportsman in training would 'be more likely to keep both mind and body under control.' Guards 'owed it to the reputation of the Force to keep fit in mind and body.'[12]

There were strong sporting traditions in the old police forces, especially in tug-of-war. In the eighteen-eighties, when discipline in the DMP was undermined by martinets, the man chosen to restore morale was the notable nineteenth-century policeman Chief Superintendent John Mallon,[13] who took personal charge of the tug-of-war team. In 1893 the Dublin stalwarts overcame all opposition on their home ground at Ballsbridge and later in the year returned from the police tournaments in Glasgow as world champions.[14] Acclaimed by the citizens of Dublin, their great victory put new heart into the DMP.

When General W. R. E. Murphy was appointed Commissioner in 1923 he found the force demoralised by its ineffectual role in a decade of political upheaval. To restore self-respect he revitalised sporting activities. The tug-of-war team immediately regained its supremacy in international competitions.[15]

The history of sport in the Garda Síochána began in Kildare, where the earliest competitions were held in September 1922. The winner of the heavyweight boxing title on that occasion was the young guard of splendid physique James Mulroy of Coolrevane, Strade, County Mayo, who won the first gold Walter Scott Medal for Valour.[16] When the new police occupied the Phoenix Park depot in December, and pending the establishment of representative bodies, O'Duffy appointed a general purposes committee to take charge of matters affecting welfare. The agenda in March included matters concerning the Garda Band and a programme for the formal opening by President Cosgrave of the restocked depot library.[17]

The guards were welcomed into the social life of town and village, not least for prowess on the sports field. In the organisation and training of football and hurling teams and the formation of boxing clubs, the Civic Guard contributed immeasurably to the healing of the wounds of civil war. The achievements of the famous Garda boxing team at home and abroad made an enormous impact.[18]

The genesis of the Coiste Siamsa may be found in the constitution of Connradh Gaolach an Gharda, founded in 1923 by a small group of enthusiasts, including O'Duffy, Chief Superintendent Mathias McCarthy, Superintendent J. A. O'Shea, Cadet John McNulty, Sergeant Sheahan, Sergeant Gardiner, and Captain Denis O'Kelly, editor of *Iris an Gharda*. A draft scheme defining its aims as the study of Irish language and history and the promotion of sport was approved at the inaugural meeting of the ardchomhairle in December.[19] As Coiste Siamsa, the cultural movement matured during the preparations for an exciting new event in the life of the force.[20]

O'Duffy's personal drive for organisation and publicity found an ideal outlet in his annual summer festival, Aonach an Gharda, held for the first time in July 1926.[21] A formal garden party in the Phoenix Park depot was attended by President Cosgrave and his ministers, senior army officers, the judiciary, and representatives of the cultural and social life of the nation. In the glare of publicity the Aonach was the perfect occasion for presenting the annual awards of the Scott Medal. The athletic events were complemented by a chess tournament, competitions in Irish dancing and drama, in singing and in conversation in Irish, and displays of arts and crafts. Members of the Garda Síochána were encouraged to wear clothing of Irish manufacture and to buy goods made at home. The Aonach in 1926 was notable for the ceremonial unfurling of a Garda parade flag, designed and embroidered by the Dun Emer Guild in Churchtown, County Dublin, which had been founded in 1902 by Evelyn Gleeson with Susan (Lily) and Elizabeth (Lolly) Yeats, the artistic sisters of W. B. Yeats and the painter Jack B. Yeats.[22]

O'Duffy was conscious of his responsibility in organising a highly visible national event, realising that any failure to live up to his ambitious plans would reflect badly on the force at a sensitive period in its short history. The event was an unqualified success.

> The Aonach stood for more than a contest in muscle and athletic skill ... Its success is a demonstration that Ireland in some measure realised her ideal in producing a type of manhood which is able to hold its own in any country in either hemisphere. The lesson must not be lost even on our own people that without self-reliance, abstinence, perseverance—in a word, without character—the race cannot hope to progress.[23]

But having ascended the heights and savoured justifiable pride in achievement, as if every triumph in life exacts a penalty, the year was to end tragically in O'Duffy's aberration in calling for rearming, which would have compromised moral authority in the new police.

PILGRIM POLICEMEN

In 1927 members of the Catholic Guild of the London Metropolitan Police on pilgrimage in Rome paraded at the Vatican for an audience with Pope Pius XI. The news fired the imagination of Archbishop Mulhern, who suggested a similar Garda pilgrimage.[24] The idea was taken up by Father William Gleeson, Jesuit chaplain of the Gardiner Street police sodality.[25] There was an immediate enthusiastic response in the recently amalgamated Garda Síochána and DMP, and a pilgrimage was planned for 1928. The Pope was 'very enthusiastic at the prospect of the first National Pilgrimage of an Irish Police Force since the introduction of Christianity in Ireland,' O'Duffy informed the Department of Justice.[26]

The government did not share the Pope's enthusiasm. O'Duffy discussed the proposal with the Minister for Justice, J. Fitzgerald Kenny, who questioned 'the wisdom of such an event.' O'Duffy intended travelling with the pilgrimage, but he had 'no personal interest ... From experience I am inclined to think my own incidental expenses would be very considerable.' In the event, the depot canteen committee voted a cash grant to cover the Commissioner's expenses. O'Friel was reluctant in urging 'some objections.' Provided it was understood that the participants would be travelling at their own expense on annual leave, the minister 'was not prepared to rule that members of the force should be officially discouraged.'

The concern in the Department of Justice was hardly surprising. The Civil War and the murderous attacks on Garda stations in 1926 were recent painful memories. A year had not passed since the assassination of Kevin O'Higgins. In the circumstances, O'Friel presumed that 'the absence of 300 policemen for holidays in another country would present no special difficulty from the point of view of police requirements in the Saorstát.' A sanguine O'Duffy expected that the pilgrimage would be 'very beneficial not only to the Garda but to the State.'

O'Friel was persuaded to arrange an advance of five pounds from the pay of the participants, the only concession asked for in return for the enormous publicity and good will for the state generated by the enterprise. The original estimate of the cost for fourteen days was stretched to cover three weeks abroad, with hotels and all meals in London, Paris, Turin, and Rome, all covered by a mere £30, with no profit for the agent, Thomas Chisholm of the Irish Travel Agency. It was all done in style as Chisholm's patriotic contribution to the success of the first great demonstration by the young state on the continent of Europe. A damask service and floral decorations were provided in the dining-car on the trains, and good family-owned hotels were chosen for their conservative respectability.

The pilgrims, 250 altogether, assembled at the Phoenix Park depot several days before departure. They were measured for new uniforms and drilled on the square. The Garda Band was on the pier at Dún Laoghaire early on a wet and windy morning in October, and the Tricolour was broken ceremoniously at the masthead to rousing cheers as the *Hibernia* cast off. Late on Sunday 14 October their train arrived at Rome Central, where the staff and students of the Irish College and their Roman friends 'accorded an almost incredibly enthusiastic welcome.'[27]

The Irish police contingent, banners aloft, their sober police uniforms resplendent with the sky-blue ribbon of the pilgrimage medal, paraded at the tomb of Italy's unknown soldier to lay a wreath. After the ceremony O'Duffy, accompanied by Father Austin Tierney, was received in audience by Benito Mussolini. The Duce was seated behind a desk on a dais at the end of a long room. Flanked by a goose-stepping military escort, the visitors marched the length of the room; following a brief exchange of pleasantries with the great man, they were marched out again. Annoyed at the Duce's haughty demeanour, and finding himself falling into step with the escort, O'Duffy muttered to his companion, 'Did you ever meet such a blithering idiot?'[28]

In a notable address to the pilgrims, Pope Pius XI defined the role of police in a Christian society.

> We have many times read, as again just now in the beautiful address presented by your distinguished General, that you are the Civic Guards ... responsible for the preservation of order, of public peace and security ... a disarmed Guard.

Disarmed, indeed, in the sense that you are provided with no material arms, but you are armed with the far more valuable weapons of vigilance, diligence and dutiful courage.[29]

In 1930 O'Duffy led a pilgrimage to the Marian shrine at Lourdes in the French Pyrenees.[30] The extraordinary Mr Chisholm of Irish Travel came up with an offer of £15 for eleven days, all expenses paid and no extras. At the grotto a phalanx of 344 normally reticent policemen of all ranks, attired in sombre civilian dress, carried votive candles in procession, singing familiar hymns with an unabashed fervour never heard from the men's side in parish churches at home. There was disappointment in Lourdes when the Irish police pilgrims did not parade in uniform. In Rome and Paris in 1928 O'Duffy had taken every opportunity to order dress parades at official and other formal functions, and the men had grown tired of the constant interruption of their holiday. Happy as they were to take part in the more intensely religious pilgrimage to Lourdes, they were determined to travel in plain clothes to protect themselves from O'Duffy's vainglorious ambitions.

A return visit to Lourdes was planned for September 1935. Commissioner Éamonn Broy notified the Department of Justice in the ordinary way, and he received a prompt positive reply from M. J. Kinnane. In April, Broy in a terse minute notified Justice that the pilgrimage would not take place.[31] There were already more than enough reasons to prevent an exodus from the country of 450 members of a police force motivated by the highest ideals. The public order crisis, with O'Duffy in his new role as leader of the Blueshirts in the eye of the storm, had not yet passed. In the circumstances it seems that the Garda authorities and their civil service masters were naïve in allowing the arrangements for the pilgrimage to go ahead.

There were other portents. A few short miles down the road from Lourdes, in Spain, one of the great political upheavals in modern European history was about to sound a clarion call for the former Garda Commissioner.[32]

THE TRIAL OF INSPECTOR BILLY O'CONNELL

It has been said of O'Duffy that in the summer of 1931 he was involved in a conspiracy to prevent the Fianna Fáil leader, Éamon de Valera, from gaining power if his party won the general election the following year. According to Conor Brady, the Commissioner approached senior army officers with a plan and, with his fellow-conspirators, had a proclamation printed at the Ordnance Survey in the Phoenix Park, calling on the people to rally behind a military government led by O'Duffy.[33] The proclamation was shown by O'Duffy to the head of the Crime Special Branch, Chief Superintendent David Neligan, in the officers' mess.

It seems that this extravagant story depends entirely on Neligan's recollection of seeing the document, as recounted in a long interview with Conor Brady. Following the army mutiny in 1924, in his role as Inspector-General of the Defence Forces O'Duffy transferred Military Intelligence from the army to the Garda

Síochána, creating in the Commissioner's office a conduit for all classified information coming to the knowledge of the state. It is more than a possibility that the document shown to Neligan in 1931 came into O'Duffy's possession legitimately and that Neligan misread the situation. (Military Intelligence was reinstated at army headquarters following the Anglo-Irish agreement on the ports in 1938, at the insistence of British Naval Intelligence.)[34]

In August of the same year, Neligan and James Hogan, professor of European and Irish history at University College, Cork, met at the RDS. Hogan belonged to the remarkable Galway family that included Colonel Michael Hogan, officer commanding the Army Volunteer Reserve, and Patrick Hogan, Minister for Agriculture in Cosgrave's administration. Professor Hogan was gathering information for a book on communism in Ireland,[35] and he sought the policeman's assistance. Neligan, who was on friendly terms with the family, cautiously obliged with copies of old Communist Party circulars, which proved useless for Hogan's purpose. On Neligan's instructions, Inspector Edward M. ('Billy') O'Connell, in charge of administration in Special Crime at Garda headquarters, made up another file of similar documents—'absolute tripe … pamphlets and general stuff,' as he described the contents afterwards. This file was to lie for months on O'Connell's crowded desk.[36]

That same August two of Neligan's detectives were involved in a fracas in the political hotbed of Kilrush, County Clare. Following an inquiry, the two men were dismissed. An emotional Neligan, apparently on his own authority, organised a collection for his men. His initiative angered the de Valera government, then less than a year in office. O'Duffy was reprimanded for 'a grave indiscretion' in authorising the collection,[37] and Neligan was suspended from duty.[38]

Only weeks earlier, in June, O'Duffy had protested to the new Fianna Fáil Minister for Justice, James Geoghegan SC, at 'a campaign of vilification' in *An Phoblacht* directed against the Detective Branch. The campaign was fuelled by Fianna Fáil committees passing resolutions

> condemning the CID [*sic*] … I appreciate and very sincerely sympathise with those members of the Garda selected by me … It is the duty of the Government to protect the members of the Detective Branch who were prepared and who are still prepared to risk even life itself so that the Government writ may run. These decent self-respecting members (the majority … Pioneers of the Total Abstinence Association) have their feelings like all of us … I respectfully suggest to the minister that Fianna Fáil Comhairle Ceanntair should be advised of the serious consequences which may result from the passing of these uncalled for resolutions.

O'Duffy's broadside was circulated to members of the government, Geoghegan confirming that he had received numerous resolutions passed at Fianna Fáil meetings 'demanding disbandment of the Detective Branch.'[39]

In a snap election in January 1933, de Valera won the overall majority that had eluded him the previous year. Over O'Duffy's head, the new Minister for Justice, P. J. Ruttledge, appointed as head of Crime Special Branch the depot commandant, Chief Superintendent Broy, who took up his new duties on 2 February. Following Neligan's fall from grace, O'Connell was 'virtually in charge of the office,' and he was 'swamped with work.' He was clearing his desk on 6 February when he discovered the file of documents intended for Professor Hogan, which he had overlooked. Putting the file into an envelope, he addressed it to 'Séamus Hogan' and gave it to one of his clerks for delivery to Colonel Hogan, as intermediary for his brother in Cork. He directed another clerk to telephone Colonel Hogan at army headquarters to tell him to expect the messenger. Hogan did not receive the telephone call, and the documents never reached him. Instead, the next day the envelope and its contents were delivered by O'Connell's clerk to Chief Superintendent Broy. O'Connell knew nothing of this but soon discovered that the documents had gone astray.

On 16 March, Broy called to see O'Duffy, who made an immediate personal report to the government. Neligan, who was still on leave, tendered his resignation, 'in accordance with instructions.'[40] In the early hours of the following morning Hogan and O'Connell were arrested on charges under the Official Secrets Act. Within a week, on 22 February, O'Duffy was removed from office. When the time came for Broy to give evidence at the trial, he entered the witness box as Garda Commissioner.

The Green Street jury returned verdicts of 'not guilty'. Colonel Hogan resumed his army career in charge of the Equitation School; he was later appointed Director of Infantry, commanded a brigade during the war years, and retired with the rank of major-general in 1945.

A different fate awaited Inspector O'Connell. Having fallen a victim of political intrigue, he was now downgraded and put back into uniform as a sergeant—not as a punishment but to correct an irregularity in his promotion in 1931.[41] He recovered his old rank in 1955 on the intervention of the Taoiseach, John A. Costello.[42]

IN THE PUBLIC INTEREST

In an age when public servants were seen and not heard, the Commissioner's public pronouncements often seemed calculated to provoke controversy. In March 1931 Superintendent John David Curtin of Tipperary arrested members of a subversive organisation on firearms charges and gave evidence at the Circuit Court in Clonmel. On Friday 20 March he carried out a late-night inspection at Golden. He was returning to his home, Friarsfield House, on the outskirts of Tipperary. At the entrance to the avenue leading to the house he stopped his car to open the gates. Standing in the glare of his headlamps, he was ambushed and shot dead.

The murder of the 29-year-old district officer was seen by O'Duffy, as reported in the *Garda Review,* as 'the most serious … since the setting up of the Saorstát.' The nation had sympathised at the loss of an 'able young officer,' but expressions of sympathy were not enough.

> You must develop a more active civic spirit and co-operate more intimately with us in the enforcement of your laws and in weeding out the callous criminals who stalk through the land. We say to the Church and to the people, if you want us to continue standing fearlessly between you and anarchy, it is your duty to take a bold and courageous stand in the cause of that peace, order and progress which you desire.[43]

The Labour Party paper *Watchword* admonished 'the responsible head of the police forces in the Free State.' The Commissioner had issued what amounted to a 'public manifesto … of a kind which the responsible minister might more properly make.' The murder of a young officer had touched 'General O'Duffy deeply as a man and as policeman … We shall not deny the credit that they do to his heart. But he … should let his head rule his heart.'[44] A civil servant in Cosgrave's office wrote on the file: 'Seen by Ministers.'[45]

In the approach to the general election in 1932, ministers in the Cosgrave administration contemplated O'Duffy's removal from office on the grounds that he had 'gradually become too arbitrary and obstinate.'[46] When the government in 1929 decided as an economy measure to close a number of remote stations and to reduce strengths in others, the Commissioner publicly stated that he was 'personally not in favour of closing any Garda station.'[47] Towards the end of 1931 he was again in open conflict with his political masters. At a time of dire worldwide financial difficulties, speculation about another reduction in pay precipitated a crisis of morale in the force. In a statement to the press, O'Duffy called for a commission of inquiry into conditions of service; the inquiry did not materialise, but no more was heard of the threat to police pay.[48]

Among the civil servants in the Department of Justice there was an ingrained distaste for publicity-seeking public servants. They were bound to have taken a jaundiced view of the Commissioner's outspokenness. In the nineteen-twenties they were unlikely to have been less prejudiced than their successors thirty years later. In 1960, in correspondence with Charles Haughey, parliamentary secretary to the Minister for Justice, T. J. Coyne diagnosed megalomania as a professional risk for policemen. 'Some of our chiefs of police have not been exempt.'[49]

As Cosgrave's ministers discussed O'Duffy's replacement there was talk of making him Irish ambassador in Washington.[50] When de Valera's second administration terminated his appointment on 22 February 1933 he was offered alternative employment as director of mineral development, a proposed new branch of the Department of Industry and Commerce. The government reassembled in the evening, de Valera reporting to his ministers that O'Duffy had declined the offer.[51]

For de Valera, the dismissal of O'Duffy was a matter of confidence. Responding in the Dáil to Cosgrave's motion of censure, he left no room for ambiguity: the Commissioner had been removed from office 'in the public interest.'[52] Upon the Government depended the ultimate responsibility for peace and order. 'We are going to see to it that those who will have the immediate responsibility will be people in whom we have full confidence. Let us note that—without any of the bunkum—full confidence.'[53]

As patriot, soldier and policeman, and as failed politician, Eoin O'Duffy was often a larger-than-life figure on the public landscape, from 1917, when he joined the Volunteers, until the sun went down on his Spanish adventure in 1937. His remarkable success as chief of police was epitomised in the wholesale closure of prisons, culminating in the abolition of the General Prisons Board in 1928.[54] Born a farmer's son on 30 October 1892 at Castleblayney, County Monaghan, he qualified as a civil engineer. Having led an active service unit in the War of Independence, he was made director of organisation and served as Chief of Staff until his appointment as GOC South-Western Command in July 1922.[55]

Elected to Dáil Éireann in 1918, he voted for the Treaty, though not without early misgivings. In his diary, Ernie O'Malley recorded a conversation with Dr Jim Ryan, who recalled that he was sitting with Dick Mulcahy at his home when news of the agreement came through from London.

> Min [Mulcahy's wife] came up in a fever of excitement, for she didn't like the Treaty. In walked Eoin O'Duffy, and he was dead against it. 'The army won't stand for that, Dick,' he said. And Dick was in a fever trying to keep O'Duffy quiet, and prevent him from talking too much ... O'Duffy was then definitely against the Treaty ...[56]

As an idealist driven by perfectionist traits, O'Duffy may have conveyed to unsympathetic observers the impression of being 'neurotic'—the verdict of Mulcahy, expressed to Robert Barton.[57] He was contemptuously dismissed by critics of his right-wing political career in the thirties as a 'bucolic idiot,'[58] a 'most curious character,'[59] an 'efficient but absurdly vain individual.'[60] The very figure of a confident soldier, as a wanted man during the War of Independence he was described in *Hue and Cry* as 'smart-looking, speaks well, walks with long strides and swings his arms.'[61] In New York for a police conference in 1923 he attracted attention as one of the romantic rebels from the old country. 'His words stream out in a sharp cackle ... When his thin lips are unsmiling they make a firm hard line at right angles to a thin hewn nose. His Irish blue eyes freeze suddenly into two points of ice.'[62]

His occasionally severe facial expression was recorded for posterity in a photograph taken in 1925 on the occasion of the amalgamation of the Garda

Síochána and the DMP. O'Duffy and his new Deputy Commissioner, W. R. E. Murphy, and Assistant Commissioners Patrick Walsh and Edward Cullen are all formally attired in number 1 dress: high collar with inset starched linen. Deputy Commissioner Coogan appears in number 2 dress, with open collar, shirt, and tie. O'Duffy's features are frozen in a scowl, as if in disapproval at the impropriety of Coogan's informality.[63]

Modern historical writing has tended to concentrate on O'Duffy's turbulent political career in the thirties. Dismissed from office and wounded in his pride, he was persuaded to throw in his lot with the remnants of Cumann na nGaedheal. It must have seemed that a new era of national endeavour had dawned for him; but 'he was too impetuous, too naïve, too forthright, and too muddle-headed to be a serious politician.'[64] A political associate, Professor Michael Tierney, wrote of

> a man who had not only won honour in peace but renown in war. His record of military achievement before the Truce was second to none, and he had been called in as Inspector General to command the army at a critical moment in 1924 (at the same time continuing to carry his responsibilities as Commissioner) ... an amiable and attractive man without any real tendency to dictatorship, but also, unfortunately, without any ideas of his own. His energy was tempestuous and undirected ... O'Duffy's later attempt to revive his [Blueshirt] movement and his intervention in the Spanish Civil War were no more than a source of pity for a man who had such a fine record as soldier and head of the Police Force, and whose career had ended so tragically. It was a tragedy in which those of us who had induced him to get involved in politics were really more to blame than he was.[65]

In the complex character of the man there was a highly developed sense of patriotic idealism that was no discredit to him. When the Provisional Government was desperately seeking a strong man to rescue the Civic Guard, O'Higgins seemed to confer on his protégé the power of a Roman governor. O'Duffy wore the mantle of office like a toga until the civil servants, determined to assert civilian control, step by step stripped away his perceived authority. If he was proud to a fault, a nation uncertain of itself had need of his vanity and had need of the determination he communicated to his men that they would succeed and that to make the effort was the patriotic duty of every member of the Civic Guard.

In the evening of his life he admitted that he had made two great mistakes. 'I did not marry, and I entered politics.'[66] He died on 30 November 1944 at the early age of fifty-two, to outward appearances a broken man, physically infirm, and half-forgotten by the generation in whose service he had spent himself in his constructive years. Towards the end of his life he made a rare appearance at a Garda Benevolent Society dance. 'His unostentatious entry to the ballroom was the occasion of a purely spontaneous ovation ... He was delighted to find that, despite the vicissitudes of politics and ideologies, the force still reciprocated the love he bore for the Garda.'[67]

O'Duffy was dead forty years and was still remembered in his parish of Mount Merrion in the south Dublin suburbs, a 'right gentleman' who did not smoke or drink and was not above organising small parish functions. Even as the sun went down he took pride in turning out well-dressed processions for the summer festivals.[68]

7

MAKING ROOM FOR REPUBLICANS

*I think something must be done at once to regularise the position and bring
order to the procedure which is being followed at present.*

A t the Fianna Fáil ardfheis on 8 November 1932, Éamon de Valera had words
of praise for the institutions of state built up by his opponents. 'To the credit
of the men in the Army, to the credit of the Civic Guard and the Civil
Service, the civil services and the forces of the State are prepared to serve elected
representatives of the people. That is a great achievement.'[1] In his acknowledgment
of the political stability he had inherited, the President of the Executive Council
made no reference to the singular contribution of the head of the Civic Guard.

In his search for a Commissioner in whom he could repose full confidence, de
Valera reached over the heads of the Garda board of management: Cosgrave's
protégé, Deputy Commissioner Éamonn Coogan; the British army soldier who
fought the republicans in the Civil War, Deputy Commissioner W. R. E. Murphy;
the former RIC officer and central figure in the Kildare Mutiny, Assistant
Commissioner Patrick Walsh; and Assistant Commissioner Edward Cullen, who
had also been appointed by the Cosgrave government.

Whatever other qualifications for the vacant office Chief Superintendent Broy
may have offered, de Valera was assured of the loyalty of a malleable Commissioner
for his purposes. In the Dáil on 14 March the leader of the opposition, W. T.
Cosgrave, asked what characteristic the government found in the new occupant of
the office that was lacking in O'Duffy. De Valera was blunt. There was one
transcendental consideration: Broy had not been chief of police under the last
administration. They wanted a Commissioner whom no section of the community
could accuse of being 'deliberately and politically opposed' to the new government
and 'likely to be biased in his attitude because of past affiliations.'[2]

In June 1932 the new Fianna Fáil administration carried out its election
promise to withhold five million pounds in land annuities owing to the British

government on sums advanced to farmers in the period 1891–1909 to buy out the landlords. In retaliation, the British imposed a 20 per cent duty on Irish livestock exports, which resulted in great hardship for the farming community and widespread public disorder.

In October, demobilised army officers raised a new organisation, the Army Comrades' Association, to defend the right of free speech at Cumann na nGael meetings, which were coming increasingly under attack by extreme republicans. Early the following year the ACA donned blue shirts to identify their followers in riots; in a more sinister development, they adopted the fascist straight-arm salute. Taking an ill-considered plunge into the political cauldron, a disgruntled Eoin O'Duffy assumed the leadership of the ACA.

The 'ambiguous relationship' between the IRA and the Fianna Fáil government emboldened the republicans in their attacks on Cumann na nGael meetings and social functions.[3] Riots became a nightly occurrence. Caught in the middle, without clear policy directions from Commissioner Broy, the overstretched police adopted pragmatic tactics, creating buffer zones between the warring sides to contain the violence. When that failed, batons were drawn, as much in self-defence as to clear the streets.

During the 1933 election campaign, de Valera called on O'Duffy to respond more directly to breaches of the peace, while the Attorney-General, Conor Maguire, exhorted the Garda to remember that the nation's honour was at stake. 'It ought to be possible for everybody to … state his programme without interference. That is fair play and justice.'[4]

Turning the heat up, O'Duffy proposed leading the ACA, now called the National Guard, in a parade on Sunday 13 August 1933 to commemorate the deaths of the founding fathers of the Irish Free State, Arthur Griffith, Michael Collins, and Kevin O'Higgins. The parade was routed to pass Leinster House. Calculating the possibility of a coup d'état, the government banned the parade. The security of Government Buildings was entrusted to Oscar Traynor, not yet in the government. Gardaí armed with rifles were posted in the vicinity of the Dáil. On 5 September the Minister for Justice, P. J. Ruttledge, reported to the government that steps had been taken to obtain military equipment from the army, including armoured cars, for use by a new Special Armed Unit of the Garda Síochána.[5]

In the erupting crisis of public order, the perceived need for reassurance on the loyalty of the police prompted the Government to pack the Crime Special Branch with Fianna Fáil supporters.[6] In advance of O'Duffy's planned trial of strength, on Thursday 10 August, Traynor began recruiting his police auxiliaries. Attested overnight as members of the Garda Síochána, the new policemen won for themselves and for the Commissioner of the day an enduring name in history as the 'Broy Harriers'.

The government decided that the economy could carry an increase of 300 in the strength of the force; before the whistle was blown, 367 were admitted.[7] The unusual recruits, hurriedly selected mainly from working-class areas in Dublin, were variously under the regulation height or over the age limit; a few were married men. Some former members of the force who had been dismissed succeeded in slipping back into the ranks.[8]

Before inquiry was made into their previous careers, and without papers or training in even basic police procedures, they were assigned at first to protection posts in the Dublin Metropolitan Division. In a dramatic account of arrival in Dublin Castle, Conor Brady describes the veteran detectives gazing 'in shocked amazement at their new colleagues dismounting from a lorry … Almost without exception, they could recognise every face as those of the men whom they had sought and pursued over the previous ten years.'[9]

The barefaced irregularities in the recruiting procedures were raised by Stephen Roche, Secretary of the Department of Justice. Roche telephoned Broy, who confirmed his own dilemma by letter on 10 August. 'I think something must be done at once to regularise the position and bring order to the procedure which is being followed at present.' The first intakes, totalling sixty recruits, had arrived, and another batch of thirty was expected the following day. Nothing was known about these men, who had been simply directed by someone 'to call at the Depot on a particular date.' Broy lamely suggested that candidates should apply in writing to the Commissioner, who should be supplied in advance with a list of 'approved candidates'. It was a matter of the most urgent necessity that immediate steps be taken to end an 'irregular and impossible position.'[10]

On 28 August, Kinnane noted on the file that McElligott in the Department of Finance had requested a written explanation, 'as full and comprehensive a submission as is possible in the circumstances emphasising the urgent nature of the matter which prevented us from giving the Department of Finance formal notice' in advance of the reopening of Garda recruiting.[11] The Department of Finance was aware that the government, on 18 August, had authorised the recruitment of three hundred new guards to meet 'certain developments at the beginning of August, including the formation of … the National Guard.' There was no provision in the Garda vote for the additional expenditure, upwards of £28,000, for which a supplementary estimate was necessary.[12]

In the new year an unhappy Roche conveyed to Broy the opinion of the Attorney-General that the new men recruited in contravention of regulations were not members of the force and could not legally exercise police functions.[13] In an attempt to keep his own house in order, he directed Broy to furnish a certificate of eligibility for every recruit; otherwise, in the case of men who did not fulfil the statutory requirements, notification for the purpose of pay was not to be sent to the clerk in charge of accounts but to Roche personally, if necessary marking communications 'secret'.[14] Roche put his case to Ruttledge. The recruitment of the new men had been approved 'informally' by the government. As accounting officer, he had no authority to pay their wages. 'The very serious situation' could be remedied only by retrospective legislation.[15]

The withholding of the land annuities from the British exchequer did not mean that farmers in debt to the government were relieved of the obligation to pay on the nail; those who refused to pay had their cattle seized. In a tradition of communal loyalty dating from the Land War in the nineteenth century, the farming community refused to co-operate with the government, and the impounded animals were auctioned at knock-down prices, to the advantage of cowboy cattle-jobbers using fictitious names, protected by the 'Broy Harriers'.[16]

As the turbulent politics of the nineteen-thirties ran their course, armed detectives fell into the habit of firing shots in the air to break up riots. It was not until 1932, after the change in government, that the Commissioner intervened to forbid the practice.[17] With O'Duffy out of office and the less disciplined 'Harriers' in action, the scene was set for potential disaster. The risk of civil proceedings on the head of the activities of illegal policemen was graphically demonstrated in the incident at Marsh's cattle yard in Cork in August 1934. A crowd had gathered for the sale of seized cattle. The yard inside and outside swarmed with guards in uniform, augmented by detectives. A lorry carrying men armed with sticks broke through the outer cordon and was immediately surrounded by guards. Without cause, the 'Harriers' recklessly opened fire, fatally wounding fifteen-year-old Michael Lynch and wounding seven others.

A civil action against Chief Superintendent Michael Fitzgerald of Union Quay and others was taken by the boy's father, Daniel Lynch. During the proceedings in the High Court, Mr Justice Hanna expressed 'surprise' that the plain-clothes men were allowed during training to 'mix with the uniformed guards for whom we have so much respect.' Ruttledge protested immediately to the Attorney-General that the remark from the bench tended to 'create the untrue and mischievous impression' of 'an undesirable class recruited in recent years with whom the ordinary police do not wish to associate.'[18] But in his judgment, delivered on 5 April 1937, Hanna excoriated the culprits as 'not real Civic Guards' and 'an excrescence upon that reputable body.'[19]

Following the murder of Superintendent Curtin in March 1931, revolvers were issued to all divisional and district officers, and the arsenal of Garda firearms was augmented from military stores.[20] The armed potential of the force now dramatically increased in response to the Blueshirt crisis. The unarmed posture of the essential Garda Síochána in uniform was seriously threatened when a company of the Special Armed Unit was given instruction in the use of Lee-Enfield service rifles, a dramatic turn in events captured by an *Irish Times* photographer.[21]

The emergence of the former Garda Commissioner as an important figure in the political arena might have posed a problem in loyalty for the Garda. But, as Conor Brady observed,

what was remarkable at this juncture was the absolute decision of the members of the force to continue in support of a government with whose policies they disagreed and whose origins they detested. It would be naïve to suggest that the Guards were all motivated by an unshakeable adherence to the strict principles of parliamentary democracy … The principles inculcated by O'Higgins and O'Duffy had gone deep into the force and the stability of the Guards in those vital months was to be one of the major factors in the resolution of the Blueshirt crisis.[22]

The ordinary decencies of life prevailed in Westport, where O'Duffy was to address a meeting. Instructions had been issued to arrest him if he appeared in the Blueshirt uniform. Approaching the town, he was intercepted by guards under Superintendent Gerald Flynn of Castlebar but was rescued by supporters. A large crowd had gathered to hear the Minister for Justice, J. Fitzgerald Kenny, and the Blueshirt leader. O'Duffy had gained the platform of planks laid on porter barrels and was beginning to speak when Superintendent Joseph Murray of Westport mounted the boards to arrest him. In the melee O'Duffy was dragged down by Garda Patrick Gill, who was concerned for the former Commissioner's safety. Taking refuge at first among the barrels under the platform, Gill succeeded in escorting O'Duffy to the Garda station. A bed supplied by a local hotel was made up in the sergeant's office, where O'Duffy received a stream of visitors before retiring for the night.[23]

In February 1937 the promised legislation to regularise Traynor's recruits was passed by the Oireachtas, indemnifying all concerned 'in the public interest.'[24] With isolated exceptions, the 'Harriers' in a surprisingly short time were assimilated as useful policemen—a tribute to common sense in the well-disciplined force bequeathed by O'Duffy and to the self-respect and resourcefulness of the new guards, a republican leavening in a largely Cumann na nGael lump. The 'Broy Harriers' stand in history as an exercise in adroit politics by a master tactician.

'FIGHTING TOOTH AND NAIL'

As Commissioner from 1933 to 1938, Éamonn Broy made a significant contribution to morale in fostering Garda sports, where he was most at home; he 'had only one love, athletics.'[25] In acknowledgment of his lifelong commitment he was elected president of the National Cycling and Athletic Association and in 1935 president of the Olympic Council of Ireland. Leaving his mark as a catalyst in the process of healing the wounds of civil war,[26] he made room for Michael Joseph Kinnane, who brought to the office of Commissioner the insights of many years of experience as assistant secretary in the Department of Justice, having watched over the development of the force since its formation in 1922.

With the arrival of a new Commissioner it must have seemed to Sergeant 'Billy' O'Connell, casualty of the Official Secrets Act affair in 1933, that deliverance was at hand. In the matter of O'Connell's legal expenses, representations were made by the Ceann Comhairle, Frank Fahy TD, and by Dan Breen TD. De Valera personally sought the views of the Department of Finance, where his intervention foundered on the well-established principle that in general the state did not pay for the defence of accused people who were found innocent by the courts.[27]

The secretary of the Department of Finance, J. J. McElligott, urged the restoration of O'Connell's former rank, and Maurice Moynihan in the Department of the Taoiseach took the matter up with Roche in Justice. O'Connell now had the head of the government and three powerful civil servants mulling over his welfare. As he had promised Moynihan, Roche talked to Kinnane, who took a strong stand: O'Connell's original promotion was irregular, and restoration of the old rank would also be irregular. Kinnane was

> fighting tooth and nail to get it into the heads of the police that irregularities are not going to happen under his regime. I told him that if I were in his position I would make the appointment, as the circumstances seem to me to be so very exceptional and cogent … If O'Connell's re-appointment as Inspector is still desired, notwithstanding the Commissioner's reluctance … the Minister for Justice should be authorised to tell the Commissioner definitely that the Government desired that the first available vacancy should go to O'Connell notwithstanding any technical difficulty, the Government accepting responsibility. I think that the Commissioner's embarrassment would be lessened if it were put to him in that way. As I have said, I would not myself stand on ceremony in the present case if I were Commissioner, but perhaps it is just as well to have a Commissioner who errs on the rigid side—the other side is so fatally easy![28]

Shortly after his appointment, Kinnane, 'fighting tooth and nail' for high standards, took a surprising initiative, writing at some length to Roche to sponsor 'a case of hardship so unusual in its circumstances' that he felt convinced it would move the minister to adopt the unorthodox course of seeking special sanction from the government to admit to the force a young man who, 'though eligible in every other respect to become a member, is yet only 18 years of age.' The boy's father, Sergeant Thomas Walsh, Roscommon, was at that very moment in hospital, 'at the brink of death.'[29]

The Commissioner eulogised the career of Sergeant Walsh, commended several times for 'meritorious conduct … zeal, energy and detective ability.' He had 'earned for himself a conspicuous place in the esteem and interest of the Force, and in the admiration and gratitude of a large section of the public.' Having to provide for an exceptionally large family, ten of whom were still living, he had managed, by outstanding industry and temperance on his own part and that of his wife, to maintain an 'exemplary standard in his way of living.' His zeal and devotion to duty had earned for him a strong recommendation for promotion. From among the men of an entire division eligible for consideration, he was selected as one of the two most suitable and deserving of the opportunity to advance. On his promotion he was routinely due for transfer to another division, but the Commissioner had been so impressed by requests he had received from 'a representative group of law-abiding people' that he had permitted Walsh to remain where he was in his new rank.

> Sergeant Walsh has been an exceptionally worthy member of the Force and an exemplary citizen. As a comrade, he has so endeared himself to his fellow-members that, I am assured, and believe, many of them look upon his illness and the plight of his family in the light of a tragedy personal to themselves and are waiting, with anxious hearts, to learn what their Commissioner and their Minister will do to help. They have already through ... their Medical Aid Fund come to the assistance of the family in meeting the heavy hospital expenses ... They are ready to give, from their Benevolent Fund, all the help they can afford ...

Kinnane found it 'extremely difficult to visualise any case in which the special authority in question could be exercised to better advantage.'[30]

Putting the case to the minister, Gerard Boland, Roche opposed discrimination 'in favour of the police as against any other branch of the public service.' Significantly, there was a similar case in his own department.

> One of the best and most popular officers [had] died prematurely leaving his wife and family almost entirely unprovided for ... If we had taken the line which the Commissioner is now taking we might have asked the Government to nominate one of the deceased officer's sons for a position in the Public Service on the grounds of public interest ... We did not do so because we thought it would be wrong and futile.

But Roche was glad to say that fortune had turned for the family, and the boy of eighteen in question was now employed as a bank clerk.

Roche detected a grey eminence at Garda headquarters: from the style of the minute he had no doubt that it was written by Assistant Commissioner Cullen. 'The Commissioner's part in the business was limited to putting his name to it.'[31] He assured Kinnane that the minister, while appreciating the 'humane motive' in the case, had rejected so wide an interpretation of 'public interest'.[32]

Following the long-expected death of Sergeant Walsh, the immediate distress for his widow and children was alleviated by his comrades in the charitable tradition of the Garda Síochána. The Department of Justice, by accident or design, now had on file a useful precedent for blocking any future attempt to drive a coach and four through the Garda appointment regulations.

NON-COMBATANTS, 1939–1946

The role of the Garda Síochána as bridge-builders in a society that was still divided by the legacy of the Civil War was demonstrated once again in the response to the outbreak of war in 1939. In the spring of 1940, as the German armies overwhelmed the Low Countries and swept across France, the part-time soldiers of the Volunteer Reserve left the towns and villages to join the colours, leaving Ireland without a home guard. In a radio broadcast on 1 June the Taoiseach called for the organisation of a Local Security Force. On Sunday 16 June national unity meetings were held in all the principal towns, the leaders of the political parties sharing a platform at a rally in College Green. In the national emergency the Garda Síochána was the keystone, the opposition leader, W. T. Cosgrave, told the vast crowd. The guards were 'good servants of the State, capable at a moment's notice of either stopping the traffic to let their children cross, or defending the State with their lives if necessary.' The country 'knew the courage of these men ...' The *Irish Times* noted a movement 'without parallel in Irish history,' a merging of all shades of creed and opinion in the task of national defence. The meeting in College Green marked 'the end of political dissension, and the beginning of true nationalism.'[33]

Kinnane delegated his most experienced headquarters officer, Deputy Commissioner W. R. E. Murphy, to organise the LSF. When the Dublin police were absorbed into the national force, Murphy personally revised police regulations to conform with the new status of the DMP as a division of the Garda Síochána. He was writing a manual of criminal investigation, which would put the rudiments of forensic science into the pocket of every garda; he had a plan to modernise traffic control in Dublin, and was developing his ideas for changing the antiquated beats that had remained unaltered for a century with an ambitious scheme of intersecting patrols. Murphy's system of 'basic beats' was tried and rejected in the nineteen-fifties as unworkable through lack of manpower, especially younger, more active guards.

Putting all other work aside, Murphy responded to the challenge of the emergency with the enthusiasm of an old soldier recalled to battle. On 4 June he circulated instructions on the 'Organisation and Duties of a Local Security Force', followed on 24 June by further instructions on the separation of military and auxiliary police functions and on 26 June and 13 July on the particular duties of an unarmed LSF. These four documents ran to a prodigious thirty-three closely typed pages, every line bearing the imprint of Murphy's personal style.[34]

A part-time force of 'at least 200,000 men' was needed. Men of all ages volunteered in their tens of thousands, including old republicans who had never before crossed the threshold of a Garda station. While the local sergeant instructed volunteers in basic police duties, the Garda roped in the farming community, bus-drivers, commercial travellers, night workers and, along the coast, volunteers in the fishing industry for observation duties. Citizens living in the vicinity of Garda stations were rostered for station and cordon duties or as messengers. The owners of motor vehicles were put on notice to hold themselves in readiness to provide emergency transport, and the location of every bicycle was listed. Armbands and distinctive lapel badges were supplied.[35] The older men and others not up to the rigours of military service opted for auxiliary police duties and wore blue denim when uniforms were issued.

While the army itself was in the throes of unparalleled expansion, Garda superintendents became directly involved as organisers of a new army reserve, which became the Local Defence Force, with a brown denim uniform. The old soldier in W. R. E. Murphy was in his element as he instructed Garda colleagues on 'modern warfare ... Persistent and unceasing offensive by advancing detachments of motorised and airborne troops ... to seize *points d'appui,* cut communications and spread panic ... It is most necessary for all those in command to ... keep constantly before their minds ... tactical principles which must guide their actions, so that in times of confusion, doubt and terror they may provide themselves with a certain guide to right action.' But the Garda would take no initiative without the approval of the responsible military officer,[36] which made sense to the practical Garda officers, who must have been relieved when responsibility for the military reserve was transferred to the army on 1 January 1941. A guard was seconded as administrative officer in each LDF area. The LSF remained under Garda control until the force was stood down at the end of the emergency in 1946.

The status of the Garda Síochána as non-combatants in the event of an invasion was raised by Kinnane, who asked for a memorandum 'authorised by the Government' to enable him to issue instructions. In February he complained at a delay in providing him with directions. He feared for his control of his force if the impression went abroad of 'any divergence of authoritative opinion' that might 'prove disastrous to the maintenance of ... discipline ... in the event of invasion.'[37] Before the end of the month he was supplied with 'very secret' instructions on the disposal of weapons and the destruction of sensitive documents if occupation by an invading force seemed probable. Gardaí were to remain at their posts to assist the civilian population, unless the army ordered an evacuation of the area.[38]

The army Chief of Staff, Lieutenant-General Daniel McKenna, disagreed with the policy of 'keeping the Garda Síochána out of the fighting,' and there was 'a good deal of support' for the views of the professional soldiers who would be in charge of operations. Kinnane himself expected that some of the best Garda officers would 'not be kept out of the fighting.' Surrounded by fighting fellow-countrymen, they would 'ignore orders,' well knowing that, however strongly they might be censured, their actions would be approved by the people and 'secretly admired' even by their superiors.[39]

Roche put forward the proposal that small coastal Garda stations might be defended as military outposts. If the local gardaí wished to remain in occupation of their stations to 'fight it out,' their decision would probably be accepted 'with gratitude.' He went further in urging that such a state of affairs might be anticipated with the fortification of selected Garda stations. The expense and inconvenience 'would be outbalanced by the satisfaction of having our guns in position ... the strongest possible indication ... of our sense of the imminence of the danger and of our determination to make a real fight of it.'

In the doomsday situation Roche envisaged, military courts would have been established 'immediately', with committees of public safety 'to deal out rough justice' for breaches of the peace. He was advised that voluntary courts, to which he was 'attached even apart from wartime emergencies,' would not function unless the local clergy consented to co-operate, a proposition for which he had 'no enthusiasm.' The Commissioner was bound to say that the ordinary decencies of life would not survive the withdrawal of guards from the districts affected, but Roche could see no reason why a country district would 'fall into chaos all at once,' considering the presence of the LDF and LSF, a military unit including at least one member of the old Garda station party, and the influence of the local clergy.[40]

Having discussed the proposals with the secretary of the Government, Maurice Moynihan, de Valera postponed further consideration 'for the present.'[41] The following year contingency instructions 'In the Event of War' were drawn up in the Department of the Taoiseach. The status of the Garda and the LSF as civilians and non-combatants was confirmed, not excluding the right of an individual garda to assist the Defence Forces 'in every way possible'; nor was a garda prevented from endeavouring 'by every means in his power' to control confusion and disorder in a war zone. They were to remain at their posts pending arrangements with 'the occupying power' consonant with international law. Responsibility for the direction of all defensive measures would rest with the army. Initiatives by individuals, 'no matter how desirable a particular course of action [might] appear,' were not to be undertaken without the approval of the army officer responsible for operations in the locality.[42] In the event, the threat of war receded, and the contingency instructions were not circulated.

The Emergency Service Medal, awarded to members of the Defence Forces and the various voluntary organisations, including the LSF, was withheld from the Garda Síochána on the grounds that as permanent public servants the contribution of members of the Garda Síochána was not voluntary. No distinction was made between soldiers of the regular army and the men who enlisted for the duration.

PART 2

8

THE ROLE OF THE REPRESENTATIVE BODY

*I regret more than I can say that the first Representative Bodies should have
any reason to believe in the uselessness of their existence.*

I n the nineteenth century, when place in the social order was still an accident of
birth, policemen were recruited, with rare exceptions, from the working class.
The principle of wages related to the value of services was hardly understood;
police pay was measured by the arbitrary yardstick of 'station in life', and policemen
shared the common lot of their class.

The economic pressures were greater for policemen, who were expected on
meagre wages to live up to higher standards of dress, residence, and social
behaviour. With increased respect for their role, they advanced in social status; but
they hardly shared in the prosperity of nineteenth-century England, despite their
exertions in bringing about the peaceful conditions essential to commercial success
that made it possible for the new industrialists to amass enormous fortunes.

While the right to combine against employers was being won by the trade
unions, the police were at the mercy of the Watch Committees. In Ireland the RIC
and DMP made humble memorials to the Lord Lieutenant. The National Union of
Police and Prison Officers, formed in 1917, attracted widespread support. The
following year the union staged a strike in London, which led to the appointment
in 1919 of Lord Desborough's Committee on the Police Service. Desborough
recommended procedures to enable the police and the police authorities to
negotiate 'matters affecting the service as a whole.'[1]

In a bid for recognition, the union called another strike. On 1 August 1919,
out of a national force of 50,000 constables, some 2,400 answered the call. The
1918 strike succeeded because the police had an unanswerable case, and the Prime
Minister, David Lloyd George, to whom the strikers appealed directly, had to give
way. After the events of 1919 General Sir Nevil Macready, just out of office as
Commissioner of the London Metropolitan Police, wrote to the *Times* that the real

cause of the second strike was the passing of the Police Act, which brought the Police Federation into existence. The men were prohibited from belonging to a trade union, and this was 'the death blow to the National Union of Police and Prison Officers, which had endeavoured ... to dominate and impose its will on all Police Forces throughout the country.' The union collapsed, and not one of the strikers was readmitted to the service.[2]

At one stroke, defining three cardinal principles, Desborough revolutionised the professional and social standing of policemen in society:

> A policeman has responsibilities and obligations which are peculiar to his calling and distinguish him from other public servants and municipal employees ...
>
> When he becomes a constable, he is entrusted with powers which may gravely affect the liberty of the subject, and he must at all times be ready to act with tact and discretion, and on his own initiative and responsibility, in all sorts of contingencies ...
>
> The burden of individual discretion and responsibility placed upon a constable is much greater than that of any other public servant of subordinate rank ...[3]

Desborough recommended representative bodies for each of the police forces, and a central council for the entire service, with the reservation that while the various ranks might meet together to discuss matters of common interest, separate representation for each rank was desirable. This view was strongly advanced by General Macready, who stated an elementary principle in management psychology: 'It is impossible that the discipline necessary to the efficiency of the Force can be maintained if the interests of superior officers are placed in the hands of the lower ranks.'[4] The Police Federation evolved nevertheless into an organisation for all ranks up to chief inspector. In the Garda Síochána, all the elected delegates, including the superintendent ranks—at the insistence of the senior officers themselves—sat as a joint body.

During the period 1923–24 matters affecting the welfare of members of the Civic Guard were referred to an ad hoc general purposes committee. Under provisions of the Garda Síochána (Temporary Provisions) Act (1923) the secretary of the Department of Home Affairs, Henry O'Friel, moved to establish representative bodies based on the British model and similar bodies provided for the RIC and DMP.[5] In November the following year regulations were made by ministerial order to enable members of the Garda Síochána 'to consider and bring to the notice of the Commissioner and (through the Commissioner) of the Minister for Justice matters affecting their welfare and efficiency, other than questions of discipline and promotion affecting individuals.'[6]

Ahead of his time, the Commissioner, Eoin O'Duffy, advanced enlightened views on management-staff relations. His ideas were not welcomed by conservative civil servants, who were much exercised in defending departmental prerogatives.

Influenced almost certainly by the endless wrangling he was himself having to contend with in his dealings with Home Affairs, O'Duffy made an extravagant proposal that would have allowed delegations to wait on government ministers. Requiring the bodies to make representations through the Commissioner to the department would involve 'considerable delay and much correspondence' and a necessity for the bodies to reconvene 'to review progress.' His own ideas would 'prevent the feelings of irritation and suspicion which invariably follow a long drawn-out correspondence.'[7]

O'Friel spelt out once again the terms of reference for representative bodies. There could be no question of the Garda communicating with any member of the government, other than the Minister for Home Affairs, and only then through the Commissioner. It would be highly undesirable to permit representations to be made 'over the head of the Commissioner'[8]—which is precisely what happened when the head of the force was excluded from conciliation and arbitration half a century later. There was nothing in the proposed regulations, O'Duffy suggested, to prevent the holding of informal conferences, 'a sort of Round Table ... a via media.' With just a hint of tartness, he added that the department was concerned that a less rigid role for the bodies 'might in some way weaken or jeopardise my position as head of the Garda Síochána ... While I acknowledge my indebtedness to the Ministry for this safe-guarding of my interests, I must say that I have no misgiving whatever.'[9] O'Duffy's 'round table' never materialised.

Two committees were established, one for chief superintendents, superintendents, and inspectors, and another for sergeants and guards. The regulations were amended in 1925 and 1927 to provide an officers' representative body and separate bodies for the supervisory ranks of inspector and sergeant, another for guards alone. Members of the several ranks in each area were balloted to form electoral colleges to select and brief the delegates on the central council. The failure to give status to the local committees was one of the causes of unrest in the force, especially in Dublin, in later years. Voting procedures were not prescribed, which was also to give rise to difficulties.

Divisional selection committees were formed haphazardly. No records were kept; local delegates were sometimes unknown to their colleagues. Intense canvassing became a feature of the process. Politically ambitious candidates, who may or may not have been those best fitted for the job, had little difficulty in getting themselves elected. The best-qualified candidates more often than not regarded the representative bodies as a distraction in the competition for promotion and opted out of the elections. Attendance at meetings of the central council was recorded as duty, and expenses were paid by the state. Domination by the officers on the Joint Representative Body eroded the influence of the lower ranks.

Following the amalgamation of the Garda Síochána and the DMP in 1925 and the merging of the two representative bodies, the rank and file on the Garda side were unhappy at the prospect of sitting with the Dublin bobbies. In the city stations there was even less welcome for the change. O'Friel made light of the perceived problems. 'Making due allowances to the feelings of the officers, n.c.o.s and men of the Dublin Metropolitan Division,' he found it 'impossible to imagine anything approaching discord or jealousy' between the representatives on either side.[10]

Unrest in the DMP was alleged by James Larkin's *Irish Worker*. Citing recent cuts in police pay, the paper endorsed a reported move to form a new Policemen's Union. A 'good opportunity' had presented itself. 'Policemen are workingmen, no different from any other wage earners ... Let them make the first move and we will be only too glad to help.' Deputy Commissioner Murphy informed the Department of Justice that while the reduction in pay was unpopular, there was no agitation. The 'burning question' was the proposed amalgamation.[11]

The problem was not simply one of friendship and common understanding. In the disbanding of the RIC and formation of the Civic Guard, significant changes in outlook had taken place in the provincial force. In Dublin in the eighteen-eighties the exchange of the top hat for a new helmet signalled no change in organisation. As they had done since they first appeared on the city streets in 1838, the constables continued to walk their beats, to the general satisfaction of the citizens of Dublin. But the world changed for the DMP after the labour unrest in 1913. Without a single substantial alteration in its general outlook and practices, and decimated by the exodus of the constables who opted to resign under the favourable terms of the Treaty, the unreformed DMP brought into the amalgamated representative bodies the psychological wounds of the head-on clash with the workers, followed by the open warfare in the city during the years of the revolution. As members of the national police force they felt insecure, suspecting the ambitions of the new Garda officers with an eye on opportunities for promotion in the city. They feared transfer to country stations, despite assurances that their conditions of service were protected. The problems lay buried for decades; in the nineteen-sixties, pent-up resentment erupted and spread like a cancer throughout the entire Garda force.

The two representative bodies elected in 1924 met for the first time in January and elected Chief Superintendent Seán McManus, Letterkenny, and Sergeant Patrick Barry, chairmen of the officers' and other ranks' committees, respectively. A young sergeant from Ballaghderreen, Patrick Joseph Gallagher, was appointed secretary to the joint body. A farmer's son and primary school monitor, Gallagher was to emerge as spokesman for his generation in the force.[12] He exerted an extraordinary influence and came to personify the representative body system, having the 'absolute trust and confidence' of the entire membership of the force. 'His respect for authority was absolute.'[13] The death of P. J. Gallagher in 1957 evoked a sense of great loss, almost of tragedy. As subsequent events were to show, the emotional reaction to his passing demonstrated both the strength and the weakness of a system that depended for its survival on one man.

At their inaugural meeting the officers put at the top of their agenda motions on pay and allowances. They recommended that the system of recruiting officers as cadets, recently introduced, be abolished, and that civilians employed as clerks at Garda headquarters be replaced by members of the force, in the interests of 'secrecy, urgency and expediency.'

The other ranks' committee, working from its first agenda, complained at delays in paying wages and the inadequacy of allowances. A motion recommending protective clothing for cycling duty was also carried.[14] O'Duffy dealt personally with resolutions touching barrack regulations, making concessions where possible; proposals involving expenditure of public funds were forwarded to the Department of Justice with his recommendations.

Until the root-and-branch reorganisation of the system of government under the Ministers and Secretaries Act (1924), senior civil servants had virtually a free hand in the administration of the new state. The extraordinary circumstances created by the contest for supremacy between the Provisional Government and the Dáil cabinet, and by the distractions of the Civil War, 'conferred inestimable advantages upon Finance in its endeavours to implement its policies throughout 1922 and 1923.'[15]

Under the influence of Joseph Brennan and T. K. Bewley, on loan from the Treasury in London, a draconian curtailment of public expenditure was both inevitable and necessary, though it would have been more acceptable if the department had been even-handed in its approach. In the search for economies the Garda magazine, *Iris an Gharda,* was identified by Brennan. Unofficial newspapers were 'calculated sooner or later to have embarrassing results' and were a burden on the taxpayer.[16] In his role as Inspector-General of the Defence Forces in the aftermath of the army mutiny, O'Duffy had an opportunity to take a swipe at one civil servant, refusing to allow the army accounting officer to examine certain accounts 'on the grounds that the moment was inopportune.'[17]

Under the patronage of the Department of Finance, the civil service operated within a magic circle of self-interest. In 1927 the minister, Ernest Blythe, appointed an economy committee, which included Henry O'Friel.[18] Spurred by the worldwide economic depression, the committee presented a report in 1931 recommending reductions in the pay of the Garda and national teachers and in old-age pensions; but economies in the civil service were not seen as justified. After deliberations lasting over four-and-a-half years, the committee 'recommended substantial cuts in all the major services, with the solitary exception of the service to which four of the five members of the committee plus the committee's secretariat themselves belonged.'[19] A 'cuts' committee in 1932 received from a deputation of higher-paid civil servants a memorandum expressing 'deep resentment at the injustice of proposed cuts in salary' and 'grave concern at the consequences.'[20] This committee, representing outside interests, was sufficiently impressed or intimidated to defend the higher officials as 'accountable for most responsible duties of a very varied nature which demanded the best brains that the country can supply.' They left the civil service untouched.[21]

SEEDS OF DISCONTENT

On 10 January 1924 Sergeant Barry's committee, representing lower-ranking guards, was still in session when the Department of Home Affairs, without notification to the representative body, announced a reduction of one pound in the pay of recruits in training. At their historic first meeting the delegates could 'hardly believe' that the consequences for the Garda Síochána had been 'seriously considered.'[22] The Desborough Report in its entirety had been adopted in Ireland by a Viceregal Commission headed by Mr Justice Sir John Ross.[23] In 1922, on the recommendation of the Police Organising Committee, the rank and file in the Civic Guard were paid the Desborough rates; but the officers of the new police had their salaries pegged below the rates enjoyed by their counterparts in Britain and in Northern Ireland.[24]

Economic realities after the Civil War compelled the government to cut back on public expenditure. In the matter of public service pay, only the Garda Síochána and national teachers were affected.[25] In the Dáil on 31 October 1923, in reply to a question from Richard Mulcahy, O'Higgins gave comparative pay rates for the RIC and the Garda Síochána. Ignoring Desborough, he fell back on the rates in 1914, when constables were paid £1 to £1 10s a week. Compared with the pre-war penury in the RIC, the new guards were handsomely paid at £3 10s, on the lowest Desborough scale.

The following year the pay of guards and sergeants was reduced by ten shillings a week, about 12 per cent, which achieved a saving of some £121,000.[26] An allowance for the use and maintenance of bicycles was reduced from six pounds to five pounds a year. The representative bodies were reconvened by telegram to rubber-stamp the first pay order made under the Garda Síochána (Temporary Provisions) Act (1923), which brought the pay cuts into force.

An accompanying memorandum set out to justify the cuts on the grounds of the cost of living (consumer price) index.[27] The JRB for the lower ranks protested that neither Desborough nor the Ross Commission had written a word about fluctuations in the cost of living: Desborough had clearly stated the intention of *raising* the status of the police, acknowledged in the new rates of pay.[28]

For the officers, McManus demanded to know what purpose the representative body served beyond a useful means of depriving members of the Garda Síochána of the right to belong to a trade union.[29] Sergeant Barry invoked the 'heroic death' of Garda Patrick Joseph O'Halloran, murdered in the bank raid in Baltinglass on 28 January, and O'Duffy's rallying cry to the beleaguered Civic Guard.

> We have made good and upheld untarnished our glorious motto, 'death before dishonour' … We have delicately and decisively smoothed the way so that Government might function, and yet our pay is to be reduced to the level of an unskilled artisan … When underpaid police perform duties attached to which are

great personal risks, the logical result is a lowering of their morale. The pride of belonging to Ireland's first National Police Force will pass away, and with it will go the cream of the country's manhood.[30]

In a conciliatory covering minute to Home Affairs, O'Duffy stood by his men. When 'youth, inexperience and the circumstances of the times' were taken into account, the resolution from the lower ranks showed evidence of 'clear thinking and calm judgement.' Their views might have been 'somewhat crudely expressed' but were deserving of consideration. Under the most trying conditions, the Garda had 'justified the confidence and more than fulfilled the expectations' of the nation. As the representative body had pointed out, it was 'not difficult to create discontent ... The Garda has not yet such a tradition as to render the whisperings of the agitator or the wrecker barren ground on which to sow the seeds of evil counsel.' As if in fear of some move against Barry and his colleagues in Home Affairs, he cautioned O'Friel: 'The present time is a period in which it is wise to hasten slowly.'[31]

On 13 February 1924 the Commissioner issued a general order to all ranks on membership of trade unions. He had received 'from sundry sources' information concerning discipline in the force that had caused him 'the greatest pain.' It had been stated,

> with what truth I am unable to say, that some of the more impulsive members of the Garda have gone so far as to suggest that any reduction in their pay should be met with action which, however permissible in the case of a trade union, is unthinkable in a disciplined force. The principle of trade unionism, excellent though it may be for those parties whom it properly concerns ... is ... of such a nature that a moment's reflection will convince the Garda of the extreme impropriety of any idea of membership by units of a police force, and lest any doubt may be entertained on the subject, owing to the absence of a specific Regulation, I wish to make it plain beyond doubt that such membership is most strictly forbidden ...[32]

On 24 June, writing again to O'Friel in defence of the bodies, O'Duffy regretted that 'in no single instance' had any of their recommendations been accepted, even in part. He had 'repeatedly pointed this out to the Ministry, and I feel more convinced than ever that a lamentable mistake has been made in not acceding to some, at least, of the reasonable requests put forward ... It is, however, now too late to remedy matters and I regret more than I can say that the first Representative Bodies should have any reason to believe in the uselessness of their existence.'[33] On receiving O'Duffy's letter, Kinnane on the same date, and with no apparent comprehension of the Commissioner's command problems, minuted O'Friel: 'After the discussion at yesterday's conference we may regard this matter as at an end.'[34]

These early exchanges set the tone in a continuing war of attrition between government departments and the Garda Síochána, which would come to a head in the Macushla Ballroom affair in 1961.

On 13 August 1925 a memorandum was prepared in the Department of Justice—perhaps at the behest of O'Higgins, who must have wondered at the endless complaints from the representative bodies, backed by O'Duffy. Though naturally self-defensive in tone, the memorandum reveals a degree of good will but also the first evidence of the breakdown in communications feared by O'Duffy when the regulations were being framed. Outside the questions of pay, allowances, and pensions, the recommendations of the representative bodies were generally accepted and appropriate action taken. But the department found it necessary to 'conform to the new economic standards and to assent to the general downward scaling of salaries' that the Department of Finance was enforcing. The Department of Justice had 'consistently pursued the policy of promoting within reason the comfort and wellbeing of the Garda.'

Individual cases of hardship (not described in the memorandum) had received sympathetic consideration; sanction had been sought from the Department of Finance for special allowances (not described), and these had been dealt with promptly and were generally successful. A cottage hospital had been provided at the Garda depot; the RIC riding school had been converted into a recreation hall. The memorandum made a particular point of an expenditure of £125 'to improve the appearance of the men's uniform,' a reference perhaps to the provision of chevrons of silver braid for sergeants in place of horizontal stripes worn as an armband in the early years, or possibly to the issue of collar badges, overlooked in the original order for uniform insignia.[35]

In the attitude of officials in the Department of Justice there was also evidence of paternalism at best. In the approach to Christmas 1936 the JRB asked for an advance of pay already earned for sergeants and guards, who were paid monthly. Though recommended by Broy, the request was turned down, 'in the best interests' of the men concerned. The wives of some hard-drinking guards may have been grateful; but in the same Christmas week, civil servants whose wages did not exceed £200 a year were given an advance of two weeks' pay.[36]

BOOT AND BICYCLE ECONOMIES IN 1929
When the national economy was again in difficulties in 1929, a lower ranks' boot allowance of £4 a year was withdrawn, and an allowance of £5 a year paid to sergeants and guards for the use of their bicycles on duty was halved, a saving to the exchequer of £40,500 in one year.[37] O'Duffy protested: the men were compelled to wear a regulation boot, and to acquire bicycles and to use them on duty as their only means of mobility in rural areas.[38] The editor of the Garda Review, William Harding, rattling the sabre for the JRB, circulated members of the Oireachtas to make the point that if guards ceased to use their bicycles in the public service, the money saved in reducing the allowance would be converted into a heavy net

increase in the Garda vote to cover the cost of public transport or the hire of hackney cars.[39] He was making a purely hypothetical case, as he well knew: in 1929 there was not even the whiff of rebellion in the Garda Síochána.

The superintendents were alarmed at the effect on morale in the force. Having successfully argued against a cut in officers' rent allowance, they offered to accept the proposed reduction as an alternative to a second attack on rank-and-file incomes.[40] Discontent in the ranks was 'born not so much out of a sense of loss,' O'Duffy wrote to the minister, J. Fitzgerald Kenny; there was a feeling throughout the force of 'ingratitude and lack of appreciation on the part of the Government for the work of the Garda.'[41] Conditions of service were governed 'by considerations of political expediency.'[42]

The Commissioner's views must not have fallen entirely on stony ground in the Department of Finance. In his budget speech in the Dáil on 24 April, Ernest Blythe expanded on the economies realised in the Garda Síochána. Recruiting had been stopped, and stations closed. But he had some cheerful news. 'The remuneration of the Guards cannot be further curtailed … Financially they are appreciably worse off than police in adjacent countries. Any further cuts would not only be impolitic … but they would be unjust to individuals who have given faithful service and allowed opportunities of entering upon other careers to go by.'[43]

The following day in the Dáil an impassioned Richard Corish TD, representing Wexford for the Labour Party, tabled a motion to annul the new allowances order. 'Here we have a force established in the arms of a revolution, showered with praises by every member of the Government … They do not yet know when they are going to reach bedrock or what their future prospects are.'[44] In the same debate the Fianna Fáil leader had little sympathy for an overmanned force. 'All the men … should have work to do, and no member of the force should be idle.' Ordinary people who were finding it very difficult to make ends meet 'think it is not fair to the community that a number of young men should be sitting on barrack walls knocking their heels … For a young man in present circumstances £3 a week is not unfair.'[45]

The fact that they were indeed relatively well off in the Ireland of the nineteen-twenties was lost in their deep-rooted sense of outrage. In despair, appealing directly to the minister, O'Duffy descended to hyperbole. Pride in the achievements of the force, 'which but a few short years ago caused the pulse of every member to throb with animation and enthusiasm has now been replaced by … disillusionment and dejection which have reduced the robust beating of that pulse to a sickly ticking.' In the Department of Justice, someone pencilled a derisive exclamation mark in the margin; but O'Duffy warned Kenny of the future consequences of the policy of resisting the men at every turn.

> It would be in the best interests of the force and the State if a change in policy came graciously and spontaneously and not as a product of long agitation and bitterness. If this is not conceded I fear the future will only bring discontent and

exasperation—a condition of things which can only make for indiscipline and inefficiency and which will certainly render the task of this Headquarters extremely difficult.[46]

In its report in October 1932 the 'cuts' committee in the Department of Finance recommended further reductions of up to 5 per cent in Garda pay.[47] The JRB feared 'a crisis without parallel in the life of the force.'[48] O'Duffy toured the provinces to meet local delegates and on his return spoke to a reporter. The Garda had always been prepared to contribute their 'just proportion' to the national economy, provided it was made clear to them that they were not being called upon to make a greater sacrifice than other state employees.

In a historic initiative that cast a long shadow, the second Garda Commissioner in his role as prophet called for a commission of inquiry into conditions of service; in vain, as already observed.[49] The further reductions in army and police pay urged by the Department of Finance were rejected by the second Fianna Fáil administration. A proposed reduction in the pay of national teachers was approved, and, significantly, the government called for reductions of up to 12 per cent in civil service pay.[50]

9

An Emphatic and Unequivocal Demand

Sound in its general line of argument, and temperate in its language.

I n the summer of 1937 the lower ranks returned to the battlefield, recapitulating in a trenchant statement all the old arguments on pay. With half the force in debt, as they alleged, they had a responsibility to call attention to a new danger.

> When a policeman's remuneration is insufficient to support himself and his family, and when he cannot legitimately augment his resources, the danger of corruption is very near. With our knowledge of the Force and our knowledge of the conditions under which our married men especially are now living, we believe that the Garda Síochána has reached a stage when the principles of honesty, which are so strongly engendered, are liable to break down.[1]

The Commissioner, addressing himself directly to the minister, P. J. Ruttledge, urged the 'most careful and sympathetic consideration' of the Garda claim; but, unwisely, he recommended the memorandum of the Joint Representative Body as 'at once sound in its general line of argument, and temperate in its language.'[2] The JRB believed it had Broy's unstinted support. The claim was published in the *Garda Review*, supported by an editorial hammering out the theme of past neglect now bearing the 'evil fruit' of discontent.[3] 'Defenceless,' they took heart from the support 'so wholeheartedly and unanimously' given by the Commissioner and the officers of the force.[4]

Summer passed, and well into the autumn there was still no reply. As the provincial press took up the scent of an emerging political story, the *Garda Review* picked up an endorsement of its warning on corruption.

When bribery lifts up its dirty head in the life of public servants it is a very dangerous form of corruption ... practically impossible to eradicate. In this country we can glory in the fact ... that officials like our police are notably free from the slightest suggestion of graft or bribery, and that is a thing we cherish most of all about the Civic Guard.[5]

There was still no reply from Ruttledge in October when Sergeant Gallagher, whose experience had taught him to be cautious in making any forecasts, conceded that a delay of four months was difficult to explain. But they had justice on their side, backed by public bodies and societies representing 'every shade of organised opinion,' pushing 'an emphatic and unequivocal demand.'[6] They were facing a crisis, which had to come sooner or later.[7] Too emotionally involved in the drama in which they were principal actors, Sergeant Gallagher and his colleagues misjudged the climate of opinion in a quiescent force; but running through their own anger were threads of incipient rebellion that only they were in a position to discern. The real crisis would be delayed for another twenty-five years, to be brought to a head by other, less conservative actors.

There was only one item on the agenda when the JRB convened at Garda headquarters in December 1937 for the second of its half-yearly meetings that year. The delegates brought 'imperative demands' from the force that 'the first and only question to be considered' was the pay claim. The meeting despatched 'an urgent memorandum' through the Commissioner to the Minister for Justice.[8] The following day the Department of Finance filed its comments on the six-month-old pay claim. There was logic in its refusal to relate Garda pay to possibly extravagant rates in other countries: the only valid comparison lay in the pay of other public servants at home, tied in with the financial resources of the state.

Recommending a partial restoration of the boot allowance, the Department of Finance sought 'countervailing saving' at the expense of gardaí in training. While scaling down recruit pay from £2 10s to £2 a week, it was confident that the force would continue to attract well-qualified candidates; with free uniform and accommodation, and after paying a mess bill of £1 a week, a recruit would receive 'substantial pocket money even during ... training and probation.'[9]

The JRB received an immediate formal acknowledgment from the Department of Justice. The delegates then sat back to await some further communication. Their patience exhausted, they requested an interview with the minister. Informed that Ruttledge was not well,[10] they asked the President of the Executive Council to meet them.[11] Having waited two weeks, speculating on the possible outcome, the delegates on 20 December were devastated by an unprecedented order to bring their meeting to an end and return to their stations 'forthwith'. The order was given by the Commissioner, who undoubtedly acted on instructions from the government.

The force was informed of the dénouement in the editorial columns of the

Garda Review. The response to their humiliation, if nothing else, demonstrated the well-rooted adherence to vocational values in the Garda Síochána in the nineteen-thirties. The order to stand down came as

> a great shock … We are not going to cavil with the drastic action of the Government. They acted as they have authority to act, and as members of a disciplined force we must accept such action in just the same way as we would accept any other order. We may resent it, deeply and naturally. We would hesitate to think, however, even for a moment, that the stern heel of discipline would be used deliberately to still the feelings of the Force on the justice of their claim that the cuts in their pay and allowances should be returned.[12]

After all their endeavours, the boot allowance was partially restored at £2 a year, 'a humiliating offer of ninepence a week.'[13] In reply to the principal claim, the Secretary of the Department of Justice, Stephen Roche, restated in pettifogging detail the policy based on the cost of living index, which by now gardaí in the most remote station might have rhymed.[14] In the nineteen-thirties the index averaged 158; in the forties, about 278. This should have resulted in an increase in Garda pay; but during the war years the force had to be satisfied with emergency bonuses, which only partly compensated for increased prices.[15]

In recommending the case made by the JRB,[16] Broy offered himself as a hostage to fortune. Given the speed of transmission of the claim from Garda headquarters to Government Buildings, on the very day it was received from its authors, it seems that it received no more than a cursory reading in the Commissioner's office and that Broy himself did not personally read the document. In the Department of Justice, the claim was cleared to Finance in little more than a week.

Ruttledge was anxious to consult the Executive Council.[17] The matter was on the agenda for the meeting on 1 October but was 'withdrawn until further notice.'[18] On 13 December the Minister for Finance, the acerbic Seán MacEntee, submitted a memorandum to the head of the government. He wished to draw attention to the accusation of official indifference to the welfare of the guards, which was undermining, in the words of the JRB, 'the principles of honesty … so strongly engendered' in the force.[19] The JRB was threatening the government, MacEntee rumbled.

> It is as if Customs Officers and Preventive Officers threatened to connive with smugglers, or as if Bank Clerks threatened to embezzle bank funds, or as if the Army threatened to mutiny unless they received increases in pay. Indeed the whole tone of the Representative Body's memorandum shows a failure to appreciate what right standards of discipline require. Yet it has already been published in the *Garda Review* for the information of the public and has already been featured in the newspapers, and must leave in the public mind the

impression that the Garda is an undisciplined Force, rather more concerned with advancing its own interests than in doing its duty to the public.

It was even more disconcerting that the memorandum was submitted by the Commissioner and was described by him as 'at once sound in its general line of argument, and temperate in its language.' If the Commissioner had 'a proper sense of discipline' he would have refused to forward the memorandum and have taken disciplinary action against the authors.[20]

The attitude of the strong-willed MacEntee foreshadowed the inevitable departure of a Commissioner who had so well served the interests of de Valera's second administration.

The government decision to replace Broy was taken the following May. The much-respected 67-year-old former RIC officer, Assistant Commissioner Patrick Walsh, was invited by de Valera to become caretaker head of the force, but Walsh declined.[21] The long-serving assistant secretary of the Department of Justice, Michael Joseph Kinnane, was then appointed.[22] He may not have entered on his new office with much enthusiasm; it was said that strong pressure was brought to bear to persuade him to take on the daunting job of head of the Garda Síochána.

THE TEACHERS AT WAR

The drive for restoration of the cuts in Garda pay took place against the background of a watershed in constitutional politics. In polls held on the same day, 1 July 1937, the government fought a general election and the referendum on the constitution, winning narrow majorities. As Minister for External Affairs, Éamon de Valera himself was stretched in the Dáil and at the same time at the League of Nations was opposing the recognition of Franco's regime in war-torn Spain.[23]

Of far more concern to Sergeant Gallagher and his colleagues was the campaign launched by the Irish National Teachers' Organisation early in 1937 for the reversal of cuts in teachers' pay.[24] The tactics of the INTO were undoubtedly followed with more than ordinary interest by the JRB. At a special congress in January 'a succession of short, forcible speeches conveyed the impression of unflinching determination.'[25]

The teachers were supported by public protest meetings in the principal towns, attended by church leaders and local politicians. The campaign was proceeding 'with persistence and vigour';[26] they were determined 'to fight ... to a finish.'[27] In June the campaign was proceeding with 'full vigour';[28] the Central Executive Committee, 'ably and enthusiastically supported by the general body of teachers,' had 'left nothing undone to bring home to the Government and the public the justice of their claims.'[29] But repeated representations to the Department of Education met with no response. In January 1938 the teachers raised the temperature with a veiled threat: their patience had 'worn very thin.'[30]

The Minister for Education, Thomas Derrig, eulogised the teachers, who were 'doing splendid and noble work—heroic work in many cases.' His sincerity was acknowledged, but 'the teachers were realists': it was money in their pockets they valued 'more than nice words.'[31]

When the matter was debated in the Dáil on a motion by Deputy Jeremiah Hurley of Cork, himself a national teacher, the minister offered to meet a deputation.[32] Following a public meeting in Ennis, the *Clare Champion* rallied mightily to the teachers' cause. The INTO had set an example of determined and persistent agitation that might well be emulated by other classes in the community. For fifty years

> this great Organisation battled with the British Treasury. It was never discouraged or dismayed by rebuffs—and, finally, it won. Under native government it was deprived of the fruits of victory and was now faced with the necessity of starting agitation all over again—they were doing this with a spirit and a courage … immensely to its credit.[33]

In April, Derrig announced the good news of a 5 per cent increase in all scaled salaries and in various grants and bonuses.[34] The increase was accepted 'as a gesture of good will.' At the INTO congress at Easter, the barren years were recalled with restrained anger. Stronger words were not printed in the *Irish Teachers' Weekly* during the course of the campaign. 'We were forced to ask, what foul act of sabotage, what unforgiveable national sin had we been guilty of to merit such treatment?'[35]

The *Garda Review* was 'sincerely glad' and extended congratulations to the national teachers on their success in recovering in part the wages lost in the 1924 cuts; but there was no concealing the bitterness at their own impotence. The teachers had succeeded where the gardaí had failed. It was not a question of one body being more deserving than another: the teachers enjoyed fundamental rights to express freely their opinions and to form associations and unions.

> They have the right collectively to negotiate, to bargain, and to withhold or dispose of their labour as they deem meet … They can promote and join political organisations, nominate or support candidates for election to the Oireachtas and to exercise the franchise; they may hold meetings, communicate their views to the press … But the Garda, a vast and important body of tremendous power and influence for good … may not advance their political views, they may not address themselves to their fellow citizens in public meetings, they are forbidden political activity and denied membership of political organisations, and in place of the powerful machinery of organised labour they are given a Representative Body which may be summoned and dismissed at the whim of authority … They are even denied the franchise. We … recognise that of its nature police service necessarily entails certain restrictions in normal human activities … But yet we

are compelled to ask ourselves whether the story would be different were the Garda as free to act as other organisations ...[36]

The outright belligerence on the Garda side had left the Government no room for manoeuvre. It is beside the point that years of indifference bordering on contempt had driven the Representative Body to desperation.

The INTO was no less determined in its campaign. While the JRB overstated its case, the teachers in their public utterances were more subtle. Supported by many influential friends, they could afford an urbane approach. The Government knew that it could depend absolutely on the passive loyalty of ordinary gardaí, who lived frugally rearing young families but were not beggared. In the minister's reply to the Garda claim the JRB was criticised for overstressing the poverty of their members: they had no reason for financial embarrassment, nor any excuse for failure to carry out their duties 'with zeal and efficiency.'[37]

There was more than a little justification for the minister's reprimand. The *Garda Review* over the years painted pictures of gardaí 'on the borderline of want,'[38] the garda wife 'struggling in a losing fight to buy food and clothing for her children,'[39] 'plight ... the only word ... adequately descriptive of the Garda way of life.'[40] The encouragement of a culture of poverty arguably undermined self-respect and confidence in the force.

Preoccupation with the fact of the pay cuts tended to cloud the central issue: the place in the social order to which gardaí were entitled, professionally and economically (their place in the social life of the community could not reasonably have been higher), judged objectively on the increasing value of their services, as defined by Desborough. In the nineteen-fifties they were to move the argument tentatively in that direction: 'an examination of Garda remuneration in relation to the standards applicable in other occupations' as 'a more equitable basis on which to adjust Garda pay than by reference to a cost of living figure.'[41] The new Commissioner had already taken a personal initiative in the matter.

AN ENLIGHTENED MANAGER

As a younger man, as principal officer and later assistant secretary in the Department of Justice, Michael Kinnane in implementing departmental policy had opposed the representative bodies. In the nineteen-forties, as Garda Commissioner, he was an older and a wiser man and, as he had begun to demonstrate in his policy of dismantling the ancient police code, an enlightened manager.

On 1 November 1946 wage-earners in all occupations participated in the first round of post-war national pay increases.[42] In the adjustment of Garda pay, the Department of Finance proposed new scales, at the same time withdrawing the emergency bonus that would have increased the pay of a garda with twenty years' service by three shillings a week, with nothing at all for men lower in the scale. Seizing the opportunity to take up the cudgels with his former civil service colleagues, Kinnane introduced a new policy in staff relations, described by the *Garda Review* as 'the first time since the establishment of the Garda that the principle of negotiation between the responsible Minister of State and the elected representatives of the Force on matters vital to Garda welfare has been conceded.' At last they were engaged in 'protracted discussions, representations, proposals and counter proposals.'[43]

It was self-evident, as Kinnane mildly observed, that what the Department of Finance suggested would do little 'to mitigate the inadequacy of Garda pay' and would be 'bound to accentuate discontent.'[44] The garda who had £3 10s on completion of training in 1922 now had just two shillings more. A junior clerical officer with seventeen years' service, married with five children, had a little over £9 a week; a garda similarly circumstanced had £5. Considering adverse conditions in the police force, the discrepancy was 'indefensible'. The police service no longer appealed to young men who in the old days were attracted by the security of employment and the prospect of a pension at a relatively early age—considerations that had been overtaken by the protection afforded by trade unions and by improved social services. The disadvantages in the police service were not sufficiently appreciated, Kinnane argued—as if the representative bodies had not been shouting the message from the rooftops for a quarter of a century.

Gardaí had to accept restrictions on their personal liberty, a severe code of discipline, and supervision by superiors and the public alike for twenty-four hours every day; they worked irregular hours of duty, night and day, in all weathers, with no payment for overtime; and at that period in the history of the force there were 'very poor' prospects for promotion. The weight of individual responsibility rested more heavily on policemen who were liable to be called upon at any time to investigate on their own initiative, a murder or a complaint of ball-playing in the street. They had to contend with the fear of public ridicule, official censure, the stress of court proceedings, and press publicity arising from blunders. In making arrests, approaching the mentally ill or intervening in public disturbances or family rows they had to overcome the fear of disabling injury, and even death in extreme cases.

The garrison system of the day compelled single men to live in barracks. In the best accommodation, conditions were unhomely and starkly uncomfortable. In official quarters it was impossible for married men to escape supervision of their domestic affairs. They had no choice of employer or place of employment; opportunities to select schools, to pursue personal or family ambitions, were severely restricted. The liability to transfer often involved family separation. These were all real disadvantages and should, Kinnane urged, be rewarded by liberal scales of pay. A sergeant's pay was 'utterly inadequate.'[45]

At the direction of the Taoiseach, Kinnane's memorandum was circulated for the information of all members of the Government.[46] The Commissioner's initiative bore fruit in the 1947 pay order.[47]

The outcome was given a guarded welcome. The reference to the lost inheritance in the Desborough and Ross Reports must have disappointed Kinnane, who may or may not have been pleased at a seeming quid pro quo for his support in the negotiations. The *Garda Review* found it 'difficult to understand the failure [in the pay order] to make provision for such a salary for the office of Commissioner ... consonant with the dignity, the duties and the responsibilities of that post.'[48]

In the approach to the second round of national pay increases in 1948 there was an expectation of a further substantial advance on the ground made the previous year. Questions were asked in the Dáil, probably inspired by the JRB taking a leaf out of the teachers' book. A perhaps unwise dabbling in politics must have whetted the expectation of a famous victory for the Garda but hardly endeared the JRB to those in the corridors of power.[49]

As if they were determined to make enemies, younger elements called a mass meeting to protest at the delay in dealing with the pay claim, to be held without consultation with the authorities in Kevin Street Garda station. The meeting was postponed when the minister, General Seán Mac Eoin, agreed to meet a deputation. A hundred or so guards who turned up were refused the use of the gymnasium; determined to make their stand, they held a short but lively 'unofficial' meeting in the barrack yard.[50]

In the event, the guards shared in the second round of national pay increases, to the bitter disappointment of the JRB. Going over the top, the *Garda Review* mourned 'the blackest Christmas' in the history of the force. Their 'high hopes— amounting to a certainty—entertained up to the very eve of Christmas' had been 'dashed in one fell swoop.' Tentative arrangements had been made personally with the minister for a Christmas advance against expected increases.[51]

The dispute had a comical side. In the Dáil the colourful Dublin deputy Alfie Byrne took on the role of champion of the force. In November he asked the minister if a 'Christmas box' was on the cards. Mac Eoin replied that he thought so— intending to convey that he hoped for a favourable decision on Garda pay before the holiday. Byrne confidently told the representative body that the minister's heart was in the right place, and they could expect an increase with 'a substantial Christmas box' in arrears of pay. In the Dáil in February 1949 Deputy Byrne pleaded 'untold hardship' in the force. In the matter of the 'Christmas box', Mac Eoin regretted what he had hinted in an aside.[52]

In the Dublin Metropolitan Division, with a tradition of rebellion dating from 1882, when the police went on strike, there were stirrings of the discontent that was to erupt in the Macushla Ballroom affair a decade later. The DMP constables in the nineteenth century worked up to nine hours a day, seven days a week, with night duty every second month, and one free day a month and ten days' annual leave. Labouring under a regime of discipline that had been reformed in other police forces, the DMP was unprepared when the Land League agitation erupted in Dublin in 1880. In two years of demonstrations, five hundred policemen were injured.

Their morale broken, they emerged from the conflict an exhausted and bewildered force. In September 1882 they held a protest meeting in the Foresters' Hall in Bolton Street. Those who were identified were sacked; by early afternoon on the same day the entire force had disappeared from the streets. The dismissed constables were reinstated by an enlightened resident magistrate, David Harrell, who followed a long line of soldiers who had commanded the force in the past. The government appointed a committee of inquiry, and pay was increased by a shilling to £1 10s a week.[53]

In 1949 feelings were 'very strong' in city stations, not least because the Garda settlement in 1948 was five months behind the civil service award in May.[54] Inflamed by the shrill protest in the *Garda Review*, gardaí in Dublin planned a march through the streets of the city.[55] 'Much churning makes bad butter,' the *Review* ruminated. The protracted negotiations the previous year had forcefully demonstrated the need for arbitration machinery, already well established in the civil service.[56]

10

INTERDEPARTMENTAL INQUIRY, 1950

Unless the police force in Dublin is speedily brought up to a strength adequate to its duties, a very serious ... breakdown will shortly occur, the responsibility for which must rest upon those who disregard the advice of those professionally concerned.

In the economic doldrums of mid-century, recruiting for the Garda Síochána was discontinued by John A. Costello's first Government on taking office in 1948. Commissioner Kinnane was alarmed. In the previous decade the strength of the city force had been increased from 968 to 1,182, with little impact on the growth in crime. 'Cycle patrols were resorted to on a wide scale for the rapid coverage of areas that could not be fully policed by foot patrols,' giving cause for 'fairly general dissatisfaction, more particularly among the ageing men who are finding the constant burden a distinct strain.' Kinnane had hoped to increase strength to a minimum of 1,200 uniformed guards; but the suspension of recruiting upset his plans in Dublin.

The problem was no less acute in the provinces. Of the 785 stations, half were operating on reduced strengths of a sergeant and three guards, an economy measure dating from 1930, when 370 stations were reduced from four guards to three. With growing demands on the force, especially from other Government departments for non-police services, units could not be expected to cope 'save by undue incursions on what should be members' private time.'

Kinnane spelt out the burdens imposed on quiescent men in a disciplined force by the revision of establishments in 1930, carried out without consultation with the representative bodies. When a small station was at full strength, a guard's official hours of duty amounted to between 75 and 80 hours a week; but when another guard was absent on leave or was sick, this was stepped up to between 90 and 105 hours. Quite apart from the inconvenience that on such occasions a married man (and three-quarters of them were married) was allowed to sleep at home only on alternate nights, the conditions of employment were 'most unreasonable and accentuated by the ageing of the men compared with the early days.'

When recruiting reopened in 1943, and after increasing strengths in Dublin and meeting other needs, he had endeavoured to level up the 'one-and-three' stations. The process had been far too slow. Even if all the small stations had been closed and the personnel redeployed it would have made the policing of country areas 'extremely difficult', given the means of locomotion available to men dependent on bicycles. Concluding, Kinnane urged a study 'of the whole question in all its implications ... not only to maintain an efficient Force but to remove the drawbacks' in the existing organisation.[1]

As the Commissioner had foreseen, the consequences of the bar on recruiting were felt immediately and most severely in Dublin. Towards the end of the following year the officer in charge of the Dublin Metropolitan Division, Deputy Commissioner Murphy, protested to Kinnane at the 'grave damage to the system of beat and patrol duty by the depletion of manpower.' From his own experience, and from discussions with police officers in other countries, he knew that the inhabitants of a city were not so much concerned with the efficiency of the police as reflected in the statistics of crime but rather looked to them to guarantee 'the amenities of living in conditions free from disorder, rowdyism, damage to property and the abuses and nuisances which so quickly arise in a city when effective police control is lacking.' The increase in street disorders and general disregard of the law would accelerate as criminals realised the ineffectiveness of the police. District officers were 'very clamantly' bringing the problems to his notice; the Department of Justice could not afford to ignore the warnings of experienced police officers. If the problems in the city got out of hand, the energy, time and manpower required to put things right would be very considerable. 'Unless the police force in Dublin is speedily brought up to a strength adequate to its duties, a very serious ... breakdown will shortly occur, the responsibility for which must rest upon those who disregard the advice of those professionally concerned.'[2]

Within days, Kinnane forwarded Murphy's memorandum, with a covering minute, to the Secretary of the Department of Justice, T. J. Coyne. The failure to replace normal wastage had already resulted in a reduction of strength in Dublin alone of about a hundred men. This was serious enough; but even if the Commissioner was authorised to resume recruiting immediately, not one recruit would be enlisted before the following April, and his training would take another six months. This would mean that no-one would be available for allocation to any station in Dublin or elsewhere before another year had elapsed, by which time wastage would be in the region of a further hundred in Dublin alone. Outside the Dublin Metropolitan Division a parallel situation was developing. Unless recruiting was resumed, there would be trouble, 'and we, the responsible Police and Civil Service Officers, will be blamed for not having taken the necessary steps in time.'[3]

In response, clearly, to Murphy's sounding the alarm, the Government in March 1950 appointed an interdepartmental committee of inquiry, the Minister for Justice, Seán Mac Eoin, himself taking the chair.[4] On the change of Government the following year Mac Eoin was succeeded by Michael Deegan of the Land Commission. An assistant secretary in the Department of Justice with the Garda brief, Daniel Costigan, joined the committee as an ordinary member; not yet forty, he brought to its deliberations energy and enthusiasm and a flair for organisation. The other members of the committee were C. S. Almond, Department of Finance, P. P. O'Donoghue SC, Attorney-General's office, and the Garda Commissioner.

The committee was presented with contradictory terms of reference: to inquire whether the force might be reorganised without increased expenditure.[5] Such an exercise in *realpolitik* was advanced by Eoin O'Duffy in 1932, when, seriously concerned at reports of loss of morale, he called for an inquiry with terms of reference 'wide enough to enable examination to be made of the question of devising if possible a less expensive police force.'[6] News of the Government's intentions coincided with the publication in October 1949 of the final report of Lord Oaksey's inquiry into police conditions of service in Britain. As Lord Justice Lawrence, Oaksey had been president of the court at the Nürnberg trials in 1945–46. A committee under an independent chairman of such standing carried immensely more weight than a mere interdepartmental group, even if chaired by a minister who was at the mercy of the electorate, as demonstrated in the early departure of Mac Eoin.[7] The appointment of the Oaksey Committee the previous year was greeted by Sergeant Gallagher as 'the biggest thing for the police since Desborough furnished its revolutionary findings in 1920'; they would follow its deliberations with 'more than academic interest.'[8]

The *Garda Review* greeted with dismay the appointment of a committee of inquiry conducting its business 'behind closed doors, relying on departmental files for its information about the Garda Síochána and having civil servants as the majority of its personnel.'[9] The committee was hamstrung by terms of reference having 'an over-riding emphasis on the obligation to save money.'[10] The strength of the force when recruiting was stopped in 1948 stood at some 7,500. The numbers were still falling a year later when the committee presented an urgent interim report recommending the immediate induction of three hundred recruits, 'with particular reference to the needs of the Dublin Metropolitan Division.'[11]

In its final report in the summer of 1951, a chapter was devoted to non-police duties carried out for other Government departments: agricultural returns, school attendance duties, weights and measures, passport applications, and the revision of voters' lists. The Joint Representative Body in the past had complained that no credit was given by way of appropriation in the Garda vote of the costs of such duties. In 1930 O'Duffy attended a meeting of ministers chaired by President Cosgrave at which he raised this question. In correspondence afterwards, forwarding a resolution from the JRB on the shedding of extraneous duties, O'Duffy revealed an unexpected dimension of his vision for the Garda Síochána. 'If it were the policy of the Government—as I contend that it should be—to perfect the Garda as the one widespread national service of the State, and its agent, representative and emissary in every town and village in the Saorstát, and then to pass to it all the State duties that it could bear and efficiently discharge, I would not recommend this resolution.' But it was clear to O'Duffy from station closures and the suspension of recruiting that this was not government policy. There was no check on the demands being made on the force. He had observed that other departments were 'punctilious in charging for every petty service'; by the same token, the Garda vote was entitled to the financial credit for services rendered to other government agencies.[12]

The 1950 committee canvassed the views of the departments affected. Agriculture stressed 'most emphatically' that in the absence of annually compiled agricultural statistics the state would be embarrassed in formulating and implementing its policy. The unique position occupied by the Garda made it possible for these duties to be carried out 'with a degree of smoothness and efficiency which could hardly be expected if new civilian staff was recruited even at the great financial cost involved.'[13] Civilian enumerators were eventually employed, at whatever cost, not without misgivings expressed by the representative bodies.

> In the interests of local knowledge, some of our present extraneous duties broaden rather than hamper [contacts] between the public and our members. The man on the walking or cycling patrol in our rural areas, like the man on the beat in our cities, is the lynchpin in police efficiency, and for this reason we feel there is a point beyond which the rigid adherence to the police function proper must impair efficiency.[14]

Sticking to its terms of reference, the interdepartmental committee decided that the shedding of extraneous duties would contribute to the more economic deployment of a smaller force. The Garda Síochána, from the date of its formation, had set out to cultivate friendly relations with the people. The performance of functions not within the ambit of police duties, strictly defined, was then welcomed as providing opportunities to meet and communicate socially with the people. The committee was satisfied that it would 'be possible for the police, whatever establishment [was decided], to perform some extraneous duties.' It made sense that guards should not be employed, for instance, as switchboard operators in certain stations, or as agents of the Censorship of Publications Board, serving lists of prohibited publications on booksellers. In rural areas the collection of agricultural statistics wholly occupied station parties for upwards of two months in the late spring and early summer, at no loss to their primary duties.

It was decided to modify various duties associated with the agricultural industry, and that guards should be relieved of responsibilities under the School Attendance Act. In another retrograde recommendation, the force was relieved of the delivery of old-age and blind pension books, a 'heavy burden'; instead, pension books were to be sent directly to pensioners by registered post. It was certainly no hardship for a guard on patrol to call on lonely elderly or disabled citizens, who invariably warmly welcomed the appearance of a visitor on such an agreeable errand. Thus was begun the dismantling of much of the good work accomplished in the pioneering years of the Garda Síochána.

Trawling the 1948 establishments, the committee found it possible to propose a saving of 714 guards in a reorganised force of 6,683. Making allowance for a new inspecting officer and other supervisory personnel, and weighing in the cost of new district patrol cars, the revised establishments were calculated to produce annual savings of £328,500.[15] Kinnane signed the report, subject to the reservation that strengths in divisions outside Dublin should not be reduced below 4,868; any further reduction in strengths could be realised only by 'a dangerous lowering of the standard of policing and by imposing unreasonable burdens on many units.' The Commissioner's reservation was noted in a memorandum for the Government, but, for whatever reason, his dissent was removed from the version of the report as printed for limited circulation.[16]

Within a few years the implementation of new policies realised a reduction in the strength of the force by one thousand to 6,500, with an administrative saving of £500,000.[17] To compensate for the loss in personnel, patrol cars were introduced in rural areas, an innovation greeted with scepticism by the JRB: there was a point beyond which increasing mobility would endanger efficiency.[18] Towards the end of the decade it deplored an acceptance of crime as inevitable, with new scientific methods and mobile units as the best response—an emphasis on cure at the expense of the philosophy of crime prevention. The man on the beat was still the strongest deterrent:

> The criminally-minded fear his living presence in uniform far more than the unseen and remote white-coated expert or mobile unit … Garda strength in many stations throughout the country was severely depleted and a number of stations in rural areas were closed … There are large areas where a uniformed Guard is seldom seen except when he dashed through the area in a car … The motorcar should supplement not supplant the station party.[19]

Failure in crime investigation was the inevitable result of 'the replacement of the man in the field by the squad car.'[20] The absence of crime was seen not as evidence of good policing but as a valid reason for closing a Garda station. In a later age, when crime seemed to be out of control, it was salutary to reflect on the vast expenditure on overtime and technology in the bid to recover what was lost when a Garda presence in peaceful communities was regarded as redundant.

THE DEPARTMENT OF FINANCE AND POLICE PROBLEMS

The interdepartmental committee, going outside their terms of reference, were unable to ignore the damp and unhealthy conditions in many of the stations they visited, or the life of monastic frugality endured by the unmarried men, who slept in tiny dormitories with curtainless windows, bare floors, and practically no furniture. They had nowhere to sit other than in the public office, or the kitchen. The accommodation did not appear to have been improved beyond that provided for the RIC in the nineteenth century; unless there was an improvement the force would have difficulty in attracting 'the right type of recruit.'[21]

The several Government departments affected by the proposals on non-police duties replied with their comments without unreasonable delay. But Costigan's pleas for co-operation fell on deaf ears in the Department of Finance. In October he sent a reminder to his opposite number in Finance, C. S. Almond. This was followed in December by a scathing letter from Coyne asking J. J. McElligott to move his department to expedite their observations.

It is evident from Coyne's letter that the committee of inquiry had been educated by their visits to Garda establishments. The structural condition of scores of Garda stations was 'nothing short of scandalous'; the furnishing of all stations was 'of the most primitive kind.' The OPW had estimated that 130 new stations were required; the cost of building 50 of the stations most urgently required would be about £440,000. Yet the amounts allowed to be spent had fallen from an inadequate £66,000 in 1948/49 to £16,000 in 1950/51, with hardly any provision in the current year. Coyne had been confident that as the recommendations were all aimed at economy, and as Almond was a member of the committee and had signed the report without reservation, they would not be held up in the Department of Finance. 'I feel constrained to say that the general attitude of your Department towards our proposals on Garda matters, notwithstanding our spontaneous efforts to secure economy, is not such as would encourage us to embark on another economy campaign.'[22]

Coyne waited in vain for a reply. In February 1952 he again wrote to McElligott, enclosing a copy of his earlier minute.

> Dear McElligott ... Would you please let me know when your Department expects to be in a position to let us have their observations ... We cannot put this matter on the long finger much longer. Apart from the pressing need to reduce rural strengths, my Minister will be very embarrassed when introducing next year's Estimates if he is not in a position to give the House [Dáil Éireann] some indication of what the Government are going to do about the recommendations of the Committee. If your Department sit on the memorandum much longer we will be forced to bring the matter to [the] Government without waiting for your observations.[23]

In May the strange attitude in the Department of Finance was taken up by the Minister for Justice, Gerald Boland, who asked his opposite number in Finance, Seán MacEntee, to intervene.

Seven years later, in February 1959, the Department of Finance having totally ignored the correspondence, Coyne showed the file to his minister, Oscar Traynor. It is not difficult to judge his mood at the time: impatience, possible anger; frustration arising from some other recent conflict with Finance. It seems that the answer may be found in protracted parallel negotiations for a scheme of conciliation and arbitration for the Garda Síochána, spanning nine years. On 25 February, Coyne wrote on the old committee of inquiry file:

> Just look at this ... I think it is a fair question to ask whether there is any justification for this way of doing business. Would any member of the Government seek to defend it? And in the end it defeats its object, as was illustrated in the case of the national school teachers some years ago who had eventually to be 'bought off' for a much larger sum than they would have been glad to take if their grievances had been promptly addressed. But the point is, do we have to do anything more than the three or four specific cases to which I have recently drawn your attention to establish at any rate a prima facie case that the Department of Finance's attitude to police problems leaves much to be desired?[24]

Traynor's private secretary wrote on the file: 'Seen by Minister, 27.2.1959.' It is, however, a fact of economic history that the presentation of Deegan's report on the Garda Síochána unfortunately coincided, in the words of Ronan Fanning, with 'the years of stagnation in which the unceasing struggle against inflation displaced economic growth as an attainable object of policy—when the slough of despond, ushered in by the crisis of 1951–52 and to endure until 1958, reached its nadir.'[25] In his history of the Department of Finance, quoting 'Silhouette' in the inaugural issue of *Administration*, Fanning throws some light on the conundrum. 'To make ends meet does not come kindly to the Irish character'; the fact that in the Irish economy

> ends have met so long did not come by kindness, but by unremitting attention to every aspect of expenditure. This has left scars far and wide over the civil service and outside it too. The zeal of those who wish to spend other people's money is great and unquenchable, and the taxpayer is not easily defended from it. But if there were those who tired of defending the pass and withdrew, J. J. McElligott was not one of them.[26]

ARCHAIC RESTRICTIONS
The Garda Síochána Code (1928) brought together in one volume all instructions that had been issued in routine orders and circulars from 1922. In the introduction,

'discipline and obedience' were defined as

> that which makes a man responsive to orders and authority; to do promptly and
> without question that which he is ordered to do; to subordinate his own ideas
> and opinions to those of the constituted authority; to fit himself instantly into that
> part of the organisation allotted to him, and to control himself in the most trying
> conditions. It makes him heedless of personal danger, strengthens his will power,
> and enables him to persevere in the accomplishment of his purpose.

The lives of the first generation of guards, on and off duty, were restricted to
an extraordinary degree. The Code provided for every conceivable contingency in
the local management of the force. Many of its more archaic rules were adapted
almost word for word from the RIC Code. Good order in barracks was
copperfastened in sixty-five separate regulations.[27]

The men worked seven days a week: reveille at 7:45 a.m., morning parade at
9 a.m., followed by the study of a programme of police duties. This class lasted for
an hour but was not counted in the return of duties performed. The day ended with
a roll-call at 11 p.m., when men not on patrol were required to parade in the day-
room.

Leave of absence of any kind, including annual leave, was 'a privilege and not
a right.'[28] Men who were not on duty were permitted to absent themselves from
barracks on recreation for no more than two hours, married men for four hours,
provided the concession did 'not impose extra duty on the unmarried men or
deprive the latter of opportunities for reasonable recreation.' In any one month an
additional twenty-four hours' leave might be granted, but not all in one period. It
was a privilege for guards to use their own bicycles in their spare time.[29] The
marriage of members of the force was regulated by no less than twenty-two separate
provisions in the Code. A man who married without permission was charged with
a breach of the regulations and transferred, at his own expense.[30]

Over the years such quaint regulations tended to become a dead letter; but
they remained available, to be invoked by overscrupulous sergeants in
circumstances that would have provoked a strike in civilian employment.

Addressing the problem of outmoded regulations, Kinnane had to move
cautiously to maintain the delicate balance between his ambition for a less
hidebound regime and the needs of a disciplined force and to avoid upsetting his
more conservative officers. In the early post-war years he made tentative changes,
designed to give more freedom to men living in the stations.[31] His initiatives were
welcomed by the *Garda Review* as 'the first step in a new deal ... From now on our
members can feel assured that their welfare will be a major consideration in the
administration of the force.'[32]

The revision of the Garda Code begun by Kinnane was advanced by his
successor in a series of historic amendments inspired by the interdepartmental

committee. The reform of the garrison system of policing inherited from the RIC released gardaí from antiquated indoor duties.

This was to have the effect of rationalising hours of duty for guards serving in the country. A daily average of seven hours' outdoor duty with a half-day on Sunday was routine. In many rural stations the hours of duty were grossly inflated, as Kinnane had pointed out, by 24-hour stints as station orderly, obligatory in the garrison system. In the nineteen-fifties in small station areas, crimes might average a mere two or three cases a year, usually petty larcenies. There was little passing traffic on country roads. The endlessly recurring indoor duty had 'a demoralising effect on the men, particularly in the smaller stations where guards [were] virtually incarcerated every second, third or fourth day' to give an ear to the telephone, which seldom rang, and to attend to callers, who were few and far between.

The changes dramatically altered the character of the police service. Generally, men not on duty were no longer compelled to return to the station at night and were free to come and go as they pleased when not required for duty.[33] The JRB welcomed the concession of a 48-hour week inherent in the curtailment of station orderly duty.

For its part, the interdepartmental committee was concerned mainly with the reduction of strengths and station closures and the employment of more guards on beats and patrols. In a convoluted minute, Daniel Costigan recalled for the Garda Commissioner that the committee had not sought authority in principle to fix the working week at 48 hours: for stations where 24 hours' continuous service was to be retained it was rather expected that the indoor duty would be performed within the shorter week, presumably in shifts.[34]

In 1929 O'Duffy opposed 'the fixing of any definite number of hours to be devoted to any particular duty … It must be clearly understood that where the exigencies of the public service require … duty must be performed without regard to time.' O'Duffy, and Broy after him, were inhibited by the activities of subversive groups and could not afford to let their guard down. 'The criminal does not work by the clock' was the constant refrain of Chief Superintendent W. P. Quinn, divisional officer, Dublin-Wicklow, afterwards (1965–67) Garda Commissioner. He believed in liberal wages for the Garda to head off the demand for overtime pay.[35]

The JRB was unremitting in its demand for reform. In no other civilised country had a police force been denied the right of a weekly rest day; the official plea that the manpower was not available was as 'untenable as it [was] unacceptable.' In the 'great world-wide movement … for the shortening of working hours,' the Garda alone was excluded.[36] The evolution in social conditions for workers generally left the Garda Síochána in a nineteenth-century time warp; the unsettled political and economic conditions in the country and the war in Europe postponed any consideration of Garda grievances.

In 1948 the force formally demanded a week of forty-four rostered duty hours. The insistence on a minimum period of outdoor duty, irrespective of the indoor duty performed, was 'one of those stupid anachronisms to which belong such relics of another age as the ... police duty class, the limitations on recreation, [and] the protracted and frequent inspection parades,' all of which were 'aggravating the general issue of crazy working hours.'[37] There the matter had to rest for another quarter of a century, when the claim was resurrected by a new, militant generation of young guards.

A NEW COMMISSIONER

With the confidence and authority conferred by a distinguished career in the civil service, Michael Kinnane took initiatives on matters a career policeman in the same office might have hesitated to address. When some more radical departures from the old regime were notified, older district officers forecast the end of discipline in the force, overlooking the fact that the seeds of indiscipline had already been sown down the years of neglect. The new generation in the force regarded some of the older officers, more settled in their ways than others, as old war-horses, though not with disrespect in most cases. On Kinnane's death in 1951 the *Garda Review* mourned the passing of a Commissioner who had dedicated himself to welfare in the force, 'so unostentatiously ... By his own personal qualities and ability he won for himself ... an affectionate regard in the hearts of all our members.'[38]

Kinnane's death was taken 'almost as a personal loss' by the rank and file. 'Police, by the very nature of their calling, tend to become conservative'; they had all the more admiration for a man who began the process of consigning to history 'many of the hidebound regulations which had been inherited from the R.I.C. ... Mr. Kinnane's outlook on the working hours problem was particularly refreshing, and his stated intention to bring Garda working hours into reasonable alignment with working hours in other occupations was not the least reason why he is so deeply regretted and so sincerely described as a great gentleman and a great Commissioner.'[39]

His recent experience on the interdepartmental committee made Daniel Costigan an obvious choice to succeed Kinnane, if the policy of modernisation was not to be retarded by conservative senior police officers.[40] Costigan's departure from the Department of Justice was said by former colleagues to have been encouraged by the second assistant secretary, Peter Berry, to facilitate his own advancement. In his relationship with the new Commissioner, Berry was often less than courteous, judging from the bullying tone of his minutes on some files. That was only the half of Costigan's difficulties in his new job. He was greeted in the *Garda Review* as 'our chief administrative officer,' a description that barely concealed the open hostility of some senior officers of long service who were outraged at being passed over again. These were men who had borne the heat of the day in the aftermath of the Civil War and in the troubled decade that followed the Fianna Fáil triumph in 1932 and whose contribution to state security during the war years was widely acknowledged. Kinnane had not interfered in operational matters, so that his senior officers as police commanders during the war years had grown in confidence. They expected that one of their number would have been chosen for the highest rank. The Government may have shied away from preferring one candidate over another to avoid an inevitable clash of personalities among the headquarters officers.

In a guarded welcome, the *Garda Review* noted Costigan's membership of the interdepartmental committee and the insights he had gained at home and on visits to police forces in other countries. 'His work and experience … must have given him a sound knowledge of the police idea.' They had disagreed with the appointment of his predecessor from the civil service. At that time, after the Broy tenure, there were circumstances in Kinnane's appointment that could have explained the reason for it: it was felt at the time that it was 'not intended to establish any principle.' In Costigan's case there were no valid reasons to explain his appointment, unless it was to be taken as a settled administrative policy. That being so, it was 'an unmerited reflection on the Force,' representing a further departure from the stated policy that the highest positions in the Garda were open to every member in every rank.[41]

A brilliant administrator, Costigan had to contend with the watershed in the nineteen-fifties precipitated by the wholesale retirement of the generation recruited in the twenties, including the loss of the older experienced officers and of the entire cadre of confident sergeants promoted and largely trained by O'Duffy. The new man desperately needed the support of his officers. The intensity of feeling among the senior officers boiled to the surface at a headquarters conference of chief superintendents in 1954, one of the Commissioner's closest colleagues telling Costigan to his face that he was not welcome. It took a man of strong character and self-assurance to meet the challenge. In a studied response, he changed the old promotion selection procedures based on seniority to offer rapid advancement to promising young sergeants employed under his own eye at headquarters, a move that only deepened the resentment of his disappointed officers. The senior officers had 'never ceased to resent the action of [the] Government in 1938 and again in 1952 in appointing civilians as Commissioners over their heads.'[42]

Costigan was hardly more than a year in office when he discovered the limitations on his authority imposed by former colleagues in the Department of Justice, whom he might have hoped to find among his few allies, a bureaucratic intervention that must have conveyed to him the full reality of his isolation. In November 1953, in an address to the Insurance Institute of Ireland, he described at length the work of the force. There was nothing controversial in what he had to say, but he was breaking new ground in projecting the unfamiliar image of the Garda Commissioner as a more open public servant. Berry, the new Secretary of the Department of Justice, appointed on the death of T. J. Coyne, took exception to his initiative, complaining that the text had not been referred to the department for sanction.[43]

COSTIGAN AND THE GARDA UNIFORM

Costigan had already established his credentials as a liberal successor to Michael Kinnane in the interest he took as a civil servant in the matter of the outmoded Garda uniform, with its buckram-stiffened high neck. In the immediate post-war years, influenced by the arrival on the streets of Dublin of visiting Allied soldiers, mainly Americans, attired in comfortable uniforms, and by the appearance of Irish soldiers in their new collar-and-tie walking-out dress, the lower ranks made a strong case for a new uniform. People had 'become uniform conscious'; and there was 'a tendency internationally to bridge the gap between officers and other ranks.'[44] Apart from the outmoded high collar, the rough texture of the cloth supplied by the Controller of Post Office Stores had been a bone of contention in the force for many years.

As a conscientious civil servant with responsibility for Garda affairs, Costigan had taken an active interest in the quality of the rank-and-file uniform. He was in sympathy with the JRB in its ambition for a common uniform for all ranks; it was 'easy to make a case for the change,'[45] but Finance would not have sanctioned the cost. It was not stated, but the loss of a distinctive uniform of good quality would not have been favoured by senior officers, who were to grudgingly concede changes introduced in the seventies under pressure from a militant Garda Representative Association.

Costigan supported the case for a better cloth. 'From my own observations even in pre-war days the material was too soft and did not look smart enough for a police uniform.'[46] In a letter to the Controller of Post Office Stores he stressed the need to improve the appearance of the uniform; 'despite difficulties,' he was 'reluctant to put the matter on the long finger.'[47] In 1950 a young guard with five years' service, Éamonn Ó Fiacháin, having sought an interview with the headquarters officer in charge of stores, presented himself in an altered tunic with an open neck and showing a shirt and tie.[48] The new uniform was made a general issue with effect from the first day of summer, 1952. Garda (afterwards Detective-Sergeant) Ó Fiacháin was also credited with having persuaded the Garda authorities to withdraw the old police helmet, worn in Dublin and Cork, as a symbol, it was alleged, of British imperialism.

From his office in the Department of Justice and subsequently as Garda Commissioner, contending with the obduracy of the Department of Finance, Costigan continued to press for better cloth. In 1954 he protested directly to the Minister for Justice. Little more than a year in office, he defined his vision for a police force: that it would be

> adequately but modestly paid ... well housed and uniformed and that in small matters, which involve little expense, it should be well looked after, in order to foster pride of profession and guard against the temptation to corruption ... Here and there an occasional member may show partiality towards a particular

publican and there may be some 'scrounging', but the vast majority of the Force are decent honourable men, and there is no danger of any rackets developing in this country while the present spirit of the Force is maintained.

The state was not doing its part. The minister himself was aware of the poor quality of uniform cloth. In 'small matters, which involve little expense,' the police force received 'the very opposite of considerate treatment.' It had taken several years to persuade the Department of Finance to sanction the allowances for the use of private cars on duty already paid to civil servants. The allowance for tailoring uniforms was well below the cost of getting the work done. The fixed allowances for heating and lighting stations were 'quite inadequate'; again, guards were meeting the deficit from their own resources. He was suggesting 'strongly' that if the Government wished to save money by reducing Garda strength and 'at the same time to have an efficient and honest Police Force,' the Department of Finance would have to adopt a different attitude towards demands for expenditure on the improvement of Garda conditions. As a first move in that direction, he suggested that the request for a better uniform cloth 'should be sanctioned forthwith.'[49]

When the Commissioner personally observed guards with soiled shirt collars, he directed his assistant commissioner in administration to make the case to the Department of Justice for an increase in the number of shirts and collars in the general issue of uniforms. After a delay of some months, he was informed that it was 'a matter appropriate for discussion by the conciliation council.' The Commissioner had no right of audience at the council; the representative bodies had not raised the matter. It seemed to Costigan that the Department of Finance was attempting to use the conciliation council to delay necessary reforms and improvements begun by the Commissioner in the public interest.[50]

TALKING UP A 'CRIME WAVE'

In 1954 the Irish Times welcomed the crime statistics for the first half of the year, recording a dramatic reduction of 29 per cent in the number of indictable crimes reported to the Garda. The incidence of housebreaking fell by no less than 32 per cent. Whatever the social and economic causes may have been, the editorial writer had 'little doubt that the principal cause [was] nothing less than good police-work.' There had been a recent intake of new recruits; the force had more men for crime prevention. Commissioner Costigan's period of office had 'conferred a practical emphasis on the increasing mobility of the force.' There were more motorised patrols. 'Nearly all experienced police officers affirm that the man on the beat was the basic and most important unit of the service. Without his trained powers of observation, patience and resourcefulness, the task of law enforcement would be virtually impossible. When he is able to work in close contact with mobile patrols, the way of the transgressor is apt to be made very hard indeed.'

In the first six months of 1954, successful detections were made in 65 per cent of the reported cases of housebreaking in Dublin.[51] Significant increases in the crime rate recorded in the Commissioner's annual reports for 1957 and 1958 gave rise to widespread public uneasiness, as reported in the press. Lurid headlines of a 'crime wave' appeared in newspapers for the first time. Ireland was 'freer of crime than almost any other country,' the Dáil was assured by the Minister for Justice, Oscar Traynor, in the debate on the estimates for his department.[52] The newspapers responded with one voice. The minister had given 'poor comfort' to the thousands of aged people living alone who did not know 'the hour of day or night' they might be beaten or robbed in their homes.[53] The recent upsurge had shocked the national 'self-righteousness over the relative absence of crime' in previous years.[54] The redeployment of the Central Detective Unit at Dublin Castle to augment units in the districts did not appear to 'recognise the vast difference between the ordinary policeman's approach and the plain clothes man's method of working.'[55] But the solution lay 'not in detection, but in prevention.'[56]

An increase in crime had been a striking feature of life in most countries in the decades after the war. It had little to do with poverty. In countries with a high standard of living there had been a similar disturbing rise in the crime rate. 'The prevention of crime is very much a moral task,' in which parents, spiritual advisers, schools and youth centres had a primary role. 'An ordered Christian home life, a reasonable measure of discipline and good social facilities' were the essential elements in any campaign to reduce crime among the young. But it was 'foolish to under-estimate the role of police in preventing as well as detecting crime,'[57] and Traynor agreed, sharing the view 'commonly expressed' that there was no substitute for the garda on the beat. Motorised patrols could not replace the man on the spot; patrol cars were useful in sparsely populated areas to ferry gardaí from place to place to carry out foot patrols.

Defending the closing of stations in remote districts, the minister must have raised conservative eyebrows at Garda headquarters. Conceding that the existence of a Garda station in any locality was 'a sort of insurance against crime and disturbances of the peace,' Traynor informed the Dáil that the decision to adopt the policy on closures was taken on the recommendation of the Commissioner and his staff. 'I think it would be entirely wrong of me to interfere with the judgement of these officers and to oppose their points of view unless I had first-hand evidence that acceptance of their recommendations would be undesirable.'[58]

The newspapers focused attention on three unsolved murders, spoiling past success in clearing up cases of homicide. Such was the level of public disquiet at the apparent inability of the Garda to bring the culprits to justice that the Deputy Commissioner and two assistant commissioners were sent to inquire into the efficiency of the Garda units in the areas affected.[59] In March, Costigan announced his intention of visiting Birmingham to study crime prevention services.[60] At a press conference in May he made it plain that the fight against crime would not be successful unless citizens co-operated with the Garda. And 'everyone knew' the identity of the culprits in the unsolved murders.[61]

An unidentified 'senior Garda officer of many years' experience' was quoted as saying that the Garda force in Dublin was too small to beat the crime wave, and its efficiency had been impaired in recent years 'by growing discontent and falling morale.' The spokesman attributed the decline to reduced effectiveness caused by the influx of young recruits replacing the experienced founder-members of the force, inadequate strengths, and conditions of service generally. These were all reasonable comments; but the opposition to Costigan among the higher echelons was never far from the surface. There was also a lack of confidence in the leadership of the force; the Commissioner had changed the time-honoured system of promotion based on seniority. 'Junior gardaí were suddenly promoted over the heads of senior men in the mistaken belief that youth in itself' was a substitute for 'the skill, astuteness, knowledge and loyalty obtained in years of service.' That had been the first 'major blow' to morale and efficiency.[62]

Costigan's meritocracy signalled a period of intense competition for promotion and a rise in the stress factor in police work. This posed a problem for a new Garda Surgeon, Dr T. A. J. Quigley, who replaced the long-serving Dr V. C. Ellis on the latter's retirement in 1957. Surgeon Quigley recognised stress as an occupational hazard for policemen, exacerbated in the Garda Síochána during a period of rapid change. He tested the medical fitness of every member of the new force and personally attended to the casualties of change.[63]

11

STRAWS IN THE WIND

Sit down, guard!

An editorial in the *Observer* (London) in 1959 commented on a recent decision by the British government to hold an inquiry into the whole field of police activities.[1] 'The police represent that element of force which is necessary even in a democratic society where government is based on consent. One of the tests of civilisation is how far that element of force can itself be civilised.' The police service reflected the way society changed. 'There was a time when the police were expected to be polite and servile to the upper classes … As a witness before [the Royal Commission on Police Powers in 1929] put it: "to represent the English police as the one unaltered element of the national life is to talk without meaning. When the times change, *all* men change with them."'[2] The editorial was filed in the Commissioner's office.

The membership of the Garda Síochána could have been forgiven for thinking the writer had in mind attitudes prevalent in the Irish establishment, where the colonial mentality inherited from the old regime in 1922 died hard. A decade earlier the Joint Representative Body, anticipating the report of the inquiry into the British police headed by Lord Oaksey, began to see in conciliation and arbitration the ideal solution to all its difficulties.[3] As expected, Oaksey recommended a police council made up of delegates from all ranks, sitting with civil servants and representatives of the local authorities,[4] and a triumvirate of independent members selected by the Lord Chancellor to govern procedure and, as a last resort, to act as a court of arbitration.[5]

In 1950 conciliation and arbitration was conceded to middle and lower-grade officers in the civil service. The JRB immediately applied for the extension of the civil service scheme to the Garda Síochána.

Having waited for action for more than four frustrating years, the JRB sought and was granted an interview with the Minister for Justice, Oscar Traynor, which resulted in an invitation to submit its own proposals for a Garda scheme; this was done in August 1955. Three years later, still awaiting a decision, the JRB protested at 'this contemptuous treatment', doubting that any other police force in the world was treated with 'the same casual contempt and indifference.'[6] Patience was further strained by the arbitrary application of civil service pay awards to the Garda Síochána.[7]

In a memorandum to the Government in 1958, the Department of Justice described discontent in the force as 'disquieting'. The procedures for investigating grievances, 'real or imaginary,' were no longer adequate; there was no valid reason for standing in the way of conciliation and arbitration.[8] Betraying its colonial mentality, the Department of Finance was 'strongly opposed' to the introduction of a Garda scheme: the force in all its ranks, 'the agency of the Government in enforcing law and maintaining order,' was expected to show 'a more unquestioning acceptance of Ministerial and Government decisions than need be required from classes already covered by conciliation and arbitration.' The department viewed with foreboding the consequences of a possible rejection by the Government of an arbitrator's award, the nightmare of 'undesirable public agitation by the police ... which could be availed of by irresponsible elements to disturb the normal reliance which [the] Government reposes in the Force.'

This was 'the paramount consideration', the Department of Justice urged in a robust rejoinder. Precisely because, quoting the Oaksey Report, a strong and efficient police force was necessary for 'the well being of the community to a greater degree than any other public service in peace time,' there was

> a stronger case for conceding arbitration to the Garda Síochána than for conceding it to any other branch of the public service ... the fact that it has not been conceded appears to be the principal cause of what has been described as 'seething discontent' in an article in the *Garda Review*[9] ... It was discontent with non-redress of grievances that led to the most serious strike in police history in England in 1919 when the authorities conceded to force much of what they had refused to concede to reason—a mistake not committed a second time by holding out on arbitration.[10]

But Finance was dogged in its opposition. Pay and conditions of service were not 'the real cause for grievance.'[11] The *Garda Review* was publishing articles 'objectionable and lacking in proper respect for the Government.'[12] The minister considered it 'inadvisable to leave the impression that a campaign of this kind was the means of securing conciliation and arbitration'—a difficult argument to sustain after a delay of eight years before the matter was addressed.

The Department of Finance had successfully resisted arbitration for higher grades in the civil service, who, like the Garda Síochána, occupied 'a special position in relation to Ministers and to the administration of the public services' and were 'liable to argue the case for the Official Side' in negotiations. Accepting this position, the Government decided in principle on a scheme for the Garda up to and including the rank of inspector, and the decision was notified to the three representative bodies.[13] The draft scheme was enclosed for consideration separately by the two committees representing the lower ranks. The document was shown in confidence, expressly not to be communicated 'to any person or body other than those for whom it is intended.'

The matter came before the December 1958 meeting of the JRB, the chairman, Chief Superintendent Tom Collins, proposing the rejection of the scheme, on the grounds that it excluded the officers. A young newcomer at the meeting, Garda Patrick E. (Éamonn) Gunn, Dún Laoghaire, representing the guards in Dublin, proposed that no decision be made until the matter was discussed by each of the bodies separately. There was no seconder for Gunn's motion, and he was ordered by the chairman: 'Sit down, guard!'[14]

Gunn's proposal to defer discussion of the conciliation and arbitration scheme offered to his rank-and-file colleagues the opportunity to speak with an independent voice. But the lower-rank delegates belonged to the generation disciplined by O'Duffy's regime of 'orders, orders, orders, and strident objurgations … to obey, obey and nothing but obey.'[15] Tragically, after decades of dominance by the officers on the joint body, and cowed by Collins, the men were incapable of asserting themselves.

In an editorial that defied the history of relations with the civil service, the *Garda Review* hoped that the concession to a section of the force would not mean the end of joint representation, which had 'served the Force and the country so well down the years.'[16] The breach of confidentiality was exacerbated in a scorching letter from the JRB. Recalling that Traynor in June 1957 had accepted the case put forward for the force as a whole, the letter expressed outrage at the exclusion of the officers and the use of 'threats against the other representative bodies concerned in the event of their furnishing, even in courtesy, a copy to the [officers' body].'[17]

The letter, signed by Sergeant Daniel Fingleton, recently appointed secretary on the death of Sergeant P. J. Gallagher, but almost certainly dictated by Collins, was returned immediately by the Department of Justice as unacceptable. The covering note from the department was also highly critical of the Commissioner. The minister was not prepared to consider a communication

> couched in language that shows a want of propriety … It is the Minister's wish that you yourself should make it a rule in future not to receive from the representative bodies any representations which impute bad faith to him or to the Government or consist of or include accusations which, to your knowledge, those making the accusations must know to be false, or are made in what appears to be a deliberately disrespectful way.[18]

The text was included in a memorandum for the Government. Given its hectoring tone, the original letter would probably have been signed by the secretary, T. J. Coyne, but it bears the literary fingerprints of Peter Berry and may have marked the beginning of the deterioration in relations between Costigan and his former colleague in the Department of Justice. As Secretary, appointed in February 1961 on Coyne's death, Berry often betrayed an overbearing manner in his correspondence with the Commissioner.

Adding fuel to the fires of outrage, the JRB pleaded that, having no direct contact with the Department of Finance, it felt duty-bound to convey the views of the force 'straight-forwardly' to the Department of Justice, and concluded with a request to the minister to receive a deputation.[19] The department once again returned the letter, directing Costigan to inform the JRB that it was mistaken in thinking that, having rejected its earlier communication, the minister was going to accept a simple denial of any impropriety: the minister would not meet a deputation until its first letter was 'unequivocally withdrawn.'[20] Sergeant Fingleton on 19 December again denied any disrespect, 'profoundly' regretting the attitude taken by the Department of Justice and restating the unacceptability of the proposal to exclude senior officers from the scheme.[21]

Having kicked over the traces, the JRB was now reined in by wiser counsels, probably through the intervention of the minister, Oscar Traynor. Sergeant Fingleton three days later wrote in more conciliatory terms, having learnt of 'the endeavours of the Minister and his Department to secure a satisfactory scheme of conciliation and arbitration.'[22] The following day the officers' body, presenting its own olive branch, 'respectfully' requested the inclusion of officers in the scheme,[23] and in its turn the joint committee for the lower ranks acknowledged the draft document but offered no comment, 'pending negotiations to include officers up to the rank of Chief Superintendent.'[24]

There was one last step to be taken before grace was restored. They dragged their feet for more than three months before conceding what amounted to an apology—a hard decision for proud men in the twilight years of their service. Convinced that conciliation and arbitration offered a last opportunity to justify the years of wasted endeavour with the prospect of enhancing retirement benefits for their own generation, the JRB, desperate to succeed, swallowed their pride.

Fighting to the end, the Department of Finance raised the issue of collective Government responsibility. The Minister for Finance was 'perturbed' at 'serious reflections on himself and on his Department,' which appeared 'all the more significant by contrast with references to the Department of Justice ... hailed as the champion of the force in its struggles with the Minister for Finance.' This distinction between the ministers implied that the doctrine of collective responsibility may not have been observed.[25]

In April the JRB made its apology and renewed its request for a meeting with the minister.[26] The response in the Department of Justice was immediate. 'In the opinion of the Minister for Justice this action of the Body, belated though it be, leaves the way clear for the question to be considered on its merits.'[27] A scheme for all ranks was approved by the Government on 15 May 1959. The JRB gave a sigh of relief. With 'a lighter heart' than they had known for 'many a day,' gratitude was extended to the Minister for Justice and his officials, and to the Government, for a 'statesman-like gesture.'

In a rare tribute to Costigan, the *Garda Review* noted the welcome from ordinary guards for the Commissioner on a recent visit to border stations. 'What most favourably impressed our members was the genuine nature of the Commissioner's solicitude for their well-being and welfare.'[28]

TOWARDS A COMMISSION OF INQUIRY
The scare headlines of a 'crime wave' in the closing years of the decade rekindled Seán MacEntee's jaundiced opinion of the force, expressed so trenchantly during the 1937 pay negotiations.[29] Now Minister for Health in Seán Lemass's Government, he was inspired in January 1960 to make representations to the Taoiseach for an inquiry into the administration and organisation of the force. MacEntee saw his opportunity in the dramatic changes taking place because of the mass retirement on age grounds of the men enlisted in the nineteen-twenties.[30] Without disclosing the identity of the writer, Maurice Moynihan in the Taoiseach's office referred MacEntee's representations to the Department of Justice, whence they were passed on to the Commissioner for observations. Responding, the embattled Commissioner paraphrased the report of the interdepartmental committee a decade earlier.[31] The Garda Síochána had been established as an unarmed civil police. From the beginning its members were encouraged to cultivate the friendship and co-operation of the people. Its tradition differed entirely from the RIC, and over the years many changes had been introduced that had 'wiped out most of the objectionable features' borrowed from the old police.

On less firm ground, Costigan argued that the Garda was no longer influenced by the 'heritage' of the DMP. In recent years, to ease the transition from the old to the new police, the age of retirement for members who were serving on the last day of 1951 had been progressively increased from fifty-seven for the lower ranks and sixty for officers to sixty-three; for those who joined afterwards, the retirement age reverted to fifty-seven and sixty, respectively. No commission of inquiry would recommend any interference with the transitory higher retiring age.

EDUCATIONAL STANDARDS
The standard of the Garda entrance examination was set at the level of the primary school leaving examination, the Primary Certificate, but many successful candidates had secondary education. The general educational standard of recruits was higher than it was for the RIC or in the early days of the Garda. It was a moot point that the Primary Certificate was too low a standard for police recruits; but any raising of

the standard would have made it impossible to get enough recruits. There was room for men whose standard of education was not very high. If all recruits had a higher standard, the better-educated 'would tire of the routine of a Guard's duties.' Raising the standard would also have the effect of excluding the intelligent small farmer's son with only a national school education. Men of this type had always been 'the backbone of the Force,' many of whom, with private study, had become the most efficient officers. Formal school education was of less importance for practical police work than general intelligence, 'self-education, and the education of experience.'

MacEntee was also concerned that the extent to which scientific knowledge was applied in crime detection had never been examined by 'independent scrutineers'. The Commissioner confidently replied that since the Technical Bureau was established in 1934, Garda experts had won international recognition for pioneering work in the science of ballistics and had built up close relations with their opposite numbers in Scotland Yard.[32] By any standard, the Garda Síochána was an efficient police force. The incidence of crime in Ireland was much lower than in Britain, and the rate of detection was higher. Press reports about a crime wave in Dublin were 'grossly exaggerated'.

Costigan felt strongly that an inquiry without reference to pay and conditions of service would be 'a definite mistake ... Arbitration is about to take place on pay, but the arbitrator cannot be expected to make a thorough examination of the needs of the police service, and the Garda representatives are unlikely to be a match in advocacy for the experts from the Departments of Justice and Finance.' As a former civil servant himself, Costigan was well qualified to make that judgment and perhaps had already begun to discern the course of events in the troubled months ahead.

COSTIGAN'S INITIATIVES

It had not been easy to bring about changes in the way the force was organised and administered. Costigan's senior officers, who had grown old in the service, 'were not readily responsive to change.' But much had been achieved, in increased mobility with patrol cars and motorcycles and extension of the radio service. The reform of the old garrison system of policing had resulted in a substantial reduction in the strength of the provincial force. A radical plan for reorganisation of the Dublin Metropolitan Division was awaiting Government approval.[33] A team of organisation and methods officers had eliminated a hundred clerical and other posts at headquarters alone. On Costigan's initiative, women members had been sanctioned and recruited,[34] and a driving school had been established.

Recruit training had been reorganised, with an emphasis on courtesy and the education of the public in law observance 'by personal example and advice.' Many of the older guards had been slow to adopt the new approach; but the effects of the new teaching were already becoming apparent. Breaking new ground, Costigan had recently enrolled two young inspectors on a management course at the Police College in Bramshill, Hampshire, the first time members of the Garda Síochána had been sent abroad for training. This initiative was criticised in the force, because of the arbitrary selection of the candidates.[35] Most controversially, the traditional system of promotion to sergeant and inspector by competitive examination was found wanting as 'unlikely to produce men best qualified to take command ... and to deal with the public.' Candidates for promotion sat instead for qualifying examinations, and their fitness for advancement was tested by selection boards.

The request for the Commissioner's observations on a commission of inquiry, received at Garda headquarters in mid-January, was dealt with by Costigan with the utmost despatch. On 2 February he replied to the Department of Justice, where his eleven closely typed pages lay on somebody's desk for two months. A reminder from the Taoiseach's office prompted the department to reply, 'regretting the inadvertence.' The Minister for Justice was in agreement with the views of the Commissioner: there was no good case for the appointment of a commission.[36] A concurrent reply to MacEntee was prepared for Lemass's signature but was not sent, as indicated on 25 April in a note in the margin: 'The Taoiseach decided today to let this matter rest—for the present at any rate.'[37]

It may be inferred that the delay in the Department of Justice and Lemass's apparent reluctance to commit himself in agreement with Costigan's views reflected a generally felt disappointment at the outcome. Costigan's defence of his stewardship disarmed his own minister and left Lemass with no room for manoeuvre, on the assumption that the Government might have appointed a commission given any encouragement from the Phoenix Park. From Costigan's point of view, to have conceded the need for an inquiry might have been interpreted as discrediting the report of the interdepartmental committee. In the light of subsequent history, the failure of MacEntee's initiative was one of the great tragedies in the history of the Garda Síochána.

ANTEDILUVIAN OFFICE PROCEDURES

The interdepartmental committee, discovering at every level in the Garda Síochána antediluvian office procedures devised for the RIC and DMP in the nineteenth century, recommended a special group to introduce modern office methods and to consider the feasibility of employing civilians. The chairman, Michael Deegan, and his colleagues may have had in mind a committee similar to their own, or a working party of organisation and methods officers. Instead, a team of management consultants was called in and given the Commissioner's enthusiastic co-operation.[38]

Over the years a large staff, including former members of the Garda boxing team after retirement from the sporting arena, had been accommodated in the JRB office. Each artificially created post was regarded as indispensable and defended against the ambitions of the new Commissioner. The men were employed mainly in posting the registers of the Benevolent and Medical Aid associations. When the veteran secretary Sergeant Gallagher died in 1957 he was replaced by Sergeant Daniel Fingleton, a weights and measures inspector. Unlike his predecessor, who was employed full-time as secretary, Fingleton combined the work with his official duties. To meet this new situation one of the office staff, Richard Rice, was promoted sergeant and put in charge of routine business.

The death of the experienced Sergeant Gallagher coincided with the presentation of the management consultant's report on the JRB office. The consultant, A. P. Guthrie, recommended replacing the registers with a card index of the membership of the two charitable associations—a straightforward if laborious task. Guthrie also introduced a new duplicate receipt-book. With the brooding figure of Chief Superintendent Collins in the background, a war of attrition began between the Commissioner's office and the JRB.[39] The new receipt-book was brought into use, but the core proposal for reform of the registers was rejected.

Costigan responded by refusing to fill vacancies in the office. As the decade drew to a close, the founder-members were retiring in rapidly increasing numbers, to be replaced by a new force of vigorous young men. Fingleton pleaded an increasing work load, aggravated by the negotiations for conciliation and arbitration then in progress. Costigan was adamant: he would not provide additional staff or fill vacancies until the consultant's recommendations had been adopted and the office reorganised.

If disgruntled senior officers, represented by Collins, had not been so preoccupied in undermining the Commissioner's authority the JRB might have acted with more confidence when its own authority was challenged. In the growing climate of good will introduced by M. J. Kinnane, the energies of the disaffected young guards might then have been contained and redirected into constructive activities more in keeping with their vocational role. In the watershed marking the standing down of the older generation in the nineteen-fifties, a new movement in the old Dublin Metropolitan District was detected by Costigan, who immediately recognised its potential for positive development in the evolving politics of confrontation within the force. Relying on paragraphs in the *Garda Review*, he learnt of the activities of the 'Dublin divisional committee'.

Otherwise the 'Dublin metropolitan selection committee', this group comprised elected local representatives, whose sole purpose under the regulations was the nomination of delegates to the two central bodies for guards and the supervisory ranks.[40] The two committees combined forces under Station Sergeant Seán Ó Colmáin as chairman,[41] with Garda P. E. Gunn as secretary.[42] Under the driving influence of these two kindred spirits, the committee acted as a de facto representative group for the metropolitan division.

Costigan read in the *Garda Review* that the Dublin committee was considering 'the question of continued association with the Representative Body' as then constituted.[43] The Commissioner may have been more than a little startled to learn that guards in Dún Laoghaire were 'fully conversant with two very pertinent Papal

Encyclicals—*Rerum Novarum,* 1891, and *Quadragesimo Anno,* 1931.' The unlikely students of Catholic sociology wished to know the views of their authorities on the principle of 'free association' for wage-earners set forth in the encyclicals.[44]

The enlightened Costigan would have hesitated to agree with his former Department of Justice colleague, Michael Wallace. In 1964 Wallace was asked for his opinion on the form of reply to be sent to a query on the legal position of members of the force engaging in politics. Inspired by Ó Colmáin, guards were attending courses on social science at the Dublin Institute of Adult Education, run by the Catholic archdiocese of Dublin. Wallace was asked if reference might be made to the 'Eccles Street premises'. Better not, he advised: social science, including industrial relations, was 'widely discussed and debated' in the institute. The relations between church and state was another popular topic, and it might be that at times the Government was subjected to 'adverse criticism on some social aspect.'[45]

Costigan was informed that Deputy Commissioner Garret Brennan, in charge of the Dublin area, had refused permission for a meeting of the Dublin selection committee, on the grounds that it was intended to debate the draft of the scheme for conciliation and arbitration, which had been released in confidence for study by the representative bodies. Costigan took a wider view, and he turned for advice to Chief Superintendent Thomas McCarthy. Described as an intellectual and stamped in a different mould from his contemporaries, McCarthy was employed as organisation and methods officer, a new post created by Costigan,[46] which had evolved as personal assistant to the Commissioner. He was among the senior headquarters officers Costigan could turn to with confidence. Was it 'reasonable for an unofficial committee to be allowed time off duty for meetings?' McCarthy replied that it was

> reasonable and desirable ... essential, that elected representatives be informed, or should take steps to inform themselves of the views of those they represent. The Regulations are silent as to how this need is to be met. The withdrawal of the present facilities [for meetings] would tend to embitter relations between the Dublin Metropolitan force and the authorities, and could have undesirable consequences. There is a moral duty on the State to take special care to ensure that members of the Garda Síochána do not suffer loss of any advantage they might win by organisation as a trade union, or by justifiable strike action.[47]

An application was received from the Dublin selection committee for permission to take up a collection to defray the costs of proposed court proceedings to have the franchise extended to members of the Garda Síochána, who were excluded from Dáil and Seanad elections, an old bone of contention. In 1930 O'Duffy had told the JRB that while he considered disfranchisement 'a slight on our individual citizenship,' he was reluctant to recommend amendment of the Electoral

Act (1923).[48] His successor, Éamonn Broy, saw 'no justification' for the restriction, but he was turned down by the minister, who feared the involvement of guards in politics.[49] The vote was conceded to members of the Garda Síochána in the Electoral Act (1960).[50]

Garda Gunn's application was rejected by Costigan, who was prepared to consider 'sympathetically' an application from the JRB 'severally or jointly for this purpose.' On the same date, 28 February, he decided that meetings of the selection committee were 'not forbidden'; but he found that in the case of the Dublin Metropolitan Division the representative body regulations were inadequate, and he proposed consulting the JRB on the matter.[51] In August 1959 the Commissioner's office invited the lower ranks to bring the inadequacies in the regulations before the JRB (with a copy to the officers' body). The Commissioner also indicated his readiness to discuss the matter with a deputation from the joint body.[52] In November 1960, in the absence of any response to his invitation, Costigan convened a conference attended by representatives of the lower ranks.

Station Sergeant Ó Colmáin handed in a paper entitled 'Constitution of the Representative Body'. Thanking the Commissioner for 'much achieved under his administration,' he warned that 'the Commissioner's influence [was] not reaching down to the ranks' and suggested that the remedy lay in 'personal contacts through works councils.' He expected 'revolutionary' proposals from a JRB sub-committee appointed to study the regulations, including the ideas on 'free association' promoted in the Papal encyclicals. These points were not addressed by him at the conference, because 'he may have been so advised.'[53]

The following April, Costigan was still waiting for the JRB to respond to his invitation to co-operate with him in amending the regulations. He asked Chief Superintendent McCarthy for a report on what had happened at the November conference. On 7 June Ó Colmáin's sub-committee made its report; whatever that document contained (the Representative Body for Guards later in the year was to adopt the report in its entirety), the JRB confined its own recommendations to an amendment permitting meetings of all four provincial selection committees. Its decision was conveyed to the Commissioner by letter dated 20 July.

It appears that McCarthy awaited developments before replying to Costigan. He did so on 17 July, probably with advance knowledge of the decision already taken by the JRB. Marking his minute 'personal', he advised the Commissioner to await the views of the representative bodies before changing the regulations. He was aware of 'widespread discontent' among the guards in Dublin; there was justification for it. Underlining a fundamental defect in the amalgamation of the Dublin police with the national force, McCarthy felt that a close study of the grievances and problems associated with service in Dublin by guards from country divisions was 'too much to hope for.' Unless reasonable facilities were afforded for consultation among guards stationed in Dublin, clandestine meetings would certainly follow. The absence of machinery for joint consultation was 'a grave defect'.

He was aware, McCarthy concluded, that the Commissioner had put out feelers to some representative body members in the hope of getting such a joint consultative council established, but without success. He urged Costigan to call the JRB into special session and to seize the initiative by putting to the meeting in person the proposal for a consultative council and, should it fail, to by-pass the elected delegates to inform the force of what had happened.[54]

Costigan left the record silent on his response to McCarthy's advice; he did not write on the file, not even the characteristic mark of his bold initials in the margin to indicate that he had at least read the document. With his back to the wall, he may have been strongly tempted to appeal to the rank and file over the heads of his officers. To have done so would probably have sparked a public demonstration by disaffected guards and have identified the Commissioner as instigator in the looming crisis. With wisdom and considerable moral courage, he resisted the temptation to seek self-justification at the incalculable cost of greater instability in the police service and in the state itself. But the question also arises whether a prudent Chief Superintendent McCarthy at the last minute, after mature consideration, might have decided to withhold his advice from an emotional Commissioner.

12

THE MACUSHLA BALLROOM AFFAIR

The bright and polite young gardaí beloved of Commissioner D. J. Costigan
… were not feeling in any form for pleasantries with the public.

The resumption of recruiting in 1952 coincided with Daniel Costigan's arrival at Garda headquarters. After a lapse of five years, 1,126 applicants responded to the announcement, of whom only 303 passed the qualifying examination, set to a new, higher standard, and 174 were called for training.[1] The new Commissioner prepared to preside over the formation of a new force as the exodus of the first generation of guards began in earnest.

In an early initiative, Costigan sent selected officers on courses at the Irish Management Institute, a move that inspired dramatic changes in recruit training programmes. The young officers returned to headquarters imbued with the principles of a new science, epitomised in revised guidelines, *Advice on the Training of Recruit Gardaí*. A new employee formed permanent attitudes towards his job, his boss and 'the company' much earlier than managers were aware; his reception and introduction to the job made all the difference in getting him off to a good start. This was equally true of new members of the Garda Síochána on their first allocation. The young men coming into the force were 'excellent types and good material for cultivation and development.' They left the depot with 'high standards of cleanliness and smartness, well instructed and warned of the pitfalls ahead of them.'[2]

Costigan discarded the century-old catechism of police duties. His predecessor in 1927 received complaints from the lower ranks that some officers were insisting on the study of definitions by rote. The 'parrot-like learning of police duties' had no educational value and tended 'to crush self-expression.' With Assistant Commissioner Walsh at his elbow, O'Duffy rejected the resolution as 'scarcely a matter for the Representative Body.' It was difficult if not impossible 'to do other than quote the text without distorting the meaning.' But he undertook to take steps to ensure that the conduct of classes would be more relaxed in future.[3]

The *Police Duty Manual* was replaced with a programme of lectures, close on a thousand pages of closely typed material bound in three volumes run off on an office stencil duplicator—a modest beginning to a radical process that evolved down the years to culminate in the Garda College in Templemore. The lectures contained 'everything a Garda [needed] to know to enable him to deal with everyday police problems' and were to be used 'in preference to any other text.'[4] When the folders were examined in the stations, doubts were expressed about the wisdom of burdening recruits with so much detail. In defence of the new departure, an instructor was heard to say that an ambitious guard would be well prepared for the sergeant's promotion examination by studying the lectures alone. But that was not the purpose of recruit training, and it raised the question of the real state of preparedness of inexperienced patrolmen for the practical demands of duty in the community.

The Joint Representative Body, with high hopes, went to arbitration in April 1960, claiming pay increases that would have given guards over £3 a week extra on a nine-year scale. Rehearsing the decades of their quarrel over Garda pay, the delegates, bloody but unbowed, raised the fraught question of the 1924 pay cuts. Relying on the old war-horse of the Desborough Report on the unique responsibilities of a policeman, they pressed yet again for parity with the RUC and British police forces. To all their arguments the official side restated its impeccable case on the integrity of the national economy. The arbitrator, T. K. Liston SC, recommended modest increases, ranging from a little over £1 a week for guards on a scale halved from twenty years.[5]

The *Garda Review* was cautious. While the new scales were 'not all that had been looked for,' they were 'a step in the right direction.'[6] A local correspondent was positively euphoric in his praise and gratitude for a 'wonderful achievement', exceeding the 'most sanguine expectations … The increase was out of all proportion to any previously won …' The names of all concerned would 'go down in the annals of the Force for what can justly be termed as the greatest achievement of all time.'[7]

The anonymous author, writing from Bray, County Wicklow, may have sensed the discontent building up in the adjoining Dublin Metropolitan Division. In a move perhaps to allay misgivings, especially among the brash younger membership of the city force, Liston's report was published in the *Garda Review* as evidence of 'the immense amount of work put by our members into the preparation and presentation of the Garda case.'[8] By way of contrast, the same issue on other pages carried without comment a summary of the recent report of the British royal commission on police pay, which recommended £910 a year for constables after nine years, an increase of £4 a week.[9]

In December 1960 a settlement of the rent allowance question was agreed by the conciliation council.[10] In lieu of the old system of token allowances for the various ranks, basic pay was increased by a new element, with an amount recovered for quarters officially provided. For sergeants and guards the increase amounted to £65 a year, subject to a deduction of £52 for official accommodation, either married quarters or the space in a dormitory occupied by single men living in barracks.

When the agreement was analysed and it was discovered that the balance of £13 would also disappear in the income tax due on the total amount, the younger men were outraged. In a curtain-raising editorial for a fateful year in the history of the force, the *Garda Review* welcomed the decision to incorporate the allowance in basic pay; but the award 'was not without some snags.' In Dublin, where housing was expensive, there was a case for a Dublin allowance, on the lines of the London allowance—the comfort of a crumb, for there was little prospect of making progress in that direction, and the JRB from past experience knew it.[11]

The editorial raised the question of an inadequate settlement arrived at in haste by the conciliation council without recourse to arbitration. The willingness of the Garda side to accept whatever was on offer was due to pressure exerted on delegates by the last of the 1922 men, who were on the brink of retirement. It was a case of the heart ruling the head. Men who had carried the burden of peace-keeping in the troubled early decades of the Free State would have been denied the increases in their pensions in the inevitable long delay in bringing the case to arbitration. It was a bad precedent, confirming Costigan's misgivings on the capacity of the JRB to manage the conciliation and arbitration machinery. In the light of the editorial of January 1961, the JRB was clearly out of touch with the mood of the younger guards concentrated in Dublin.

The conciliation council reconvened in October to consider the Garda case for application of the eighth round of general pay increases. Agreement was reached on the basis of the award already applied in the civil service; guards with less than six years' service received no increase.[12] On top of the mismanagement of the rent allowance claim, the exclusion of the younger guards from the eighth round was the last straw.

'THE COMMISSIONER'S ORDER WILL BE IGNORED'

In late October 1961 the newspapers reported widespread dissatisfaction among the younger guards. 'The bright and polite young gardaí beloved of Commissioner D. J. Costigan over the past five years were not feeling in any form for pleasantries with the public.'[13] A protest meeting at Fitzgibbon Street station was forbidden.[14] The men reconvened in a laneway, where the organisers explained their position. An exodus of older guards reaching the age limit was expected the following year. The pay award 'would greatly benefit men on the verge of retirement'; but the future of the force depended on the new generation, who were starting their careers 'under the shadow of frustration.'[15] The young guards were 'the chaps who do the night duty, get the black eyes and broken teeth.'[16]

A rumour that plans were afoot for a 'go-slow' in the enforcement of traffic regulations and the detection of minor offences was headlined in the newspapers as 'a dramatic turn in the pay dispute.'[17] 'The most obvious effect of their attitude occurred in the capital at rush-hour [on Thursday evening]: long lines of traffic moved at snail pace through the centre of the city.' By Monday the go-slow had ended, according to a newspaper report.[18]

The announcement on Friday 3 November by a 'secret committee'[19] of a mass meeting in the Macushla Ballroom in Amiens Street the following afternoon brought the crisis to a head. Support for the Dublin guards was pledged by colleagues in Counties Cork, Limerick, and Monaghan. The minister, Charles Haughey, was 'perturbed' at the news from the provinces.[20] Having consulted some of his Government colleagues, he decided that no statement would be made on behalf of either the Government or the Minister for Justice: the responsibility for restoring discipline lay with the Commissioner. He directed Costigan to issue to the force a circular letter warning that attendance at unauthorised meetings would be regarded as a grave breach of discipline, warranting dismissal.[21]

Costigan that evening responded as directed. The representative bodies were the authorised channel for the communication of the views of the force to their authorities and the minister, and it was an offence to call or attend any unauthorised meeting concerning the force. Disciplinary action would be taken for attendance at unauthorised meetings or for any other action that offended against the disciplinary regulations. Invoking the ultimate sanction, the Commissioner warned that disobedience would warrant dismissal. But he felt it was not necessary to remind guards of their solemn declaration: he could 'rely on the loyalty and good sense of all members to abide strictly by the regulations of the force.'[22]

The response of the organisers was swift and forthright. 'I can tell you that the Commissioner's order will be ignored. The meeting will take place as planned,' a member of the 'secret committee' told a reporter.[23] What followed was much less a planned revolt than a spontaneous eruption of pent-up discontent. A total of 815 men, including many mature guards, turned up at the Macushla Ballroom. Superintendent Timothy O'Brien, the avuncular district officer at Store Street, accompanied by Inspector Albert Dawson, entered the hall but withdrew when requested to leave.

No arrangements had been made for the orderly conduct of the meeting. Conflicting voices shouted suggestions on procedure. From a balcony a prominent local politician, Seán Loftus, attempted to address the frustrated men. In the confusion the slight young figure of Garda John Marrinan, stationed at Rathfarnham in the south city suburbs, mounted the stage and called the meeting to order. A recent graduate of Trinity College, with a degree in commerce, Marrinan was employed on plain-clothes duties as an escort to the former President of the Executive Council of the Irish Free State, W. T. Cosgrave. He was not immediately recognised and did not come to notice until he took the chair at a subsequent meeting organised in Cork.[24]

When the meeting settled down, Marrinan supervised the election of a committee of thirty-six, including representatives from the Dublin area and other districts. The proceedings ended with an expression of 'grave dissatisfaction' at the exclusion from the pay order of guards with short service, and demands for the resignation of the representative bodies and for an independent commission to inquire into pay and conditions of service. The *Irish Times* called the dispute 'undeniably the most serious of its kind to have faced any Government since 1922.'[25]

In a flurry of activity on Sunday 5 November, Haughey twice met the Secretary of the Department of Justice, Peter Berry, and the Commissioner, while Costigan had separate meetings with his headquarters officers and superintendents from the Dublin districts. The memorandum prepared for the Government meeting the following Tuesday probably understated Haughey's 'serious dissatisfaction' at the report of the Macushla Ballroom meeting provided by Superintendent O'Brien. Only one of the ringleaders was identified, although there were about thirty on the platform; 167 of the 815 who attended the meeting were identified by inspectors on duty at the entrance.[26] Haughey's impatience may have been understandable; but in all the confusion, standing briefly inside the door at the back of the hall before he was excluded, it would have been impossible for O'Brien afterwards to make anything like a full report, and the handful of inspectors who accompanied him could not have been expected to identify the hundreds of young men from city and country districts who were determined to gain admittance to the hall without being recognised.

It is clear from the memorandum that Costigan had already lost the initiative and was being carried along by events. The decision to prefer disciplinary charges was taken in the Department of Justice.

> The Commissioner accepted, as a disciplinary measure to be exercised by him that each of the 167 men who had been identified as being at the meeting would be charged with a disciplinary offence under the regulations, would be required in due course to give an assurance as to his future conduct, would be fined the maximum fine of £10, and would, within four weeks, be transferred to a country station.[27]

The charges were preferred immediately. One of the offenders, having consulted senior counsel, John A. Costello, pleaded—for the first time in Irish police history—his constitutional right to fair procedures. The Attorney-General advised the Government that such an appeal would be upheld by the Supreme Court.[28] 'As the person statutorily responsible for the general direction and control of the Garda Síochána,' Costigan put out a further statement, which, in the light of his stated views on deficiencies in the representative body regulations, must have caused him the gravest misgivings.

To ensure that the gardaí have an adequate method to ventilate their grievances and promoting their welfare, the law provides for the election in a democratic manner of three representative bodies to look after the interests of the various ranks. In these elections ... every garda has a vote and the system is carefully designed to ensure the widest possible representations ...

The Commissioner was on firmer ground attacking the reported proposal for a go-slow on duty.

The holding of the meetings was a serious breach of the disciplinary regulations and will be dealt with as such. The proposal to adopt 'go-slow' tactics is infinitely more serious and if tolerated would lead to chaos. It will be readily realised that individual members of the force cannot be permitted in any circumstances to take to themselves the right to decide to what extent they will do their duty and pick and choose the individual citizens in relation to whom they will enforce the law.

Any member of the force who engages in conduct of this nature will be dismissed. I believe that what has occurred constitutes a threat to the very existence of the Garda Síochána as a disciplined force with all the implications— that is, for the preservation of law and order. I shall not hesitate therefore to use every resource available to me to bring the present situation to an end.[29]

The 'secret committee' responded immediately, circulating to all guards a letter of their own, disowning the activities of the hotheads. It was their 'unanimous decision' that members were not to withhold their services or 'in any way disaffect or cause disaffection.' They were resolved to 'uphold the highest traditions of the force' and deprecated 'any suggestion made by irresponsible sections of the force to the effect that members of the Garda Síochána would overlook certain minor offences in an effort to bring pressure to bear on the Authorities.' They also called for the resignation of the representative bodies, on the grounds that they were not properly constituted.[30]

At the Government meeting two days later, 9 November, it was 'informally agreed' that the Minister for Justice would give statutory consent 'as requested by the Commissioner' for the dismissal of eleven identified ringleaders;[31] the scapegoats were directed to have their belongings packed and to vacate their stations by midnight.[32] This was the beginning of a personal tragedy for Costigan, leading to a deterioration in his health and eventual removal from office. Isolated as he was by the disloyalty of some of his senior officers, who withheld their support, while subjected to the unremitting pressure for action, in recommending the dismissal of the ringleaders he was widely believed to have acted against his own better judgment. Within days he had to reinstate the eleven men in their jobs, for the commander of a disciplined force a public humiliation, which brought him close to the breakdown to which he eventually succumbed.

In the highly charged mood in the stations, and in anticipation of the sackings, an inchoate protest in the form of mass resignations mushroomed throughout the city. The signed letters were collected by individuals acting on the vague authority of the 'secret committee'. The Commissioner made it known that resignations tendered in connection with the agitation would be accepted. When the ringleaders were dismissed, the protest collapsed; in Marrinan's own station at Rathfarnham, the letters of resignation collected locally were conveniently 'lost'.[33]

A second mass protest meeting was called for Sunday afternoon. 'We can call out 85–90 per cent of the men,' a belligerent spokesman told a reporter.[34] Late on Saturday, Assistant Commissioner W. P. Quinn and his senior officers met at Dublin Castle to consider whether the second demonstration would go ahead at the Macushla Ballroom or elsewhere in the city.[35]

Even as they were meeting, a tragedy was unfolding in Stradbrook Road, Blackrock, County Dublin. Quinn had not left his office to return to his home in Bray when the news broke that his wife had been killed in a traffic accident. As a mark of respect, the demonstration planned for later in the day was called off. A notice was posted at the Macushla Ballroom: 'Meeting postponed due to unforeseen tragic circumstances.'[36] The pavements outside the ballroom were crowded with spectators, who watched as 'several hundred gardaí in plain clothes' arriving for the meeting read the notice and walked away.[37]

If their initiative in the early hours of Sunday 12 November had not promoted the moves being made behind the scenes for a settlement, the good will it generated must have given heart to the peace-makers. On Tuesday the press welcomed the intervention of the Archbishop of Dublin, Dr John Charles McQuaid, in the role of mediator. Having been given a guarantee that discipline had been restored, Haughey invited the dismissed men to make individual applications for reinstatement. The Commissioner was prepared to reappoint the eleven guards, each one giving a personal undertaking that he would not take part in any further acts of indiscipline. The eleven expressed 'deep appreciation and gratitude' to Archbishop McQuaid and to 'Mr Haughey on his readiness to accept their guarantees to His Grace.' It was unfortunate that guards whose first loyalty was due to the Commissioner as head of the force took 'the opportunity of respectfully assuring the Minister of their loyalty to him.'[38]

In its leading article the *Irish Times* reflected the universal sense of relief. Nobody who valued the 'Civic Guard' and who acknowledged the part it had played in the history of the community could feel otherwise than relieved that a settlement of an 'unnecessary and potentially damaging disagreement' was in sight. The Minister for Justice had played 'a properly conciliatory part by offering to reconsider the dismissal of the guards whose part in the dispute had brought down on their heads the full wrath of authority.' It could of course be argued that neither the minister nor the younger guards had acted with a true sense of responsibility in the earlier stages of 'this unfortunate row.'[39] The *Irish Press* was more generous.

'Throughout the dispute the men conducted themselves with admirable restraint. They showed complete awareness of where their first duty lay.'[40]

The *Irish Independent* addressed the issue of trade unionism and the police service.

> It is always a delicate question to decide the extent to which trade union rights should be extended to the police, who of their nature cannot be allowed to strike. But the very fact that they are deprived of the workers' strongest weapon is an argument for giving them latitude in other directions. In particular, restrictions on freedom of speech and discussion in common should be kept to a minimum. Otherwise, as we have seen, the result is the development of 'secret committees' and a general air of conspiracy which in the long run could have a more damaging effect on public confidence and the morale of the force itself than open insubordination.[41]

Archbishop McQuaid wrote personally to the Taoiseach, Seán Lemass. 'May I thank you for the bigness with which you handled the Garda settlement. The Minister has achieved something that could not otherwise have been obtained—a genuine loyalty. And it will help him at the beginning of what, please God, will be a most successful term of office.'[42] Lemass replied immediately, thanking the archbishop 'most sincerely' for his letter. 'Permit me to say that it is, of course, to Your Grace, over and above everyone else, that the outcome was due, and I should like to express my deep appreciation for Your Grace's timely and fruitful intervention in the affair, which was causing us all a great deal of worry. I will inform the Minister of your kind references to him, from which I am sure he will derive both pleasure and encouragement.'[43]

While still within a week of the crisis, the Department of Justice considered it too early to evaluate the situation clearly, but in its memorandum to the Government on 7 November it summarised the causes of the 'widespread indiscipline in the Garda Síochána.' Other workers had been successful in defying established negotiation procedures. It was felt throughout the force that the JRB was not committed to advancing the interests of guards with short service, while their senior colleagues were looking out for themselves. The JRB had not kept members informed on the business of the conciliation council, while the *Garda Review* had exerted a bad influence, consistently stressing the disadvantages and none of the advantages in matters of pay and conditions of service. Single guards had resented deduction from their wages for the sub-standard accommodation provided.

Finally, and perhaps most significantly, the memorandum suggested that senior officers who were recruited and promoted to high rank in the formative years of the force were 'not of high calibre.' There had been evidence from time to time that they had not given the Commissioner their full support. This was not particularly related to the Commissioner personally but because the senior officers had never ceased to resent the action of the Government in 1938 and again in 1952 in appointing civilians as Commissioners over their heads.[44]

In the Dáil the Roscommon deputy John McQuillan blamed the minister for the crisis: it was not the Commissioner who was responsible but the minister, who was pretending to be 'the good boy'.[45] Seán Treacy TD, South Tipperary, asked for an assurance that the representative body would be abolished, 'being the whole source and cause of all [the] unpleasantness.'[46] Moving the second reading of the Garda Síochána Bill (1961), which provided for an increase of twenty-one in the establishment for inspectors in the Dublin Metropolitan Division, Haughey, in a colourful turn of phrase, made what was in effect a plea to the rank and file. Every guard 'carried gold braid in his tunic pocket … The young man of ability who applied himself to his career in the force with diligence, zeal and energy could look forward to a very promising future.' But he had to emphasise that only a certain proportion of those who were qualified to advance could attain promotion; it was inevitable that some members would be disappointed. 'What can and must be avoided is that natural and human disappointment should be transformed into a sense of frustration or injustice leading to discontent.' This could be done only if the system of promotion was 'just and equitable and every member of the force can feel that he [would] get a fair crack of the whip.'

It was expected that in the following six years, because of retirements, it would be necessary to fill close on nine hundred vacancies in the sergeant and higher ranks.[47] The luck of the draw as a factor, conceded by the minister, was fairly understood by every reasonable member; but the perception persisted that the system was sometimes distorted by political intervention and by favouritism.

The JRB for many years had been advocating an adequate memorial to members of the force who had been murdered on duty, to replace a bronze plaque at the guard-room unveiled by Kevin O'Higgins in 1927, shortly before he was himself assassinated. A proposal to erect a monument at a cost of £5,000, approved in principle in 1948, was deferred on grounds of economy. In the wake of the Macushla Ballroom crisis, Haughey reactivated the proposal in a submission to the Department of Finance; he wanted the memorial erected 'forthwith'. In view of recent difficulties with the Garda Síochána it was 'a most appropriate time to announce the intention.' The cost having doubled since the proposal was first made, the Department of Finance wondered whether the JRB (which had no funds) might not bear half the cost. A memorial to the soldiers killed in the Congo, recently unveiled by President de Valera, had cost a mere £138, and the army was likely to 'take a poor view' of a 'much more elaborate' Garda memorial. In less than a month after the Macushla Ballroom affair, Haughey won the support of his Government colleagues. Wasting no time, he took the opportunity of his Christmas message to the force to announce the generosity of a grateful Government.[48]

In a perfect climate of opportunity, it seemed that the minister and his civil servants were determined to strike when the iron was hot. Early in January,

Haughey announced a ten-year plan to provide new stations and a thousand houses for married guards, at a cost of £3½ million.[49] The transfer of Garda training from the overcrowded Phoenix Park depot to McCann Barracks in Templemore, County Tipperary, in the summer of the following year was also awaited, though it was not realised until 1964.

The Dublin Metropolitan District was confined within boundaries drawn in 1836, with some outward adjustments in more recent years. In an apparent move to neutralise the perception of the close-knit metropolitan division as a seedbed of rebellion, the city commander, Assistant Commissioner Quinn, was directed to reorganise the division to include the greater Dublin area, with common promotion lists for the entire force and liability to transfer to any part of the country for guards in all ranks. This was accomplished in the new Dublin Metropolitan Area.

In December the Department of Justice announced the appointment of an informal advisory committee to assist the minister in drafting new regulations for the representative body.[50] Anticipating the development, the *Irish Times* recalled that the representative body had taken an initiative earlier in the year. 'An important contribution to the problem' would be a document presented to the Commissioner by a committee set up by the representative body itself—a harking back to Station Sergeant Seán Ó Colmáin's participation in the conference called by Costigan in November 1960 and the presentation of a report to the Commissioner the following July.[51]

BACK AGAIN TO THE DRAWING-BOARD

The old JRB early in January 1962, mending fences, put in a new pay claim for all ranks. There was not a hope of recording agreement at conciliation. Before the claim could be heard at arbitration, elections under revised regulations[52] changed the face of representative body politics with the return of a central council of confident young guards who were determined to go their own way.[53] John Marrinan was elected its first general secretary and quickly became the standard-bearer for the rank and file. For close on thirty years he was a prominent figure in the force, making ground for all ranks in his negotiations on basic pay and conditions of service. Showing its independence, the new body disowned the composite pay claim, which was then withdrawn in its entirety. At the insistence of the guards, the scheme for conciliation and arbitration was amended to allow for negotiations by the three bodies acting separately. This and other amendments to the scheme were reluctantly accepted on behalf of the JRB by Chief Superintendent Tom Collins, 'for the time being as a matter of expediency.'[54]

In April the Representative Body for Guards lodged its own pay claim, followed by the supervisory and superintendent ranks with separate claims. The public response was sympathetic, as reflected in the newspapers. 'The guards ... have served us well and we must therefore consider whether we, the taxpayers, have rendered adequate thanks.'[55] At arbitration, the claim was conceded in full on the lower points in the pay scale, with generous increases recommended for guards with longer service. Calculating the probable impact on efforts by the Government to curb competition in wage negotiations, recently addressed in a strategic document, *Closing the Gap,* the Department of Finance reacted in alarm: the awards were 'unique ... without parallel' in the public service.[56]

In the Department of Justice the pragmatic view was taken that the arbitrator, Judge Frederick Mangan of the District Court, had not accepted the findings on the status of guards in the community reported by the chairman of the board in 1960. The award was 'overgenerous', but the minister had no option in the matter. 'Rejection of the findings would give rise to such widespread dissatisfaction in all ranks that the machinery of law enforcement would seriously suffer.'[57]

The following January, the ninth-round increase throughout the public service gave guards in the lowest rank a new maximum of £18 4s, an increase of £8 17s or 19½ per cent in a little over four years since the first award at arbitration in December 1960.[58] Determined to hold on to their hard-won new status, the RBG two years later made another pay claim, based on increases granted to other workers that had disturbed recently established relationships, citing in the first place loss of ground compared with the pay of entry-grade clerical workers.

THE RATE FOR THE JOB

In its response to the 1963 claim for parity with clerks, the official side countered with a potentially damaging case based on educational qualifications. Virtually all the groups listed in the Garda claim required the Leaving Certificate as a minimum qualification, compared with sixth standard in national school for Garda recruits. Quoting from the report of the management consultants, Urwick Orr, the counter-claim described clerical work in the Garda Síochána as 'low-grade' and capable of being done 'as speedily and as accurately by the cheapest clerical labour, not by policemen.'[59]

Mangan clearly was not impressed; but the broadside from the official side had far-reaching consequences for the Garda Síochána. The problem in the community at large was soon to be resolved by the Quinn Tribunal on remuneration in clerical employment, which established the principle of the 'rate for the job', transcending unrelated educational standards.[60] Instead of depending on the worth of a guard in real terms, cogently argued in claim after claim, the RBG campaigned for higher educational qualifications for recruits. As a consequence, candidates with higher qualifications began to take the place of the recruits who were traditionally the backbone of the service: young people with innate characteristics of stoic courage, more amenable to discipline, which made a policeman 'responsive to orders and authority; to do promptly and without question that which he is ordered to do; to subordinate his own ideas and opinions to those of the constituted authority.'[61]

In its submission to the Commission on the Garda Síochána in 1968, the Department of Justice defended the status quo.

It would not be right for the State to deprive a young man who has a good primary education of an opportunity of competing for entry to the Garda Síochána. Experience has shown that he can absorb the training and make his progress right through the ranks to the top. In the past many people without formal educational qualifications have made their mark in the Force and will continue to do so.[62]

The principle of the rate for the job, defined by the Quinn Tribunal, was endorsed in January 1970 by the Conroy Commission, which included as an ordinary member the author of the tribunal report, the economist Gerald Quinn.[63]

THE SERGEANTS MAKE THEIR OWN MARK

In the autumn of 1962 the newly elected representative bodies convened at Garda headquarters for their half-yearly meetings. Traditionally, the chairman of the officers' body was returned unopposed as chairman of the Joint Representative Body, and Chief Superintendent Collins was duly nominated by his own committee. In a highly symbolic gesture of independence, the RBG nominated Garda Patrick Lally, Oldcastle, County Meath, the most junior of all the delegates, who was elected chairman,[64] setting the scene for the growth of competing vested interests in the force.

The 1924 pay cuts had had another, undetected effect in the enhancement of the relative position of the superintendent ranks in the pay structure, emphasising inherited social as opposed to functional differences in the officers-and-men syndrome.[65] The emergency bonuses and subsequent flat-rate increases in the pay of public servants during the war years had the contrary effect of compressing differentials, especially in the middle ranks. In 1965, following the successful conclusion of negotiations at arbitration on a pay claim by guards, the Representative Body for Inspectors, Station Sergeants and Sergeants[66] presented a pay claim to establish realistic differentials for these ranks.

This claim represented the first comprehensive definition of the duties of the sergeant rank in particular.[67] In response, the official side argued that the sergeant was a 'chargehand' and not a 'supervisor'. On this vital issue the arbitrator, William Sandys, ruled in favour of the Garda side.[68] But, as Sandys had already reported on the pay of superintendents and chief superintendents, blocking any upward movement in the scales for inspectors and, consequently, for sergeants, he made recommendations in line with his award to guards.[69]

For the wrong reason—to defeat a pay claim—the official side at arbitration in 1966 stumbled on a reality in Garda management. From the nineteen-fifties onwards, with the retirement of the older sergeants, under pressure of rank-and-file militancy and the erosion of authority in the primary group in the organisation of the force—the Garda station party[70]—the new men became the mere chargehands defined for the arbitrator by the civil servants. The reality remained that 'the job of supervisor is not only one of the most important in industry; it is also the most difficult.'[71]

CHURCH AND STATE

The consequences for the Garda Síochána, the Government and the community of the breakdown in discipline and of the years of disenchantment with the leadership of the force following the Macushla Ballroom affair would have been more serious were it not for the energy of one man who was not a member of the force. At a turning-point in Garda history, when respect for authority had been all but whittled away, the unofficial Garda chaplain, Father Clarence Daly, C. P., acted as a buffer between the men and their officers, a debt acknowledged privately by successive Commissioners. The charismatic Passionist spent every waking hour calling at the stations, visiting hospitals and the families of sick men in their homes, and practically every other evening presiding at social functions. In extraordinary times, recognising the vital role he was playing, his superiors were reluctant to upset the relationship of mutual affection he had built up with the force. The respect of the rank and file for the big, bluff priest was all the greater for his outspoken honesty. Preaching at the annual mission at Mount Argus, his advice to guards to distance themselves from politicians was a recurring theme.[72]

In 1982, on the occasion of the diamond jubilee of the force, he accompanied Commissioner Patrick McLaughlin and a company of Garda pilgrims to Rome. Welcoming the policemen and their families, Pope John Paul II echoed the exhortation of his predecessor, Pius XI, addressing O'Duffy and the 1928 Garda pilgrims. They were celebrating sixty years of dedicated service to their country in a tradition of

> vigilance, diligence, zeal and dutiful courage. In the contemporary world the task of the police is certainly not an easy one. It required a sense of vocation, of committed dedication to the safety and well-being of your fellow-citizens. It requires that you recognise and consider yourselves as an important and effective moral force for good at work in your society.[73]

13

THE INCONSISTENCY OF SPECIAL PAY

To paraphrase an old saying, every recruit-garda should feel at the outset of his career that he carried a Commissioner's baton in his holdall.

I t was wholly unjust that the Garda Commissioner should have been held accountable for the conflict between the membership of the Garda Síochána and the Government and the tension within the representative bodies that contributed to the rebellion in 1961. The Macushla Ballroom affair finally overtook Daniel Costigan, and he resigned on 5 February 1965.

In his replacement by Deputy Commissioner William Quinn, a career policeman who had risen through the ranks,[1] the new generation of guards won a victory. The Minister for Justice, Brian Lenihan, made the most of the shift in Government policy, trumping the promise of his predecessor, Charles Haughey, of 'gold braid' for young men of ability: advancement would be on merit alone, and, 'to paraphrase an old saying, every recruit-garda should feel at the outset of his career that he carried a Commissioner's baton in his holdall.'[2]

The Representative Body for Guards, meanwhile, presenting its case to the Mangan Tribunal in 1963, defended the integrity of basic pay. Its members received no shift pay, overtime, 'on call' money, or other recognition of onerous working conditions. But there were 'good reasons' for not introducing supplementary payments of this kind:

> It would be totally inconsistent with the status of police as a service, the efficiency of which depends upon the maintenance of morale and esprit de corps, that the constable should be meticulously paid at agreed rates for anything over and above a 'normal' working week ... The proper way to bring the constable's remuneration into line with modern conditions is to pay him at a rate which fully recognises the exacting nature of the police way of life and, in addition, fairly compensates him for his inability to increase his earnings outside.

On receiving a new claim two years later for more rest days, the Department of Justice enthusiastically endorsed the earlier RBG position on basic pay: Mangan had taken all this into account.[3] The claim was renewed in 1967, this time for a 48-hour week with free days, the loss of a free day to be compensated either by time off or overtime pay. Breaking new ground in Garda management-staff relations, the Commissioner, Patrick Carroll,[4] appointed an all-ranks working party under Chief Superintendent John Coakley.[5] The initiative, which restored the fractured unity of the Joint Representative Body, was also an interesting experiment in shared responsibility. Peter Berry, Secretary of the Department of Justice, may have seen an opportunity to implement official policy with the support of the rank and file, but the professional integrity of ordinary policemen was equal to the challenge.

The committee was appointed in November 1967 and reported the following May, plunging the Department of Justice and the Commissioner into controversy over the terms of reference. An interim report in February had drawn Berry's fire. The minister was 'at a loss to understand' how the misconceptions had occurred. Harking back to the interdepartmental inquiry of 1950, Berry reinterpreted Coakley's terms of reference to suit policy in the Department of Justice. 'The principal task of the Committee was to advise on the extent to which, by a re-allocation of existing strengths and re-assessment of opening hours ... of stations, a reduction (to be specified) in hours could be granted without additional expenditure on increased manpower and without detriment to adequate policing.'

The interim report recommended modest increases in strengths and the employment of civilians in Garda offices. In reply, the Department of Justice declared itself 'confident' that Coakley would be guided to 'the correct lines.' The minister was 'accordingly shocked' to find in the final report that the recommended additional strength had practically doubled, deviating further from the terms of reference.

Berry stressed 'the necessity for ruthlessness' in reallocating strengths. Officials in his department had investigated the situation in County Wexford, a division served by 165 sergeants and guards in thirty stations, a ratio of one policeman to 574 people. Coakley was recommending an increase from 165 to 171; instead, as the civil servants sought to demonstrate, it was possible to achieve a *reduction* in strength of 17, closing no less than nine stations.[6]

This informal study was based on a report by the consultants Urwick Orr dating from the nineteen-fifties.[7] In an attempt to provide frustrated civil servants with a benchmark for Garda strengths outside the Dublin Metropolitan Area, Urwick Orr in 1958 devised a formula based on local population, operational area, and reported crimes: one duty guard to 750 people, 6,000 acres, and two indictable crimes.[8] The consultants attempted to arbitrate with finality on the future needs of the force without regard to crime prevention, any increase in reported crimes, the growing traffic problem, or other demands. Police authorities in other countries, despite long years of study, had failed to discover 'any formula or specific approach

Éamonn Broy, Garda Commissioner 1933–38.

Garda motorcycle units, Dublin Castle, mid-1930s.

Garda patrol cars, Dublin Castle, mid-1930s.

M. J. Kinnane, Garda Commissioner 1938–51.

A typical station party: Kanturk, Co. Cork, 1947; Superintendent Jeremiah Holland, Sergeant W. J. Keegan, Sergeant Francis Brennan.

Recreation in a typical station day-room, 1940s. Card-playing for small stakes was permitted by barrack regulations. The guard in the waterproof coat was either ready for or returning from patrol.

Chief Superintendent Patrick Carroll, Crime Branch (*left*), and Superintendent G. Lawlor, Technical Bureau, with a visiting Indian police officer, *c.* 1950.

Superintendent Dan Stapleton and Detective-Garda F. P. McGrath, forensic laboratory, Technical Bureau, *c.* 1950.

Daniel Costigan, Garda Commissioner 1952–65.

Headquarters conference, 1954. Front row (*from left*): Chief Superintendent F. Burke, Surgeon V. C. Ellis, Assistant Commissioner P. J. Carroll, Deputy Commissioner W. R. E. Murphy, Gerald Boland, Minister for Justice, Commissioner D. Costigan, Mr Justice Thomas Teevan, Deputy Commissioner G. Brennan, Assistant Commissioner T. Woods, Chief Superintendent H. Duffy.

Oscar Traynor, Minister for Justice, inspecting a guard of honour in Dublin Castle, *c.* 1959.

Women gardaí: the first recruit class, 1959, with their instructor, Sergeant D. Prissick, Liverpool City Police.

A group of visiting police officers at Garda Headquarters, *c.* 1960, with Chief Superintendent Tom Collins (*seated, third from left*), Chief Superintendent H. O'Mara (*standing, extreme left*), Deputy Commissioner P. J. Carroll (*sixth from left*), Deputy Commissioner T. Woods (*seventh from left*), and Superintendent P. O'Neill (*extreme right*).

Passing-out parade of recruits in the Phoenix Park Depot, *c.* 1960; Commissioner Daniel Costigan and Peter Berry, secretary, Department of Justice, taking the salute.

The signing of the Garda Conciliation and Arbitration Scheme, 1959. *Seated (from left):* Inspector H. Nangle, Chief Superintendent Tom Collins, Commissioner Daniel Costigan, Deputy Commissioner G. Brennan, Assistant Commissioner T. Woods; *standing:* Superintendent D. Corcoran, Garda M. Egan, Garda P. E. Gunn, Sergeant D. Fingleton, Chief Superintendent T. McCarthy.

The Representative Body for Guards, 1962. *Seated (from left):* P. Nolan, Mallow; John Marrinan, Rathfarnham (general secretary); P. E. Gunn, Dún Laoghaire (chairman); C. Ryan, Kiltyclogher; J. Fitzgerald, Naas. *Standing:* P. Courtney, William Street, Limerick; N. Scott, Tralee; P. Lally, Oldcastle (chairman, JRB); J. Scott, Claremorris; J. Lee, Dunglow; M. Harlow and R. Keating, Pearse Street, Dublin.

The Representative Body for Inspectors and Sergeants, 1965. *Seated (from left):* Sergeant D. Fingleton, Headquarters (treasurer); Inspector Seán Ó Colmáin, Dún Laoghaire (chairman); Sergeant T. Murphy, Training Centre (secretary); Station Sergeant J. Connolly, Chapelizod; *standing:* Inspector P. Crowley, Mullingar; Inspector J. Loakman, Wexford; Sergeant J. Kelly, Clifden; Sergeant Gregory Allen, Headquarters (general secretary); Sergeant K. McCready, Kilmainham; Inspector J. F. Murray, Galway.

The Garda badge, limestone medallion in granite by Michael Biggs, 1966, at Garda Headquarters.

William P. Quinn, Garda Commissioner 1965–67.

Patrick Carroll, Garda Commissioner 1967–68.

Michael J. Wymes, Garda
Commissioner 1968–73.

Patrick Malone, Garda Commissioner
1973–75.

The author as Garda archivist with P. J. Carroll and Assistant Commissioner Seán Sheehan, Head of Research and Planning, 1975.

Edmund P. Garvey, Garda Commissioner 1975–78, with Assistant Commissioner J. M. McAleenan and Patrick Cooney, Minister for Justice, Training Centre, Templemore, *c.* 1976.

Patrick McLaughlin, Garda Commissioner 1978–83.

Father Clarence Daly, C. P., Garda chaplain and peace-maker, 1956–83.

that can be applied ... to estimate the number of constables required in any area for beat duties.'9 Berry found it 'difficult to understand' why the consultants' report was not 'in the forefront of their deliberations,' suggesting that the Commissioner should consider sending back the report to enable the 'glaring omission to be rectified.' He required the Commissioner to be 'ruthless in making the best possible use of manpower.'10

Writing to Berry on the same date (their letters crossed), Carroll spelt out the aims of police: the protection of life and property, the preservation of public peace and good order, and the prevention and detection of crime. The formula recommended for Garda deployment provided 'anything but a sound basis on which to decide the working of the Garda Síochána.' How any approach to this matter could ignore the preventive side of police was difficult if not impossible to understand, 'and no practical police officer would do so.'

The force had proved its efficiency in every aspect of its work through the dedication of all ranks, 'in most cases without regard to time or personal interests or the extent of the workload involved because their primary consideration was to do their job.' Down through the years, changes had been introduced 'long before the consultants appeared on the scene and subsequently with specific regard to the consultants' recommendations.' He listed the progress made: divisions and districts abolished, stations closed or redefined as sub-stations, with a net reduction in total strength.11

In July, with considerable misgivings, Carroll recommended new lists of station closures, guided by Coakley's conclusions, the views of his senior officers, and 'more especially' Government policy.

> By closing more stations and sub-stations there will be further large areas where the public will be exposed to the activities of criminals who can operate without serious risk of detection ... There is bound to be a substantial increase in crime and a fall in the rate of detections ... Every station closed or reduced and every sub-station closed deprives the inhabitants of those areas of the feeling of security which is at present provided. In every area there are people who take full advantage of the distance between their victims and the nearest Garda station. Furthermore, in their attacks on property, criminals using motor transport and aware of the location of Garda stations will have much more freedom of action and run less risk of detection than is the case at present.

There was also the possibility that the annual criminal statistics might be mistakenly viewed as a balance sheet reflecting the effectiveness of the Garda Síochána. The figures did not accurately reflect the crimes committed: a complete assessment of crime could never be made, as many crimes were never reported.12

With its foot firmly in the door, the RBG had no intention of allowing administrative warfare to undermine its historic claim for a shorter working week. Endorsing the thrust of the 1950 interdepartmental committee, Coakley recommended an end to the traditional garrison or 24-hour standby system of policing rural areas. In its place it envisaged a round-the-clock centralised service based on district headquarters, with 'hot line' telephones at outlying stations and a nationwide radio service and mobile patrols to support depleted strengths in the satellites.[13]

Boldly recommending the closure of some of the more remote stations and the creation of new sub-stations,[14] the committee proposed for the redeployed force a working ratio of one guard to a thousand people. With doubtful wisdom, Coakley recommended the abolition of the police duty class, taking the view that it was 'the personal duty of established personnel to keep themselves up-to-date on current law, regulations and procedure so as to be able to efficiently perform their duties at all times,'[15] at best a pious platitude.

Coakley's acceptance of civilian clerks and the employment of civilians in other non-police roles was a significant concession in a conservative organisation. Seizing the opportunity, the Department of Justice soon afterwards advertised vacancies in the force for a new category of Garda civilian clerks, leaving it to the Commissioner to decide on their employment.[16]

A COMMISSION OF INQUIRY

Early in 1967, following the collapse of the middle ranks' pay claim, Berry invited the chairman of the JRB, Chief Superintendent William O'Halloran, to broker an agreement on a new pay structure between the various interests, suggesting a reduction of two increments in the superintendents' pay scale to allow the inspectors and sergeants to move upwards in the scales. The sergeants and inspectors invited the officers of the other bodies to a meeting in the Ashling Hotel in Parkgate Street. On behalf of the chief superintendents, who were not directly affected, O'Halloran agreed to the proposal. The initiative failed, the spokesmen for the lower ranks and for the superintendents stating their intention to claim for their own people any advantage won by the middle ranks.

During the discussions, the RBG delegates, John Marrinan and his chairman, Jim Fitzgerald of Naas, unexpectedly questioned the need for supervision of their members, on the grounds that they derived their duties from common law and the statute law and not from the Garda organisation. They were prepared to consider the proposed new pay structure if the references in the pay claim to the sergeant's supervisory role were removed.[17] The new generation of young guards, it seemed, was unwilling to enter any agreement that might undermine their own negotiating position.

Berry's intervention was misunderstood in the force. When the Government Information Bureau early in 1968 stated that no Garda pay claims awaited hearing by the conciliation council, an unnamed Garda sergeant protested that the secretary of the Department of Justice had 'reopened negotiations' on the middle ranks' pay claim.[18] The issue made headlines again a year later when a well-attended open meeting of inspectors and sergeants in the Garda Club discussed the failure of their claim for wider differentials. In a further statement, the Department of Justice denied reports in the newspapers that the arbitrator in 1966 had suggested that 'if the economic situation improved, the claims of non-commissioned officers should be treated as a matter of urgency … No such recommendation was made by the arbitrator.'[19] The representative body resigned on the issue in 1974, when discontent was 'arguably stronger in the middle ranks' than it was 'either at the top or the bottom.'[20]

EQUATING POLICE WITH FIREMEN

A recommendation by the Labour Court in August 1968, conceding to striking Dublin and Dún Laoghaire firemen effective parity with Garda pay, drew a protest from the RBG, which had a new pay claim pending. The court made its judgment without reference either to police duties and responsibilities or to the working conditions in the Garda Síochána.[21] On the other hand, it saw 'substantial similarities' between certain recruitment and employment conditions in the fire service and the Garda Síochána.[22]

In a rare intervention, Carroll backed the representative body, repudiating on behalf of the Garda Síochána the decision of the Labour Court to equate the duties of gardaí with those of firemen. Having invoked Desborough on the responsibilities and obligations of a policeman 'peculiar to his calling,'[23] Carroll cited the recently published report of President Lyndon Johnson's Commission on Law Enforcement and Administration of Justice (1967). In many cities in the United States police wages were tied to those of other government employees. It had been a tradition for police and fire service wages to be identical; but

> police compensation should be based solely on the nature of work being performed by various classes of personnel within the department as well as within the entire structure of local government. Since policemen and firemen perform entirely different jobs, neither service should base its salaries upon those of the other. If, considering all factors, firemen require higher salaries, they should be so compensated. The opposite should also be true.[24]

Within days, on 28 August, the JRB called for the appointment of a commission to inquire into pay and conditions of service. The Government conceded in principle, provided the force accepted a settlement of its current pay claim in line with increases already given to civil servants and other public service workers.[25] Re-enacting the Macushla Ballroom protest seven years before, this time under the aegis of their representative body, three thousand guards, packing two halls in the Garda Club, welcomed the promise of a commission but 'rejected outright' the proposed pay increase. The appointment of a chairman for the arbitration board had been hanging fire for some time. Referring the matter to the Government, the Department of Justice complained that the representative bodies had been 'engaging in propaganda' within the force and in the public press to give the impression that the official side had been 'dilatory' in attending to their claims. They were well aware of the 'very magnitude' of the issues: £800,000 for a 'status' pay increase, a further £1,000,000 a year to finance a claim for improved working conditions, 'if the existing scale of law enforcement was to be maintained.' If the Government was to 'withstand a further barrage of propaganda' an arbitrator would have to be appointed 'as soon as possible.'[26]

The *Irish Independent* supported the Garda case.

> For many years Gardaí have been trying to get their grievances righted. Because they cannot form a trade union or employ trade union tactics their campaign has been carried on in muted tones and to the accompaniment of a loss of morale. Money, hours, conditions—one only has to name the complaint and the Garda can tell a frustrating tale—but only in private, since he is debarred from making too public what can be described at suitable moments as confidential information …

The guards needed an assurance that the 9 per cent offered was an interim measure and that the proposed commission would not be ignored when it stated (what could be proved without a commission) 'that conditions are completely below the standards required in a complex, modern world.'[27]

Under the confident leadership of John Marrinan and his colleagues, a crisis was avoided. In September the Government appointed a commission under Judge J. C. Conroy to make recommendations on the remuneration and conditions of service in the Garda Síochána.[28]

'TREATED LIKE SCHOOLBOYS'

By the summer of 1969 Conroy had taken evidence from the various interested parties and was visiting police establishments abroad. The representative bodies, including the RBG, were satisfied with the progress being made when the newspapers once again were full of the sound and fury of discontent, this time in a district in the western suburbs of Dublin.

In Crumlin, which included Sundrive Road, the local force was riven by a revolt against the authority of a new commander, Superintendent Michael Fitzgerald, an officer of unimpeachable integrity. His rigid personality tended to antagonise colleagues throughout his service; an unhappy reputation as a martinet when he was chief instructor in the Training Centre followed him to the city and acted as tinder to a bonfire in the situation at Crumlin.

Fitzgerald discovered a legacy of slack administration and a district force performing below reasonable standards. To turn his district around, he personally supervised his men when his less than enthusiastic sergeants failed to co-operate. On the morning of the general election in June 1969 the early shift in both stations in the Crumlin district threatened to report sick, protesting at 'Captain Bligh-style discipline'.[29] The superintendent was so strict on inspection that it was 'almost impossible to satisfy him.'[30] The Commissioner, Michael Wymes,[31] having received a joint deputation from the representative bodies for the lower ranks, appointed Assistant Commissioner James McDonagh to investigate the men's complaints.

The uneasy peace may have held until Wymes had considered McDonagh's report, but the transfer a month later of a young guard, Cornelius O'Connor, to a station in County Cork, for no reason in the opinion of his colleagues, was the last straw. Crumlin was suddenly back in the headlines with a vengeance when over seventy guards rostered for duty at 6 a.m. failed to appear on parade. When the afternoon shift paraded for duty, twenty-eight guards reported sick. A meeting of five hundred city-centre guards pledged support for the men in Crumlin, and other meetings were planned as the dispute intensified. The newspapers picked up their angry voices: they were being 'treated like schoolboys ... In this day and age when man is big enough to set his sights on the moon, an officer of the Garda Síochána should be big enough to see that a 1922 code of discipline is outdated.'[32]

A provision in the Garda Síochána (Discipline) Regulations (1926) that an offence against discipline would be aggravated by a denial of the charge was gravely unjust.[33] As part of the legacy of the RIC, such a draconian provision had long been outmoded; the Garda authorities were fully aware of the defect and had been ignoring it for decades. In the nineteen-fifties Costigan tried, and failed, to interest the Department of Justice in amending the statutory regulations. In his frustration, presenting to the department the heads of new discipline regulations, he encroached on the business of the civil servants and for his trouble was spurned by Peter Berry, just as in his efforts to get the representative body regulations amended he was ignored by the JRB under Chief Superintendent Tom Collins.

But in the essential matter of deportment in a uniformed force there was nothing in the code of exemplary conduct to offend reasonable men among the guards up in arms in Crumlin. In an editorial, the *Irish Independent* latched on to the theme of antique regulations. The unprecedented upsurge in unrest in the Garda was not caused by trivial grievances: the calibre of the men involved was such that a wave of unrest among them could not be regarded as 'the fretting of immature men showing lack of judgement.' For the Garda Síochána to operate within a framework administered by the Department of Justice,

> the relationship should have been sufficient to ensure that legitimate complaint was reasonably considered ... Allowing for the special nature of Garda work it could at least have watched for signs of antiquity, rules and regulations thoroughly outmoded by modern standards, and repugnant to the present mentality of everyone ... It is futile to blame one man or a few men if they are administering rules still operated by the Department of Justice or at any rate allowed to remain on the books.[34]

In a statement issued by the Government Information Bureau, the Department of Justice quickly denied any fault in not bringing the disciplinary regulations up to date. The matter had been 'under active consideration for a considerable time,' in consultation with the Garda authorities; the men's representatives had chosen to refer the matter to Conroy, hence the delay.[35]

The other newspapers took a more balanced view, the *Irish Times* considering that the dispute did not turn on any general objection among the guards, nor was any alteration in the regulations being called for. 'The trouble might be described as a domestic one.'[36] The *Irish Press* asked what had gone wrong in Crumlin that seventy-seven guards had 'simultaneously in all but name … gone on strike?' The people who had heard on the radio

> a senior garda saying that he was afraid to be two minutes late in reporting for duty—even if he had been delayed by performing a service for one of the public—must have been considerably taken aback … Discipline must be upheld of course; this central fact cannot be overstated, but for discipline to be effective it must be respected and accepted. In the present situation it obviously isn't, but the logic of the situation is easier to state than enforce. If the object of the men's ire is removed … what happens to the morale and behaviour of the rest of the Force's upper echelons?[37]

The revision of the discipline regulations was anticipated by the *Irish Times*. Attitudes to authority had changed. The new generation was not as impressed by rank and title as its parents were, but moral authority and natural leadership were universally recognised and respected. Among the Garda there was 'a widespread feeling' that the civil servants in the Department of Justice were exercising 'far too much influence over the force … It may be nothing more than a strong suspicion, but it is not improving morale.' The newspaper echoed Costigan's dream of a joint consultative council. Judge Conroy was a chairman who commanded respect. His commission was made up of four esteemed men but did not include any representative of employee interests. This was surely a defect.[38]

An overflow meeting in the Garda Club on 26 July called for the removal of Superintendent Fitzgerald and the cancellation of Garda O'Connor's transfer.[39] Reporting the meeting, the *Sunday Independent* editorialised in defence of the guards as 'men of standing … not likely to take the action they have without a burning feeling of suffering from injustice.'

Within days, the crisis was defused, on the intervention once again of Wymes, who announced that the officer at the centre of the row would be transferred from Crumlin, at his own request. But O'Connor's transfer had 'nothing whatever to do with the general issue.' The young guard was urged to defy the order, but O'Connor at another crowded meeting in the city disarmed the hotheads by announcing his departure for Killeagh, County Cork. His address was 'greeted by mixed cheering, handclapping and booing. Several of the more militant members accused him of being selfish and having turned his back on the movement just when it was gathering momentum to gain better pay and conditions.'[40]

Assistant Commissioner McDonagh's report on the state of discipline in the Crumlin district was not published, leaving an honourable officer to suffer in silence. In the sixties the times were out of joint for conscientious officers. Having served throughout his career in country divisions, Superintendent Fitzgerald was uncomfortable in the milieu of the Dublin metropolitan force, with its different traditions. He was accommodated at Garda headquarters, and was later promoted. His temporary replacement in Crumlin, Superintendent Daniel Devitt, had given all his service in city stations, including a long stint in the vital rank of station sergeant, and was more in sympathy with the pragmatic outlook of men who worked the challenging Dublin beats.[41] For the moment the dust had settled; but Fitzgerald's humiliation in Crumlin cast a long shadow.[42]

CONROY AND A PANDORA'S BOX

Sought in vain by O'Duffy in his time, and by Costigan, the commission of inquiry was, not unreasonably, perceived as the product of rank-and-file agitation. Conroy was largely driven by the RBG. The minutes of evidence were delivered at Garda headquarters every evening and were studied and analysed. To protect the office of Commissioner from appearing to side with the Department of Justice, and to avoid conflict with the representative bodies in a quarrel not of the Commissioner's making, critical observations on tendentious and inaccurate statements by witnesses were not communicated to the department. Presented with a *fait accompli*, Wymes distanced himself from the proceedings, to the chagrin of Peter Berry. At Berry's insistence, Wymes put in a brief appearance and made a circumscribed statement.[43]

The Conroy Report was published in January 1970 and made a notable contribution to stability and peace in the police service. Banishing the ghost of Desborough's report on the British police, Conroy described the occupation of a guard as 'unique'[44] and defined for the Garda Síochána its own 'qualities of a policeman': courageous, mentally alert, honest and fair in his dealings with everyone, tactful and courteous; dedicated, with a great sense of personal responsibility, capable of acting decisively and with authority.[45] But for the rising generation, the idealism that motivated the founder-members of the force was tempered by defensive attitudes in a burgeoning affluent society. Products of a regime of harsh discipline introduced when recruit training was transferred to the isolation of Templemore in 1964, the new men taking up duty at their first stations readily paid what amounted to union dues to a rampant representative body.

Conroy made over fifty separate recommendations on practically every aspect of life in the force, including pay and allowances, standards of accommodation, recruitment, education and training, promotion, the discipline regulations, uniforms, and the employment of civilians. The report proposed a Consultative Council, to include the elected delegates of all ranks and representatives of the Garda Commissioner and of the Departments of Justice and Finance.[46]

Conroy confirmed the status of sergeants as supervisors.[47] But the psychological problem of the loss of confidence in front-line leadership was not resolved, assuming it emerged in the evidence, nor could it have been resolved in the short term by any pay increase alone. The restoration of the confidence that distinguished the older generation of sergeants remained a challenge for the management and, not least, for a representative body prepared to commit itself to the status of its members in the best professional sense.

A decade had passed since the Macushla Ballroom affair. A little-publicised committee of inquiry into conditions of service appointed in 1962 by Charles Haughey inspected many Garda stations. The chairman, Monsignor Thomas Fehily, director of the Dublin Institute for Adult Education (who had acted as intermediary between Archbishop McQuaid and the Government in the peace negotiations the previous year), reported privately to the minister. The report was not published, but it was known that Fehily and his colleagues were shocked by what they saw of the living and working conditions in the stations they visited. In 1970 Conroy could still describe some official accommodation as 'sub-standard and not fit to live in.' While it was conceded that the Office of Public Works was making progress within financial constraints, there had been 'a slowness in providing proper accommodation' and a baffling reluctance to make judgments on obviously unsuitable buildings.[48]

The long-standing claim for a shorter working week was a primary bone of contention. The Garda management was not faultless in the build-up of resentment. In the response to the public order crisis in the nineteen-thirties it was vital to deploy large concentrations of guards to contain excitable crowds at political meetings. A quarter of a century or so later men were still being sent to race meetings and football matches in greater numbers than were necessary and were often left to their own devices on empty perimeter roads in all weathers. At holiday resorts during the summer months, local units, augmented at weekends by men from adjoining stations, worked extended hours without recompense; they saw no merit in the provision for time off, which was not always available to them anyway. Their claim for a five-day, forty-hour week with paid overtime was probably the last straw for a hard-pressed Government in its decision to appoint the commission on pay and conditions of service.[49]

In recommending a 42-hour week, Conroy set down the conditions for the payment of overtime.[50] However painstakingly the proposals were drafted, it was clear to Commissioner Wymes that Conroy had presented a Pandora's box, with horrendous pitfalls for the Garda management. In a flurry of activity, the Commissioner's personal assistant, Chief Superintendent John McAleenan, prepared a submission to the Department of Justice on the need for a statutory Pay and Allowances Order to govern the payment of overtime. Instead, the problems were addressed through the conciliation and arbitration machinery: the representatives of the rank and file and the supervisory ranks on one side and of the Departments of Justice and Finance on the other, the Commissioner making no contribution and depending on the civil servants for information. The arrangements agreed at conciliation were circulated by the Commissioner in a directive on annual leave, rest days, hours of duty, overtime pay, and night duty allowance,[51] completing the revolution of the guards.

The overtime bonanza, at two extremes, resulted in many individuals making small fortunes, but guards in special employment did not share in the pay-out. The breach of the traditional integrity of basic pay created jealousies as the attention of the force was focused on opportunities to enhance incomes, a wasting competitive spirit that was bound to subvert and did rapidly undermine morale. In 1973, as if designed for the purpose, a greatly simplified computerised payroll replaced the ancient manual pay-sheets written out by station sergeants. Like the legendary salt machine, the new payroll facilitated the payment of overtime and other new allowances. To monitor overtime, a new layer of expensive bureaucracy was established at Garda headquarters.

A measure of the demoralisation that set in was the virtual eclipse of the Garda Síochána as a preventive force, as patrols disappeared off the streets. Apart from the occasional sighting of a patrol car, citizens could travel the length of the country without encountering a uniformed guard. To judge the situation for himself, Wymes personally monitored patrols in the provinces—whether on his own initiative or at the direction of the minister is not clear—and subsequently called for station diaries and patrol books.[52]

The chaos in the Garda Síochána resulting from the introduction of a system of secondary wages contained a core historical lesson. Conroy identified the conflict between the Department of Justice and the Garda Síochána, including by inference the problems that had been allowed to fester in the area of conditions of service, that might have been resolved if the department down the years had not held the representative bodies at arm's length. Conroy defined the dichotomy as 'a vagueness, causing uncertainty and ineffectiveness [in] the relationship between the Department and the Commissioner,' a malaise that 'permeated the Force.' Concluding, the commission strongly urged an examination of the 'role, organisation and personnel policy of the Force and, in particular, its relationship with the Department of Justice.'[53]

Copies of the report were circulated on Friday 23 January. Before the representative bodies had time to study the 250-page document in detail, word went out that Conroy had recommended an increase in basic pay of £2 a week,[54] and the force was up in arms again, with renewed threats by guards to report sick. Welcoming the report, Marrinan deprecated the reaction as 'impetuous'.[55] A sober assessment appeared in the editorial column of the Irish Press. It was 'incredible' that

Judge Conroy's commission was 'the first since the foundation of the force … The rank-and-file were likely to find that the recommended "fringe benefits" were even more valuable than the pay increases.'[56]

The *Garda Review* in February acknowledged the 'sense of fairness' that had guided Conroy. In a comment on the confused anger that had greeted the report, it recalled the following month the years of frustrated endeavour. It was not surprising that 'pent-up feelings … could not be dispelled without some angry reaction.' Marrinan in a newspaper interview wondered whether the Government 'really, in good faith,' intended to implement the recommendations.[57] The RBG warned that if action was not taken by 1 April its members would ballot an agreed course of action, a statement described by the *Irish Times* as 'unusually stiff'. It was doubtful whether the Government fully appreciated that it was due to the Representative Body alone that the force was held back from all-out strike.[58] According to the *Garda Review,* the Government would have been 'astounded' to hear the criticisms of the representative bodies as 'too moderate, too restrained and too willing to see the difficulties' of the management.[59]

On the initiative of the militant RBG, the old representative body structures were soon to be reorganised according to separate vested interests as staff associations. The new Garda Representative Association would have 'more elbow room, more participation in the running of the force.' It would 'negotiate as an independent entity' in its own right, 'within the force but not part of its structure.'[60] In the flush of its recent achievements, the GRA entertained an unreal ambition of independence in a disciplined force.

On the retirement of M. J. Wymes in 1973 he was succeeded as Commissioner by Patrick Malone. A conscientious and self-effacing administrator, Malone stabilised the Garda Síochána in stressful times. He established the Garda Museum and Archives in 1974.[61]

14

A PROPHET NOT WITHOUT HONOUR

A strict disciplinarian, immensely proud of his force ... who did not waste words.

The humiliation of Superintendent Fitzgerald in the Crumlin affair in 1969 cast its shadow a decade later at an open meeting in the Garda Club convened to discuss club business. It was known beforehand that Commissioner Edmund Garvey, as club president, was to attend. Garvey was at loggerheads with the Representative Body for Guards. As if inviting confrontation, he had shown his displeasure by withdrawing from the *Garda Review* the Commissioner's traditional Christmas message to the force, against the strong advice of one of his senior headquarters officers, and instead circulated his greetings personally to members of the force on a slip of paper in their pay envelopes.[1]

The hall was crowded for the meeting, younger guards making up the bulk of the attendance. Garvey's arrival was greeted with an unprecedented stamping of feet until the building resounded with their mutiny. The initiative was retrieved for the Commissioner and a semblance of dignity restored when some of the older members present courageously repudiated the hotheads;[2] but the public display of indiscipline must have been a factor in the decision by the Government to remove from office a Commissioner with a reputation as 'a strict disciplinarian, immensely proud of his force ... who did not waste words.'[3]

In January 1978 Garvey was summoned to the Department of Justice to be told by the minister, Gerard Collins, in the presence of the secretary, Andrew Ward, that the Government wished to have his resignation within two hours; failing that, he would be removed from office. No explanation was given. 'The end of Commissioner Garvey's service as head of the Garda Síochána came swiftly and with no finesse.'[4]

Acknowledging the former Commissioner's 'deserved reputation as a man who wanted action and results,' the representative bodies were barely forgiving. 'It would be hypocritical to suggest that we always saw eye to eye with the former Commissioner. He had his own way of doing things and it often clashed with our wishes. We will not rake over old embers. Suffice it to say that we will remember Mr Garvey with respect for his many achievements; we will not agree that he steered the Garda Síochána in the right direction.'5

The best-informed observer of Garda affairs, Conor Brady, was in no doubt that Garvey was

> subjected to pressure quite unlike anything his predecessors had experienced from their political masters. He was sent in by the Coalition Government because he was, as [the former minister] Patrick Cooney put it, 'a tough cop.' He was given the task of countering decades of indolence at Garda Headquarters, decades of browbeating the force from the Department of Justice, decades of demoralisation among the rank and file of the gardaí themselves.6

The Government had been dissatisfied with Garvey's handling of allegations of heavy-handedness by some members of the force in the treatment of prisoners. In what became known as the fingerprint affair, failures in the investigation of the murder of the British ambassador, Christopher Ewart-Biggs, and his secretary, Judith Cook, in a land-mine explosion at Stepaside, County Dublin, on 21 July 1976, had given rise to great concern. The RBG for its part had expressed dissatisfaction with the Commissioner's attitude to discipline.7 It was also revealed that the Minister for Justice had only recently become aware that Garvey had endeavoured, without success, to persuade the Director of Public Prosecutions to proceed against the editorial board of the Garda Review under the Offences Against the State Act for 'usurping the functions of government.'8

The editorial in the Garda Review of June 1976 had attacked official attitudes to 'crime and criminality'. Within days of a decision by the representative body to seek the right to strike, the Minister for Justice, Patrick Cooney, in the Dáil had played down the level of violence and criminality in modern Ireland. The representative bodies had become 'increasingly disillusioned … by this head-in-the-sand mentality.' It was not confined to the crime problem: in matters of welfare, force morale, public attitudes towards the force—right across the board, the Garda Síochána was faced with 'enormous and rapidly worsening problems,' which were ignored right up to Government level.

In February 1977 another remarkable editorial reflected the bellicose mood among the lower ranks. Commenting on a speech on law enforcement by the minister, who was visiting the Training Centre for a passing-out parade, the Garda Review wondered what Cooney was talking about in exhorting the guards to 'stay within the law.' Why had the minister with responsibility for running the police force come to the Training Centre to give advice on the functions of police and the courts? 'Mr Cooney proclaimed himself and the force as a whole to be against police misbehaviour.' But ministers of state did not pick their subjects for public address without first carefully considering the implications. The minister was addressing a problem that could do the Garda Síochána 'untold and possibly irreversible damage.'

The seventies were the years of the 'heavy gang' allegations. The *Garda Review* believed that the force had an unblemished record, and it did not accept that there was or had been any widespread problem of misbehaviour in the matter of securing convictions. Cooney had not suggested that there was; the problem was not that of guards exceeding their powers, it was 'rather a problem of public confusion fed by a gullible and uninformed media ... taken in by people whose interests are served by breaking down public confidence in the police.' The law of evidence as it stood and the right to silence were obstacles to the investigation of crime.

Whatever the reasons for the loss of his job, Garvey, believing his integrity had been impugned, fought a successful action in the courts against the state.

THE RESPONSE TO SUBVERSION

The report of the Conroy Commission in January 1970 was timely, coming on the threshold of a decade that would see the discipline of the Garda Síochána tested in ways that had not been seen since the Civil War or the Economic War and its consequences in the next decade. The fall-out from the collapse of the Northern state encouraged subversive elements to contemplate attacks south of the border. Within months of the Conroy Report, on 3 April 1970, an armed gang raided the Royal Bank of Ireland in Arran Quay, Dublin. The crew of a patrol car, Garda Richard Fallon and Garda Paul Firth of Mountjoy station, were first on the scene. The five armed and masked robbers were leaving the bank as Garda Fallon, with reckless courage, attempted to impede their escape and was shot dead. He became the first casualty of peace in his generation in the force since the murder of Dublin-born Detective-Garda George Mordant, aged forty-five, a former railway guard, who was shot dead attempting to arrest a wanted man in Donnycarney, Dublin, on 24 October 1942.

As a young man, Fallon left his father's farm in County Roscommon to join the force. At forty-four, the father of five children, for conspicuous bravery in confronting armed criminals he was posthumously awarded the gold Scott Medal. His funeral from the policemen's church of St Paul of the Cross, Mount Argus, evoked an outpouring of public grief not witnessed since the homecoming of the Irish soldiers who died in the Niemba ambush in the Congo in 1960. The Garda Band, which had been stood down in a notional cost-saving exercise, voluntarily re-formed to lead the cortege. The remains of Dick Fallon, draped in the Tricolour, were followed it seemed by every guard in the country who was not on duty, an awesome phalanx stretching from College Green to the Parnell Monument. In the stilled streets the sound of marching feet seemed to many the death-knell of peace in Ireland.

The spill-over from the Northern troubles, testing the Garda to the limits of its capacity, heralded the rise of organised crime. In the last year of the previous decade the Garda Commissioner in his annual crime report recorded 147 crimes of 'robbery and assaults with intent to commit robbery,' including 12 cases of robbery with firearms. In 1970 the figures were 215 and 17; the number of robberies increased dramatically year by year to 1979, when 1,020 were recorded, including 228 armed robberies, or 252 when 'aggravated burglaries with firearms' were included. The plague of armed crime continued to rise into the following decade.

The murder of Garda Fallon was followed on 8 June 1972 by the death of the veteran Inspector Samuel Donegan of Cavan, killed by a booby-trap bomb left on the roadside at Drumboghanagh on the Cavan-Fermanagh border.

On 11 September 1975 another name was added to the roll of honour. Garda Michael Reynolds of Clontarf, Dublin, was on night duty. In the afternoon, with his wife and young daughter, he left his home in Artane on a shopping expedition. At about the same time the Bank of Ireland in Killester was raided by armed criminals. Garda Reynolds was passing the shopping centre in Killester when a car with four occupants drove out in front of him and sped off. Believing that the car might have been stolen, Reynolds set off in pursuit, blaring his horn. The chase through the north city suburbs ended on foot in St Anne's Park. Leaving his wife and child in the car, Reynolds overtook his quarry. Tackling one of the gang, he was shot by an accomplice. The former builder's labourer from County Galway, aged thirty, died later in hospital and, like Fallon, was posthumously awarded the gold Scott Medal for valour. Once again bereaved members of the Garda Síochána packed the Passionist church at Mount Argus. They marched to the limits of the city on the first leg of the journey to Garda Reynolds's native Ballinasloe, where Edmund Garvey, barely a week in office, walked behind the coffin. 'He was one of the finest men we had,' the new Commissioner told the *Irish Times*. 'He showed great courage in anything he did, and nothing would deter him from his duty. In following the killers he showed a complete disregard for his own safety.'

It was inevitable that the renewed violence would provoke criticism of the unarmed posture of the force. Speaking both for his own representative body and for the force generally, John Marrinan silenced the critics. 'Essentially we are an unarmed force and I think that the public outrage which will follow the killing of this officer will be protection for our members in the future.'[9]

But the list of martyrs continued to grow: Garda Michael Clerkin, aged twenty-four, from County Monaghan, stationed at Portarlington, killed in a booby-trap bomb at Garryhinch, Portarlington, on 16 October 1976; in the following decade Garda John Morley, aged thirty-eight, and Garda Henry Byrne, aged twenty-nine, both from Knock, County Mayo, and stationed at Castlerea, shot in pursuit of armed bank-robbers at Aghaderry, County Roscommon, on 7 July 1980; and Garda James Quaid, aged forty-three, from County Limerick, stationed at Wexford, shot while attempting to make an arrest at Ballyconnick, County Wexford, on 13 October 1980.

On 20 February 1982 Garda Patrick Reynolds, aged twenty-four, from Boyle, stationed at Tallaght, Dublin, was in a party of guards surrounding suspected premises when he was shot dead; on 11 April 1983 Sergeant Patrick McLoughlin, aged forty-two, from Mullingar, stationed at Dunboyne, County Meath, was shot dead answering a night call at his home; on 10 August 1984 Garda Francis Hand, aged twenty-seven, from County Roscommon, stationed at Dublin Castle, escorting a mail van at Drumcree, County Meath, was ambushed and shot dead; on 27 June 1985 Sergeant Patrick Morrissey, aged forty-nine, from County Cavan, stationed at Collon, County Louth, was shot dead in pursuit of two armed criminals.

The murder of the British ambassador in July 1976 was followed three years later, in August 1979, by the murder of Lord Mountbatten, a crime that horrified the nation. The following year, on 6 January, in a sinister development, the head of the Forensic Science Laboratory, Dr James Donovan, was seriously injured by a bomb planted in his car. The kidnapping of the Dutch industrialist Tiede Herrema on 3 October 1975 at Monaleen, County Limerick, and the seventeen-day armed siege at the house in Monasterevin where he was held captive, absorbed the energies and creative imagination of the entire force.

The successful conclusion and the arrests in the Herrema case did not deter a new gang of desperate criminals, who seized the supermarket director Donald Tidey at Stocking Lane, Rathfarnham, County Dublin, on 24 November 1983. Twenty-two days later, on 16 December, in the gun battle that accompanied the rescue of the hostage in Derrada Wood, near Ballinamore, County Leitrim, a soldier, Private P. J. Kelly of Athlone, aged thirty-six, and Recruit-Garda Peter Sheehan from County Monaghan, aged twenty-three, were shot dead.

In the face of a crisis of such proportions a robust response was expected. In his autobiography, Garret FitzGerald recalls that the assassination of the British ambassador 'provoked widespread demands for tougher action against the IRA.'[10] The new Commissioner in his day was a tenacious and successful detective. In the response to the spate of violent crime in the nineteen-seventies Garvey became a focus of the demand for action. Officers in all ranks of similar character, personally known to the author, classmates and close colleagues, were equally dedicated and tenacious detectives in their pursuit of criminals; nothing short of a vigorous response to violent crime was demanded by the community at large. Wives and growing families became accustomed to the frequent absence from home of husbands and fathers, taken away when a serious crime was reported, following their quarries night and day until the last scrap of evidence was collected and the culprits arrested. A classmate, Chief Superintendent John Courtney, in his retirement spoke for all his colleagues when he publicly acknowledged the 'tolerance, understanding and support' of his family, without which he could not have carried out his duty effectively.[11]

Courtney epitomised the tenacity and wholehearted dedication of the members of the Serious Crime Squad (unofficially the Murder Squad). 'In my time in charge of the Murder Squad I didn't tolerate slackers or hangers-on. Many couldn't stick the pace and disappeared off the investigation team altogether. I was very happy to get rid of them. Officers who made excuses of going on holidays, or whatever, were dropped. I wanted total commitment.'12

Accusations by unscrupulous criminals of assault during interrogation became commonplace. The mythical Garda 'heavy gang' was a media invention, resulting from the use of the term in a different context by defence counsel, Patrick McEntee SC, in a murder trial in Cork.13 In the Garda Reynolds murder trial one of the accused, having complained of ill-treatment, refused to give evidence under oath. In other cases the alleged victims had no such scruples. Reports in the *Irish Times* of 'Garda brutality' in the interrogation of suspects by a 'heavy gang' were read by a 'distressed' Garret FitzGerald, then Minister for Foreign Affairs. He was approached by 'two responsible members of the Garda Síochána,' who went over Garvey's head to complain of the activities of some of their colleagues. His informants, representative body delegates but not members of the RBG, conceded that 'many of the allegations were false ... concocted by subversives to undermine the Gardaí and in the hope of avoiding conviction for offences of which they were guilty.' FitzGerald's colleague in the Department of Justice, Patrick Cooney, was 'unsympathetic' to the allegations.14 The investigating officers endured the calumnies in disciplined silence. The allegations hurt Chief Superintendent Courtney 'very much, given the effort which I and my colleagues had put into combating crime and helping to preserve the security of the State, often at risk to our lives.'15

The activities of subversive groups taxed the Garda Síochána beyond its resources. To meet the threat to the stability of the state, the Government authorised the employment of the Defence Forces in aid of the civil power 'when it became clear that the Gardaí organised and equipped as they are could not act as a sufficient deterrent to armed elements within the State.'16 To guarantee the supremacy of the civil authority, members of the Garda Síochána always accompanied military parties so called out. Over a quarter of a century the people became accustomed to the sight of convoys of Garda and military vehicles and the appearance of mixed parties of guards and soldiers at check-points.

'A PLAIN, BLUNT MAN'

Against the background of unremitting warfare in the battle against crime, the single-minded Garvey was outraged by the activities of the representative bodies, forever articulating the mood of discontent in the ranks and giving few examples of positive leadership. In a tribute at his retirement function on 30 May 1980 one of his close friends, Assistant Commissioner Daniel Devitt, extolled the virtues of a deeply religious man whose humanity in seeking the rehabilitation of criminals and finding them employment was a by-word in the city. His address in the crowded banquet room in the Burlington Hotel testified to the traditional intense loyalty among the fraternity of the Dublin police.

When the author was stationed in Rathfarnham in the old Dublin-Wicklow Division in the nineteen-fifties he met colleagues living in the sub-district who worked on the other side of the Dodder in the Dublin Metropolitan Division, as it then was. The river formed a kind of frontier: though the same uniform was worn on both sides, attitudes to the job, formed by history and contrasting conditions of service, made the guards on opposite banks almost strangers to each other. If Superintendent Leo Maher, the Dublin-born district officer in Rathfarnham, with his spick-and-span regimental outlook, epitomised the reformed Constabulary tradition, Dan Devitt personified the legacy of the DMP, characterised by a loyalty among comrades that must have been unique in the police forces of Ireland.

Davitt's valedictory speech at the former Commissioner's presentation is a piquant contribution to a controversial period in Garda history. No 'whiz-kid academic,' Garvey was 'a plain, blunt man who ... never had any time for cant or claptrap.' Why was he removed from office? In a strong attack on unnamed enemies, Devitt pulled no punches. 'A prophet, it is said, is not accepted in his own country. Jealousy of his ability, his uprightness and his integrity made lesser men come to the conclusion that he should be removed from office. His ability in all aspects of policing, administrative and operational, was in my view approaching closely to genius. And, as the great Dublin writer Jonathan Swift once said, "When a genius comes on the scene, all the dunces conspire against him."'[17]

TOWARDS A MODERN POLICE FORCE

At the height of the agitation in the nineteen-seventies for early implementation of the Conroy Report, the Commissioner's personal assistant, Chief Superintendent John McAleenan, reading disturbing newspaper headlines, remarked that the Garda Síochána was a great organisation, well founded and administered with justice; otherwise it would not have been possible to withstand the upheavals within and the blows struck by its enemies in the community. They really should have been on their knees, but, bad as the situation was, battered and bruised, they would pull through.[18] The force survived the crisis because, in the opinion of a well-informed observer, Mr Justice Hugh O'Flaherty, 'the Garda Síochána occupy a special place in Irish life and culture as well as in the affection of the people. The force, like our language, is part of what we are.'[19]

The Serious Crime Squad was revitalised in the nineteen-sixties by Chief Superintendent (afterwards Commissioner) Patrick McLaughlin, who 'recruited the best and brightest to that squad' and established 'standards of expertise and efficiency to rival any force in the world.' McLaughlin brought 'high ethical standards' to his work; and John Courtney was moulded in the same good tradition.[20] Courtney and his colleagues achieved a success rate in crimes solved of 'over 90% ... higher than any other police force in the world.'[21]

The foundations were laid in the establishment and development of the

Technical Bureau from modest beginnings. In 1903 Sergeant William Henry of the RIC and a DMP constable were sent to Scotland Yard for training in the new science of fingerprints. On their return to Dublin they were employed by the General Prisons Board to establish fingerprint records in the old Habitual Criminals Registry. Henry was in charge of the registry when the Board was dissolved; he was one of the administrative staff absorbed into the Department of Justice in 1928, when the registry was transferred to Garda headquarters.

The records of the Habitual Criminals Registry were not intended for crime investigation purposes. To meet police needs, single-fingerprint bureaus had recently been established in each of the prison areas. In the prisons, fingerprints were taken in duplicate; the ten prints in the second set were cut out and classified separately. The local bureaus were merged in a new office at Garda headquarters, and members of the force were trained in the arts of fingerprint comparison, presumably by Henry. The central registry became the nucleus of the Technical Bureau.

In 1931 the Commissioner invited suggestions from members of the force for the improvement of any phase of police work.[22] A young detective-sergeant, George Lawlor, stationed in Galway, contributed a progressive essay based on private study of crime detection methods practised abroad.[23] His ideas on the training of selected guards in the practical application of these skills prompted the establishment of a specialist unit under Chief Superintendent Garrett Brennan. As a key man, Lawlor was recalled from Galway. Brennan recruited a ballistics expert, Commandant Daniel Stapleton of the Army Ordnance Corps, who was appointed to the force in the rank of superintendent.

Stapleton won international recognition for the Technical Bureau with pioneering work in forensic science. He discovered that the fracture patterns in broken glass made it possible for mere fragments to be matched and presented as evidence in court. When wartime scarcities and restrictions on public transport resulted in an epidemic of bicycle thefts, the manufacturer's frame number was the only means of identifying a rebuilt bicycle. With the number filed off, it seemed that detection was impossible, until Stapleton found a means of bringing up the number and retaining it for the time necessary for a photograph to be taken.

The investigation of the notorious Nurse Mamie Cadden abortion case in 1956, in which a young woman died, was a field day for the forensic scientist. The suspect's flat in Hume Street, Dublin, and the street outside were fine-combed for evidential dust, fibres, blood stains, and human and animal hair. It might be said that the Technical Bureau came of age in the successful prosecution of the Nurse Cadden case. Requests for details came from Scotland Yard, from the Sûreté in Paris, and from police forces as far afield as India and America.[24]

In the early sixties a visionary Chief Superintendent McLaughlin sought expansion of the Technical Bureau to provide a forensic science service; but it was not until 1972, under pressure of the unfolding tragedy in Northern Ireland and its knock-on effects in the whole country, that his voice was heard. His ideas were referred for investigation by the National Science Council. In 1975 Dr James Donovan was appointed to head a new National Forensic Science Laboratory, which has grown over the years into an institution employing some fifty scientists and laboratory technicians. Under the leadership of Dr Donovan, a founder-member of the European Forensic Science Institute, papers by members of his staff are published from time to time in international scientific journals. The vital importance of the work carried out by the laboratory was immediately recognised by organised criminals, resulting in the attack on its director.[25]

But successful as a police force may be in clearing up crime, often perceived as the more romantic side of police work, the employment of detectives was historically regarded as an indication of failure in its preventive role. The innovation of a Criminal Investigation Department came in England in 1842, thirteen years after the foundation of the London Metropolitan Police. At the direction of the Home Office, a cadre of two inspectors and six sergeants was put into plain clothes to specialise in crime detection. They were to grow in numbers over the years into the great establishment known to the world as Scotland Yard. The first Commissioners, Charles Rowan and Richard Mayne, 'disliked detection on principle, and only yielded to its adoption on what they deemed superior authority.'[26]

In his *Handbook of General Instructions,* Rowan was at pains to impress on the minds of the new constables the 'great end' of his new departure.

> It is to be understood, at the outset, that the principal object to be attained is the Prevention of Crime. To this great end every effort of the Police is to be directed. The security of person and property, the preservation of the public tranquillity, and all the other objects of a Police Establishment, will thus be better effected, than by the detection and punishment of the offender, after he has committed the crime. This should constantly be kept in mind by every member of the Police Force, as a guide for his own conduct. Officers and Police Constables should endeavour to distinguish themselves by such vigilance and activity, as may render it extremely difficult for any one to commit a crime within that portion of the town under their charge.[27]

It would obviously be impracticable to commit the immense resources in manpower necessary to investigate to a conclusion every one of the less serious crimes against property—already an economic 'black hole'—taking account of the increase in the prisons vote, without weighing at all the incalculable social loss in going down that road. It seems that society has grown to tolerate its losses, cushioned by householder insurance policies. Garvey believed that 'even though we are law-abiding in Ireland we are not very security-conscious.'[28] His observation might be read as an endorsement of successful crime prevention policies in the past, when a society grown accustomed to the ways of peace could rest safely with its doors on the latch day and night.

The fear of detection and imprisonment is a strong deterrent for all but the most hardened criminals, for whom the thrill of competition with the law can be a way of life. By the same token, recidivists driven by the scourge of the drug lust are indifferent to the consequences of a life of crime. For the law-abiding population the very existence of the police force serves the preventive principle, but not beyond the point where the police become conspicuous by their absence on regular beats and patrols. Occasional sightings of police only confirm the problem in the public mind; and when the uniform and not the individual wearing it becomes the point of reference, there is a real danger of a breakdown in confidence.

The introduction of Neighbourhood Watch in the nineteen-eighties was a timely response to the crisis. Essentially an exercise in promoting Garvey's security consciousness in the community, the scheme is 'designed to encourage the community to become involved in the prevention of crime … in close liaison with the Garda Síochána.'[29] But the professional police content in the programme—1 per cent of total Garda time, according to an official survey[30]—is barely sufficient to meet the wider need of crime prevention. The sub-district of Dundrum in the south Dublin suburbs, with a population approaching fifty thousand, is divided into six areas, with a guard in each area assigned to community relations duties. The guard facilitates his street co-ordinators, keeps in touch with residents' organisations and social clubs, and generally makes himself known in his area. At one guard to eight thousand people in an urban area, the police presence is thin on the ground when the remainder of the station party are employed on indoor duties, on a fixed-point protection post, and on motorised patrols.

The restoration of foot patrols is essentially a matter of political will. An honoured place in social history awaits the Minister for Justice who can succeed in modifying trade unionism and in rekindling vocational motivation in the police service. The cost of a grand programme of crime prevention would be recouped in the closing of prisons and in a healthier society. The effectiveness of the preventive response is amply demonstrated whenever, following a spate of serious crime, public outcry compels the authorities to deploy uniformed guards in sufficient numbers to operate cordons and patrol the area affected, but only until the particular crisis has passed.

Matching the experience of police managers the world over, having to contend with cuts in resources when, 'curiously enough,' Neighbourhood Watch 'is successful in preventing crime, this itself may cause residents to be less interested' in the commitment to civic responsibility.

RESEARCH AND PLANNING
In his submission to the Conroy Commission, the Commissioner, supported by the representative bodies, brought up the idea of a Research and Planning Unit at Garda headquarters.[31] Great things were expected of this forward-looking proposal for a

full-time unit dedicated to the study of police methods, including modern communication facilities. The new unit would be staffed by Garda officers 'and by civilians trained in technical and management techniques.'[32] Anticipating Conroy, Commissioner Wymes in the summer of 1969 appointed Chief Superintendent John McAleenan to head the unit. An application was made for the appointment of a systems analyst and an expert in communication technology. The systems analyst arrived, but instead of the communications expert Wymes had asked for, the Department of Justice attached to the Commissioner's office a civil servant who presented his credentials as an expert in administration. If it was not a studied insult, the civil servants were at least insensitive to men of McAleenan's experience. The new arrival was ignored by the Garda officers.

McAleenan and his colleagues applied themselves to the preparation of a submission on a national radio system, urging an initial study of systems already surveyed and installed by state agencies and commercial interests. The project was considerably delayed when the Department of Justice invited the Department of Posts and Telegraphs to become involved. After months of experimental field work, the P&T technicians withdrew. A decade later, Professor John Scanlan's Radio Advisory Committee[33] installed a nationwide communications and command and control system of the latest type, with a modern technicians' workshop, at a cost of over £30 million.

The security crises precipitated by the Northern troubles were showing no sign of abating. When it seemed that the radio project, vital for the police service, might run out of steam for want of money, Deputy Commissioner E. J. Doherty protested that the cost was not the main criterion: the Government had to consider that the consequences of not having an adequate communications network could well be the death of another guard.

Relying on its own resources, the Research and Planning Unit launched ambitious plans to computerise administrative and forensic science records, and among other projects devised schemes for rural policing, adopted in the eighties, and for regionalisation of the management structure, long delayed but eventually introduced in the following decade. Members of the unit were assigned to organisation and methods duties, to the codification of Garda regulations, revision of the Garda Guide, and the production of a criminal investigation manual.

In his role as organisation and methods officer, the author recommended the creation of a Garda Archive, to preserve the Commissioner's official papers, then in danger of destruction because of the pressing need at the time for office space. The proposal was accepted by Commissioner Patrick Malone, and the author was assigned to the project. The Garda Museum, an ambition of long standing, was realised when the prime mover, Assistant Commissioner Seán Sheehan, was appointed in 1974 to head Research and Planning and added the museum to the author's remit.

The unit was still finding its feet when the Irish Independent in the same year reported 'a major management survey' of the Garda Síochána, to be undertaken by a firm of consultants. The Garda was 'taking the opportunity to press for a study [of] the relationship between them and the Department of Justice,' recommended by Conroy. With manpower stretched to the limit because of border duty, increasing crime problems in urban areas, and the need for guarding important buildings and installations, 'the use of the latest and tightest managerial systems [was] vital.'[34]

The dust had not settled on Urwick Orr when the Department of Justice resurrected the idea of an inquiry by consultants as the best way to meet pressure from the representative bodies for resolution of the dichotomy in the relationship between the department and the Garda Síochána detected by Conroy.

The commission had been inhibited by its terms of reference from looking at factors beyond pay and conditions of service influencing morale.[35] They would have failed in their duty did they not 'strongly urge that an examination be carried out by appropriately qualified people into the role, organisation, and personnel policy of the Force and, in particular, its relationship with the Department of Justice.'[36] To tease out the conflicts in traditional relationships, the Commissioner was happy to accept the good offices of the proposed consultants—but not as arbiters of the role of the Garda Síochána in society. The 'appropriately qualified people' selected by the Commissioner from the most experienced Garda officers were already at work in the Research and Planning Unit. It was unthinkable that any member of the Garda Síochána would be invited to investigate the organisation and personnel policy of another Government department, over the heads of civil servants.

In the event, a firm of management consultants, Stokes Kennedy Crowley, was employed to carry out a survey of the force. Unlike Urwick Orr in the fifties, SKC formed an amicable working relationship with the Garda personnel in Research and Planning. The consultants engaged in much serious talk of mathematical formulas for the measurement of police work, based on experience in other countries and the consultants' own studies. Computer programs would determine the value of a guard in economic terms by reference to crimes and offences committed and other incidents dealt with in the course of beats and patrols. There was intense discussion also of response times, of the time it took for guards to answer calls for assistance. There were few governments in the world that had not engaged in this pointless exercise—pointless because the premise was invalid. Police cost-effectiveness can be understood only in the context of the first principle of crime prevention. It is a paradox for Garda management that historically, success in its primary role was self-defeating, leading to station closures and other economies.

In the matter of deployment of personnel, the consultants offered one useful formula: it took five guards to man any given post over a period of twenty-four hours in the operation of a forty-hour week.

To conclude its investigations, SKC invited a senior civil servant and Garda members of the Research and Planning Unit to accompany its experts on a tour of police establishments abroad. In one working week of five days, the consultants swept through police headquarters in the Netherlands, Norway, Sweden, and Denmark. The *Garda Review* five years later was not impressed. At a cost of 'no less than a quarter of a million pounds,' highly qualified consultants were employed to examine how the force was being managed, but their report had not yet seen the light of day.[37]

15

A Memorandum of Understanding

What's a policeman worth?

In October 1978 lines were being drawn again on old battlefields. With a new national wage agreement in prospect, the Government expressed alarm at the way the previous agreement had been used by many interests to extract additional benefits, to the detriment of the common good.[1] Claims for substantial pay increases had been lodged by the four Garda representative associations, supported by newspaper reports of a proposed ban on overtime.

On 6 October, as the Government discussed the renewed threat to Garda discipline, the new Commissioner, Patrick McLaughlin,[2] received John Marrinan and his colleagues in an attempt to resolve the crisis. Following an unsuccessful meeting, the Garda Representative Association formed a steering committee to investigate options for industrial action. The *Irish Times* posed the question: 'What's a policeman worth?' The Government was in a dilemma. If it breached the national pay agreement it risked demands for parity from other groups; standing firm and offering nothing, there was a greater risk of a serious confrontation with the guards themselves. The inconsistency of special pay in a police force had come to haunt the body politic. 'The guards did very well when they were 6,000 strong and there was a lot of overtime for those who wanted it. Now they are 9,000 strong and the overtime has all but dried up.'[3]

A recommendation by the arbitration board in December 1974 that overtime be paid to senior officers was the kernel of a long-drawn-out dispute with the Superintendents' Association. The extraordinary proposal to downgrade functional status in the senior ranks inherent in changing the basic principle of inclusive pay was rejected by the superintendents. As the official side dourly held the line on the principles of the scheme for conciliation and arbitration, the association in May 1978 began proceedings in the High Court claiming infringement of their constitutional rights. A proposal by the Government to refer the dispute to the

Devlin Committee was also rejected, the association citing Devlin's function: the adjudication of claims by senior civil servants and others who were excluded from conciliation and arbitration.[4]

Following a Government meeting on 17 October, the Minister for Justice, Gerard Collins, met the officers of the four associations, representing all ranks up to chief superintendent. With the offer of a new, broadly based inquiry on the table, the stalemate with the officers ended and the threat of industrial action by the lower ranks was called off. In November, Dr Louden Ryan, professor of political economy at Trinity College, Dublin, was appointed to head a review committee.[5]

The inclusion in Ryan's terms of reference of the possibility of a Garda cadet system put the representative bodies on their guard. The force favoured instead higher entry standards, linked to a system of accelerated promotion.[6] McLaughlin had recently announced plans for the creation of a Garda College, 'an institution to teach police science, management and various related disciplines at third level … the police equivalent of the Military College at the Curragh.'[7]

The Ryan Report was published in May, favouring guards with long service, who were awarded the lion's share. Angry headlines were made, again by the younger members, who found that their pay had been increased by a token award. They were not appeased by an unprecedented trebling of the rent allowance.[8] There was no public sympathy for any form of protest. The Ryan Report had offered the force a very fair deal; if it was rejected it would be 'a poor reflection on their own judgement and sense of reality.'[9] Ryan's concern for the welfare of the experienced guard without prospects of advancement also had an impact on the pay of the supervisory ranks, who were incensed: Ryan had 'insulted the intelligence and responsibility of the Garda Sergeant.'[10]

The report acknowledged that disparities in earnings between members of the same rank arising from unsocial hours and overtime payments had created serious problems for the management. It was 'difficult if not impossible' to employ personnel 'to maximum efficiency … The tendency towards fragmented and sectional interest' was 'endangering the ethos of the Force and weakening its cohesion.'[11]

The lower ranks felt that their views on the more effective deployment of the force were not valued, their officers standing on the long-discredited view that the rank and file 'should not concern themselves with matters relating to overall efficiency.' To counteract such perceptions, Ryan recommended the reconstitution of Conroy's moribund Joint Consultative Council with an independent chairman.[12] In its deliberations the force would be able to 'achieve more fully the primary objective of the vast majority of its members—to be good policemen.'[13]

PRIMARY LEADERSHIP ERODED
The vacuum in the exercise of authority in the nineteen-sixties left ordinary guards floundering—men and women of good will with the best interests of their

profession at heart. The decade of the eighties was heralded in a blunt editorial in the *Garda Review,* prompted by a recommendation in the Ryan Report on recruit selection procedures. It regretted a loss of the sense of vocation in Ryan's new affluent society. In the recent past the force could pick and choose candidates from among school-leavers; if they were still getting many fine recruits, it was no thanks to the old selection system. The Garda were getting some 'sorry base characters', rejects from organisations whose standards had been lifted higher with the rising educational profile in the community, young men 'whose personal lives were in such a mess' that a well-paid and secure place in the Garda Síochána was seen as 'a refuge from their problems.' They were getting, frankly, young men who would 'not be had anywhere else.' The selection system was unable to catch unsuitable candidates when they turned up at their local Garda station 'possessed of the right physical requirements and a certain basic level of education.'[14]

The renewed offensive reflected views already expressed by the *Garda Review* in the period before the Ryan Report, albeit in language described by Collins in the Dáil on 28 February as 'unfortunate'.[15] The editorial had confused two quite distinct matters: character or personality defects and educational attainments. In the view of the Commissioner, on his own judgment the modern recruits were as good as their predecessors; 'in all probability' they were better. The great majority of recruits had the Leaving Certificate; of those who had not, 'every single one' had successfully competed against applicants with the Leaving Certificate. Moreover, three hundred candidates with the Leaving Certificate had failed in the last examination.[16] But 'there was never any question about that': the minister was asked simply to agree that a higher standard of education was essential.[17]

The new demand for higher educational qualifications seriously challenged the 'qualities of a policeman' defined by the Conroy Report. Examination results were no guide to that courage and honesty, no yardstick of that 'great sense of personal responsibility'[18] in Conroy's definition. In a unique occupation, these and other qualities of adaptability and common sense were more vital attributes of a good policeman than academic success.

The guard without higher educational certificates was not on that account less endowed with inborn intelligence, nor lacking in practical ability: he was probably more experienced in the ways of the world and of greater value as a peace officer. It was not among people of that high calibre that the so-called rejects of other organisations were found in the Garda Síochána. Some candidates more highly qualified than the job required might have felt cheated having to work side by side for the same wages with less privileged colleagues. The demand for higher entry standards was more part of a strategy for improving pay and conditions than a real commitment to raising the professional standing of the force. In an earlier age, when clerical jobs in the public service, the ESB and other state industries were highly prized by a burgeoning middle class, the pursuit of equality in educational standards was forced on Garda representatives. Levels of formal education offered a convenient measure in pay negotiations, until the Quinn Tribunal defined the principle of the rate for the job.

The erosion of leadership in the front line of operations was the most pressing problem for the Garda management. As the pioneer in industrial research George Elton Mayo discovered in the Hawthorne experiments,[19] when cohesion was lost in the primary group—in the Garda Síochána, the sergeant and his party of guards— morale suffered in the organisation as a whole. The supervision of work was diminished when the primary leader identified too closely with the people in his group and lost caste as a result. The gap in the chain of command must have called into question the quality of reports arriving on the Commissioner's desk from the work-place. That was more likely to have been the real cause of instability in the Garda Síochána during the years of transition in mid-century.

In a confused response to the crisis, demands were made for increased manpower and more resources in the form of modern technology. In Britain it was forecast that the police would have to contend with technological change similar to the revolution that had overtaken coal-miners, dockers, and railwaymen; but the police were spending a small fraction of their budget on research and development compared with the commitment by the armed services.[20] It was plainly ridiculous to make comparisons of that kind between industry and, for that matter, the war machine, drawing its very life-blood from technological advance, and a service concerned primarily with people and the frailties of human nature.

It was not that the police could survive without the benefits of modern science; but society had to be wary that demands for more technology did not obscure the real issues, including the critical problem of alienation, which occurred when the supervision of work collapsed, local knowledge deteriorated, and the police tended to become isolated in the community. An even greater problem within the Garda Síochána was the loss of identity with its own historical psyche, which began with the emergence of trade unionism in the sixties.

The radicalism inherent in the trade union movement can have no place in the uniquely disciplined institution of the police service, distinguished as it must be by an essential conservatism. But society was reluctant to pay the price of removing the police service from the market. That price included vastly improved pay and conditions of service, guaranteed by an agreed formula to ensure that policemen, on account of their discipline, were not left behind in the general scramble for more money.

Historically, when discontent in the ranks boiled over, the roots could always be found among the city police, whose arduous working conditions contrasted sharply with service in rural districts. There was no respite for the Dublin bobby working the old three-relief system, with its unremitting duty demands and disruption of domestic life: working until ten at night, rising at five the following morning every other day for the early shift at six, with night duty one month in three. The public office in a city station resembled a military command post in wartime, with people getting forms signed, reporting lost or stolen property, or making complaints of various kinds, while prisoners, drunk and sober, were being brought in, distracting the station house officer and his assistants.

Complaints against guards for discourtesy are an occupational hazard in any city. In the sixties, when discipline was undermined by the Macushla Ballroom affair, there was an upsurge in such reports as unwary guards in increasing numbers responded unwisely to taunts, adding to the normal pressures of police duty.[21]

The predictability of the duty roster suited most of the guards in the metropolitan division. In rural districts the day's work was usually broken into two tours of duty, the patrolmen making their leisurely way on foot or cycling on country roads, well known to their neighbours who lived in isolated houses along the way. Occasionally, once or twice a month, patrols went out after midnight, when, hopefully, a neighbour, abroad in the small hours about his lawful business, would spread the news that the guards were on the prowl, reassuring the people. The exigencies of service were well served by a system that allowed routine duties to be performed as required.

In the spring and autumn, agricultural statistics were collected; in the evenings the guards were made welcome at card games in some houses, which kept a station party in close touch with the people. The social dimension in the role of a village policeman was attractive to guards who were predisposed to a quiet life. In most stations, sergeants arranged patrol times to suit men who might wish to accompany their wives and families on shopping expeditions in the provincial towns or when they needed the daylight hours to till their gardens or to cut turf for the winter fuel supply.

A way of life that had survived from the nineteenth century disappeared after the Conroy Report, with the introduction of the wholly unnecessary three-relief system. New conditions, including the increased mobility of travelling criminals, aided by modern communications, made change inevitable, but not to the extent brought about by the clamour in the metropolis. In country districts there was no demand for special allowances. The crisis in Dublin could have been avoided if the representative bodies, instead of seeking to break down basic pay, had presented to Conroy a claim for a special Dublin allowance, in acknowledgment of the arduous working conditions in the city. Such an allowance, similar to the London allowance, had been claimed, year in year out, since the amalgamation of the two police forces in 1925 but equally consistently had been turned down.[22]

A MEMORANDUM OF UNDERSTANDING

Against the backdrop of the conflict with Commissioner Garvey, the representative bodies sought a means of shaking off the shackles of discipline they believed had led to the crisis in the force in the sixties and had inhibited their activities in the recent past. At the time, they were discussing with the Department of Justice amendment of the statutory regulations to replace the representative bodies with new staff associations. Alongside these deliberations they negotiated an informal 'memorandum of understanding', which defined the role and status of delegates as having a responsibility, with the Garda management, in solving personnel problems at the local and national level.

The memorandum conceded that elected representatives should be 'immune from the Garda disciplinary code.' It was agreed that legal difficulties would make it difficult to insert such a provision in the regulations, 'which in any event would be incompatible with the status of a representative as a member of the Force.' It was acknowledged that a delegate, to be effective, must be given the latitude to speak his mind openly. Provided he did not exceed 'bona fide representative body duty or act in a way seriously incompatible with his duty as a member of the Force,' his work as a representative body spokesman would not make him liable to disciplinary action.[23]

Disciplinary proceedings if begun would not be maintained without the consent of the Minister for Justice. But this seriously undermined the authority of the head of the force, who had the statutory duty of maintaining discipline. Moreover, while the memorandum was being negotiated over his head, the Commissioner depended on civil servants, who had no direct responsibility, to protect his interests. The resulting contradiction between the new freedom for some guards to buck the system and their membership of the Garda Síochána was bound to send the wrong signals down the ranks. The concession was abused when representative body officers strayed from their brief to make public pronouncements on the political issues of the day.

In the post-war years, policemen allowed themselves to be demoralised by the pressures of social change, putting at risk their unique professional integrity; their leaders participated in debates with agendas set by sociologists, penologists, and others. Drawn into debate on matters belonging to other disciplines, the Garda appeared to have no authentic voice of its own, and the vital contribution it had to make was lost by default. Politicians who were most in need of instruction heard only distorted views on the essential role of the police.

The supervisory middle ranks would go so far down the road of response to crime after the event as to speak with satisfaction of 'success' in filling prisons as a valuable contribution by the Garda Síochána to the solution of the problem,[24] without apparently realising that the new stance began to identify the modern guard with the Bow Street Runners, the 'thief-takers' of the eighteenth century.[25]

In the nineteen-fifties, police methods were becoming more sophisticated. Yet the first principle, that of visibility—unarmed police in uniform working closely with the community, not isolated in stations or cruising in patrol cars or dashing like fire brigades to the scene of crimes after the event—continued to be the bedrock of successful law-and-order policies. A quarter of a century later, the new generation of guards had become so radicalised as to be willing to compromise their inheritance. The pressures on the force in the troubled seventies were not greater than had been endured by the new police in the decade of the Civil War. When guards in Dublin were held at gunpoint by armed criminals, the *Garda Review* questioned whether the unarmed policeman was any longer 'a practical ideal': 'We do not want to become an armed force, but a state of affairs now exists which may well modify our attitude. We are no less committed to the ideal of an unarmed Garda Síochána, but a state of affairs may now be upon us where some additional recourse to arms may be the lesser of two evils.'

Rejecting any role for the army in crime prevention, the journal advocated armed Garda flying squads. Crime was a job for the guards. 'If we need guns ... then we may have to have them. And if some of us are to be issued with guns ... let them be the right kind, and let us be adequately trained in their use.'[26]

The *Irish Independent* reported anger in the force at the growing number of incidents in which members of the force had been held at gunpoint, and painted a grim picture of armed guards as 'fearless crime-fighters on our streets.'[27] The *Irish Times* responded cautiously. The people had 'rightly regarded the unarmed garda as a symbol of their good citizenship.' The suggestion of a limited armed response to serious crime seemed a sensible one, yet

> it could have symbolic significance in a community which has always had to work hard to keep the gun out of politics and public life. It might well be, when the passage of years allows an overview of today's events, that arming even a section of the gardaí could be seen as playing straight into the hands of the gunman. Maybe it is not right to try to fight fire with fire, so to speak. Maybe the people should simply accept the losses and stick by their principles ...[28]

The general secretary of the Association of Garda Sergeants and Inspectors, Sergeant Derek Nally, agreed it was 'facile' to suggest that arming the Garda would of itself reduce the incidence of serious crime. He called for 'new laws on evidence, more money and manpower.' Collins opposed 'arming the force as a whole,' but he 'could not tolerate gardaí being pushed around by armed youngsters.'[29]

There the matter was allowed to rest until, two years later, an innocent bystander was shot in a gun battle. A gang of four armed criminals raided a public house in Grand Canal Street, Dublin, and made off in a Post Office van, with a Garda patrol car in pursuit. The gang was intercepted by detectives at Merrion Gates, where shots were exchanged. David Smith, an insurance clerk from Sallynoggin, standing at a bus stop, was caught in the crossfire. Realising the danger, he was shouting, 'I'm only waiting for a bus!' when he was hit. The incident reverberated in the *Irish Times,* the emphasis shifting away from the editor's former advice to the community to 'accept the losses and stick by ... principles.' The preservation of the unarmed ideal had been 'one of the successes of our independence'; but the Garda was finding that it was

> no longer possible to maintain the ideal in its purest form ... The public therefore

must accept the fact that some gardaí will be armed and will be mandated to use those arms for the foreseeable future.

If there are any doubts about the circumstances in which the gardaí may fire they should be cleared up now—and it does appear that there is some confusion on this issue. The general public and indeed the gardaí themselves are entitled to know precisely what to expect if they find themselves involved in situations in which firearms are used. The shooting of Mr David Smith was a terrible and costly mistake. It is fortunate that his condition now appears to be improving somewhat. But there must be no repetition of such accidents. They are preventable.[30]

The author, as a serving member of the force then researching Garda history in his employment as archivist, felt compelled to write to the editor in defence of the ideal. Accidents in the use of firearms were *not* preventable.

> This was foreseen in 1922 by the first Commissioner, Michael Staines. The rifles and sword bayonets of the RIC had been discarded, but each member of the new police would be armed with a revolver for personal protection. In making arrests 'great restraint' was advised. At the same time, they were 'not to allow authority to be flouted or defied.' When it was necessary to take action, there was to be 'no hesitation or indecision in doing what was necessary ...'

The instructions to the new police were explicit. In every case in which a firearm was used, an inquiry would be held. 'It would be incumbent on the member of the Guard concerned to justify his action, both then and before the ordinary tribunals of the country.' Staines underlined the dilemma for an armed police; his warning was even more relevant in the age of the rapid-firing handgun. Should a fatal accident occur as a result of a change in policy, the member of the Garda Síochána involved, and he alone, would go to the stocks. He might be exonerated in law, the newspapers reporting the cold fact; but outside his own home no-one would know his anguish.

The Defence Forces were recruited, trained and specially disciplined to carry and use arms. The members of the Garda Síochána were not soldiers. What was at stake was the moral authority of government. Staines in 1922 had defined the role of the Civic Guard in terms of the moral authority of an unarmed police; Pope Pius XI, addressing members of the Garda Síochána in Rome in 1928, had redefined principles of moral authority for a police force in a Christian society, 'valid for all time.'[31]

The contradictions in the memorandum of understanding were soon apparent. The author was made the subject of a disciplinary investigation; he escaped on giving an undertaking to seek approval for any future communications to the press.

The murder of Garda Patrick Reynolds on 20 February 1982 drew the fire of the *Sunday Tribune*. 'Are we living in cloud cuckoo land with an unarmed police force? ... It is no argument to claim that the arming of the police would escalate the crime war. This is a war that society—and the Garda Síochána—must win ...'[32] The Association of Garda Sergeants and Inspectors, in its journal, *Horizon,* hit back with a trenchant editorial, 'No guns':

> The frustration felt by members of the force ... was echoed by many civilians who fear that the level of crime is becoming an alarming threat to the stability of society. The most disturbing outcome ... of the death of Garda Reynolds has been the subtle but growing campaign on the part of sections of the force and the media to bring about the general arming of the Garda Síochána ... To encourage the belief that the time has come to 'escalate the war'—for the gardaí to take up arms in order to defeat crime—is not only ludicrous but extremely dangerous ... Arming the Guards is a simplistic and unsatisfactory solution to a highly complex problem. Such a course would create far more problems for the force than it might ever solve. The overwhelming confidence and support of the public for the gardaí might well be placed in jeopardy ...[33]

VERY HIGH POLITICS INDEED

Under the protection of the memorandum of understanding, the Association of Garda Sergeants and Inspectors at its conference in Bantry in 1982 proposed changes in the extradition laws to facilitate the transfer to Britain or Northern Ireland of members of subversive organisations charged with serious crimes[34] and called for a definition of 'political offence' and the amendment of the Criminal Law Jurisdiction Act (1976) to allow joint interrogation of suspects by the Garda and the RUC.[35] The intervention of the AGSI in the national debate left the force as a whole open to legitimate criticism, and this was understood by the general secretary of the GRA, John Marrinan, a fraternal delegate at the conference. Extradition was an 'extremely delicate and sensitive matter,' and he was not 'in the business of politics.'[36]

The *Irish Independent* made the point that in a democracy it was unsatisfactory when the police acted as 'a pressure group for law reform.' Known terrorists, 'some of them murderers of fellow-policemen,' were being 'allowed to roam free ... under protection of the law they violate with impunity'; but while they sympathised with the Garda authorities, there was an alternative. The legislation provided the police forces in both jurisdictions with a formidable weapon to bring subversives to justice, irrespective of whether they were apprehended north or south of the border.[37]

In the opinion of the *Irish Times,* the Government hardly thanked the AGSI for raising the question of extradition 'so sharply' at the conference. 'Some members of the Fianna Fáil party in particular may be a bit uneasy at the strong sense of solidarity with their RUC colleagues ... expressed at the same meeting ... The senior gardaí have moved into very high politics indeed.'[38]

Defending its stand, the AGSI cited the legislation, which defined its role as 'representing members of the Garda Síochána in all matters affecting their welfare and efficiency,'[39] and went on to make a sweeping interpretation of the extent of its responsibility. 'Clearly the associations have a duty ... to do all in their power to further not just the "welfare" but also the "efficiency" of their members. Their remit, therefore, is quite extensive and undoubtedly covers such matters as the reform and administration of the law, the prevention and detection of crime and related matters.'[40] The association conceded that the legislation was not specific on how these objects were to be achieved; but the statutory regulations[41] provided for annual delegate conferences that had 'the right, guaranteed under the Constitution, to freedom of expression.'[42]

Whatever the merits of the case for review of the law on extradition, the intervention in the debate by a serving member of the Garda Síochána added nothing to either the primary welfare or, strictly in that context, efficiency in the force, which are central to the *raison d'être* of the associations.

In 1982 Commissioner McLaughlin, at the GRA conference in Ennis, proposed that the duty roster be redesigned to facilitate the redeployment of guards for beats and patrols at times of peak demand. He was heard 'with some trepidation by delegates who [felt] that tampering with traditional duty patterns could lead to exploitation.'[43]

The concept of the Garda Síochána as whole-time employment had also been lost. In the police service there is a unique temptation to distraction when members engage in other occupations. In 1982 the Labour Party deputy Jim Kemmy complained of double-jobbing in Limerick. The *Garda Review,* relying on the regulations, replied that guards were entitled, like other citizens, to use their spare time in profitable activities 'that do not conflict with their official duties.'[44]

THE EXEMPLARY ROLE OF THE POLICE

The function of the police as guarantors of public order is axiomatic; but in the philosophy of the police their role as exemplars in society is hardly recognised. In the classroom, up to comparatively recent times, little if any time was given to the study of the philosophy behind legal structures already well catered for in training programmes; there was not enough emphasis on the principle of organising well-disciplined citizens in a police service to project objective social behaviour. The exemplary role, defined in a sociological study in England in the nineteen-fifties,[45] emerged in a debate in the Department of Justice in 1960, begun by Charles Haughey, then parliamentary secretary to the Minister for Justice. Haughey described as 'one of the most disquieting features of Irish life' recent widely reported cases of refusal by onlookers to assist guards in difficulties arresting criminals. He suggested a public relations programme to 'popularise' the police.[46]

It appears that no role for the police themselves was envisaged in the minister's programme. A photograph appeared in the *Evening Press* on 6 March 1962 showing the housing officer, Superintendent Edmund Garvey, inspecting the reconstructed Bridewell station in Dublin. Haughey personally telephoned the Commissioner to complain that Garvey 'had allowed himself to be photographed,' adding that he had intended to open the new Bridewell himself. The Commissioner's private secretary, Superintendent John McAleenan, eventually tracked down the housing officer in Athlone. Garvey explained that he had been asked by an official in the Department of Justice to meet the reporter and to facilitate the press photographer.[47]

Responding to the minister's invitation for comments on his PR proposal, the Secretary of the Department of Justice, T. J. Coyne, offered strong views on the behaviour of individual guards as the cause of negative public perceptions of the force. Standards of absolute honesty and truthfulness in giving evidence in court were 'somewhat deficient'; courtesy was lacking, 'particularly amongst older men in Dublin where there is a bad tradition … Appearance and bearing, to say nothing of their general conduct when on or off duty can have a great influence … Respect is increased by the sight of a smart and well-conducted policeman, and proportionately diminished by the spectacle of the slouch, unshaven, dirty, ill-conducted.' It was a matter of training and discipline. There was room for improvement, though Commissioner Costigan was doing all he could to uphold and maintain the highest standards.

This was a damning indictment, a litany of failure in supervision, on the eve of the Macushla Ballroom affair close on forty years ago. It may be taken that the secretary of the Department of Justice was reliably informed.

The matter of deportment is a problem for modern society as a whole. What is tolerable in domestic life becomes a serious problem in the courtroom, where the drama of the law is enacted. The author and his contemporaries in the generation of transition in the nineteen-forties wore their best uniforms and were informally inspected by district officers present in court as prosecutors. While the majority of Garda witnesses in the uniformed force present themselves in an acceptable manner, a minority in need of haircuts or wearing their uniforms indifferently hardly enhance the solemnity of the occasion. Appearing in denims and anorak, a detective-garda might be indistinguishable from defendants in criminal cases; older detectives continue to present the suited, collar-and-tie image that was once *de rigueur.* Concerned senior officers suggested that the fall in standards coincided with the development of the university-style Garda College following the implementation of the Walsh Report on Garda training in the mid-eighties.

The Dublin Metropolitan Charge Court deals with some 3,500 cases a week. In recent memory the same volume of work was processed in months. Remand prisoners are arraigned before the court at the rate of 14,000 a year. In a crime-prone society, the pressures on Garda witnesses are self-evident. Though some older judges tend to be critical of the decline in old-fashioned deportment, in general judges are said to be sympathetic to work-stained Garda witnesses who, day in, day out, contribute to an orderly society, a distinction being made between detectives investigating ordinary crime, who might be expected to make a better effort, and colleagues following the trail of drugs-related and similar crimes, who frequently appear in court with prisoners straight from the scene of searches.

By common consent, standards of deportment and dress markedly improve in the higher courts. But the reality remains that commitment to the exemplary role is most dramatically visible to society in the crowded district courts. Transcending standards in general appearance, deportment is critically judged by the confidence of police witnesses at the solemn moment of attesting to their evidence in court.

Public relations were 'tricky'. The ultra-conservative Coyne warned against 'the cult of the individual ... Police officers should not be seen or heard in the press or on radio any more than necessary.' He was opposed to 'letting the Commissioner address clubs or associations or deliver lectures or get himself photographed doing this or that.' He was 'dead against ... the Commissioner building himself up consciously or unconsciously by publicity.'

When the Joint Representative Body in 1965 proposed the appointment of a Garda public relations officer, Commissioner William Quinn replied that every member of the Garda Síochána was a PRO in his own right. A self-respecting police force had no need of commercial sales techniques: if it failed to live up to high standards there was nothing a public relations officer could do to cover up its deficiencies.[48]

In the closing years of the twentieth century, the new lawlessness spawned by the rising drug culture challenged the international police community to rededicate themselves to the primary objectives of their profession. Police training the world over was underpinned by the fundamental though narrowly expressed concept of their function defined by Rowan and Mayne for the New Police in 1829, institutionalised in the Dublin Metropolitan Police in 1836. Yet the exemplary role was implicit in their vision of crime prevention as the only rational way to an orderly society.[49]

That vision was all but lost in the endless wrangling over conditions of service, as O'Duffy had feared. The father figure in the story of the Garda Síochána, ahead of his time, broke himself on the wheel of his perfectionist nature striving to make the politicians and their administrators see the sense of allowing the rank and file to be part of the process of moulding the service, accepting and living with the inevitable mistakes by academically unqualified policemen as a small price to pay for ensuring the survival of the lodestar of philosophy. O'Duffy instinctively sensed the core values, but half a century would pass before philosophy as distinct from practice was taught in the classroom.

A PHILOSOPHY FOR THE MODERN GARDA

Even as the force celebrated its golden jubilee in 1972 it began to seem that the downturn in its fortunes had made a return to the drawing-board a serious option. Conroy's proposal for an examination of the 'unclear relationship' between the

Garda management and the Department of Justice might have arrested the decline. Against all the odds, successive Commissioners, with considerable skill and avoiding public controversy, rose above the negative influences inherent in the conflict. The Garda Síochána barely survived the crisis of transition precipitated by the departure of the founder-members, who put down the deep roots of enduring tradition inherited by the modern force.

The establishment of the Garda College on the foundations of the old Training Centre was a watershed in the development of the police service. The appointment in 1984 of a highly qualified Garda Training Committee, under Dr Tom Walsh as chairman, was greeted in the *Garda Review* as 'a matter both of surprise and of very deep significance … Neither the GRA nor any of the Associations representing other Garda ranks [were] represented on the committee.'[50]

In 1987 the committee in its Report on Probationer Training defined for the first time a philosophy for the modern garda.[51] The citizen expected police officers

> to have the wisdom of Solomon, the courage of David, the strength of Samson, the patience of Job, the leadership of Moses, the kindness of the Good Samaritan, the strategical training of Alexander, the faith of Daniel, the diplomacy of Lincoln, the tolerance of the carpenter of Nazareth and finally an intimate knowledge of every branch of the natural, biographical and social sciences. If he had all these he might be a good policeman.

An examination of the work carried out by a station party in any one week would demonstrate that this was 'no exaggeration, but a fact …'[52]

It is the role of the Garda Síochána to prevent and detect crimes and offences, to protect life and property and to maintain public peace and good order and to do so without fear, favour, malice, or ill-will. Through statute and common law, society had conferred on individual guards the powers of interception, of search and arrest, that can ultimately lead to depriving a citizen of the precious right of personal liberty. In the exercise of discretionary powers, a great deal of stress is placed on individual guards, who are seen by many people as first interpreters of the law.

'The achievement by the Garda Síochána of such extraordinary objectives … demands innovation and imagination' in the administration of the Garda College and also dedication and motivation on the part of the guards themselves. 'Irish society today is characterised by an increasing population, higher levels of education, higher standards of living and higher expectations among its young people. Simultaneously there is a high level of unemployment and the opportunities to achieve desired goals and status are restricted.'

In an age of moral decline, increasing numbers of young people are turning to drugs or drink and inevitably drifting into criminal behaviour, 'either to avoid facing reality or to have the material things they could not otherwise have. Hence the success of the police [in maintaining] peace and social order … necessitates the development of high professional standards in the Garda Síochána. It will require of gardaí the capacity to know the society they serve, and to understand the communities which make up that society.'[53]

To achieve these aims the Garda Síochána needs a new and different 'memorandum of understanding' to remind the guards themselves of the high ideals expected of them and to afford the people an opportunity to state the positive contribution to Irish society of their own police. As Henry O'Friel declared on the inception of the force in 1922, 'the importance of the Civic Guard in social and economic life cannot be exaggerated.'[54]

As citizen police, servants of the people, the Garda Síochána has lived up to its undertaking to win respect based on moral authority. By their courage in rejecting force of arms and unreasonable numbers in their ranks they gave the first example in the process of taking the gun out of political life, demonstrating in that commitment that the exemplary role of the police in Irish society was no empty philosophical definition. In a rebellious age that the founder-members of the force would not recognise they show vocational respect for legitimate authority in a disciplined force. In their public and private lives, on duty and participating in community and social activities, individual guards continue to give of their best to society in witnessing to ideal law-abiding citizenship. In such a 'memorandum of understanding' lies the guarantee of a contented police force in a peaceful and stable society.

Appendix 1

NOMINAL LISTS

POLICE ORGANISING COMMITTEE
Appointed by Provisional Government; inaugural meeting 9 February 1922, Gresham Hotel, Dublin.
(Sources: Garda Archives, Walsh Papers; National Archives, HA 99/15, HA 235/329, S9048; recollections of P. J. Carroll.)

Brennan, James, RIC, head constable, Headquarters
Brennan, Patrick, TD, Volunteers, Commandant, Co. Clare
Broy, Edward, ex-DMP, sergeant, CID
Foley, J. P., RIC, head constable, Belfast
Galligan, John, RIC, sergeant, Tipperary SR
Harte, Patrick, RIC, sergeant, Roscommon
Kearney, John, RIC, district inspector, Boyle
Kelly, Michael, DMP, inspector, E Division, Donnybrook
Lynch, Martin, Volunteers, Co. Clare
McCarthy, Mathias, RIC, acting-sergeant, Chichester Street, Belfast
McCormack, Michael, RIC, sergeant, Letterkenny
McElligott, Thomas J., ex-RIC, sergeant
McGetrick, Thomas, RIC, district inspector, Howth
Maher, Jeremiah, ex-RIC, sergeant, Naas; Volunteers, Co. Kildare
Neary, Thomas, DMP, constable, A Division, Kevin Street
Prendeville, Edmund, RIC, sergeant, Clonmel
Ring, Michael J., Volunteers, Commandant, Co. Mayo
Riordan, Patrick, RIC, district inspector, Union Quay
Shea, P. (not identified)
Staines, TD, Michael J., Sinn Féin
Walsh, Patrick, RIC, district inspector, Letterkenny

CIVIC GUARD DEPOT
RDS showgrounds, Ballsbridge, Dublin (21 February 1922); Artillery Barracks, Kildare (15 May 1922).

Headquarters officers
Staines, Michael J., TD, Commissioner (president, mess committee)
Walsh, Patrick, Deputy Commissioner
Brennan, Patrick, TD, assistant commissioner
McCarthy, Chief Supt Mathias, barrackmaster
McCormack, Chief Supt Michael, accounting officer
Brennan, Supt James, assistant barrackmaster
Harte, Supt Patrick, assistant accounting officer
Maher, Supt Jeremiah, private secretary
O'Connor, Supt Bernard, receiving and measuring officer

Depot staff
Ring, Chief Supt Michael J., depot commandant (mess committee)
Haugh, Supt Patrick J., adjutant

Company officers and police duty instructors
Burke, Supt Francis
Byrne, Supt John J.
Galligan, Supt John
Hallinan, Supt Daniel
Keane, Supt John
Kelleher, Supt John P.
Liddy, Supt Seán, TD
Lynch, Supt Martin (mess committee)
McCrudden, Chief Insp. Robert
Neary, Supt Thomas
Prendeville, Supt Edmund (mess committee)

KILDARE MUTINY
Committee formed in Ballsbridge, March 1922, to agitate for expulsion of RIC officers (fourteen members, the following identified.)
(Sources: National Archives, HA 235/329; S9048.)

Daly, Thomas P., Cork, president*
Sellars, Patrick (Sonny), secretary (replaced a former RIC constable named Strickland)
Brannigan, Sgt J. J. [82], Galway
Byrne, Sgt John J. [187], Dublin
Collison, Malachy, Tipperary*

Coy, Sgt Patrick [174], Galway
Doyle, Seán, Wicklow*
Hennessy, Sgt M. [15], Limerick
Kilroy, Sgt Thomas [138], Galway
O'Brien, Seán, Tipperary*
O'Halloran
Ryan, E. J.*
*Deserted Civic Guard to join Rory O'Connor in Four Courts.

Officers whose expulsion was demanded by Daly's committee
Brennan, Head Constable James
Kearney, Dist. Insp. John (resigned in Ballsbridge)
Maher, ex-Sgt Jeremiah
O'Connor, Dist. Insp. Bernard
Prendeville, ex-Sgt Edmund
Walsh, Dist. Insp. Patrick

Officers elected by Daly's committee to take over Depot, Kildare
(including Newbridge, occupied by Civic Guard 16 May 1922).
(Sources: National Archives, HA 235/329, Kildare Inquiry; Seán Liddy, An Síothadóir, December 1962.)

Brennan, Assistant Commissioner Patrick, 'Commissioner'
Haugh, Supt Patrick J., 'assistant commissioner'
Liddy, Supt Seán, 'adjutant'
Lynch, Supt Martin, 'commandant'
McCrudden, Chief Insp. Robert, 'chief superintendent'

'Company officers'
Coy, Sgt P. [174], Galway
Cronin, P.
Doyle, Sgt P. [221], Dublin
Kennedy, Sgt M. [346], Tipperary
Kilroy, Sgt T. [138], Galway
Leonard, Sgt D. A. [178], Leitrim
Minogue, Sgt M. [206], Clare
O'Brien, Sgt J. [576] ,Tipperary
O'Neill, A.
Rochford, Sgt J. [97], Clare

Scanlan, Sgt J. J. [697], Clare
Turner, Sgt P. [193], Clare
(In brackets, number in nominal register, Garda Archives.)

Officers who accompanied Commissioner Staines from Kildare to Little Denmark Street, Dublin, 16 May 1922
(Source: National Archives, HA 99/15.)

Brennan, Supt James
Burke, Supt Francis
Byrne, Supt John J.
Galligan, Supt John
Harte, Supt Patrick
Keane, Supt John
McCarthy, Chief Supt Mathias
McCormack, Chief Supt Michael
Maher, Supt Jeremiah
Neary, Supt Thomas
O'Connor, Supt Bernard
Prendeville, Supt Edmund
Ring, Chief Supt Michael J.
Walsh, Deputy Commissioner Patrick

Supt Daniel Hallinan, Supt P. (John J.?) Kelleher and Supt George O'Dwyer remained on duty in Kildare and Newbridge.

OFFICERS ALLOCATED TO DIVISIONS
(Source: UCD Archives, RM, P7b/293, memo from O'Duffy to Department of Home Affairs, no date, *c.* 1 November 1922, compiled apparently before lists published in *Thom's Directory,* 1923.)

Chief superintendents
Cullen, Edward, Union Quay, Cork
McManus, Seán B., Letterkenny
Maher, Jeremiah, Naas

Superintendents (as divisional officers)
Brennan, James, Waterford
Burke, Francis, Drogheda
Clinton, Patrick, Thurles

Direen, Thomas, Limerick
Hallinan, Daniel, Wicklow
Hannigan, James, Tralee
Haugh, Patrick, Wexford
Keegan, Hugh, Galway
Liddy, Seán, Birr
Lynch, Martin, Kilkenny
Muldoon, Richard, Sligo
O'Duffy, Éamonn, Bandon
O'Dwyer, George, Ennis
O'Mara, Henry, Castlebar
O'Neill, Alex., Mullingar
Robinson, Thomas, Roscommon
Walsh, Nicholas, Howth

Acting superintendent (acting divisional officer)
Murphy, Jeremiah, Monaghan

CIVIC GUARD LISTS
(Source: *Thom's Directory*, 1923.)

Kevin O'Higgins TD, Minister for Home Affairs
P. McGilligan MA BL, private secretary
H. J. Friel (Ó Frighil) BA, Secretary
P. Sheehan, assistant secretary (establishment not formed)

Garda Síochána
(Expected strength: 4,500; enrolled: about half that number)

O'Duffy, Gen. Eoin, Commissioner
Coogan, Edward, Deputy Commissioner
McCarthy, Chief Supt Mathias, commandant
Ellis, Dr E. V., surgeon
Brennan, Supt James, barrackmaster

The following lists, rearranged alphabetically (with necessary corrections in parentheses), were probably made *c.* November 1922, during the period of transition between temporary depots, hence the numbers of superintendents and inspectors listed as stationed at Kildare, Ship Street, and Collinstown. The RIC depot, Phoenix Park, was taken over by the Civic Guard on 17 December 1922 but apparently not occupied until 1 January 1923.

Superintendents
Brennan, Garrett, Waterford
Burke, Francis, Drogheda
Clinton, Patrick J., Collinstown, Co. Dublin
Cullen, Edward P., Cork (chief superintendent)
Direen, Thomas, Limerick
Galligan, John, Ship Street, Dublin
Hallinan, Daniel, Naas
Harrington, J. (John H.), Tralee
Harte, Patrick J., Finance (Headquarters)
Haugh, Patrick J., Wexford
Keane, John, Monaghan
Keegan, Hugh (Hugh J.), Galway
Kelleher, John (John J.), Wicklow (chief superintendent)
Liddy, Seán, Birr (temporary)
Lynch, Martin, Kilkenny
McManus, S. B. (Seán), Letterkenny (chief superintendent)
Maher, Jeremiah, Ship Street, Dublin (chief superintendent)
Neary, Thomas, Sligo
O'Connor, Bernard, Recruiting (Headquarters)
O'Duffy, Edward (Éamon), Bandon
O'Dwyer, George, Clare
O'Mara, Henry, Swinford
Prendeville, Edmund, Ship Street, Dublin
Robinson, Thomas, Roscommon
Stack, William (William J.), Kildare
Walsh, M. J., Dublin (Dublin-Wicklow)

Inspectors
Allen, William, Howth
Bergin, James J., Thomastown
Breen, William, Carrick-on-Shannon
Burns, William, Ship Street, Dublin
Carberry, James S., Kildare
Casey, P. H. (Patrick Hugh), Headquarters
Casserly, Thomas F., Collinstown, Co. Dublin
Conway, Patrick, Bruff
Cooney, John (John J.), Kildare
Courtney, J. (J. C.), Portumna

Creagh, Richard (Richard F.), Kildare
Cronin, Denis, Cork
Cronin, Patrick, Kilrush
Dowd, Michael, Cavan
Doyle, P. (Patrick), Kells
Fahy, Peter, Cork
Farrell, John, Newcastle, Co. Limerick
Feeney, M. A. (Martin), Thurles
Feore, John, Kildare
Finnegan, Joseph (Patrick?), Ship Street, Dublin
Fitzgerald, M. (Michael), Cappoquin
Geary, William, Carrickmacross
Glennon, Patrick, Maryborough (Port Laoise)
Gunn, Thomas, Drogheda
Harrison, J., Ballyshannon
Hayden, Thomas (Heydon, Richard?), Dunglow
Hughes, John, Ship Street, Dublin
Hunt, James, Ship Street, Dublin
Jones, F. (Francis), Ship Street, Dublin
Keaney, John, Athlone
Keenan, J. J. (John), Headquarters
Kelly, J. G., Kildare
Kelly, John, Athy
Kissane, R. (Richard), Kildare
McCabe, Edward, Enniscorthy
McCrudden, Robert, Boyle
McGann, Henry, Carlow
McGrath, Martin, Ship Street, Dublin
Madden, James, Bray
Meehan, P. (J. J.), Headquarters
Millar, Edward, Collinstown, Co. Dublin
Mitchell, Patrick J., Killaloe
Molloy, J. J. (John), Ballinasloe
Moore, J. J. (John), Bailieborough
Muldoon, Richard, Longford
Murphy, Jeremiah, Mullingar
Murray, Frank, Transport, Ship Street, Dublin
Murray, Joseph, Kildare
O'Boyle, Bryan (Bernard), Dundalk

O'Byrne, Louis, Collinstown, Co. Dublin
O'Halloran, Cornelius, Kildare
O'Neill, James (Séamus), Collinstown, Co. Dublin
O'Neill, Patrick, Ship Street, Dublin
O'Reilly, A. (Andrew), Castlerea
O'Reilly, Peter, Gort
Reynolds, J. H. (John), Ennistimon
Rochford, Pierce (Pierce P.), Monaghan
Ryan, James, Killarney
Smith, Loftus H., Buncrana
Stapleton, A. G. S. (A. J. P.), Ship Street, Dublin
Tarpey, Edward, Dunlavin
Tobin, E. M. (Edmund),Ship Street, Dublin
Twomey, D. (Tuomey, Denis), Galway
Tyrrell, John (John J.), Collinstown

Definitive lists are published annually in the *Garda Síochána Directory,* beginning 1 January 1925.

Appendix 2

BARRACKS ATTACKED IN THE CIVIL WAR

The following is a possibly incomplete list of centres where incidents were reported between December 1922 and November 1923 as attacks on barracks and repeated attacks on the same premises or interception of patrols. (Sources: gleaned from National Archives, Home Affairs file H99/109, and *Iris an Gharda*, 1923.)

Adare	Broadford
Ahascragh	Brosna
Ardmore	Bruree
Askeaton	Callan
Athboy	Carlow
Athy	Carrickbeg
Bagenalstown [Muine Bheag]	Carrickmacross
Ballickmoyler	Carrigaholt
Ballina	Carrigallen
Ballinamore	Castleblayney
Ballineen	Castleconnell
Ballinrobe	Castledermot
Ballintra	Celbridge
Ballyferriter [Baile an Fheirtéaraigh]	Clane
Ballyheigue	Claregalway
Ballylinan	Clonmel
Ballyporeen	Coachford
Baltinglass	Croghan
Bandon	Delvin
Birr	Derrybrien
Blessington	Dromahair
Borris	Drumlish

Dundrum (Co. Dublin)

Dungarvan

Dunlavin

Dunshaughlin

Edgeworthstown

Elphin

Ennis

Feakle (Co Roscommon)

Foxrock

Glaslough

Graiguenamanagh

Granard

Greenfort

Gweedore [Gaoth Dobhair]

Hacketstown

Inistioge

Kilbarry

Kilkee

Killaloe

Killann

Killarga

Killimor

Kilrush

Kiltoom

Lawrencetown

Liscannor

Lisdoonvarna

Macmine Junction

Macroom

Maryborough [Port Laoise]

Milford

Millenthorna

Monivea

Moylough

Mullinavat

Naas

O'Brien's Bridge

O'Callaghan's Mills

Pallaskenry

Passage East

Portlaw

Rathfarnham

Rathkeale

Rathowen

Rooskey

Roscommon

Shanaghlish

Shannon Harbour

Shercock

Swanlinbar

Swords

Thomastown

Toornafulla

Tuam

Tullow

Tyrrellspass

Urlingford

Wexford

Wolfhill (Co. Kilkenny)

Wolfhill (Co. Laois)

Woodford

Youghal

Appendix 3

Selected Letters of Appreciation

(Edited from the original letters in the National Archives, file H235/132.)

In November 1922 Commissioner Eoin O'Duffy forwarded to the Minister for Home Affairs, Kevin O'Higgins TD, a letter he had received from E. C. H. Knox, collector of taxes, Inishowen, County Donegal, expressing appreciation for the assistance he had received from members of the Civic Guard as he collected money owing to the Provisional Government—'a sample of the many reports I am receiving from the public.'

> It is most encouraging to receive unsolicited testimonials of this nature regarding the carrying out by the Civic Guard of what was deemed to be an almost impossible task.

A selection of similar letters received by O'Higgins and O'Duffy was filed in the Department of Home Affairs.

From S. O'Brien, chairman, Roscrea District Council, 4 November 1922:

> In Roscrea where all was chaos accompanied by an absolute contempt for any form of law, a complete change has been effected. The licensing laws had been so abused ... and Sunday trading had become a gross and positive scandal. Three or four licensed houses were notorious for all-night harbouring of the worst and most irresponsible elements ... Silently and unobtrusively Inspector [Martin] Feeney has changed all this and with a tact and courtesy that cannot be too highly commended. It is no exaggeration to say that crime is now virtually non-existent in the Roscrea Police Area.

From Colonel-Commandant A. McCabe, Boyle Military Barracks, 8 November 1922:

> The Guards in Sligo and other areas around here are conducting themselves and their work very creditably. I think their success is entirely due to the fact that they are unarmed, and I hope there will be no change in this policy in the future no matter what occurs.

From District Justice Patrick O'Donoghue, Newcastle, County Limerick, 2 December 1922:

> Without any pretence whatever I can frankly say that your Guards in my district are most exemplary and receive very praiseworthy comments from all.

From District Justice Dermot Gleeson, County Clare, 8 February 1923:

> I have been genuinely struck by the high character and self-respect shown by the Guards in the entire area and to their splendid discipline and efficiency. A more sober, more respected or more efficient body of men one could not see than the Guards in this county.

From District Justice T. A. Finlay, Roscommon, 17 April 1923:

> Throughout my entire district all ranks have shown a wonderful spirit in face of the hardships which they have to endure. Every day they are commending themselves more and more to the people by their bearing, their conduct, their quick detection of crime and their absolutely impartial enforcement of the law.

From J. W. Buggy, Sub-Sheriff's Office, Clonmel, September 1923, commenting on the recent general election:

> My Presiding Officers are unanimous in stating that the Elections were the best handled and quietest in memory, due to the tact, courtesy, efficiency and fairness of your force on the day of polling. I consider this tribute from 238 men representing all shades of opinion to be a very high one for an infant force to have gained on the first attempt.

From Micheál Ó hAonghusa (Michael J. Hennessy) TD, County Cork, 1 January 1924:

> The Garda serving in East Cork have proved themselves a very creditable body of men, temperate in their habits, efficient and industrious in their work and equal to the discipline imposed by regulations.

From J. B. O'Driscoll, Killaloe Slate Quarry Company, Nenagh, 14 January 1924, acknowledging assistance in labour trouble:

> Nothing could be more prompt or efficient than the services rendered us by the Civic Guard. The thing that impressed us most was the very wholesome respect for the majesty of the law that Sergt. O'Shea and his men have instilled in the minds of the people since they arrived here.

Resolution of the Grand Jury of County Cork, 15 February 1924:

> We congratulate the Civic Guard on the prompt manner in which they lay hold of criminals. They do so with an expedition worthy of a very much older body and they show that as a police force they are second to none. We are proud of them.

From W. Flanagan PC, Killeigh, County Offaly, 17 June 1924:

> I have found the Civic Guard a most capable, well-conducted, disciplined body of men, anxious to carry out the law without straining it, and to act on all occasions up to the high ideals set before them. I would like to refer especially to Sergt. Michael O'Connor, Tullamore, to whose tact, general efficiency and keen devotion to duty is largely due the popularity of and confidence in the Civic Guard in Offaly.

Resolution of the Grand Jury of County Galway, 24 June 1924:

> We wish to place on record our appreciation of the manner in which Sergeant James Daly has performed his duties since the advent of the Guards in Galway. The sergeant by his tact, energy, capability and uprightness has won the approval of all the well-disposed members of the community, and the law-breaker has found in him a firm but just upholder of the law.

Appendix 4

ROLL OF HONOUR, 1922–1996

Garda HENRY PHELAN [1347], Callan, Co. Kilkenny, 8 November 1922; born 24 December 1900, Co. Laois; farmer's son. On 28 October 1922 a Civic Guard party including Garda Phelan opened a station in Callan and started a hurling team; he was in Mullinahone, Co. Tipperary, buying hurleys when he was shot dead.

Sgt JAMES WOODS [2358], Scartaglen, Co. Kerry, 3 December 1923; born 25 March 1900, Co. Clare; farmer's son. Shot dead in an armed raid on the barracks in Scartaglen.

Garda PATRICK JOSEPH O'HALLORAN [651], Baltinglass, Co. Wicklow, 29 January 1924; born 15 May 1896, Co. Galway; railway signalman. Shot and mortally wounded, 28 January 1924, Baltinglass, attempting to arrest armed bank-robbers.

Sgt THOMAS GRIFFIN [814], 7 May 1924; born 12 April 1899, Cork; mechanic. Garda JOHN MURRIN [3919], 19 October 1924; born 23 March 1898, Co. Donegal; merchant. Carrick-on-Suir, Co. Tipperary. Shot and mortally wounded, 6 May 1924, at Cregg, Carrick-on-Suir, attempting to arrest an armed criminal.

Garda THOMAS DOWLING [5708], Fanore, Co. Clare, 28 December 1925; born 5 July 1896, Co. Kilkenny; carpenter. Ambushed and shot dead at Craggagh, Fanore, in reprisal for his enforcement of the distilling laws.

Sgt JAMES FITZSIMMONS [2566], St Luke's, Cork, 14 November 1926; born 23 May 1903, Belfast; electrician. Garda HUGH WARD [5633], Hollyford, Co. Tipperary, 16 November 1926; born 14 February 1897, Co. Meath; farmer's son. On the night of 14 November 1926 many Garda stations were attacked by armed gangs. Sgt Fitzsimmons was shot dead and Garda Ward mortally wounded.

Garda TIMOTHY O'SULLIVAN [6670], Knock, Co. Clare, 11 June 1929; born 27 November 1896, Co. Cork; baker. Killed by a booby-trap bomb at Tullycrine, Co. Clare.

Supt JOHN CURTIN [783], Tipperary, 21 March 1931; born 10 October 1902, Co. Cork; engine-driver. Ambushed and shot dead outside his home in Tipperary.

Garda JOHN ROCHE [4905], Union Quay, Cork, 4 January 1940; born 11 June 1905, Co. Limerick; farmer's son. Shot and mortally wounded, 3 January 1940, arresting a wanted man at MacCurtain Street, Cork.

Sgt PATRICK McKEOWN [DMP 11919], Blackrock, Co. Dublin, 17 August 1940; born 9 April 1901, Co. Armagh; labourer. Garda RICHARD HYLAND [8333], Dublin Castle, 16 August 1940; born 26 October 1903, Co. Kildare; shop assistant. Garda Hyland was shot dead, Sgt McKeown mortally wounded, attempting to arrest wanted men in Rathgar, Dublin.

Sgt DENIS O'BRIEN [8288], Dublin Castle, 9 September 1942; born 17 June 1899, Dublin; clerk. Ambushed and shot dead outside his home at Ballyboden, Co. Dublin.

Garda MICHAEL WALSH [6658], Cavan, 1 October 1942; born 14 March 1901, Co. Mayo; groom. Shot dead, Ballyjamesduff, Co. Cavan, attempting to arrest a wanted man.

Garda GEORGE MORDANT [6712], Dublin Castle, 24 October 1942; born 24 September 1897, Dublin; railway guard. Shot dead, Donnycarney, Dublin, attempting to arrest a wanted man.

Garda RICHARD FALLON [9936], Mountjoy, Dublin, 3 April 1970; born 18 December 1926, Co. Roscommon; farmer's son. Shot dead, Arran Quay, Dublin, attempting to arrest five armed bank-robbers.

Insp. SAMUEL DONEGAN [8586], Cavan, 8 June 1972; born 20 November 1911, Co. Longford; farmer's son. Killed by a booby-trap bomb on the border at Drumboghanagh, Newtown Butler, Co. Fermanagh.

Garda MICHAEL REYNOLDS [17673], Clontarf, Dublin, 11 September 1975; born 9 February 1945, Co. Galway; builder's labourer. Shot dead, Raheny, Dublin, attempting to arrest two armed bank-robbers.

Garda MICHAEL CLERKIN [18189], Portarlington, Co. Laois, 16 October 1976; born 23 May 1952, Monaghan; clerk. Killed by a booby-trap bomb at Garryhinch, Portarlington.

Garda JOHN MORLEY [15543], 7 July 1980; born 6 October 1942, Knock, Co. Mayo; farmer's son: with Garda HENRY BYRNE [18300], 7 July 1980; born 24 March 1951, Knock, Co. Mayo; shop assistant. Castlerea, Co. Roscommon. Shot dead at Aghaderry, Co. Roscommon, in pursuit of armed bank-robbers.

Garda JAMES QUAID [13497], Wexford, 13 October 1980; born 16 November 1937, Co. Limerick; factory worker. Shot dead at Ballyconnick, Co. Wexford, attempting to arrest a wanted man.

Garda PATRICK REYNOLDS [21281], Tallaght, Dublin, 20 February 1982; born 16 December 1958, Co. Roscommon; farmer's son. Garda Reynolds was in a party surrounding premises near Tallaght suspected of being a hiding-place for stolen property when he was shot dead.

Sgt PATRICK McLOUGHLIN [14679], Dunboyne, Co. Meath, 11 April 1983; born 9 December 1941, Mullingar; shop assistant. Answering a night call at his home in Dunboyne, was shot dead by an armed man.

Recruit-Garda PETER SHEEHAN [23589], Training Centre, Templemore, Co. Tipperary, 16 December 1983; born 24 September 1960, Monaghan; engineer-technician. Was taking part in a joint Garda-Army search for kidnappers at Ballinamore, Co. Leitrim, when he found their hiding-place and was shot dead.

Garda FRANCIS HAND [20594], Dublin Castle, 10 August 1984; born 29 August 1957, Co. Roscommon; farmer's son. Escorting a mail van at Drumree, Co. Meath, ambushed by an armed gang and shot dead.

Sgt PATRICK MORRISSEY [14545], Garda Headquarters, Dublin, 27 June 1985; born 7 March 1936, Co. Cavan; builder's foreman. Shot dead at Collon, Co. Louth, in pursuit of two armed men who had made an abortive raid on a post office.

Garda JEREMIAH McCABE [15860], Henry Street, Limerick, 7 June 1996; born 22 November 1943, Ballylongford, Co. Kerry; student. Shot dead on escort duty by an armed gang at Adare, Co. Limerick.

Appendix 5

THE CORROFIN HOAX

Reproduced from carbon copy of typescript among Mulcahy papers, UCD archives
(RM P7a/202).

*Copy of Inspection Minute by Deputy Commissioner Coogan—Corofin Garda Station,
11th May 1923*

Visited station in conjunction with Divisional Tour, Sergeant W. Lennon, 231, and
station party present. When I entered the Sergeant sat glowering at me and refused
to call the party to attention. I called the party to attention and Garda O'Neill tried
to rise and fell into the fireplace. I asked the Sergeant to account for the state of
affairs existing at the station and he replied in a manner as would do justice to the
worst corner boy in the slums of London.

I searched the barracks and found that a seizure of poteen (three gallons) made
on the previous day had been almost consumed by the station party. The barrack
servant sat with a baton in her hand protecting the remainder of it and refused to
move. She also had possession of the station books and records and refused to allow
me to inspect them. In my examination of the barracks I found that the w.c. was
filled with station records, apparently used by the station party on their visits there.
I heard noises coming from the rear of the cells. When I went to investigate I found
three young ladies there. I took statements from them and they complained that
when passing the barracks they were forcibly taken in by Sgt. Lennon and Guards
Bourke and O'Toole—for a purpose better imagined than described.

In the kitchen of the station Guard Bourke caught me by the uniform and
would not let me go until I promised to refund him a fine of £5.0.0 imposed on him
and have the record of same erased.

When I returned to the front of the Barracks I found the Sergeant urinating
from the front door into the street and he started to argue with me on the footpath
with his person exposed.

On leaving the station I was approached by a local trader who demanded that
I make the party pay some of their Mess Account for the preceding twelve months,
now amounting to some £70.

The whole situation at Corofin was disgraceful. I returned to Tuam and had all the station party suspended immediately.

I hope that the Divisional Officer will ensure that these men discharge their local debts before they themselves are discharged from the Force.

Sgd. E. Coogan
Deputy Commissioner

NOTES

ABBREVIATIONS

AGSI   Association of Garda Sergeants and Inspectors
CSO   Central Statistics Office
DMA   Dublin Metropolitan Area
DMD   Dublin Metropolitan Division
DMP   Dublin Metropolitan Police
GA   Garda Archives
GRA   Garda Representative Association
JRB   Joint Representative Body
MA   Military Archives
NA   National Archives
PRO   Public Record Office
RB   Representative Body
RBG   Representative Body for Guards
RBISS   Representative Body for Inspectors, Station Sergeants, and
            Sergeants
RIC   Royal Irish Constabulary
UCD   Archives Department, University College, Dublin

Note

The Garda magazine from February 1922 appeared as *Iris an Gharda*; it reappeared in 1924 as *Guth an Gharda* and in 1925 as *Garda Review*, then reverted to its original title as *Iris an Gharda* before resuming its identity as *Garda Review*. All references in the notes refer to the magazine as *Garda Review*.

Chapter 1 (pages 3–6)

1. Lecky, 164–94, found in Palmer.
2. 26 George III (1815), cap. 24. See also Walsh, *The Irish Police* 3: 'The term "police" arrived in the English language in the mid-eighteenth century . . . '
3. Parl. College Green, PD, vol. 13, 59, found in Palmer.
4. Garda Síochána [Guard of the Peace], raised in 1922 as the Civic Guard.
5. Carroll, 'Notes for a history of police in Ireland'. P. J. Carroll (1897–1982), Deputy Commissioner. Born Clones, Co. Monaghan; son of an RIC constable; educated as a teacher, St Patrick's College, Dublin. Senior cadet, 1923. Administrator with vast knowledge of police duties and procedures and a meticulous eye for detail. His published *Notes* awakened an interest in Irish police history, which found expression in the creation of the Garda Museum and Archives in the nineteen-seventies.
6. 25 George III (1814), cap. 131. The Peace Preservation Force was raised in 1816.
7. *Parliamentary Papers,* 1837–38 (735), vol. 46, 571.
8. Broeker, *Rural Disorder and Police Reform in Ireland,* 199.
9. PRO (London), CO904/174/4. See Allen, 'Arms, the DMP and 1916'.
10. Home Office (London), Inspector-General RIC circulars, 1921–22. (County Inspector's office, Roscommon; probably retrieved by souvenir-hunter, 1922.)
11. Former RIC members in Civic Guard: assistant commissioner 1, chief superintendents 6, superintendents 8, inspectors 11, sergeants 80, guards 23 (undated manuscript, NA, H99/243). See also 4/407/1, 3 Jan. 1924: RIC members resigned or dismissed, recommended for admission to Civic Guard but not recruited.
12. Fedorowich, 'The problems of disbandment of the Royal Irish Constabulary'. (My thanks to Timothy O'Neill for this reference.)
13. Members of the Civic Guard were given retrospective legal sanction by the Garda Síochána (Temporary Provisions) Act (1923), section 22 [8 Aug. 1923].

Chapter 2 (pages 7–30)

1. Minutes of Provisional Government, 17 Jan. 1922, NA, G1/1.
2. Collins and railway dispute: author's notes, provenance mislaid.
3. Contemporary newspaper reports.
4. Forester, *Michael Collins,* 278.
5. Curran, *The Birth of the Irish Free State,* 160. Griffith summoned the dormant parliament of 'Southern Ireland' sanctioned by the Government of Ireland Act (1920); on 14 January a sufficient number of pro-Treaty deputies and the four Trinity College representatives met in the Mansion House to approve the Treaty and elect a Provisional Government. Under Collins as chairman, the new government overlapped the Dáil cabinet in membership and functions.

Ministers attended meetings of both cabinets until Cosgrave merged the Dáil cabinet and Provisional Government on the assembly of the Third Dáil, 9 September 1922.

6. Statement by Staines, Military History Bureau; copy in possession of Staines family. Staines put out the Tricolour on the GPO in 1916; this claim is disputed by O'Mahony in *Frongoch: University of Revolution,* 71: 'Gearóid O'Sullivan, Cork [Adjutant-General, 1919–1921] had the honour of hoisting the Tricolour over the GPO.' As brigade quartermaster, Staines was more likely to have provided the flag and to have hoisted it himself.

7. O'Mahony, *Frongoch: University of Revolution,* 57.

8. Taylor, *Michael Collins,* 96. See also army appointments, UCD, RM P7b/56, 27.

9. The Dáil courts were clandestine tribunals of petty sessions, with higher district courts in the parliamentary constituencies; prominent citizens served as magistrates, backed by part-time constables drawn from the ranks of the Volunteers.

10. Kildare mutiny inquiry, NA, H235/329. Warrant of appointment, 12 July 1922, O'Sheil and McAuliffe, GA. Kevin R. O'Sheil SC, born Omagh, 1891, son of Francis Shields, solicitor; educated Mount St Mary's Jesuit college and TCD. Standing Committee, Sinn Féin; judicial commissioner, Dáil Land Court; legal secretary, Provisional Government; assistant legal adviser, Executive Council, Irish Free State, and member of committee on Free State constitution; delegate, League of Nations, 1923; Land Law commissioner, 1923–1963. Author of *The Making of a Republic* (1922); and see *Irish Times,* 7 Nov. 1966 (start of a series of articles). Obituary, *Irish Times,* 16 July 1970.

11. UCD, RM P7/B/29, 180, 24 July 1922.

12. Draft documents, manuscript amendments, UCD, RM P7/A/41, 24 June 1921. See also Kotsonouris, *Retreat from Revolution*; also Maguire, 'The Republican courts', on the Republican courts and police.

13. UCD, RM P7/B/59, 162, 28 July 1922.

14. UCD, RM P7/B/29, 66, 6 Aug. 1922.

15. Horgan, *Seán Lemass,* 22.

16. *Dáil Debates,* 28 Feb. 1922, 118. Austin Stack, a 'simple, kindly, dearly loved' man (Pakenham, *Peace by Ordeal,* 83), was captain of the Kerry football team; leader of Sinn Féin prisoners in hunger strike in Mountjoy Prison on the death of Thomas Ashe in 1917. Stack himself was forcibly fed; he held out until prisoner-of-war status was conceded. Companion of Asst Commr Patrick Brennan, Meelick, Co. Clare (Gaughan, *Austin Stack,* 75–82).

17. *Dáil Debates,* 1 Mar. 1922, 136.

18. NA, H99/35, 6 Sep. 1922.

19. NA, H99/35, 21 Sep. 1922.

20. Coogan, *De Valera,* 435.

21. RIC officer's journal, Walsh Papers, GA.

22. *Constabulary List and Directory, 1921.*
23. RIC, establishment records, 1816–1921, NA, HO184 (microfilm; original in PRO, London).
24. 'The RIC: a plea for reform', *Constabulary Gazette,* 1907.
25. Conversation with Con Walsh, son of Patrick Walsh.
26. Walsh Papers, GA, D791/1922, 8 Mar. 1922. See also Fedorowich, 'The problems of disbandment of the Royal Irish Constabulary'.
27. Walsh Papers, GA, D795/1922, 15 Mar. 1922. See also Fedorowich, 'The problems of disbandment of the Royal Irish Constabulary', 36. The Auxiliaries were stood down on 13 January 1922. The RIC was formally disbanded on 31 March 1922, but this was not completed until August; in Northern Ireland disbanding was delayed until the Royal Ulster Constabulary was established in June 1922.
28. Younger, *Ireland's Civil War,* 243.
29. Conversation with ex-Chief Supt Tom Collins, who had close associations with Fine Gael.
30. Activities of 'Truce heroes': Béaslaí, *Michael Collins and the Making of a New Ireland,* vol. 2, 37. See also Chief Supt Dónal O'Sullivan (retired), Tralee, a lifelong student of the RIC, in *Síocháin,* Dec. 1997, 77. O'Sullivan records eighty-two attacks from December 1921 to February 1922, resulting in twelve deaths and twenty-seven serious injuries. On 17 March gunmen invaded Galway Hospital and shot dead two policemen who were recovering from injuries.
31. Béaslaí, *Michael Collins and the Making of a New Ireland,* vol. 2, 376–7.
32. UCD, RM P7/A/63–73.
33. Walsh Papers, GA.
34. Walsh Papers, GA.
35. Manuscript note directed to Dist. Insp. Walsh, Walsh Papers, GA.
36. A comprehensive list of members of the Police Organising Committee and of other members of the RIC and DMP who took part in the organisation of the Civic Guard does not appear to have survived; but see appendix 1 for nominal lists reconstructed from various sources, including O'Duffy, 'History of the Garda Síochána', *Garda Review,* Mar. 1929, 331; manuscript notes, Walsh Papers, GA; Department of Home Affairs files, NA, H235/329 and S9048; and conversation with Dep. Commr P. J. Carroll, who joined the force as a cadet in 1923.
37. O'Duffy, 'History of the Garda Síochána', *Garda Review,* Mar. 1929, 331.
38. Conversation with Mulcahy.
39. Conversation with Gerard McElligott, son of T. J. McElligott.
40. NA, 4/107/1, 14 Jan. 1924.
41. Copy of letter of resignation, 20 May 1919, Walsh Papers, GA.
42. UCD, RM P7/A/40, 8–10.

43. NA, 4/107/1, 14 Jan. 1924.
44. NA, 4/107/1, 14 Jan. 1924.
45. Conversation with Con Walsh, son of Patrick Walsh.
46. O'Kelly, *Salute to the Gardaí.*
47. NA, H99/111, 29 Dec. 1922.
48. Neligan, *The Spy in the Castle.* In the reorganisation of the army in 1922, Neligan (born Templeglantine, Co. Limerick, 1899, died 4 Oct. 1983) was appointed Director of Intelligence, with the rank of colonel, with responsibility for the Protective Corps and Criminal Investigation Department, operating out of Oriel House, formed to protect the lives and property of people who supported the Provisional Government. A CID badge issued by Oriel House was withdrawn when it fell into the hands of the Irregulars; no such badge was ever issued or used by the Garda Detective Branch (see Department of Justice file, NA, 4/269). In 1923 Neligan rejoined the DMP as chief superintendent, G Division; he took charge of the Garda Special Branch on the amalgamation of the two police forces in 1925; suspended from duty in 1932, having authorised a collection for detectives dismissed for ill-treating prisoners, and re-employed in the Land Commission.
49. Neligan, *The Spy in the Castle,* 78. Broy (born Rathangan, 1887; died 21 Jan. 1972) 'had only one love, athletics, and one hate, the British Empire.' His job as typist in the detective office in Brunswick Street (Pearse Street) gave him the opportunity to make copies for Collins of confidential reports; the discovery of these papers in a flat in Dawson Street led to his arrest. He attended the early meetings of the Police Organising Committee, describing himself as 'captain on the staff of GHQ'; appointed adjutant, Army Air Services, with the rank of colonel. He resumed his police career in 1923 as civilian secretary of the DMP; moved to Garda Headquarters as chief superintendent, Crime Branch, 1925; Commissioner, 1933–38.
50. Seán Kavanagh, *An tÓglach* (reprinted in *Irish Independent,* 1 Mar. 1968).
51. Gaughan, *Austin Stack,* 194.
52. Gaughan, *Austin Stack,* 188.
53. Kildare inquiry, Prendeville evidence, NA, H235/329.
54. Report of Police Organising Committee, 17 Feb. 1922. On the same day the Postmaster-General, J. J. Walsh, put on sale the first postage stamps of the new state, British stamps overprinted *Rialtas Sealadach na hÉireann* [Provisional Government of Ireland]. Collins wrote to Kitty Kiernan: 'The stamp on this was the first Irish Free State stamp ever licked by a member of the Free State Provisional Government' (Ó Broin, *In Great Haste,* 125).
55. Civic Guard Organisation Scheme, no date, NA, H99.
56. RIC and DMP, *Report of Committee of Inquiry, 1914.* Reservation by M. F. Headlam, Treasury remembrancer: '... Economies in organisation might

almost certainly be possible by amalgamating [the DMP] with the Royal Irish Constabulary. There seem to be no reasons, except historical reasons, for maintaining two Forces ...'

57. Home Office (London), RIC Inspector-General, circulars, 1920–21.

58. NA, H99/174, 29 May 1923.

59. NA, H99, Police Organising Committee. The new rates of pay recommended for the RIC and DMP by the Ross Inquiry (1919) and applied in the Civic Guard in 1922 were taken from the Desborough Report: constables, £3 10s to £4 10s; sergeants, £5 to £5 12s; inspectors, £360 p.a.; superintendents, £475 to £650 p.a. (without police experience, starting at £300); chief superintendents, £700 to £900 p.a. (without police experience, starting at £500.).

60. Deletion of reference to Freemasons: Allen, 'Arms, the DMP and 1916' (part II). See also Constabulary and Police (Ireland) Act (1916), third schedule; Garda Síochána (Temporary Provisions) Act (1923).

61. O'Duffy to Home Affairs, 29 Dec. 1922, NA, H99/111.

62. Provisional Government minutes book, 27 Feb. 1922, NA, G1/1.

63. Mansergh, *The Unresolved Question,* 25: 'D. P. Moran denounced Griffith and his "Green Hungarian Band" for having a misconceived order of priorities. They had nailed their flag to the masthead, not of a separatist Gaelic republic, but to the monarchical 1782 constitution which "had sent us adrift in a new world which persuaded Irishmen to make the greatest sacrifice in our power—the sacrifice of our national character." He meant the Gaelic language, for him the essence of nationhood—something which "mere political independence, a parliament in College Green ... will not necessarily bestow."'

64. Chief Supt M. McCarthy, *Garda Review,* June 1937.

65. *Garda Review,* Feb. 1948, 255.

66. *Garda Review,* Feb. 1948, 271.

67. Government departments in the Irish Free State were known as 'ministries' up to 1924. To avoid alternating references to the same body by different names, the term 'department' is used throughout.

68. NA, G1/2, 27 July 1922. The new insignia incorporating the legend *Póilíní Áth Cliath* [Dublin Police] was designed by John F. Burke, a pupil in Blackrock College, Blackrock, Co. Dublin. The various badges and buttons were replaced by the Garda insignia on the amalgamation of the DMP with the national force in 1925. The schoolboy artist joined the Passionists at Mount Argus, Dublin, spiritual home of policemen since 1893; as Father Edmund Burke, he was for many years editor of *The Cross.*

69. Information supplied by correspondents in reply to an inquiry published in the national press and by the writer and artist Timothy O'Neill. John Francis Maxwell (1880–1948) was an illuminator in the monastic tradition, and he published a textbook for his students. The contract for the new Garda insignia

was given almost certainly to John Ireland, uniform clothing manufacturers, of Ellis Quay, Dublin, which had long association with the old police. In 1923 Maxwell was commissioned to design the Walter Scott Medal, the Garda decoration for bravery. Compelled by family circumstances to leave the classroom, he took on the job of managing Lightfoot's fruit and vegetable business in the Dublin market. As a printed device the badge appeared first in the masthead of *Iris an Gharda* (February 1923), designed by J. J. O'Reilly. The cast-iron station plaques were made by the Duthie and Large foundry, Athy, from a mould by Herbert Painting, headmaster of the local technical school. Born and educated in England, Painting was not in sympathy with Celtic art forms, with the result that Maxwell's design was not fully realised. In 1966 the sculptor Michael Biggs, finishing the memorial at the entrance to Garda Headquarters, revealed the original concept in two limestone medallions set in the granite plinth.

70. NA, G1/1, 17 Jan. 1922.

71. NA, H99/176, 20 Apr. 1923.

72. Arthur Codling of the Department of Finance was not satisfied: the department had not been consulted. The expenditure on the station badges was approved, the bill for a thousand badges coming to £253, including £5 for an overproduction of twenty-six badges. See also NA, Department of Justice, 4/269, 7 Nov. 1922: Staines agreed to pay the artist's fee of £5, which had not been paid by November, when Maxwell lodged a claim for that amount. Dep. Commr Coogan considered the fee excessive; Maxwell was 'persuaded to accept £3.3s.0d.'

73. 'Establishment of Depot. Proposed Prov. Govt. have RIC Depot evacuated and by a certain early date' (note, among other manuscripts, taken during discussions of the Police Organising Committee, GA, Walsh Papers, unsigned manuscript, 15 Feb. 1922).

74. NA, G1/1, 10 Feb. 1922.

75. NA, H99/10, 18–20 Feb. 1922. The Civic Guard was in occupation of the RDS premises from 18 February to 1 May, at a rent of £50 a week; presenting a bill for £550, including repairs, Bohane stated that £75 a week had been charged to the British military for the same facilities (NA, H99/139).

76. Curran, *The Birth of the Irish Free State,* 164.

77. Garda nominal register, GA; also D94/1922.

78. Recorded conversation by the author with Christina Allen-McAvinia. Patrick McAvinia's certificate of service, endorsed by his county inspector, GA. McAvinia served twenty-five years in the Garda Síochána and is recognised as the first member of the force, notwithstanding that his number was 2 in the register; he retired as detective-sergeant in Drogheda, 1947.

79. NA, H99/174. The Police Organising Committee employed twelve recruiting officers, with one assistant each, at £7 and £4 10s a week, respectively, plus travelling expenses.

80. O'Duffy, 'History of the Garda Síochána', *Garda Review,* Mar. 1929, 331.
81. NA, H99/30, 4 Sep. 1922.
82. The principal disbanding centres were Mullingar Barracks and Gormanston Camp.
83. Early correspondence dealing with RIC stores, NA, Department of Justice, 4/140.
84. Kildare inquiry, evidence book II, NA, H235/329, 44. The armbands were green for sergeants, blue for inspectors, 'another shade' for officers.
85. GA, Walsh Papers.
86. Correspondence, 9 Aug–10 Oct., NA, H99/52; see also H99/228.
87. GA, Walsh Papers, ref. 821, 27 Mar. 1922.
88. The old *Constabulary Manual* had long become dated as the Oireachtas over the years passed legislation imposing new and varied duties on the Garda Síochána.
89. Reddy, *The Murder File,* 5. See in particular (p. 10) Sgt George Lawlor's blueprint for the Garda Technical Bureau (1931), based on self-taught crime investigation skills. See also *Garda Review*, Nov. 1960. George Lawlor (1897–1961), Monasterevin, Co. Kildare; grocery manager; Irish Volunteers, 1917–1922; Civic Guard 1923. Detective-superintendent in charge of Technical Bureau.
90. NA, H99/10, 12 Apr. 1922.
91. NA, G1/2, 7 Apr. 1922.
92. Undated memo, NA, H99/10. See also Costello, *A Most Delightful Station,* chap. 10–31.
93. NA, G1/2, 10 Apr. 1922.
94. Correspondence, 1 Jan.–8 Apr. 1922, NA, H99/2.
95. Notes in pencil among miscellaneous manuscripts, no date, made by P. Walsh, apparently during deliberations of the Organising Committee, GA, Walsh Papers. Brennan was proposed by Kearney, seconded by McCormack; McCormack proposed by McElligott, seconded by Prendeville; Galligan proposed by Kearney, seconded by Foley. See also Staines evidence, NA, H235/329.
96. NA, G1/1, 10 Mar. 1922.
97. Staines evidence, NA, H235/329.
98. GA, Walsh Papers, ref. 821, 27 Mar. 1922.
99. Appointments, GA, Walsh Papers, 3 May 1922. See also Walsh evidence, NA, H235/329, also Inquiry Report, NA, S9048.
100. NA, G1/1, 17 Jan. 1922.
101. NA, H99/39; also GA, Walsh Papers, ref. 821, 27 Mar. 1922.
102. NA, H99/39; also GA, Walsh Papers, ref. 821, 27 Mar. 1922.
103. *Irish Independent,* 23 May 1922. See also NA, H99/243, undated manuscripts. Eventually only 129 former RIC members joined the new police: assistant

commissioner 1 (disbanded); chief superintendent 6 (disbanded 4, retired 2); superintendent 8 (disbanded 2, resigned 4, pension 1, retired 1); inspector 11 (disbanded 2, resigned 9); sergeant 80 (disbanded 5, resigned 71, dismissed 3, deserted 1); guard 23 (resigned 20, dismissed 3).

104. NA, H99/22, 31 July 1922.

105. NA, H99/22, 3 Aug. 1922.

106. NA, DE1/4, 21 Mar. 1922.

107. *Irish Independent,* 25 Mar. 1922.

108. Kildare inquiry, Evidence of P. Sellars, NA, 235/329.

109. Daly is not named in Tom Barry's *Guerilla Days in Ireland.* His self-appointed protest committee of fourteen included a former RIC constable named Strickland as secretary, a shadowy figure, soon to be replaced by Patrick (Sonny) Sellars [159], former battalion vice-commandant, 1st South-Eastern Galway Brigade (inquiry, evidence of John O'Mara). The other committee members, identified at the inquiry by the men themselves or by other witnesses, were John O'Mara, formerly captain, East Limerick Brigade; Seán O'Brien and Malachy Collison, both from Co. Tipperary; Seán Doyle of Co. Wicklow; E. J. Ryan; Sgt John J. Byrne, Dublin, soon promoted superintendent; Sgt J. J. Brannigan [82], Sgt Patrick Coy [174], and Sgt Thomas Kilroy [138], Co. Galway; Sgt M. Hennessy [15], Co. Limerick; and a man named O'Halloran. (The numbers in brackets are taken from the general register in the Garda Archives. The register taken into use at the Ballsbridge depot and continued in Kildare was apparently lost; the second register, opened in the Ship Street or Phoenix Park depots, does not include the names of members who left the force before the second register was compiled.) Kilroy and Hennessy worked in the recruiting office under the former RIC man Bernard O'Connor, who was listed by Daly for expulsion from the Civic Guard.

110. Kildare inquiry, evidence of Thomas Kilroy, NA, H235/329.

111. Kildare inquiry, evidence of Patrick McNamara, NA, H235/329.

112. Liddy, 'Smothered history'.

113. Kearney was appointed district inspector, third class, on 19 Aug. 1916; first class, 18 Jan. 1921.

114. MacColl, *Roger Casement,* 208.

115. O'Sullivan, 'The fate of John B. Kearney'. Ex-Chief Supt O'Sullivan, Tralee, has made a study of the life and times of Head Constable Kearney.

116. MacColl, *Roger Casement,* 211.

117. Reid, *The Lives of Roger Casement,* 355–6.

118. O'Sullivan, 'The fate of John B. Kearney'. Kearney afterwards sent the watch direct to Casement's defence counsel, George Gavan Duffy. In fear for his life, Kearney took refuge in England, where he was employed sorting and putting

away the records of the RIC. He lost two sons in the Second World War and died a tragic figure in 1946.

119. *Dáil Debates,* 28 Feb. 1922.
120. O'Sullivan, 'The fate of John B. Kearney'.
121. Kildare inquiry, evidence of Staines, NA, H235/329.

Chapter 3 (pages 31–48)

1. J. A. O'Connell [566], Garda nominal register, GA. Promoted sergeant in November 1922, he served in a number of small stations in Co. Mayo, finally as duty sergeant in Ballinasloe, where he resigned in 1934.
2. Kildare mutiny inquiry, evidence of Patrick Brennan, NA, H235/329. Quotations from other witnesses are taken from minutes of evidence on this file.
3. Kildare mutiny inquiry, evidence of J. A. O'Connell, NA, H235/329.
4. Pay in the Irish police forces was substantially increased in 1919 in line with recommendations of the Desborough Committee in England. Historically, the rank and file of the RIC were not well paid, but the money arrived regularly every month, which put the constables in a privileged category in rural communities struggling to survive on smallholdings or dependent on casual labour.
5. Walsh in cross-examination of Brennan, NA, H235/329.
6. GA, D308, 15 June 1922.
7. Staines's letter of resignation, 16 May 1922, GA, Walsh Papers; see also NA, H235/329. In evidence at the inquiry, Sellars named Walsh, James Brennan, McCarthy, McAvinue and the DMP man Neary as the group selected by Daly.
8. O'Connell, NA, H235/329.
9. The eight signatories of the ultimatum delivered to Staines, according to J. A. O'Connell at the inquiry, included T. P. Daly, Seán O'Brien, E. J. Ryan, Malachy Collison, and Seán Doyle—all members of Daly's committee.
10. 'Depot days at Kildare', *Garda Review,* July 1948.
11. O'Connell, NA, H235/329.
12. O'Connell, NA, H235/329.
13. Ring and Brennan, NA, H235/329.
14. O'Connell, NA, H235/329.
15. McNamara, NA, H235/329.
16. Liddy, NA, H235/329.
17. Liddy, NA, H235/329.
18. Ring, NA, H235/329.
19. McNamara, NA, H235/329.
20. O'Connell, NA, H235/329.

21. Liddy, 'Smothered history'.
22. James Brennan, NA, H235/329.
23. Costello, *A Most Delightful Station,* 338.
24. Supt John J. Byrne, NA, H235/329. As Sgt Byrne, this witness was on the Ballsbridge deputation that waited on Brennan to protest at the employment of RIC officers.
25. GA, Walsh Papers; also NA, H235/329.
26. Report of Kildare mutiny inquiry, NA, H235/329.
27. Routine Orders, 17 May 1922, preserved by Garda Patrick Finlay [51], now in Garda Archives. See *Garda Review,* May 1950; also Liddy, 'Smothered history'.
28. NA, H99/15, 27 June 1922.
29. Frank Murray [183], NA, H523/329.
30. M. J. Ring, NA, H523/329.
31. Keane, NA, H523/329.
32. Keane, NA, H523/329. 'Jim Staines', probably Martin James Staines (935), b. 1900, Kilcorkey, Ballinagar, Co. Roscommon, motor driver.
33. Keane, NA, H523/329.
34. From the evidence of Ring, O'Mara, and Liddy, NA, H523/329.
35. Coy, NA, H523/329.
36. Liddy, 'Smothered history'.
37. Typescript notes for an address by Michael Collins on his visit to Kildare, NA, S9048.
38. Brennan, NA, H235/329.
39. McAvinue, NA, H235/329.
40. The Carmelite priest 'Father Brady' has been identified by the historian Father Peter O'Dwyer OCarm as probably Michael Andrew O'Grady OCarm (1868–1932).
41. Younger, *Ireland's Civil War,* 270–338. The famous *Mutineer* seized in Templemore was renamed *Ex-Mutineer* when recaptured by government forces. See O'Malley, *The Singing Flame,* 81: the Irregulars travelled to Kildare in 'a Crossley tender, the armoured car and a line of motorcars.'
42. NA, H235/329, Haugh.
43. O'Malley, *The Singing Flame,* 82.
44. 887 DS, 28 June 1922, NA, S9048.
45. Sellars, NA, H235/329.
46. Liddy, NA, H235/329.
47. Liddy, 'Smothered history'.
48. NA, H99/60.
49. NA, H99/23, 22 June 1922.
50. Recorded conversation by the author with Mrs Angela O'Dwyer.
51. NA, H99/123, 18 Dec. 1922.

52. NA, H99/158, 17 Jan. 1923.
53. The warrant signed by Michael Collins appointing O'Sheil and McAuliffe as a commission of inquiry is in the Garda Archives.
54. UCD, RM P7/B/38, 266, 18 July 1922.
55. Report and minutes of evidence, NA, H235/329.
56. Bernard O'Connor, one of the five officers named in Daly's ultimatum, joined the RIC in 1889; rising through the ranks, was appointed district inspector in 1915; stationed in Edenderry when the Anglo-Irish war started; forced to resign, apparently on suspicion of his nationalist sympathies.
57. NA, G1/3, 17 Aug. 1922. Named as successor to Michael Staines: Cmdt Seán Ó Muirthile, governor of Kilmainham Prison; as Lt-Gen. Ó Muirthile was Quartermaster-General, 1923–24. See also UCD, RM P7b/56, 27.
58. NA, G1/3, 22 Aug. 1922.
59. *Iris an Gharda*, vol. 1, no. 1, 26 Feb. 1923. A Garda magazine was recommended in the O'Sheil-McAuliffe report 'as a vehicle for a cohesive force' to counter what it described as the 'very dangerous feature of personal allegiance [among] comrades-in-arms' in Co. Kildare.
60. NA, H99/8. Civic Guard strength in May was not greater than 1,500; but conflicting figures, one as low as 910, were given at the inquiry by Asst Commr Brennan.
61. *Iris an Gharda*, 24 Sep. 1922. An Seabhac (Pádraig Ó Siochfhradha, born Dingle, 1883, died Dublin, 1964) knew Joe Ring personally; always 'in good spirits, never captious or vindictive. An uncharitable word I never heard fall from his lips. In spirit, he was unspoiled, candid and genially humorous. In the darkest days, there was always in his face a ripple of sunshine. I saw him sad but once. He was on his way to see his old home, burned to the ground a few nights previously by the Black and Tans. "As the night is bright," he said, "I will steal down alone and have a look at it." The martial tread of his fighting column will never again re-echo through his native hills. The scolding blackbird may roost in peace, and the red grouse in the purple heather undisturbed. Wood and stream, and western sea are hushed in sorrow … Mayo, you dare not claim | A braver man than Ring' (*Mayo News*, found in *Iris an Gharda*, 24 Sep. 1922).
62. GA, A41/10/26, 30 Oct. 1922.
63. McNamara [269], personal record, GA.
64. Coy [174], personal record, GA.
65. GA, D588, 24 Jan. 1923.

Chapter 4 (pages 49–72)

1. NA, G1/2, 27 June 1922.
2. Minutes, Provisional Government, 12 July 1922, NA. (And see Coogan,

Michael Collins, 393.)

3.   Paddy Brennan probably never ceased to be a soldier at heart, wishing to emulate his famous older brother, Brig-Gen. Michael Brennan, afterwards Chief of Staff of the Defence Forces. Posing for a rare photograph in the summer of 1922, Paddy Brennan modelled the new Garda officers' uniform, cut from the pattern for army officers, which survives to this day.

4.   Department of Finance (B. W. Gilbert) to Department of Home Affairs, 5 Sep. 1922, NA, H99/148.

5.   O'Connell, Staines, Kildare mutiny inquiry, NA, H235/329.

6.   NA, G1/2, 15 July 1922.

7.   UCD, RM P7/B/29, 227, 17 July 1922.

8.   NA, G1/2, 17 July 1922. See also UCD, RM P7/B/29, 227, 17 July 1922.

9.   UCD, RM P7/B/38, 268, 19 July 1922.

10.   UCD, RM P7/B/38, 215.

11.   UCD, RM P7/B/38, 263.

12.   UCD, RM P7/B/38, 263.

13.   UCD, RM P7/B/38, 215, 24 July 1922.

14.   UCD, RM P7/B/38, 31 July 1922.

15.   UCD, RM P7/B/38, 31 July 1922.

16.   J. F. Sides, UCD, RM P7/B/38, 20 July 1922.

17.   UCD, RM P7/B/31, 14, 3 Aug. 1922.

18.   Brennan's reports, UCD, RM P7/B/38, 21 July 1922.

19.   Kavanagh, UCD, RM P7/B/38, 2 Aug. 1922; see also RM P7/B/34, 203, 2 Aug. 1922.

20.   UCD, RM P7/B/31, 17.

21.   Brennan's reports, UCD, RM P7/B/31, 24 Aug. 1922.

22.   UCD, RM P7/B/29, 66, 6 Aug. 1922.

23.   Forester, *Michael Collins,* 327 (PRO (London), CO38573).

24.   UCD, RM P7/B/31, 17.

25.   Younger, *Ireland's Civil War,* 362.

26.   Younger, *Ireland's Civil War,* 393. W. R. E. Murphy: born Bannow, Co. Wexford, 1890; educated Queen's University, Belfast, and University College, Dublin. In 1923, as Maj.-Gen. Murphy, lately GOC Kerry Command, appointed Commissioner of DMP; Deputy Commissioner, Garda Síochána, 1925. Organised the Local Security Force (1939–1946); his thirty-three closely typed pages of instructions on the role of the LSF, including the bones of a treatise on modern warfare, can only have startled the Garda sergeants who were appointed as liaison officers (GA, LSF). Retired 1955; died 1975.

27.   UCD, RM P7b/69, 171.

28.   Younger, *Ireland's Civil War,* 372.

29.   UCD, RM P7b/69, 152. The reporter recorded national army casualties as six

dead, twenty injured. See Younger, *Ireland's Civil War*, 373: 'several dead on both sides' and uncounted combatants injured.

30. UCD, RM P7b/69, 147. O'Duffy to commander in chief, 23 July 1922. And see Younger, *Ireland's Civil War*, 373: O'Duffy issued a 'fulsome proclamation in which he lauded the victory of the national army.'

31. UCD, RM P7b/68, 159.

32. UCD, RM P7b/68, 117 (122).

33. Forester, *Michael Collins*, 334.

34. UCD, RM P7b/68, 42.

35. UCD, RM P7b/29, 164.

36. UCD, RM P7b/71, 41, 6 Sep. 1922.

37. NA, G1/3, 26, 31 Aug. 1922.

38. UCD, P7b/70, 2, 1 Sep. 1922.

39. UCD, P7b/70, 2, 1 Sep. 1922.

40. UCD, RM P7b/70, 1, 2 Sep. 1922.

41. UCD, RM P7b/48, 145, 4 Sep. 1922.

42. UCD, RM P7b/71, 41, 6 Sep. 1922. See also O'Duffy, *Garda Review*, Aug. 1928, 860. On receiving O'Duffy's acceptance of his appointment as Commissioner, O'Higgins made his first appearance as Minister for Home Affairs in Kildare, addressing the assembled staff and recruits.

43. Younger, *Ireland's Civil War*, 248.

44. UCD, RM P7/B/27, 13 Aug. 1922.

45. Addressed 'Dear General'—presumably Mulcahy.

46. The occupation of Dublin Castle by the Civic Guard on 17 August 1922 was recorded by press photographs; the parade was led by Staines, entering by the Palace Street gate, another part of the parade entering the Lower Castle Yard.

47. P.J.G. [P. J. Gallagher], 'Without Prejudice', *Garda Review*, Dec. 1955.

48. *Clare Champion*, 14 Apr. 1923.

49. Éamonn Coogan BL BSc BComm: born Castlecomer, 1896; sometime principal, Limerick School of Commerce; Irish Volunteers, 1914; associate of Michael Collins; inspector, Department of Local Government, under W. T. Cosgrave; removed from office in controversial circumstances, 1936; reappointed chief superintendent; retired 1941. Entered politics for Fine Gael in Dún Laoghaire Borough Council; elected to Dáil Éireann for Carlow-Kilkenny, 1944; nominated in general election of 1948; died 1948.

50. NA, H99/29, 3 Sep. 1922.

51. NA, H99/29, 19 Sep. 1922. The first parties of civic guards were sent to Athlone, Ballinasloe, Buncrana, Bruff, Carlow, Cavan, Clones, Ennis, Galway, Granard, Kilkenny, Letterkenny, Limerick (William Street, Frederick Street, and John Street), Longford, Maryborough (Port Laoise), Monaghan, Mullingar, Naas, Roscrea, and Wicklow.

52. NA, H99/29, 4 Oct. 1922.

53.   NA, H99/29, 22 Nov. 1922.
54.   Carbon copy of document, NA, H99/29, Oct. 1922.
55.   NA, H99/152.
56.   Garda Síothchána, General Order No. 9 (1922): Raids and Attacks on Civic Guard Barracks (21 Nov. 1922), 21–4.
57.   NA, H99/109, 5 Dec. 1922. See appendix 2 for barracks attacked during the Civil War.
58.   NA, H99/109, 23 Dec. 1922.
59.   NA, H99/109, 25 Dec. 1922.
60.   NA, H90/114, 14 Dec. 1922.
61.   NA, H99/109, 23 Dec. 1922.
62.   NA, H99/109, 30 Dec. 1922.
63.   NA, H99/109, Jan. 1923.
64.   NA, H99/109, 2 Jan. 1923.
65.   NA, H99/109, 24 Dec. 1922.
66.   NA, H99/15.
67.   GA, A46/11/26, 20 Feb. 1923. The raiders did not actually burn down the school.
68.   NA, H99/109, 20 Jan. 1923.
69.   NA, H99/29, 20 Dec. 1922.
70.   NA, H99/29, undated.
71.   *Iris an Gharda*, 2 Apr. 1923.
72.   *Iris an Gharda*, 24 Oct. 1923.
73.   *Guth an Gharda*, 21 Aug. 1924. James Mulroy (1899–1986), the first unarmed policeman in Irish history to be decorated for bravery. A farmer's son from Straide, Co. Mayo, he fought in the War of Independence, and joined the Civic Guard in 1922. The donor of the medal for valour, the philanthropist Walter Scott (1861–1935), was born in Montréal of Scots-Canadian parents. Starting as a messenger boy in the grocery trade in Boston, Mass., he moved to New York, where he made his fortune. He used his money to sponsor college scholarships, to endow hospitals, and to strike medals for police bravery. The New York Police Department conferred on him the title of Honorary Commissioner. O'Duffy met Scott at a police conference in New York in 1923 and was charmed by Scott's interest in the new Irish police force. The endowment of the medal in a bond worth about £250 was a small enough gesture for a man of the donor's wealth in return for the honour of having his name inscribed on the Garda decoration 'in perpetuity'. In the perspective of history it may be thought that the institution of a privately endowed medal was a *faux pas* on Duffy's part. Taken off guard in a social encounter, he committed his government at home. He may perhaps have pre-empted the good will of Cosgrave, O'Higgins and the other ministers, who might have found it difficult to turn down a recommendation from the Commissioner, despite certain opposition in Finance.

74. Sgt Francis McCague [2614], reports of attacks on barracks and patrols, NA, H99/109.
75. *Iris an Gharda,* 2 Apr. 1923.
76. NA, H99/109, 6 Nov. 1923. Sgt John Mulvey (1678), 1899–1959, Lanagh, Ballintogher, Co. Sligo, farmer; Irish Volunteers.
77. Monthly Confidential Report, NA, H99/125, 22 Feb. 1923. This is the first such report presented by the new police. The crimes and offences causing the greatest problems were: attacks on police barracks, railways, roads and bridges, and post offices; the interception of postmen, with letters seized and returned *Censored by IRA*; illicit distilling; incendiary fires; the kidnapping of court witnesses; women's hair shorn; livestock stolen; and land seized and grazed by 'gangs of scoundrels'. A change in the pattern of crime was reported, with attacks increasingly directed at economic targets—a 'deadly weapon'. See appendix 2 for barracks attacked during the Civil War.
78. NA, H99/109, 22 Dec. 1922.
79. *Iris an Gharda,* 9 Apr. 1923.
80. *Iris an Gharda,* 23 Apr. 1923.
81. NA, Department of Justice, 4/28, 1a, 3 Feb. 1927. Armed robberies in all areas excluding Dublin: 1923, 996; 1924, 368; 1925, 266; 1926, 137.
82. NA, H99/109, 16 Jan. 1923.
83. *Irish Independent,* 19 Jan. 1923.
84. O'Duffy, 'Attack on Civic Guard Barracks at Baltinglass', circular letter, 2 Jan. 1923, GA, Civic Guard, miscellaneous papers.
85. GA, personal file 651. Patrick Joseph O'Halloran was transferred to the Dublin-Wicklow Division on 17 November 1922 and presumably posted at once to Baltinglass. Born Co. Galway, 1896; signalman on Great Southern and Western Railway; joined Civic Guard at RDS, Ballsbridge, Mar. 1922. Died 29 Jan. 1924.
86. *Guth an Gharda,* 21 Aug. 1924.
87. UCD, RM P7/A/33, 17 Dec. 1921.
88. PRO (London), CO904/174/4. See Allen, 'Arms, the DMP and 1916'.
89. NA, H99/64, 6 Nov. 1922.
90. NA, H99/64, 10 Oct. 1922. Protection posts: College of Science, inspector and 30 guards; Government Buildings, inspector and 10 guards; Ormond Quay, inspector and 4 guards; OPW, St Stephen's Green, inspector and 6 guards; Shelbourne Hotel, inspector and 5 guards; Leinster House, inspector and 14 guards; Treaty rooms, 2 guards. All arms: 38 rifles, 30 revolvers.
91. NA, H99/64, 9 Jan. 1923.
92. NA, H21/16, 10 Mar. 1924.
93. NA, H21/16, 19 Mar. 1924; also 2 Apr. 1924.
94. NA, Department of Justice, 4/28, 1a, 9 Feb. 1924. Chairman of JRB, Chief Supt S. B. McManus.

95. O'Duffy, General Order No. 1, NA, H99/23, 21 Sep. 1922.
96. Garda Síothchána General Order No. 1 (1922); cancelled Nov. 1922.
97. NA, S5260, Department of Justice, 4/28, 1a, 6 Dec. 1926.
98. O'Friel to Department of Finance, 24 July 1925, NA, 4/28, 1a.
99. Conversation by the author with ex-Sgt Andrew Eustace, a member of the Limerick contingent, GA.
100. *Garda Review,* Feb. 1926, 162.
101. O'Duffy, 'History of the Garda Síochána', *Garda Review,* Mar. 1929, 338.
102. NA, S5260, 6 Dec. 1926.
103. NA, S5260, 6 Dec. 1926.
104. O'Friel to Executive Council, NA, S5260, 24 Jan. 1927.
105. Brady, *Guardians of the Peace,* 197.
106. *Irish Times,* 23 Jan. 1934 (report with photograph); also Brady, *Guardians of the Peace,* 226.
107. NA, Cab.1/5, 5 Sep. 1933.
108. O'Higgins to O'Duffy, NA, Department of Justice, 4/28, 1a, 3 Feb. 1927.
109. NA, S5260, 6 Dec. 1926. Some passages of O'Duffy's submission may have been written by such a conservative figure and Irish Party sympathiser as Asst Commr Walsh. See GA, Walsh Papers: views on promiscuity in the social life of rural Ireland, typescript, no date, not signed.
110. See Gorer, *Exploring English Character*: 'I wish to advance the hypothesis that one of the techniques by which the national character of a society may be modified or transformed over a given period is through the selection of personnel for institutions which are in continuous contact with the mass of the population in a somewhat super-ordinate position ...'
111. O'Duffy, 'History of the Garda Síochána', *Garda Review,* Apr. 1930, 420.
112. NA, S5260, 6 Dec. 1926.
113. NA, S5260, 6 Dec. 1926.
114. De Vere White, *Kevin O'Higgins,* 258.
115. De Vere White, *Kevin O'Higgins,* 231.
116. Conversation with Chief Supt Thomas Collins, who joined the Civic Guard as a cadet in 1923. Chairman of JRB; after retirement in the nineteen-seventies he became an active member of Fine Gael. See Chief Supt Leahy, personal papers among unregistered officers' files, GA. Leahy was a member of the London Branch of the Gaelic League and the GAA. In 1922 he applied for membership of the Civic Guard. 'My primary object is not to improve myself materially, for my prospects are sufficiently satisfied in the Civil Service, but to serve the Government of the Irish Free State ... and generally to serve to the best of my ability my own country ...' The correspondence was dealt with personally by Deputy Coogan, a former civil servant himself, who could be relied on to recognise the value of Leahy's experience. He assured Leahy of the Commissioner's wish to admit him to high rank in the force.

117. Account of assassination: de Vere White, *Kevin O'Higgins,* 240–2.
118. O'Higgins memorandum, 3 Oct. 1924, GA, CM 2550/49.
119. W. R. E. Murphy to O'Friel, 20 Aug. 1924, GA, CM 2550/49.
120. O'Friel to Murphy, 27 Aug. 1924, GA, CM 2550/49.
121. Author's notes, provenance mislaid. See O'Malley, *The Singing Flame,* 145: Oriel House had 'an unsavoury record ...' See also Department of Justice, Circular 6. Sep. 1922, NA, H99/35.
122. 'Police Dept., General H'qrs, 24 Brunswick St.,' to each brigade police officer: enlistment form for Civic Guard enclosed, returnable to Capt. Ennis, Oriel House. See also Department of Justice, 4/269, 21 Aug. 1929, Neligan to Department of Justice: CID badge found in a London street, struck 1922/23 for Oriel House but never used. NA, H235/13.
123. Accounts of tensions in the DMP that arose in part from an initiative taken by the Jesuits in the post-Emancipation period to care for the spiritual welfare of the Dublin constables, NA, CSORP 1858/11753. See also Allen, 'The Jesuits and the DMP'.
124. Allen, *The Passionists and the Policeman in Ireland.*
125. *Irish Catholic Directory.* Canon Joseph Burke, parish priest, Aughrim Street, Dublin, was the last of the RIC chaplains.
126. NA, H235/13, 19 Sep. 1922.
127. In the historic group photograph 'Ireland's Unarmed Police Force, The Civic Guard, Collinstown, 20th Nov. 1922' (GA), Father Dunlea is seated beside O'Duffy.
128. NA, H235/13, 1 Jan. 1923.
129. Father Theobald Mathew (1790–1856), 'Apostle of Temperance'. See also photograph of Father Patrick McAuliffe, chaplain, *Iris an Gharda,* 13 Aug. 1923.
130. In RIC times the Sunday Mass parade to Aughrim Street church was a familiar sight for residents of the North Circular Road. The tradition was resumed by the Civic Guard when Father McAuliffe returned to his parish in June 1924.
131. Supt J. J. Bergin, *Garda Review,* Dec. 1939. In the period 1922–1931 nine gardaí were murdered; 1940–42, six; 1970–1996, fourteen; a total of twenty-nine, all ranks, were murdered on duty in the period 1922–1996. See appendix 4, Roll of Honour.
132. *Iris an Gharda,* 18 Apr. 1923. See also *Irish Catholic Directory,* 1924, 566.
133. *Iris an Gharda,* 30 Apr. 1923: Sgt James McGee, Elton, Knocklong, Co. Limerick; Insp. J. J. Bergin, Callan, Co. Kilkenny. Also Sgt (afterwards Chief Supt) John Collins, Ahascragh, Co. Galway, report on an objection by a member of the station party to the service taking place, GA, provenance mislaid. The ceremony of consecration by the local curate having been conducted in a bedroom, in deference to the complainant, O'Duffy found no grounds for complaint.

134. Garda James Brennan, district clerk, Wicklow, 26 Apr. 1985, GA. The only surviving copy of Staines's valedictory circular was discovered by Brennan in a store and deposited by him in the Garda Archives. The idealism of the age was epitomised in verse by Kenneth Reddin, one of the new district justices, in *Iris an Gharda,* 6 June 1923:

> Gentleness;
> And to the weak, and whom the world hath smitten,
> All courtesy of your manhood.
> Strong be your arm to vindicate
> Against the strong; nor let resentment tell your blow,
> But right alone, inexorable.

CHAPTER 5 (PAGES 73–96)

1. RDS, Ballsbridge, 18 Feb. 1922; Artillery Barracks, Kildare, 25 Apr.; Denmark Street, 17 May; Ship Street, 17 Aug; Phoenix Park Depot, 17 Dec.
2. NA, H99/27.
3. NA, H235/329, 31 Aug. 1922.
4. NA, H99/102, NA.
5. MA, 2/25928, 17 Dec. 1922.
6. O'Duffy, 'History of the Garda Síochána', *Garda Review,* May 1929, 54.
7. O'Duffy, 'History of the Garda Síochána', *Garda Review,* June 1929, 652–69.
8. O'Duffy, 'History of the Garda Síochána', *Garda Review.* See also NA, S3108, 15 June 1923. In the summer of 1923 the supply of uniforms ran out, leaving 1,200 recruits without uniform. Recruits were not allowed to go into the city in plain clothes, to protect 'innocent young lads from the country' from the 'many temptations in Dublin.' In uniform they were readily identified by the provost-sergeants; it was because of this close supervision 'that their conduct afterwards in the country [was] so admirable' (O'Duffy).
9. O'Duffy to Representative Body, GA, letter among bundle of petitions on conditions of service in the nineteen-twenties.
10. *Freeman's Journal,* 13 Aug. 1923.
11. NA, H99/131, NA.
12. NA, H99/131, NA.
13. Return of expected strength to 30 Sep. 1922: surgeon 1, bandmaster 1, chief superintendent 5, superintendent 20, inspector 10, sergeant 100, guard 1,550, NA, H99/8, 23 Aug. 1922. Figures extrapolated from monthly returns prepared at the Ship Street headquarters, probably not completely reliable.
14. Garda Síochána (Temporary Provisions) Act (1923), first schedule: maximum establishment: Commissioner 1, Deputy Commissioner 1, assistant commissioners 2, surgeon 1, chief superintendents 25, superintendents and inspectors 140, sergeants 950, guards 4,400. See also Garda Síochána Act (1924), first schedule: maximum establishment: Commissioner 1, Deputy

commissioner 1, assistant commissioners 2, surgeon 1, chief superintendents 27, superintendents and inspectors 150, sergeants 1,200, guards 4,918. (Before 1925, superintendents and inspectors were counted together as district officers.)

15. NA, H99/228, 8/26 Feb. 1924.
16. Police Forces Amalgamation Act (1925), third schedule: maximum establishment: Commissioner 1, Deputy commissioners 2, assistant commissioners 2, surgeon 1, chief superintendents 29, superintendents 157, inspectors 60, station sergeants (Dublin) 44, sergeants 1,350, guards 6,000.
17. O'Duffy to Supt O'Connor, 1 Nov. 1922; author's notes, provenance mislaid.
18. Depot commandant, Chief Supt M. McCarthy, to Supt O'Connor, 30 Oct. 1922 (provenance mislaid): 'This should not have happened.' Timothy Ward [1771]: born Drumhubbrid, Drumcong, Co. Leitrim, 1900; service in Irish Volunteers; joined Civic Guard 1 Sep. 1922 and 2 Oct. 1922; sergeant, 1 Oct. 1923; retired 21 Dec. 1963.
19. O'Duffy to Department of Justice, anticipating reopening of recruiting in 1929, NA, Department of Justice, 4/107/1, 11 Dec. 1929. See also NA, H99/202 (on 4/107/1), 28 Mar. 1931. The upper age limit of twenty-seven enabled 'failures in other walks of life to fall back on Garda ... dead weight in police force. At 19–20 years recruits were docile, impressionable; discipline readily becomes second nature.'
20. O'Duffy to Supt O'Connor, 6 Nov. 1922; author's notes, provenance mislaid. The original ad hoc rules of entry were codified in the Garda Síochána (Designations, Appointments and Discipline) Regulations (1924).
21. NA, H99/228, 26 Feb. 1924.
22. O'Duffy to Department of Justice, NA, H99/202 (on 4/107/1), 28 Feb. 1931; and O'Duffy to Minister for Justice, 4/107/1, same date.
23. O'Duffy to Department of Justice, NA, H99/228, 8 Feb. 1924.
24. Kinnane to Secretary, Department of Justice, NA, 4/31 (part 2), 6 Apr. 1944.
25. Garda Síochána (Appointments) Regulations (1937).
26. Report of Chief Supt H. Duffy, NA, Department of Justice, 4/107C, 1 Dec. 1942.
27. Memorandum of Department of Justice for Department of the Taoiseach, 22 Feb. 1943.
28. O'Duffy to Department of Home Affairs, NA, H99/147, 21 Feb. 1923; exchange of internal minutes on the file in Home Affairs. The correspondence arose on an application from a former member of the Connaught Rangers for membership of the force, accepted on the recommendation of Kevin O'Higgins; an earlier application from Cpl Joseph O'Donoghue from Dublin, who served in the same regiment, was also accepted. 'If you have a few dozen other former members of the Connaught Rangers of the type of O'Donoghue, send them along' (O'Duffy, NA, H99/80, 10 Nov. 1922).

29. O'Duffy to Supt O'Connor, 19 Mar. 1923; provenance mislaid.
30. O'Friel to O'Duffy, NA, H99/82, 20 Nov. 1922.
31. O'Duffy to Minister for Home Affairs, NA, H99/82, 25 May 1923.
32. O'Duffy to Home Affairs, NA, Department of Justice, 4/107/1, 14 Jan. 1924.
33. O'Duffy to Home Affairs, NA, Department of Justice, 4/107/1, 14 Jan. 1924.
34. O'Duffy to Department of Justice, NA, Department of Justice, 4/107/1, 28 Feb. 1927.
35. Broy to Department of Justice, NA, Department of Justice, 4/107A, 4 Dec. 1936.
36. Minutes, Minister for Finance, NA, 4/107A, 28 Jan. 1937.
37. Mulcahy to Home Affairs, NA, H99/29, 3 Sep. 1922; also UCD, RM/P7/B/71/189.
38. O'Duffy to Home Affairs, NA, H99/29, 19 Sep. 1922.
39. *Garda Review,* July 1951, 621.
40. *Garda Review,* Feb. 1951, 239.
41. *Garda Review,* Sep. 1955, 795; Aug. 1954, 675; Aug. 1958, 695. See Tom Garvin, 'Revolutionaries turned politicians', *Irish Times,* 6 Dec. 1997: 'The cost of rebuilding infrastructure and compensating victims of the IRA was borne by taxpayers. In effect, the Civil War took several billion pounds (in today's value) out of the economy in nine months at a time when GNP was less than a third of what it is now.'
42. O'Duffy, reports, NA, H99/29, 3–10 Oct. 1922.
43. O'Friel to OPW, NA, H99/29, 23 Apr. 1923.
44. Hanson to O'Friel, NA, H99/29, 24 Apr. 1923.
45. Hanson to O'Friel, NA, H99/29, 24 Apr. 1923.
46. *Dáil Debates,* debate on Civic Guard (Acquisition of Premises) Bill, 19 June 1923, col. 2050; second reading, col. 2308; col. 2487. O'Higgins estimated that 75 per cent of the old barracks had been destroyed. See Pakenham, *Peace by Ordeal,* 40.
47. NA, H99/29, 12 May 1923.
48. NA, H99/29, 24 Apr. 1923.
49. NA, H99/29, 8 Sep. 1923.
50. Conversation with ex-Det.-Supt James Hunt, Ballyhaunis (a constable in the RIC, resigned on patriotic grounds; self-employed as a hackney car driver; joined Civic Guard on the invitation of Michael Staines; recruiting clerk; as Insp. Hunt, housing liaison officer, 1922–23; detective-superintendent, Special Branch, 1925). On one memorable occasion Hunt met a young sergeant and party of guards arriving from the depot with their stores. The landlord, a local shopkeeper who had promised a house, unexpectedly withdrew the offer, directing Hunt to another house he owned, outside the village. The guards would find the door unlocked, and he would not object if he discovered afterwards that they had moved in. They found the doors wide

open and the house in use as a shelter for cattle. Undaunted, the men borrowed shovels and with youthful enthusiasm and copious buckets of water from a nearby well cleaned out the only home available to them. Before nightfall they had a fire going and their beds made up. It was not an isolated experience. See Hunt to Commissioner, Conditions in Stations in Co. Longford, NA, H99/29, 6 Oct. 1923.

51. GA, A44/17/26, 13 Dec. 1924.
52. GA, A44/17/26, 20 Oct. 1924.
53. O'Duffy to JRB, GA, A44/17/26, 29 Nov. 1929.
54. *Garda Review*, Oct. 1929, 1168. O'Duffy suggested an inquiry: 'If left in the hands of the Board of Works little progress could be anticipated, having regard to that Department's evident indifference to the needs of the Garda in the matter of accommodation.'
55. Hanson to O'Friel, NA, H235/166, 18 Nov. 1929.
56. Divisional inspections by Headquarters officers, various reports fom the 1920s, bundled in one file, GA.
57. UCD, RM P7a/202. A carbon copy of a similar typescript was shown to the author as a young garda stationed at Oilgate, Co. Wexford, in 1952.
58. Coogan, *Ireland Since the Rising*, 48. The opportunity to cast the Garda Síochána in a bad light was seized by Proinsias Mac Aonghusa: 'One of the myths of this State is the great work done by the unarmed Civic Guards in the years following the Civil War ... A look at Tim Pat Coogan's [book] is sufficient to realise how undisciplined many guards were in those years' (*Irish Times*, 24 Oct. 1970). With acknowledgment to Coogan, the hoax was quoted by a former member of the force, Séamus Breathnach (*The Irish Police*, 118–19): 'Undoubtedly the best yardstick for measuring the prevailing lack of morale is the description of Assistant Commissioner [*sic*] Coogan's inspection minute of 1923 in respect of a Garda party in the west of Ireland.' Edna O'Brien published the full text of the bogus document in *Mother Ireland* (London: Weidenfeld and Nicholson 1976, 97–8).
59. *Garda Review*, Feb. 1975.
60. Patrick Joseph Carroll, son of an RIC constable; headed the class of Garda cadets recruited in 1923; in 1939 joined the close-knit community of Headquarters officers as a newly promoted assistant commissioner in charge of B Branch (personnel).
61. 'Lough Erne' (letter), *Garda Review*, Oct. 1929, 1153.
62. 'The Brightening of Barrack Life', *Garda Review*, Apr. 1926, 306.
63. *Garda Síochána Code, 1928*, chap. 25, Miscellaneous Disciplinary Regulations (932, 401).
64. Letter from M. McGuinne, 135 Springfield Road, Belfast, NA, H99/49. His son, Michael Leo McGuinne, was an adjutant at Portobello Barracks, Dublin (MA).

65. NA, H99/49.

66. General Order 14/1922, published in *General Orders, 1922* (1923). As an earnest of his resolve, O'Duffy dismissed the entire station party at Ballina and four guards at Trim and published his decisions (*Iris an Gharda,* 14 May 1923).

67. General Circular 22; also *Iris an Gharda,* 16 Apr. 1923.

68. *Iris an Gharda,* 9 Apr. 1923.

69. *Guth an Gharda,* 21 Aug. 1924.

70. See Roll of Honour (appendix 4): Garda Thomas Dowling, murdered at Fanore, 28 Dec. 1925.

71. UCD, RM P7/B/293, 3 Feb. 1923.

72. UCD, RM P7/B/293, 3 Feb. 1923.

73. UCD, RM P7/B/293, 3 Feb. 1923.

74. UCD, RM P7/B/293, 3 Feb. 1923.

75. NA, Department of Justice, 4/107/1, 25 May 1923.

76. NA, H99/228, 17 July 1924.

77. *Constabulary List and Directory, 1914,* 187–9: Regulations under which gentlemen are admitted as cadets of the RIC. See also *RIC Code* (6th edition), 1911, regulations 662–81. From the text it appears that the code did not hinder the allocation of cadets to districts after six weeks: if a cadet was not allocated within six months, the Inspector-General was informed.

78. *RIC Code* (6th edition), 1911, regulation 1431.

79. RIC and DMP, *Report of Committee of Inquiry, 1914* (Sir David Harrell, chairman; M. F. Headlam, Treasury; R. F. Starkie RM), also conversation with William Comerford, son of Dist. Insp. Francis Comerford, Tuam, on social and economic problems for head constables promoted to district inspector. If married with a family, a grant of £80 was made for uniform and equipment and for horse and vehicle.

80. RIC and DMP, *Report of Committee of Inquiry, 1914.*

81. NA, H99/228, 17 July 1924.

82. NA, H99/228, 17 July 1924.

83. Chief Supt McManus to Commissioner, NA, H235/166, 11 Jan. 1924.

84. NA, H99/228, 17 July 1924.

85. NA, H99/228, 26 Mar. 1924.

86. Memorandum of Department of Justice for the Government, 4 Sep. 1940, NA, 4/107, on 4/218.

87. Department of the Taoiseach to Department of Justice, NA, Department of Justice, 4/107, 20 Sep. 1940.

88. Memorandum of Department of Justice, 4 Sep. 1940, NA, 4/107.

89. NA, H99/34.

90. NA, H99/34, 31 Mar. 1923. ·

91. NA, H99/8, 20 June 1922.

92. NA, H99/8, 14 June 1922.
93. NA, H99/45. The first formal, if crude, Civic Guard estimates for 1922/23 were detailed as: salaries, £450,000; allowances, £65,000; subsistence, £30,000; travelling, £30,000; clothing, £50,000; accoutrements, £5,000; barrack rents, £12,000; furniture, £21,000; fuel and light, £4,000; incidental, £2,000; transport, £33,000; telegrams, £500; escorts, £150.
94. NA, H99/89. The bicycles were ordered from John O'Neill Ltd, Lucania Works, at £10 12s 6d each, for resale at £11, repayable at £2 a month. The order for the bicycles was presumably placed by the accounts officer, Chief Supt McCormack, who was among the officers sacked by O'Duffy: see NA, Department of Justice, 4/107/1, 14 Jan. 1924.
95. Dáil Éireann, Committee of Public Accounts, Second Interim Report, 19 Dec. 1924, NA, Department of Justice, 4/140 (RIC Stores).
96. Coogan to Home Affairs, NA, Department of Justice, 4/140, 23 Apr. 1924.
97. Internal minutes on file, NA, H99/145, 13 Dec. 1922.
98. NA, H99/145, 18 Dec. 1922.
99. NA, H99/145, 21 Dec. 1922.
100. A, H99/145, 21 Dec. 1922.
101. Memorandums among a batch of early circulars, GA, 15 Nov. 1922 and 2 Apr. 1923.
102. NA, H99/95, 24 Jan. 1924.
103. NA, H99/118, 16 Jan. 1923.
104. O'Duffy to Minister for Justice re James Geoghegan, applying to leave the country with Irish athletes for the Olympic Games in Los Angeles, NA, H99/151, 24 June 1932.
105. Manuscripts of Patrick Walsh, c. 1950, on the organisation of St Joseph's Young Priests' Society, GA, Walsh Papers.
106. Department of Finance circular E7, 1 May 1922, GA, Walsh Papers.
107. GA, Walsh Papers.
108. O'Duffy to Home Affairs, GA, Walsh Papers, 13 Jan. 1923.
109. GA, Walsh Papers, 28 Aug. 1923 and 20 Feb. 1924. Supt Michael Horgan, Co. Sligo, former district inspector, instructor, and depot schoolmaster. Temporary instructors: J. F. Duignan, M. J. Lyons, Thomas McGetrick. As district inspector at Howth, McGetrick was seconded to the Police Organising Committee and made a significant contribution as chairman of the sub-committee on conditions of service before he removed himself. A man of gentle disposition, he was fifty-six when he took on the job of instructing the Civic Guard recruits.
110. GA, Walsh Papers, 3 Mar. 1924.
111. NA, H99/132, 26 Oct. 1923.
112. NA, H99/132, 26 Oct. 1923.
113. O'Higgins to Blythe, NA, H99/132, 2 Nov. 1923.

114. O'Friel appended to O'Higgins, NA, H99/132, 2 Nov. 1923.
115. NA, H99/132, 5 Jan. 1924.
116. Contemporary newspaper reports.
117. Editorial, *Garda Review*, Aug. 1937.
118. NA, H99/118, 5 Mar. 1923.
119. NA, H99/118, 23 May 1924, and following correspondence.
120. NA, S2123A, 11 Dec. 1926.
121. NA, 4/30/2, 9 July 1928.
122. John Mackin (1892–1960), born Cullyhanna, Co. Armagh; Irish-language teacher and Gaelic League organiser; present at Rotunda for the inaugural meeting of the Volunteers, 1913, and took part in the Howth gun-running the following year. Emigrated to America, 1914, joining Volunteer organisation and Gaelic League in New York. Returned 1920; Irish-teacher, Co. Wicklow VEC. Civic Guard, 1923; Irish instructor, Depot school. As chief superintendent, Galway, 1934, organised the new Galway West division, to be administered in Irish; collaborated with District Justice Seán Mac Giollarnáth in the introduction of Irish in courts in the new Irish-speaking division. As Depot Commandant, 1939, directed recruiting for the auxiliary police, Taca Síochána, later absorbed in the regular force. See obituary, *Garda Review*, Sep. 1960.
123. O'Duffy to Department of Justice, 23 Feb. 1928, NA, Department of Justice, 4/31; also S5975.
124. NA, H99/228, 17 Jan. 1924.
125. *Garda Review*, vol. 1, no. 1, Dec. 1925, 52.
126. *Garda Review*, Feb. 1926.
127. O'Duffy, *Garda Review*, 1 Nov. 1929; Linguaphone Irish course.
128. Editorial, *Garda Review*, Nov. 1929, 1221.
129. Coogan, 14 May 1925, NA, Department of Justice 4/31. See 'Sheen', letter to the editor, *Garda Review*, Nov. 1929, 1251: 'What is being done for the language in the Garda Síochána? Apart from talking a whole lot about it—telling us to learn it and have a great love for it and all that it stands for—is there ever a word about the native speaker when promotion comes along? In 1923, we were dispatched to ... the Gaeltacht ... there to remain hidden away without ever a word about us ...'
130. O'Duffy, 29 Feb. 1928, NA, 4/31.
131. Comhdháil Náisiúnta na Gaeilge to the Taoiseach, 29 Feb. 1944, NA, 4/31.
132. Author's notes; provenance mislaid.
133. Routine Order 11/47, quarter to 30 Sep. 1947, 2.
134. The author, who joined the Garda Síochána in November 1947 with national school Irish, was out of his depth struggling with the strange terms in the translated *Police Duty Manual*. Failing the monthly examinations, he was paraded before the depot commandant, Chief Supt Harry O'Mara, who threatened transfer to the Aran Islands, and left the matter there.

CHAPTER 6 (PAGES 97–108)

1. *Irish Times,* 24 Feb. 1933.
2. John Mallon, foreword to Rules of DMP Obsequies Association (1897), GA.
3. NA, H99/223, 18 Oct. 1923.
4. O'Duffy to Representative Body, 2 Feb. 1928, among RB resolutions of the nineteen-twenties, GA.
5. *Garda Síochána Code,* 1928, part II: Finance Regulations, regulation 220. The Garda Síochána Act (1924), section 18, provided for the payment into the Reward Fund of (inter alia) 'all fines, penalties ... damages awarded ... or otherwise payable to any member of the Garda Síochána on any summary conviction.'
6. NA, 235/166/1, 28 June 1929.
7. O'Duffy to Department of Justice, 21 Oct. 1929, NA, 235/166/1.
8. NA, 235/166/1, 11 Feb. 1930.
9. *Garda Review,* Jan. 1933.
10. *Garda Review,* June 1933.
11. See J. Anthony Gaughan, *Olivia Mary Taaffe, 1832–1918: Foundress of St Joseph's Young Priests' Society,* Tralee: Kingdom Books 1995.
12. O'Duffy, 'History of the Garda Síochána', *Garda Review,* Oct. 1929, 1122.
13. John Mallon, who had recently enhanced his reputation in bringing to justice the culprits in the Phoenix Park murders: born Flurrybridge, Co. Armagh, 1838; draper's assistant; joined the DMP in 1858. Having worked as a clerk in the Commissioner's office, he was hand-picked for the Detective Division. Assistant commissioner, 1893, the first policeman from the ranks to be admitted to the Dublin Castle establishment. His biographer, Frederick Moir Bussy, described him as a good Catholic and nationalist. On his choice of career he was advised by his parish priest, Canon Murphy of Meigh: 'I don't think the duties of policeman are congenial to your nature ... If you are called upon to do things that are not right, don't do them; and if you leave the service, leave the knowledge you have gained ... behind you.'
14. The constables on the rope in 1893 were William Ashe, William Bannon, James Carroll, Andrew Heffernan, James Hourihan, Thomas McBennett, Daniel Mahony, George Thackaberry, Edward Timlin, and a famous giant, Maurice Woulfe; captain: Insp. Denton Booth; coach: Denis Carey of Kilfinnane, Co. Limerick.
15. Under Insp. Denis Hurley the revived tug-of-war team won the Wembley Cup in 1924 and were champions of Britain and Ireland, 1924–28.
16. *Irish Independent,* 17 Sep. 1922, 3 (photograph and caption). The Civic Guard competitions were held in Kildare in September 1922. The results, including James Mulroy's heavyweight title, were not recognised by Coiste Siamsa.
17. General Purposes Committee, 4 Feb. 1923; *Iris an Gharda,* 5 Mar. 1923. See also *Iris an Gharda,* 2 Apr. 1923. The committee: Chief Supt M. McCarthy,

depot commandant; Chief Supt J. Brennan, barrackmaster; Supt Thomas Casserly, adjutant; Supt J. Galligan, president, officers' mess; D. J. Delaney, director of music; Chief Insp. J. J. Tyrrell; Insp. Byrne; Sgt McMahon; Sgt McGrath; Sgt Desmond; Garda Byrne; Garda (afterwards Supt) R. Hayes. The ad hoc committee was instrumental in having the RIC cavalry riding school reconstructed for use as an oratory during the period of intensive recruiting in 1923–24; the building was later used for indoor sports and as a dance hall and a venue for concerts to raise funds. The committee depended on contributions of a shilling a year from members of the force.

18.   Coiste Siamsa, *Jubilee Souvenir: 50 Historic Years of Sport in the Garda Síochána, 1922–1972,* 64.

19.   Scheme of organisation, Connradh Gaelach an Gharda, *Iris an Gharda,* 8 Oct. 1923. See also revised scheme, *Iris an Gharda,* 12 Nov. 1923; P.J.G. [P. J. Gallagher], *Iris an Gharda,* 10 Dec. 1923; inaugural council, *Iris an Gharda,* 17 Dec. 1923; and *Iris an Gharda,* 28 Apr. 1924.

20.   See Manning, *The Blueshirts,* 71: O'Duffy 'loved organisation and revelled in publicity.'

21.   *Garda Review,* Aug. 1926. See also *Aonach an Gharda Souvenir Programme, 14–18 July 1926,* 120.

22.   A royal blue flag of Irish poplin fringed in gold, double-sided; embroidered in front with the Garda badge with the arms of the four provinces, save that for Connacht the arms of the city of Galway are used instead; reverse: embroidered in gold to represent a sunrise, formerly believed to be the ancient symbol of the Fianna, representing the dawn of freedom. The restored flag is now laid up in the officers' mess at Garda Headquarters, Dublin.

23.   Editorial, *Garda Review,* Aug. 1926.

24.   NA, Department of Justice, 235/257, 16 Nov. 1927. 'Archbishop Mulhern', probably Bishop Edward Mulhern, Dromore. When the author was in Rome in 1981 in connection with the Garda diamond jubilee pilgrimage the following year he was shown an illuminated address presented to the Pope by the London policemen.

25.   Mr Gleeson, the Jesuit scholastic in James Joyce's *A Portrait of the Artist as a Young Man* (chap. 1): 'The round shiny cuffs and clean white wrists and fattish white hands and the nails of them were long and pointed … So long and cruel they were, though the white fattish hands were not cruel but gentle.' (I am indebted to the publisher's reader for this insight.)

26.   NA, Department of Justice, 235/257, 28 Apr. 1928; all correspondence.

27.   *Garda Review,* Dec. 1928.

28.   The experience was shared by Father Austin Tierney with confrères at the Passionist monastery, Mount Argus, Dublin, and told to the author by Father Clarence Daly, Garda spiritual director, 1957–1983.

29.   Full text of the papal address: *Garda Review,* Jan. 1929. The illuminated

address presented to the Pope was designed and executed by M. Fitzpatrick, Dublin. The text was not filed at Garda Headquarters; the original document in the Vatican Archives is not yet catalogued.

30. NA, 235/257, 19 Mar. 1930. See also *Garda Review*, Nov. 1930.
31. NA, 235/257, 19 Feb. 1935.
32. O'Duffy, *Crusade in Spain*.
33. Brady, *Guardians of the Peace*, 167–9. See also Coogan, *De Valera*, 434–5: it was all 'only talk.'
34. Cmdt Peter Young, Military Archives.
35. Hogan, *Could Ireland Become Communist?*
36. Evidence at the trial of Col. Hogan and Insp. O'Connell (23–24 Feb. 1933), as reported in the newspapers, NA, S2396.
37. Minutes of Executive Council, 1/5, 16 Dec. 1932, NA.
38. Brady, *Guardians of the Peace*, 172–6.
39. NA, S2206, June 1932.
40. Brady, *Guardians of the Peace*, 176. Neligan was afterwards accommodated in the Land Commission as a nominal clerk, without any duties being assigned to him.
41. O'Connell's irregular promotion anticipated special provisions for detectives introduced in the Garda Síochána (Promotion) Regulations (1943), including promotion to inspector for a sergeant who had shown 'consistently meritorious service in Detective Branch and ... special zeal and ability in the performance of his duties.'
42. Garda Síochána (Promotion) (No. 2) Regulations (1955): 'A sergeant who formerly held the rank of inspector and who lost that rank on being removed from the Detective Branch otherwise than as a punishment under the Garda Síochána (Discipline) Regulations, 1926, shall be deemed to have passed [the necessary examinations] and shall be eligible for promotion to the rank of inspector.'
43. *Garda Review*, Oct. 1931; *Irish Times*, 9 Oct. 31. For the best account of the murder of Curtin see O'Sullivan, 'The murder of Superintendent John Curtin', 125–33.
44. *Watchword*, 23 Jan. 1932.
45. Manuscript minutes, 10 Oct. 1931, NA, S6196.
46. Ernest Blythe, Vice-President of the Executive Council of the Irish Free State and Minister for Finance under W. T. Cosgrave; *Irish Times*, 2 Nov. 1970.
47. *Irish Independent*, 14 Dec. 1929.
48. *Irish Independent*, 8 Feb. 1932. Garda pay was cut in 1924, allowances in 1929.
49. Coyne to Charles Haughey TD, 15 June 1960, NA, 4/483.
50. Brady, *Guardians of the Peace*, 167.
51. NA, G2/10, 22 Feb. 1933; *Dáil Debates*, 14 Mar. 1933, vol. 46, col. 798.

52. *Dáil Debates,* vol. 46, col. 764, 14 Mar. 1933.
53. *Dáil Debates,* vol. 46, col. 796, 14 Mar. 1933.
54. Gregory Allen, 'The General Prisons Board, 1877–1928', *Irish Law Times,* 17 Sep. 1977.
55. Army appointments, 1919–1924, UCD, RM P7b/56, 27.
56. Ernie O'Malley notebooks, UCD, RM P17b/103.
57. Ó Broin, *Protestant Nationalists in Ireland,* 191. Barton revealed his own emotional turmoil in a letter to Dorothy Stopford in March 1922: 'Many a time I have wished I had died in Portland Gaol before I got mixed up with those cursed [Treaty] negotiations.'
58. Author, provenance mislaid.
59. Proinsias Mac Aonghusa, *Irish Times,* 24 Oct. 1970.
60. De Vere White, *Kevin O'Higgins,* 232.
61. *Iris an Gharda,* 16 Apr. 1923.
62. *Garda Review,* May 1926.
63. Historical collections, GA. See *Garda Síochána Code, 1928,* chap. XI, regulation 453.
64. Manning, *The Blueshirts,* 162.
65. *Studies,* autumn–winter 1971, 396–7.
66. Ex-Supt Thomas Noonan in O'Kelly, *Salute to the Gardaí.*
67. P.J.G. [P. J. Gallagher], *Garda Review,* Jan. 1945.
68. Conversation with the late Paddy Licken, Stillorgan, Dublin.

CHAPTER 7 (PAGES 109–118)
1. Coogan, *De Valera,* 435.
2. *Dáil Debates,* vol. 46, col. 764, 14 Mar. 1933.
3. Brady, *Guardians of the Peace,* 184.
4. Brady, *Guardians of the Peace,* 187.
5. NA, Cab.1/5, 148, 5 Sep. 1933.
6. For accounts of political tensions in the nineteen-thirties see Manning, *The Blueshirts,* Brady, *Guardians of the Peace,* 172–83, and Lee, *Ireland,* 178–80.
7. Roche (Secretary of Department of Justice) to Minister for Justice, 12 Sep. 1934, NA, 4/107/1.
8. Roche (Secretary of Department of Justice) to Minister for Justice, 12 Sep. 1934, NA, 4/107/1.
9. Brady, *Guardians of the Peace,* 199.
10. Broy to Roche, 12 Sep. 1934, NA, 4/107/1.
11. Kinnane manuscript, NA, 4/107/1, 28 Aug. 1933.
12. Kinnane to Department of Finance, 2 Sep. 1933, NA, 4/107/1.
13. Roche to Broy, 9 Mar. 1934, NA, 4/107/1.
14. NA, 4/107/1, 16 Nov. 1934.

15. Roche to Minister for Justice, NA, 4/107/1, 12 Sep. 1934.
16. Coogan, *De Valera*, 477.
17. O'Duffy, circular to divisional officers, NA, 4/28 (1b), 25 Nov. 1932.
18. NA, S9878. The Attorney-General, Patrick Lynch, 'had formed a very strong and definite view on the course of the trial' and signalled his intention of appealing to the Supreme Court in the event of an adverse judgment. 'The police themselves of their own accord and without official prompting warmly repudiated' the slight on their colleagues 'in their semi-official magazine.'
19. Brady, *Guardians of the Peace,* 223.
20. NA, Cab.1/3, 140, 11 June 1931.
21. *Irish Times,* 23 Jan. 1934.
22. Brady, *Guardians of the Peace,* 194–5.
23. Recorded conversation by the author with Patrick Gill.
24. Garda Síochána Act (1937) [26 Feb. 1937]: 'An Act to establish the validity of the admission of certain past and present members of the Garda Síochána ...' See also Garda Síochána (Appointments) Regulations (1937) [15 Mar. 1937].
25. Neligan, *The Spy in The Castle,* 78.
26. Brady, *Guardians of the Peace,* 198.
27. McElligott to Moynihan, 22 Feb. 1939, NA, S2396.
28. Roche to Moynihan, 11 Nov. 1939, NA, S2396.
29. Kinnane to Roche, 24 Oct. 1938, NA, Department of Justice, 4/107/1. (Sgt Thomas Walsh, Knappabeg, Westport, attested 1923; served at Cloone, Castlerea, Co. Roscommon.)
30. See Garda Síochána (Appointments) Regulations (1937), section 4 (2), special cases 'in the public interest.'
31. Roche to Minister for Justice, 8 Nov. 1938, NA, Department of Justice 4/107/1.
32. Roche to Kinnane, 9 Nov. 1938, NA, Department of Justice 4/107/1.
33. *Irish Times,* 17 June 1940.
34. Small collection of papers among LSF memorabilia, GA.
35. Lapel badge: black enamel, gilt harp and letters *CA,* for Caomhnóirí Áitiúla [Local Protectors].
36. Small collection of papers among LSF memorabilia, GA.
37. Kinnane to Secretary of Department of Justice, 14 Feb. 1941, NA, S12273.
38. Garda circular CM 2217/40, 28 Feb. 1941, NA, S12273.
39. Roche to Ó Muimhneacháin [Maurice Moynihan], Secretary of Department of the Taoiseach, 25 Feb. 1941, NA, S12273.
40. Roche to Ó Muimhneacháin [Maurice Moynihan], Secretary of Department of the Taoiseach, 25 Feb. 1941, NA, S12273.
41. NA, S12273, 12 Mar. 1941, manuscript in margin.
42. 'In the event of war', manuscript, Department of the Taoiseach, 4 Aug. 1942, NA, S12273.

CHAPTER 8 (PAGES 121–130)

1. Desborough Committee, 550.
2. See Reynolds and Judge, *The Night the Police Went on Strike*; see also O'Duffy, 'History of the Garda Síochána', *Garda Review*, Feb. 1930, 218–19.
3. Desborough Committee, 550.
4. Macready, General Order, 8 Mar. 1919, quoted by Reynolds and Judge, *The Night the Police Went on Strike*.
5. Constabulary and Police (Ireland) Act (1919).
6. Garda Síochána (Representative Body) Regulations (1924), and regulations made in 1925 and 1927; also NA, H99/215. For procedures in biennial elections see Routine Order 98/60, quarter to 31 Dec. 1960, 86.
7. NA, H99/215, 29 Aug. 1923.
8. NA, H99/215, 12 Sep. 1923.
9. NA, H99/215, 14 Sep. 1923.
10. NA, H99/215, 22 Dec. 1927.
11. NA, H235/91.
12. V.C. [Garda Vincent Collins], obituary, *Garda Review*, Jan. 1958. P. J. Gallagher was 'an able advocate who liked a fight … tenacious and seldom lost an argument … He stretched the rules in the cause of charity and humanity.' Gallagher died on 27 November 1957.
13. Editorial, *Garda Review*, Jan. 1958.
14. Representative Body correspondence, 1923–1931, NA, H235/166; additional papers on H235/166 (1)–(7).
15. Fanning, *The Irish Department of Finance*, 55.
16. Fanning, *The Irish Department of Finance*, 116.
17. Fanning, *The Irish Department of Finance*, 117.
18. Fanning, *The Irish Department of Finance*, 198. The economy committee (not to be confused with an economic committee formed about the same time): J. J. McElligott and J. J. Healy, Department of Finance; Diarmuid O'Hegarty, Secretary of the Executive Council; and Henry O'Friel, Department of Justice; secretariat, Department of Finance officials.
19. Fanning, *The Irish Department of Finance*, 200.
20. Fanning, *The Irish Department of Finance*, 229. The 'Cuts Committee': Philip O'Connell, a director of the Agricultural Credit Corporation (chairman); Laurence Cuffe, cattle salesman; Dónal O'Connor, chartered accountant; G. Gordon Campbell and Edward Gallen, farmers.
21. Fanning, *The Irish Department of Finance*, 232–3.
22. NA, H235/166, 13 Jan. 1924.
23. Report of Viceregal Commission on Reorganisation and Pay of the Irish Police Forces, 1920 (Ross Commission), *Parliamentary Papers, 1900–1949*, 552.
24. Kevin O'Higgins, in reply to Richard Mulcahy, *Dáil Debates*, 1923, vol. 5, cols. 430–2. See also Department of Justice memorandum, 16 June 1937, NA,

S9967A. Desborough Report scales were adopted for the Civic Guard 'administratively' in April 1922.

25. Editorial, *Garda Review*, May 1938.

26. *Iris Oifigiúil*, 26 Feb. 1924.

27. Garda Síochána (Pay and Allowances) Order (1924). And see CSO, consumer price index, table 1. Between 1914 and the immediate post-war period the index varied from 100 to 130 (1914 = 100) and then fell to between 80 and 85. Garda pay was accordingly adjusted to meet this reduction. The revised rates, based on eighty-five points, were payable within the range 70–100, not subject to 'trifling or temporary fluctuations.' See also memorandum of Department of Justice for Executive Council, 16 June 1937, NA, S9967A; memorandum accompanying 1924 pay order, *Garda Review*, Feb. 1938, 319; and *Dáil Debates*, 1929, vol. 29, cols. 1652–5.

28. NA, 235/166, 5 Feb. 1924.

29. Chief Supt McManus, 8 Feb. 1924, NA, H235/166.

30. Sgt Barry, undated appendix A attached to O'Duffy, 18 Feb. 1924, NA, H235/166.

31. O'Duffy, 18 Feb. 1924, NA, H235/166.

32. O'Duffy, 'History of the Garda Síochána', *Garda Review*, Feb. 1930, 221.

33. NA, H235/166, 24 June 1924.

34. Kinnane manuscript, 24 June 1924, NA, H235/166.

35. Unsigned memorandum for Secretary, Department of Justice, 13 Aug. 1925, NA, H235/166.

36. *Garda Review*, Jan. 1937.

37. Memorandum of Department of Finance for Executive Council, 8 Dec. 1937, NA, S9967A.

38. O'Duffy to Secretary, Department of Justice, 19 Oct. 1929, NA, H235/166/1.

39. Harding's letter, filed in the President's office by Michael MacDunphy for information of the Executive Council, 7 May 1929, NA, S5873.

40. RB officers to Commissioner, 15 Nov. 1929, NA, H235/166/1.

41. Commissioner to Minister, 28 Jan. 1930, NA, H235/166/1.

42. Commissioner to Minister, 24 Oct. 1930, NA, H235/166/3.

43. Blythe, *Dáil Debates*, vol. 29, cols. 765–6.

44. *Dáil Debates*, vol. 29, col. 1652–5.

45. *Dáil Debates*, vol. 29, col. 1678.

46. O'Duffy to Minister, 5 May 1931, NA, H235/166/4.

47. Memorandum of Department of Justice for Executive Council, 16 June 1937, NA, S9967A.

48. P.J.G. [P. J. Gallagher], *Garda Review*, Dec. 1931, 31.

49. *Irish Independent*, 8 Feb. 1932.

50. Fanning, *The Irish Department of Finance*, 237–8.

CHAPTER 9 (PAGES 131–139)

1. Memorandum of RB (Sgt T. Larkin, chairman; Insp. M. P. Horan; Station Sgt R. Butler; Garda P. E. Maguire; Garda M. N. McFeeley; Garda P. J. Ramsbottom; Sgt P. J. Gallagher, secretary), 4 June 1937, NA, 9967A.
2. Broy to Ruttledge, 5 June 1937, NA, 9967A.
3. *Garda Review*, July 1937, 867–71.
4. Editorial, *Garda Review*, July 1937.
5. Editorial, *Garda Review*, Sep. 1937.
6. *Garda Review*, Oct. 1937, 1279.
7. Editorial, *Garda Review*, Nov. 1937.
8. Editorial, *Garda Review*, Jan. 1938.
9. Memorandum of Department of Finance for Executive Council, 8 Dec. 1937, NA, S9967A.
10. NA, G2/15. See also Government minutes, Dec. 1937; Government meetings: 7 Dec., Ruttledge present; 14 Dec., absent; 21 Dec., present.
11. Editorial, *Garda Review*, Jan. 1938.
12. Editorial, *Garda Review*, Jan. 1938.
13. Editorial, *Garda Review*, Jan. 1938.
14. Reply to Garda claim, approved by Government on 7 Jan. 1938, NA, S9967A, also in *Garda Review*, Feb. 1938, 319.
15. Department of Justice memorandum, 30 Nov. 1942, NA, S9967A; Department of Finance memorandum, 20 Nov. 1944, NA, S9967B, also 12 Nov. 1945; Garda Síochána Pay Order (1945) [Jan. 1945].
16. Broy to Minister, 5 June 1937, NA, S9967A.
17. Department of Justice to Department of Finance, 16 June 1937, NA, S9967A.
18. Moynihan, 2 Oct. 1937, NA, S9967A.
19. JRB, 4 June 1937, NA, S9967A.
20. MacEntee to de Valera, 13 Dec. 1937, NA, S9967A.
21. Conversation with Con Walsh, eldest son of Patrick Walsh.
22. Government minutes, 24 May 1938, NA, G3/1. Michael Joseph Kinnane, fourth Garda Commissioner, 1938–1952: born Co. Galway, 1888; educated Blackrock College, Blackrock, Co. Dublin; joined British civil service in London, 1908; Dublin, Department of Home Affairs, principal officer, 1922; assistant secretary, 1928. Dealing directly with Garda matters, he gained valuable insights into the problems of the force. Died in office, 10 July 1952.
23. Keogh, *Ireland and the Vatican*, 127–32.
24. *Irish School Weekly*, 30 Jan. 1922, 107: 1922, grants for teaching of Irish withdrawn; Nov. 1923, 10 per cent reduction in salaries and emoluments; Mar. 1926, gratuities for instruction of monitors withdrawn; Mar. 1929, fees for instruction in maths and rural science withdrawn, elementary evening schools closed; Mar. 1933, reduction in salaries under Temporary Economies Act; Mar. 1934, 9 per cent reduction in salaries.

25. *Irish School Weekly,* 6 Feb. 1937, 138.
26. *Irish School Weekly,* 3 Jan. 1937, 3.
27. *Irish School Weekly,* 15 May 1937, 487.
28. *Irish School Weekly,* 5 June 1937, 559.
29. *Irish School Weekly,* 1 Jan. 1938, 3.
30. *Irish School Weekly,* 1 Jan. 1938, 3.
31. *Irish School Weekly,* 21 Jan. 1938, 75.
32. *Irish School Weekly,* 2 Apr. 1938, 319.
33. *Irish School Weekly,* 16 Apr. 1938, 367.
34. *Irish School Weekly,* 23 Apr. 1938, 391.
35. *Irish School Weekly,* 23 Apr. 1938, 402.
36. Editorial, *Garda Review,* May 1938.
37. Minister's reply to Garda claim, NA, S9967A; also in *Garda Review,* Feb. 1938, 319.
38. *Garda Review,* Jan. 1949.
39. *Garda Review,* Nov. 1950.
40. *Garda Review,* Jan. 1951.
41. *Garda Review,* Nov. 1950.
42. The first round of post-war national pay increases came into effect on 1 November 1946; second round, 1 November 1948; third round, 15 January 1951; fourth round, 1 November 1952; fifth round, 1 November 1955; sixth round, 1 April 1958; seventh round, 15 December 1959; eighth round, various dates in 1961 (information from Department of Finance).
43. *Garda Review,* Apr. 1947.
44. Kinnane to Department of Justice, 4 Nov. 1946, NA, S9967B.
45. NA, S9967B.
46. Manuscript minutes, undated: 'Circulated at today's Govt meeting at direction of the Taoiseach at the request of the Minister for Justice', NA, S9967B.
47. Garda Síochána Pay Order (1947) [July 1947]: guards, £3 10s to £6 7s 6d in twenty-five years; sergeants, £6 12s 6d to £7 10s in five years.
48. Editorial, *Garda Review,* Apr. 1947.
49. *Dáil Debates,* vol. 113: Alfred Byrne TD, col. 35; P. J. Burke TD, col. 747; Alfred Byrne TD, col. 1388; Seán Dunne TD, col. 1528.
50. NA, S9967C; *Irish Independent,* 18 Dec. 1948. Deputation received by the Minister for Justice, Gen. Mac Eoin: Chief Supt Thomas Collins, Sgt P. J. Gallagher, Garda J. J. Conway, DMD, Garda M. T. Egan, Cork, and Garda J. Flynn, Port Laoise.
51. *Garda Review,* Jan. 1949. See NA, S9967C, 31 Dec. 1948: gardaí awarded 11s from 1 Jan. 1949.
52. *Dáil Debates,* vol. 114, col. 175.
53. DMP: Committee of Inquiry, 1883, *House of Commons Papers, 1883.*
54. 'Fear na Cathrach', *Garda Review,* Feb. 1949, 298.

55. *Irish Times,* 11 Jan. 1949. The protest march was prohibited by the Commissioner.
56. Editorial, *Garda Review,* June 1949.

CHAPTER 10 (PAGES 140–154)

1. Kinnane to Secretary of Department of Justice, GA, B694/48, 2 Mar. 1948; copy of minutes, initialled, among miscellaneous unclassified correspondence.
2. Dep. Commr W. R. E. Murphy to Commissioner, 12 Sep. 1949, GA.
3. Kinnane to Coyne, 17 Sep. 1949, GA.
4. NA, Department of Justice, 4/321/2.
5. NA, Department of Justice, 4/321/2. Terms of reference: to inquire into duties, organisation, and strength; whether the force might be reorganised by reduction in the cost of the force, without interfering with proper policing or incurring greater expenditure on alternative methods of performing non-police duties; at what rate recruiting should be opened to maintain the strength considered necessary.
6. *Irish Independent,* 8 Feb. 1932.
7. Report of Committee on Police Conditions of Service (Oaksey Committee), part I, Apr. 1949, *Parliamentary Papers,* vol. 19, 251; part II, Nov. 1949, vol. 19, 379. For the Lord Justice Lawrence insight the author is indebted to the publisher's reader.
8. P.J.G. [P. J. Gallagher], *Garda Review,* June 1948.
9. *Garda Review,* Apr. 1950.
10. *Garda Review,* Aug. 1950.
11. Report of Commission of Inquiry, July 1951, para. 2, NA, Department of Justice, 4/321/2; strengths, 1948–1951, para. 22.
12. O'Duffy to Minister for Justice, 28 Jan. 1930, NA, H235/166/2. See also draft report, appendix IV, all non-police duties, seventy separate requirements, various Government departments, NA, S7989C/2. See also Walsh, *The Irish Police,* 1–3, on 'the inclusion of social and economic matters in the police remit . . . It would be fair to say . . . that the concept of police, as originally understood, comprised the organised protection of the health, welfare, security and morality of the citizenry, as well as the regulation of industry, commerce, the professions, agriculture and the environment in the interests of the common good.'
13. NA, 4/321/2, 23 Nov. 1951.
14. *Garda Review,* Oct. 1953.
15. NA, Department of Justice, 4/321/2; but see Report of Committee of Inquiry, para. 22: strength on 30 Apr. 1948: 7,510. Also para. 305, Headquarters and Depot; para. 306, DMD; para. 307–10, other divisions.
16. Draft report, NA, S7989C/2, 57: footnote, 'Paras. 304–310 subject to

reservation by Mr. Kinnane.' At p. 72, Kinnane's minute dated 31 July 1951 entering his caveat. See also NA, Department of Justice 4/321/2.

17. Press conference, D. Costigan, Dublin newspapers, 2 May 1959.
18. *Garda Review*, Oct. 1953.
19. *Garda Review*, Mar. 1959.
20. *Garda Review*, Aug. 1960.
21. Report of Commission of Inquiry, 1950, para. 291.
22. Coyne to McElligott, 5 Dec. 1951, NA, Department of Justice, 4/321/2.
23. Coyne to McElligott, 7 Feb. 1952, NA, Department of Justice, 4/321/2.
24. Coyne to Minister for Justice, 25 Feb. 1959, NA, Department of Justice, 4/321/2.
25. Fanning, *The Irish Department of Finance,* 493, encapsulating Patrick Lynch, 'The Irish economy since the war', 199.
26. Fanning, *The Irish Department of Finance,* 59–60 (quoting 'Silhouette', *Administration,* vol. 1, no. 1, 70).
27. *Garda Síochána Code, 1928,* chap. VI, Barrack Regulations.
28. *Garda Síochána Code, 1928,* chap. V, rule 155.
29. *Garda Síochána Code, 1928,* chap. VI, Barrack Regulations, rule 16.
30. *Garda Síochána Code, 1928,* chap. XXI, rules 794–815.
31. Routine Orders 21/1947; 13/1949; 25/1950; 21–23/1951; 22/1952.
32. *Garda Review,* Nov. 1949.
33. Routine Order 72/1960.
34. Costigan to Commissioner, 20 Sep. 1951, NA, Department of Justice 4/321/2.
35. Routine Order B16, 31 Mar. 1929.
36. *Garda Review,* May 1936.
37. *Garda Review,* July 1949.
38. Editorial, *Garda Review,* Aug. 1952.
39. P.J.G. [P. J. Gallagher], 'Without prejudice', *Garda Review,* Aug. 1952, 707.
40. Daniel Costigan: born Derryfadda, Kealkill, Co. Cork, 1911; educated St Finbarr's College, Farrenferris; entered civil service, 1929, executive officer, Department of Posts and Telegraphs; administrative officer, Department of Justice, 1935; assistant secretary, Department of Justice; Committee of Inquiry into Garda Síochána, 1951–52; Garda Commissioner, 1952; recruited first women gardaí, 1959; returned to civil service, 1965; died 10 Sep. 1979. As the civil servant in the Department of Justice responsible for the censorship of publications, Costigan had proved himself an enlightened official. When the Censorship Board in 1951 banned Graham Greene's novel *The End of the Affair* he argued against the severity of the decision, pointing out that the Committee on Evil Literature, on whose recommendations the legislation was based, had not recommended that the test should be whether a book 'might have a bad influence on an adolescent' (Dermot Keogh (editor), *Irish Democracy and the Right of Freedom of Information,* vol. 1 (Cork University Press, Cork); reviewed by Joe Carroll, *Irish Times,* 3 Apr. 1996).

41. 'Without prejudice', *Garda Review,* Aug. 1952.
42. Department of Justice for Government, 7 Nov. 1961, part IV, para. 19 (j), NA, S16841, B/61; also discussions with members of the force who were close to developments at the time.
43. Text of Costigan's address: *Garda Review,* Dec. 1953, 65–71. Berry's reprimand: author's recollection.
44. RB (Sgt P. J. Gallagher) to Commissioner, 15 Nov. 1948, NA, Department of Justice, 4/100/4.
45. Costigan, internal minutes, 13 Jan. 1949, NA, Department of Justice, 4/100/4.
46. Costigan to Controller, P&T Stores, 20 Oct. 1950, NA, Department of Justice, 4/100/4.
47. Costigan to Coakley, Controller, P&T Stores, 24 Jan. 1951, NA, Department of Justice, 4/100/4.
48. *Irish Times,* 22 Aug. 1951. Éamonn Ó Fiacháin, Garda sergeant, Dublin; born 1925, son of a DMP constable; educated at St Vincent's CBS; trained as a fitter. Garda Technical Bureau, ballistics. A pioneer environmentalist and member of the Gaelic League. As a young garda on traffic duty in Grafton Street he epitomised the efficiency of the Dublin pointsman. In 1950 an expatriate Irish writer, Mary Frances McHugh (*Thalassa,* 1931), commissioned Seán Keating PRHA to draw Ó Fiacháin's portrait, which is now in the Garda Museum.
49. Costigan to Minister for Justice, [1] Jan. 1954, NA, S7989C/2.
50. Costigan to Peter Berry, Secretary, Department of Justice, 18 Aug. 1960, NA, 4/100/4 (1948–1963), A29/3/60.
51. *Irish Times,* 16 July 1954.
52. *Dáil Debates,* vol. 174, col. 770. The increase in crime in 1957 was 14,000, in round figures. In 1958 a further increase of 18 per cent was recorded.
53. *Irish Independent,* 24 Apr. 1959.
54. *Cork Examiner,* 5 May 1959.
55. *Cork Examiner,* 3 Nov. 1959.
56. *Irish Times,* 2 May 1959.
57. *Irish Press,* 10 June 1960.
58. *Dáil Debates,* vol. 174, col. 770–1.
59. The officers sent to the scene of the three unsolved murders were: Asst Commr F. Burke (Hannan, Wexford, Mar. 1958); Asst Commr P. J. Carroll (Fitzpatrick, Kilbride, Feb. 1958); Dep. Commr T. Woods (Moore, Raemore, Tralee, Nov. 1958).
60. *Irish Times,* 17 Mar. 1959.
61. *Evening Mail,* 1 May 1959.
62. *Evening Herald,* 11 Nov. 1959.
63. Thomas Ambrose Joseph (Joe) Quigley (1919–1993), Garda Surgeon, 1958–1984; Carna, Co. Galway, both parents national teachers. Commandant, Army Medical Corps; athlete, track events and hurling. A

distinguished philatelist with an international reputation, member Post Office Philatelic Advisory Committee.

CHAPTER 11 (PAGES 155–165)

1. Interim Report of Royal Commission on the Police, 1960 (Willink Commission), *Parliamentary Papers,* vol. 20, 333.
2. *Observer* (London), 27 Nov. 1959, found among newspaper cuttings, 2 Mar. 1959–30 Dec. 1962, GA.
3. *Garda Review,* Feb. 1949.
4. Report of the Committee on Police Conditions (Oaksey Committee), part II, Nov. 1949, Police Council for Great Britain, para. 377, *Parliamentary Papers,* vol. 19.
5. Arbitration, *Parliamentary Papers,* vol. 19, para. 378.
6. *Garda Review,* July 1958.
7. *Garda Review,* Aug. 1958.
8. Memorandum of Department of Justice for Government, 20 Sep. 1958, NA, S16465A.
9. *Garda Review,* Aug. 1958.
10. Memorandum of Department of Justice for Government, 20 Sep. 1958, NA, S16465A.
11. Department of Finance to Government, 22 Sep. 1958, NA, S16465A.
12. NA, S16465A.
13. NA, S16465A.
14. Conversation with P. E. Gunn.
15. O'Duffy, 'History of the Garda Síochána', *Garda Review,* June 1929.
16. *Garda Review,* Dec. 1958.
17. Memorandum 4/38/34 of Department of Justice, 3 Jan. 1959 (appendix), NA, S16465A.
18. Text in Department of Justice to Commissioner, 12 Dec. 1958 (p. 9), NA, S16465A.
19. JRB to Commissioner, 16 Dec. 1958, NA, S16465A, listing such outstanding grievances as conciliation and arbitration, pay, rent and locomotion allowances, denial of the franchise, and standards of accommodation and of uniform and equipment.
20. Department of Justice to Commissioner, 18 Dec. 1958, NA, S16465A.
21. RB to Commissioner, 19 Dec. 1958, NA, S16465A.
22. 22 Dec. 1958, NA, S16465A. The reappointment of Oscar Traynor to the Department of Justice in Seán Lemass's first Government was welcomed by the *Garda Review* (July 1959): 'The force would be less than human if it were not pleased to have retained as its Minister one with whom it has had such cordial and happy relations. The Garda Síochána is particularly grateful to Mr.

Traynor for having secured for it … conciliation and arbitration.'

23. Garda officers to Commissioners, 23 Dec. 1958, NA, S16465A.

24. JRB, lower ranks to Commissioner, 23 Dec. 1958, NA, S16465A.

25. Memorandum of Department of Finance for Government, 5 Jan. 1959, NA, S16465A.

26. RB to Commissioner, 7 Apr. 1959 (appendix), NA, S16465A.

27. Memorandum of Minister for Justice for Government, 9 Apr. 1959, 4, para. 7, NA, S16465A.

28. *Irish Times,* 7 May 1959, quoting *Garda Review.*

29. MacEntee to de Valera, 13 Dec. 1937, NA, S9967A.

30. MacEntee to Lemass, 13 Jan. 1960, NA, S7989C/3/94.

31. Costigan to Secretary, Department of Justice, 2 Feb. 1960, NA, S7989C/3/94.

32. See Reddy, *The Murder File*; also John Healy, 'Science Beats Criminal' (series), *Irish Press,* beginning 22 Mar. 1954.

33. Commissioner's circular B2/13/60, 27 May 1964, NA, S14043B/2/95. The DMP district, whose boundaries were altered only slightly since they were drawn in 1836, was extended to embrace Howth and large areas of Rathfarnham and Bray, with consequent territorial reorganisation beyond the boundary of the new greater Dublin area.

34. *Irish Times,* 24 Apr. 1959. Two hundred women were interviewed for eighteen vacancies.

35. The inspectors selected for the course at the Police College, Bramshill, were Patrick McLaughlin, Technical Bureau, and Seán Sheehan, Letterkenny, who rose through the ranks to commissioner and assistant commissioner, respectively.

36. Department of Justice to Department of the Taoiseach, 16 Apr. 1960, NA, S7989C/3/94.

37. Manuscript on Lemass, unsigned letter, 25 Apr. 1960, NA, S7989C/3/94.

38. Urwick Orr and Partners (Ireland) Ltd, 1956 to 1958.

39. Author's notes, *c.* 1968, from Garda files, destroyed in a general clearance to provide office space, before an archival policy was adopted in 1974 and before the enactment of the National Archives Act (1986).

40. Garda Síochána (Representative Bodies) Regulations (1927).

41. Station Sgt Seán Ó Colmáin (1917–1982), member of a Dublin family of blacksmiths; joined Taca Síochána (the auxiliary police raised on the outbreak of war in 1939 and later absorbed into the permanent force). He was posted to a city station, where he emerged as an indefatigable organiser in the forefront of every good endeavour. Early in his service he became active in representative body affairs; he is credited with winning the right for gardaí to vote in Dáil and Seanad elections. An Irish-language enthusiast, he organised a scholarship scheme to send the children of gardaí to the Gaeltacht; invited President de Valera to officiate (see NA, Department of the President, 98/1/57,

and *Irish Times,* 27 June 1959). He retired as superintendent, Baltinglass.

42. P. E. Gunn, Dún Laoghaire; secretary, DMD selection committee, 1956–58; elected to RB 1958; chairman of RBG 1962–65.

43. Meeting of the DMD selection committee, Kevin Street station, 9 July 1958: *Garda Review,* Aug. 1958, 766.

44. 'Servienda Guberno', *Garda Review,* Jan. 1959, 197. The students of papal encyclicals among the Donnybrook gardaí were also probably attending the Dublin Institute for Adult Education.

45. NA, Department of Justice, 4/425, 19 May 1964. As finance officer at Garda Headquarters, Michael Wallace had a unique rapport with members of the force. On his recall to the Garda desk in the Department of Justice he was feted by the president and members of the officers' mess.

46. *Irish Independent,* 11 Jan. 1954.

47. Author's notes: see note 39 above.

48. JRB, O'Duffy, 28 Jan. 1930, NA, H235/166/1.

49. Memorandum of Department of Justice for Executive Council, 21 Oct. 1936, NA, S9297A.

50. Author's notes, Commissioner to B Branch, 28 Feb. 1959: see note 39 above; also *Irish Times,* 10 Feb. 1959. An application by Station Sgt Ó Colmáin for inclusion on the voters' register was refused, the Dublin County Registrar ruling that under existing legislation the applicant had no rights.

51. Author's notes, Commissioner to B Branch, 28 Feb. 1959, .

52. Author's notes, Commissioner to B Branch, 18 Aug. 1959.

53. Author's notes, Commissioner to B Branch, 7 Dec. 1960.

54. Author's notes, McCarthy to Costigan, 17 July 1961. There was no record on the file (no longer available) of the Commissioner's response to Chief Supt McCarthy.

CHAPTER 12 (PAGES 166–178)

1. *Irish Times,* 24 Dec. 1953.

2. Routine Order 65/1960, half year to 31 Dec. 1960, 45–54.

3. Representative Body to Commissioner, 28 Apr. 1927, NA, H235/166.

4. Routine Order 65/1960, 52. The *Police Duty Manual* remained in use in the stations as a convenient guide to basic duties.

5. Memorandum 4/314/6 of Department of Justice for Government, 21 Feb. 1960, NA, S16841A. The Garda members on the arbitration board were Chief Supt T. Collins, Wexford, and Garda Malachy Egan. See Garda Síochána Pay Orders, 1924–1975.

6. Editorial, *Garda Review,* June 1960; also 'Senex', p. 529: 'Our first experience of Conciliation and Arbitration points towards certain lessons for the future … Our triumphs will go hand in hand with disappointments …'

7. 'Viator', *Garda Review*, June 1960, 579.
8. *Garda Review*, Jan. 1961, 145–51.
9. *Garda Review*, Jan. 1961, 153–4; see also Interim Report of Royal Commission on the Police, 1960 (Willink Report), Nov. 1960, *Parliamentary Papers*, vol. 20, 333.
10. Unofficial news item, Department of Justice, Dec. 1960, NA, S16841A.
11. *Garda Review*, Jan. 1961.
12. Memorandum 4/314 of Department of Justice for Government, 7 Nov. 1961, appendix B, NA, S16841, B61. See Garda Síochána Pay Orders, 1924–1975.
13. *Sunday Review*, 29 Oct. 1961.
14. *Irish Independent*, 2 Nov. 1961.
15. *Evening Press*, 2 Nov. 1961.
16. *Evening Herald*, 2 Nov. 1961.
17. *Irish Times*, 3 Nov. 1961.
18. *Evening Press*, 6 Nov. 1961.
19. *Daily Express*, 3 Nov. 1961.
20. *Irish Independent*, 3 Nov. 1961.
21. Memorandum 4/314 of Department of Justice for Government, NA, S16841, B61.
22. *Irish Times*, 4 Nov. 1961.
23. *Irish Times*, 4 Nov. 1961.
24. John Marrinan to the author.
25. Editorial, *Irish Times*, 6 Nov. 1961.
26. Memorandum 4/314 of Department of Justice for Government, NA, S16841, B61. According to John Marrinan, the one 'ringleader' identified was probably the late Dónal Murphy, who was believed to have circulated the notice of the proscribed meeting and booked the hall.
27. Memorandum 4/314 of Department of Justice for Government, NA, S16841, B61.
28. Memorandum 4/314 of Department of Justice for Government, NA, S16841, B61.
29. *Irish Times*, 6 Nov. 1961.
30. *Evening Herald*, 9 Nov. 1961.
31. Manuscript, 9 Nov. 1961, NA, S16841, B61.
32. *Irish Independent*, 10 Nov. 1961.
33. Author, recollected from conversations.
34. *Irish Times*, 11 Nov. 1961.
35. *Sunday Independent*, 12 Nov. 1961.
36. *Irish Independent*, 13 Nov. 1961.
37. *Irish Press*, 13 Nov. 1961.
38. *Irish Independent*, 15 Nov. 1961.
39. *Irish Times*, 14 Nov. 1961. In a television interview, Ivor Kenny, IMI and a

member of the Conroy Commission, commented that the protesting young gardaí might consider if they had chosen the right career.

40. *Irish Press,* 14 Nov. 1961.
41. *Irish Independent,* 14 Nov. 1961.
42. Manuscript, Archbishop McQuaid, 15 Nov. 1961, NA, S16841, B61.
43. Lemass, 16 Nov. 1961, NA, S16841, B61.
44. Memorandum 4/314, 7 Nov. 1961, NA, S16841, B61.
45. *Dáil Debates,* 16 Nov. 1961, vol. 192, col. 519: McQuillan.
46. *Dáil Debates,* 16 Nov. 1961, vol. 192, col. 523: Treacy.
47. *Irish Times,* 17 Nov. 1961.
48. NA, S17189/61; also *Garda Review,* Dec. 1961.
49. *Irish Times,* 9 Jan. 1962.
50. Press release, Department of Justice, *Irish Independent,* 5 Dec. 1961. Advisory Committee on Regulations of Representative Bodies: Richard McGonigle SC, William H. Gill, M. H. Gill and Son Ltd; Philip Cassidy, Dublin Institute of Catholic Sociology. In November the Minister for Justice stated that he was being urged to institute an inquiry into 'the workings of the negotiating machinery available to members of the Garda Síochána.' He could 'not undertake any such examination [until he had received] an assurance from the Commissioner that discipline had been fully restored' (*Irish Independent,* 10 Nov. 1961).
51. *Irish Times,* 18 Nov. 1961. Filed in Commissioner's office; in the margin Supt J. M. McAleenan, private secretary, noted: 'This document is presumably the paper of 20.7.'61 on file B2/27/60.'
52. Garda Síochána (Representative Bodies) Regulations (1962).
53. *Irish Times,* 21 Sep. 1962, photograph of new RBG: Patrick Nolan, Mallow; John Marrinan, Rathfarnham, Dublin (general secretary); P. E. Gunn, Dún Laoghaire (chairman); Chris Ryan, Kiltyclogher; James Fitzgerald, Naas (co-opted in place of Éamon Ó Fiacháin, Headquarters, promoted sergeant); Patrick Courtney, William Street, Limerick; Niall Scott, Tralee; Patrick Lally, Oldcastle (elected chairman of JRB); James Scott, Claremorris; John Lee, Dunglow; Micheál Harlowe, Pearse Street, Dublin; Richard Keating, Pearse Street, Dublin. (Marrinan, Harlowe and Keating were members of the 'secret committee'.)
54. Author's notes from files destroyed.
55. *Irish Times,* 28 Jan. 1963: 'The Civic Guard [sic] is a body of men with a history unique in this country. It was established under the guidance mainly of Kevin O'Higgins to serve two purposes. These were the restoration of a universal respect for the law after the Royal Irish Constabulary had suffered almost total rejection by the people; and the acceptance by the same people of a force which was prepared, unarmed, to protect civic rights in a community completely set at odds by civil strife. Its success was, and is,

manifest. There is no body of opinion now prepared to question the loyalty, integrity or efficiency of the Civic Guard in spite of the many stresses imposed on it by the birth, youth and maturing of a new State. The Guards, in short, have served us well, and we must therefore consider whether we, the taxpayers, have rendered adequate thanks ...'

56. Memorandum of Department of Finance, 15 July 1963, NA, S16841, B95.
57. Memorandum of Department of Justice, 12 July 1963, NA, S16841, B95.
58. Conroy Report, appendix 230a; also Garda Síochána Pay Orders.
59. Urwick Orr and Partners (Ireland) Ltd, survey of Garda administration, 1956–58, GA.
60. Gerard Quinn, Tribunal of Inquiry, Remuneration of Clerical Recruitment Grades in the Public Sector, Dublin: Stationery Office 1960.
61. *Garda Síochána Code, 1928,* introduction.
62. Conroy Report, para. 680.
63. Conroy Report, 'rate for the job', para. 288–91.
64. P. E. Gunn (chairman of RBG, 1962–65) to author.
65. Conroy Report, appendix 230; also Garda Síochána Pay Orders. On the base of 100 points for a garda at the top of the scale, superintendents in the period 1922–23 had 243 points; the pay cuts the following year increased this relativity to 271 points. In the post-war movement in favour of workers on low incomes, including gardaí, the superintendents' relativity was reduced to 187 points, which was not substantially disturbed by the Conroy Report.
66. Representative Body of Inspectors, Station Sergeants and Sergeants, elected 1965: Insp. Seán Ó Colmáin, Dún Laoghaire (chairman); Sgt T. A. Murphy, Training Centre (secretary), Sgt Gregory Allen, Headquarters (general secretary); Insp. P. Crowley, Mullingar; Insp. J. Loakman, Union Quay, Cork; Insp. J. F. Murray, Galway; Station Sgt J. Connolly, Chapelizod; Sgt J. Kelly, Clifden; Sgt N. K. McCready, Kilmainham; Sgt D. Fingleton, Headquarters (treasurer).
67. RBISS Pay Claim, 1965, bound volume, GA.
68. The author, with Insp. J. F. Murray, Galway, represented the RBISS on the arbitration board.
69. Conroy Report, para. 371. And see 'Fear Fada', *Garda Review,* Sep. 1966: 'The rumours going the rounds are as uncomplimentary as they are incorrect ... The only fact we are sure of is that Sgt G. Allen has been reverted from his R.B. post. This decision coupled with the absence of any official statement on the pay claim has given rise to a certain amount of speculation ... Some time ago I saw a copy of the report on which the NCO claim was based. It is a comprehensive document, and the arguments in our favour are put forward with that ruthless logic I'm sure the Official Side in the talks will find somewhat disconcerting. Is it here the difficulties and delays arise, or is it something more sinister that does not bear the telling?' (The representative

body in fact felt bound by the confidentiality rule in conciliation and arbitration.) The same correspondent (*Garda Review,* Dec. 1966) captured the mood of disappointment in the middle ranks: 'After all the case building and skirmishing over a period of 14 months, the mountains laboured and brought forth a mouse.'

70. Brown, *The Social Psychology of Industry,* 72: 'The primary group rather than the isolated individual should be the basic unit of observation in all industrial research.'

71. Brown, *The Social Psychology of Industry,* 104.

72. Joseph (Clarence) Daly, Passionist priest, 1928–1998; Castlerea, Co. Roscommon, grandson, son and nephew of constables in the RIC; spiritual director, Garda Síochána, 1956–1983. In 1947 he joined the Congregation of the Passion at the Graan, Enniskillen, taking the name of an obscure seventh-century Austrian saint. At his funeral service Father Ralph Egan, himself a former Garda chaplain, recalled that Clarence stamped his own strong character on a name associated with an ineffectual character in whimsical literature. In stature he was a big man, with a bluff personality that perfectly matched the manners of workaday policemen. Stepping down in 1983, he spent the remainder of his life as a director of retreats. A popular pulpit orator, he preached an annual charity sermon in the United States on behalf of Concern America; for this work he won the Michael Doheny Humanitarian Award.

73. *L'Osservatore Romano,* 22 Apr. 1982. See also *Garda Review*, May 1982.

CHAPTER 13 (PAGES 179–190)

1. William Patrick Quinn: born Inniskeen, Co. Monaghan, 1900; educated St Mary's, Dundalk; service in Irish Volunteers, War of Independence. Joined the Civic Guard in 1922; replaced the murdered Supt John David Curtin as district officer, Tipperary, 1931. Rose through the ranks to become the first rank-and-file member of the force appointed to the highest office: Commissioner, 1965–67; died 10 Jan. 1978.

2. *Irish Times,* 6 Feb. 1965.

3. Department of the Taoiseach 97/6/587, 3 June 1965, NA, S16841B. Memorandum of Department of Justice for the Government (RBG: 'It has been said …'), provenance not shown.

4. Patrick Carroll (1903–1975); Stradbally, Co. Laois; clerk, battalion staff officer, national army; joined Civic Guard in 1923 and rose through the ranks. Police duty instructor; collaborated with former District Inspector, Michael Horgan, RIC, in adapting the *RIC Guide* (Andrew Reed) for use in the Garda Síochána (1934). Commissioner, 1967–68; closely identified with representative bodies; first Commissioner to address rank-and-file elected assemblies.

5. Copy of papers, including Report of Commission of Inquiry, 24 May 1968, GA, RP 1/2/05. Chief Supt J. Coakley, Ennis (chairman); Supt E. J. Doherty, Union Quay, Cork; Supt J. J. McNally, Cavan; Sgt N. K. McCready, Kilmainham; Sgt T. A. Murphy, Training Centre; Garda John Marrinan, RBG; Garda D. McNamara, Thurles; Det.-Garda B. A. Sheehan, Central Detective Unit; Det.-Garda T. O'Leary, Central Detective Unit; Sgt A. J. Mulligan, Blessington (secretary). Terms of reference: 'to undertake by research and discussion into Divisional, District and Sub-District policing arrangements considered necessary to meet changes arising from the introduction of the Reduced Working Week as claimed by the Representative Body for Guards ...' The committee was to report to the Commissioner on the methods recommended, the disposal of resources in personnel, transport, and equipment, and the employment of civilians.

6. Peter Berry to Commissioner, 21 June 1968, GA, RP 1/2/05.

7. Report of Urwick, Orr and Partners (Ireland) Ltd (Guthrie Report), GA, 21/1958.

8. GA, RP 1/2/05, Coakley, para. 15, 16. The ratio of gardaí to the population in 1958 was 1:620, 'appreciably higher than that of reasonably comparable forces,' in Guthrie's view. Compare Guthrie's proposed ratio of 1:750 with the ratios in England and Wales of 1:509 in the boroughs, 1:637 in the counties (Report of Committee of Chief Constables of England and Wales, 1962; Coakley, para. 17).

9. Coakley, para. 17; Report of Committee of Chief Constables of England and Wales, 1962. See also the American authority, Wilson and McLaren, *Police Administration*, p. 365: 'A distribution of the patrol force based on an absolute measure of the need in terms of minutes of time necessary to perform a satisfactory quality of service seems to be impractical . . . There has not yet been developed an absolute measure of the time needed for a satisfactory routine preventive patrol, and (with the exception of patrolmen whose duties are entirely inspectional) most of a patrolman's time is spent in this type of patrol . . . There likewise has not yet been established a standard optimum patrol strength . . . An absolute measure of the required patrol time must be based on complete data . . . Time and location data are unknown in some cases; the proportion with missing data may be high.'

10. Author's notes, Berry to Commissioner, 15 Mar. 1968, GA, RP 5/126/24.

11. Carroll to Berry, 15 Mar. 1968, GA, RP 5/126/24. During the nineteen-fifties and sixties, two divisions and eleven districts were abolished; sixty-one stations were closed, and fifty re-formed as sub-stations. Strength of country divisions at end of 1950: 5,046; end of February 1968: 3,934, a reduction of 1,112. As 267 had moved into the new DMA in January 1964, the net reduction in the provinces was 845.

12. Copy, Dep. Commr A. I. Flood to Secretary, Department of Justice, 31 July

1968, GA, RP 1/2/05. It was proposed to close a further sixteen stations and eighteen sub-stations and to re-form thirty-seven stations as sub-stations.

13. Coakley (para. 147) stressed as 'basic essentials' the maintenance of necessary strengths at district headquarters stations, adequate transport, a radio system, and outside telephone facilities at outlying stations.

14. Coakley (para. 38) proposed the closure of thirteen stations and fifteen sub-stations and the creation of thirty-seven new sub-stations.

15. Coakley, para. 133.

16. Author's recollection.

17. Author's recollection. See Walsh, *The Irish Police*, 13–14: the Garda Síochána as a body does not enjoy a legal personality distinct from that of its individual members; also p. 67: the status of a garda as a member of an organised and disciplined force of police under the leadership of a chief officer.

18. *Irish Independent*, 22 Jan. 1968.

19. *Irish Times*, 20 Jan. 1969.

20. *Garda Review*, Apr. 1974.

21. *Sunday Press*, 18 Aug. 1968.

22. *Irish Times*, 24 Aug. 1968. In reply to a request from the Labour Court for advice on recruitment and training in the Garda Síochána, a clerk at Garda Headquarters routinely drafted a short letter giving the sort of information that might have been found in a recruiting poster; and the letter was dispatched. On such evidence, it seems, the Labour Court made its momentous decision equating pay in the Fire Brigade with Garda rates. (Author)

23. Lord Desborough (1918), adopted in Ireland by Lord Ross (1919): 'A policeman has responsibilities and obligations which are peculiar to his calling and distinguish him from other public servants and municipal employees.'

24. *Irish Times*, 24 Aug. 1968, from the Report of President L. B. Johnson's Commission on Law Enforcement and Administration of Justice, *Task Force Report: The Police*, 1967, 135.

25. *Irish Times*, 13 Sep. 1968. In August the RBG had two claims at arbitration, one for a 162 per cent pay increase, the other for a 52 -day week.

26. Memo, Department of Justice to Government, 29 Aug. 1968, NA, S16755, 99/1/314.

27. *Irish Independent*, 12 Sep. 1968.

28. Commission on the Garda Síochána (Conroy Commission): J. C. Conroy, senior Circuit Court judge, chairman of Civil Service Arbitration Board, also headed an inquiry into the remuneration of bank officials; Ivor Kenny, director, Irish Management Institute; Patrick Noonan, president, Incorporated Law Society; Gerard Quinn, lecturer in economics, UCD, chairman of Tribunal on Remuneration of Clerical Grades in the Public Service; William P. Quinn, former Garda Commissioner.

29.   *Irish Times,* 19 June 1969.

30.   *Evening Herald,* 17 June 1969.

31.   Michael John Wymes: born Drogheda, son of an RIC constable, 1907; died 19 Dec. 1989. Joined the Garda Síochána and rose through the ranks; detective-superintendent, Central Detective Unit; assistant commissioner, DMA; Commissioner, 1968–73. In an unprecedented move by the Government, he was nominated Commissioner months before his predecessor, Patrick Carroll, was due to retire.

32.   *Irish Press,* 26 July 1969. '1922 code': see note 33.

33.   Garda Síochána (Designation, Appointments and Discipline) Regulations (1924), section 16; re-enacted in Garda Síochána (Discipline) Regulations (1926).

34.   Editorial, *Irish Independent,* 28 July 1969.

35.   *Irish Independent,* 29 July 1969.

36.   Editorial, *Irish Times,* 26 July 1969.

37.   Editorial, *Irish Press,* 26 July 1969.

38.   Editorial, *Irish Times,* 30 July 1969.

39.   *Sunday Independent,* 27 July 1969.

40.   *Irish Press,* 1 Aug. 1969.

41.   See Devitt, *Never Bet,* 91–2.

42.   *Garda Review,* Oct. 1969. Michael Fitzgerald (1924–1981), chief superintendent; Drumcollogher, Co. Limerick, farmer; Garda Síochána, 1945. Of uncompromising honesty, he was given to secret acts of charity. 'A stickler for discipline . . . he set a very high standard for himself . . . not . . . the wisest of men in dealing with subordinates' (Devitt, *Never Bet*). In assessing the career of such controversial figures as E. P. Garvey and Michael Fitzgerald, definitive verdicts must await the judgment of historians when the restricted papers of the period are made available for research.

43.   Author's recollection.

44.   Conroy Report, para. 21.

45.   Conroy Report, para. 27–9.

46.   Conroy Report; see summary of recommendations, 216–24.

47.   Conroy Report, para. 371.

48.   Conroy Report, para. 826–7.

49.   Conroy Report, para. 726, 750.

50.   The cost of the Conroy recommendations approved by March 1970 was £1.75 million a year; the reduction in hours of duty would cost another £1.1 million (Minister for Justice, quoted in the *Irish Independent,* 14 Mar. 1970).

51.   Author's notes: Garda Headquarters circular A72/30/70, Apr. 1973.

52.   Author's recollection.

53.   Conroy Report, para. 1266–7.

54.   Conroy Report, para. 318, 328. On the maximum pay for a garda (£23 7s 3d

for men, £20 8s 9d for women, on 1 June 1969) Conroy recommended a new maximum of £25 7s 3d for men and £22 8s 9d for women, together with a restored rent allowance of £2 a week for married members and £1 a week for single members.

55. *Sunday Independent,* 25 Jan. 1970.
56. *Irish Press,* 24 Jan. 1970.
57. *Evening Herald,* 10 Mar. 1970.
58. *Irish Times,* 13 Mar. 1970.
59. *Garda Review,* Sep. 1976.
60. *Garda Review,* Oct. 1977. See also *Garda Review,* Oct. 1980: the old JRB had 'outlived its effectiveness ... The spirit of healthy rivalry which motivated the ... separate bodies during the 'sixties and 'seventies was a major factor in improving Garda pay and conditions all round ... Each group feels it has certain prerogatives and privileges to protect. Some of these are real. Some, not to put too fine a point upon it, are illusory; hangovers from days gone by ...'
61. Patrick Malone, Commissioner, 1973–75; born 1910, Riverstown, Dundalk, son of a farmer; educated Dundalk CBS. Garda Síochána 1931; rose through the ranks. As chief superintendent, Crime Branch, he was a witness at the arms trial, 1970.

CHAPTER 14 (PAGES 191–203)

1. *Garda Review,* Dec. 1976. Edmund Patrick Garvey (1915–1989); born Ballinlough, Co. Roscommon. Motor mechanic; joined Taca Síochána, 1940, and rose through the ranks. In the Central Detective Unit earned a reputation in the investigation of serious crime. Energetic in promoting welfare: member of the Garda Club; Garda housing officer. Commissioner 1975–78, during the period of paramilitary activity in the state. In 1975 was made a member of the Orange Order by the government of the Netherlands for the rescue of the kidnapped Dutch industrialist Tiede Herrema.
2. Author's recollection.
3. *Irish Times,* 20 Jan. 1978.
4. Editorial, *Irish Times,* 20 Jan. 1978.
5. *Garda Review,* Feb. 1978.
6. *Irish Times,* 21 July 1978, 8.
7. Dick Walsh, *Irish Times,* 20 Jan. 1978.
8. Don Buckley, *Irish Times,* 20 Jan. 1978, 6. Editorial board of *Garda Review:* Garda Jim Fitzgerald, GRA; Garda John Marrinan, GRA; Insp. Patrick Culligan, AGSI; Sgt Derek Nally, AGSI; Supt Laurence McKeon.
9. Reddy, *Murder Will Out,* gives a comprehensive account of the Reynolds murder and subsequent trial.

10. FitzGerald, *All in a Life,* 312.
11. Courtney, *It Was Murder!,* 6.
12. Courtney, *It Was Murder!,* 133.
13. Courtney, *It Was Murder!,* 129–30.
14. FitzGerald, *All in a Life,* 313.
15. Courtney, *It Was Murder!,* 5.
16. Duggan, *A History of the Irish Army,* 280.
17. Devitt, *Never Bet,*146.
18. Author.
19. Courtney, *It Was Murder!,* ix.
20. Courtney, *It Was Murder!,* ix.
21. Courtney, *It Was Murder!,* 5.
22. Routine Orders, Sep. 1931.
23. Det.-Sgt George Lawlor [1932], 'Crime detection', *Garda Review,* Nov. 1960.
24. The success of the specialists, and the reputation won for the Garda Síochána, is documented by Tom Reddy in *Murder Will Out* and *The Murder File* and by John Courtney in *It Was Murder!*
25. Conversation with Dr James Donovan.
26. Reith, *A New Study of Police History,* 221.
27. Reith, *A New Study of Police History,* 135.
28. Reddy, *Murder Will Out,* 162.
29. *Neighbourhood Watch: Crime Awareness Works* (promotional pamphlet, with a foreword by Commr P. J. Culligan).
30. *Communiqué* (Garda Headquarters), reported in the *Sunday Tribune,* 12 Apr. 1998. All preventive activities, including mainly motorised patrols, recorded as accounting for 35 per cent of all Garda time.
31. Conroy Report, 1189.
32. Conroy Report, 1193.
33. Radio Advisory Committee: Prof. J. O. Scanlan, UCD (chairman); A. C. Deenan, ESB; K. O'Connell, RTE; P. McDonagh, Limerick RTC; Dep. Commr E. J. Doherty; D. Mathews, Department of Justice; B. Lenihan, Department of Finance.
34. *Irish Independent,* 26 Oct. 1974.
35. Conroy Report, 1264.
36. Conroy Report, 1266.
37. *Garda Review,* Aug. 1980.

CHAPTER 15 (PAGES 204–217)

1. *Irish Times,* 5 Oct. 1978.
2. Patrick McLaughlin: born Malin, Co. Donegal, 1921; costing clerk; educated St Eunan's College, Letterkenny. Garda 1943; head of Technical Bureau,

1961–67. Tactful successor to his predecessor, Edmund Garvey, taking over in 1978. Directed Garda organisation for papal visit, 1979. Instituted the annual Garda pilgrimage for peace in Ireland to the Marian shrine at Knock, 1979; led the Garda pilgrimage to Rome on the occasion of the diamond jubilee of the Garda Síochána, 1982. Resigned in 1983 with Dep. Commr T. J. Ainsworth as a result of the telephone-tapping affair involving Government ministers.

3. Editorial, *Irish Times*, 12 Oct. 1978.
4. *Irish Times*, 16 May 1978.
5. Report of Garda Committee of Inquiry (Ryan Committee) (Dr W. J. L. Ryan, Roderick O'Hanlon, Gerard Quinn, Seán Ó Murchú, Redmond Power), Apr. 1979.
6. *Garda Review*, Nov. 1978.
7. *Garda Review*, Nov. 1978.
8. Gardaí with two years' service, £3,599–3,675 (6 per cent); after five years, £3,998–4,275 (11 per cent); on nine-year scale, long-service increment at fifteen years: pay increased from £4,375 to £5,200 (18 per cent). Rent allowance: £631 married, £423 single. Sergeants: £4,852, increased to £5,750; inspectors: £5,335, increased to £6,600. Superintendents and chief superintendents, who did not receive overtime pay, were awarded a new maximum of £8,775 and £10,875, respectively. The increases, including pay and rent allowance, were estimated to cost £14 million in a full year.
9. *Irish Times*, 12 May 1979.
10. Sgt Derek Nally, *Irish Times*, 12 May 1979.
11. Ryan Report, 9.3, 9.4.
12. Ryan Report, 9.6.
13. Ryan Report, 9.28.
14. *Garda Review*, Jan. 1980. See also Ryan Report, para. 8.51: 'There is scope for improvement in the procedures by which recruits are selected … It would be desirable to supplement the present examination which applicants must take by aptitude and other tests to assess their suitability for a career in the Force …'
15. The minister speculated that the editor was 'not necessarily the writer of the article.' John Marrinan, in a letter to the editor of the *Sunday Press*, 16 Mar. 1980, admitted that he was the author.
16. *Dáil Debates*, vol. 318, col. 999.
17. *Garda Review*, Feb. 1980.
18. Conroy Report, 27–9.
19. Brown, *The Social Psychology of Industry*.
20. Evans, *The Police Revolution*.
21. Author.
22. *Garda Review*, Jan. 1961: the last reference to a Dublin allowance.

23. Directory of rules, regulations and procedures relating to the GRA and to the rights and obligations of its members, 43.
24. Editorial, *Irish Times*, 4 Jan. 1997, and subsequent correspondence between George Maybury and the author, beginning 14 Jan. 1997.
25. Reith, *A New Study of Police History*, 26: Bow Street Runners.
26. *Garda Review*, July 1978.
27. *Irish Independent*, 26 July 1978.
28. *Irish Times*, 26 July 1978.
29. *Irish Times*, 5 Aug. 1978.
30. *Irish Times*, 2 Oct. 1980.
31. Gregory Allen to editor, *Irish Times*, 8 Oct. 1980.
32. *Sunday Tribune*, 21 Feb. 1982.
33. *Horizon*, Mar. 1982.
34. Report of the fourth annual delegate conference, Bantry, *Horizon*, Apr. 1982.
35. *Irish Times*, 1 Apr. 1982.
36. *Irish Times*, 1 Apr. 1982.
37. *Irish Independent*, 1 Apr. 1982.
38. *Irish Times*, 2 Apr. 1982.
39. Garda Síochána Act (1977).
40. Editorial, *Horizon*, Apr. 1982.
41. Garda Síochána (Associations) Regulations (1978).
42. Editorial, *Horizon*, Apr. 1982.
43. *Garda Review*, Mar.–Apr. 1982.
44. *Garda Review*, Nov. 1982.
45. Gorer, *Exploring English Character*.
46. Correspondence of Haughey, Coyne, and others, 9–22 June 1960, NA, 4/483.
47. Manuscript, McAleenan to Costigan, 7 Mar. 1962, filed among press cuttings, GA.
48. Author's recollection.
49. Reith, *A New Study of Police History*, 135.
50. Editorial, *Garda Review*, Jan. 1985.
51. *Garda Training Committee: Report on Probationer Training* (1987), 251.
52. *Garda Training Committee: Report on Probationer Training* (1987), para. 4.1, quoting Prof. August Vollmer, *The Police and Modern Society*.
53. *Garda Training Committee: Report on Probationer Training* (1987), para. 4.3.
54. Correspondence, 9 Aug.–10 Oct., NA, H99/52; see also H99/228.

BIBLIOGRAPHY

PRIMARY SOURCES

Garda Síochána Archives (Record Tower, Dublin Castle): various papers, including the small but valuable Patrick Walsh Collection.
Military Archives (Cathal Brugha Barracks, Dublin): various papers.
National Archives (Dublin): files of the Department of Justice (incorporating the Department of Home Affairs) from 1922.
University College, Dublin: Richard Mulcahy Papers and O'Malley Papers.

JOURNALS

Garda Review, 1925–1935; 1969–
Guth an Gharda, 1924
Horizon (journal of the Association of Garda Sergeants and Inspectors), 1980–82 (continuing as *Garda News*)
Irisleabhar an Gharda, 1922–24; 1935–1969
Síocháin (journal of the Garda Pensioners' Association), 1972–
An Síothadóir (journal of the Garda Pensioners' Association), 1962–1971

BOOKS AND ARTICLES

Alderson, John, *Policing Freedom*, London: Macdonald and Evans 1979.
Allen, Gregory, 'Towards a model police service', *Garda Review*, Apr. 1974.
Allen, Gregory, 'Soldier and sensible lawyer', *Garda Review*, July 1974.
Allen, Gregory, 'The Tavistock angle', *Garda Review*, Sep. 1974.
Allen, Gregory, 'Police, pay and politics', *Garda Review*, Jan. 1975.
Allen, Gregory, 'Status and police', *Garda Review*, June 1975.
Allen, Gregory, 'Arms, the DMP and 1916', *Garda Review*, Aug. and Sep. 1977.
Allen, Gregory, 'Unarmed force by accident', *Police Chief* (New York), Sep. 1977.
Allen, Gregory, 'The General Prisons Board, 1877–1928'; *Irish Law Times*, 17 Sep. 1977.
Allen, Gregory, 'The New Police, London and Dublin: the birth of the Dublin Metropolitan Police', *Police Journal* (London), L/4, 1977.

Allen, Gregory, 'The Jesuits and the DMP', *Pioneer,* July–Aug. 1985.

Allen, Gregory, *The Passionists and the Policeman in Ireland, 1893–1993,* Dublin: Passionist Publications 1993.

Allen, Mary, *The Pioneer Policewoman,* London: Chatto and Windus 1925.

Barry, Tom, *Guerilla Days in Ireland,* Tralee: Anvil Books 1981.

Béaslaí, Piaras, *Michael Collins and the Making of a New Ireland,* Dublin: Phoenix 1926.

Beckett, J. C., *The Making of Modern Ireland, 1603–1923,* London: Faber and Faber 1966.

Brady, Conor, 'The policeman's lot', *Irish Times,* 19–21 Aug. 1969.

Brady, Conor, 'Call from Conroy', *Irish Times,* 5 Feb. 1970.

Brady, Conor, 'The professional policeman', *Irish Times,* 6 Feb. 1970.

Brady, Conor, *Guardians of the Peace,* Dublin: Gill and Macmillan 1974.

Breathnach, Séamus, *The Irish Police from Earliest Times to the Present Day,* Tralee: Anvil Books 1974.

Brennan-Whitmore, William J., *With the Irish in Frongoch,* Dublin: Talbot Press 1917.

Brewer, John, *Royal Irish Constabulary: An Oral History,* Belfast: Institute of Irish Studies, Queen's University, 1990.

Brewer, John, *Inside the RUC: Routine Policing in a Divided Society,* Oxford: Clarendon Press 1991.

Broeker, Galen, *Rural Disorder and Police Reform in Ireland, 1812–1836,* London: Routledge and Kegan Paul 1970.

Brown, J., *The Social Psychology of Industry,* Harmondsworth (Middx): Penguin 1954.

Brown, J., *Techniques of Persuasion,* Harmondsworth (Middx): Penguin 1963.

Bunn, Frank, *Letters to a Young Constable,* Stoke-on-Trent 1947.

Carroll, Patrick, 'Notes for a history of police in Ireland' [a series of articles based on original research], *Garda Review,* 1961–62.

Childers, Erskine, *The Constructive Work of Dáil Éireann, No. 1, The National Police and Courts of Justice,* Dublin: Talbot Press 1921.

Commission on the Garda Síochána [Conroy Commission], *Report on Remuneration and Conditions of Service* (Prl. 933), Dublin: Stationery Office 1970.

Coogan, Tim Pat, *Ireland since the Rising,* London: Pall Mall Press 1966.

Coogan, Tim Pat, *Michael Collins,* London: Hutchinson 1990.

Coogan, Tim Pat, *De Valera,* London: Hutchinson 1993.

Costello, Con, *A Most Delightful Station,* Cork: Collins Press 1996.

Courtney, John, *It Was Murder!,* Dublin: Blackwater Press 1996.

Critchley, T., *A History of Police, England and Wales,* London: Constable 1967.

Critchley, T., *The Conquest of Violence,* London: Constable 1970.

Curran, Joseph, *The Birth of the Irish Free State, 1921–1923,* Birmingham: University of Alabama Press 1980.

Curtis, Robert, *The Irish Police Officer,* London: Ward and Lock 1861.

Curtis, Robert, *The History of the Royal Irish Constabulary*, Dublin: Moffat 1869.

Denman, Robert, 'Unionization of police: the New York experience', *Police Chief*, Dec. 1969.

de Vere White, Terence, *The Story of the Royal Dublin Society*, Tralee: Kerryman 1955.

de Vere White, Terence, *Kevin O'Higgins* (second edition), Tralee: Anvil Books 1986.

D 83222 [Walter Mahon-Smith], *I Did Penal Servitude*, Dublin: Metropolitan Press 1946.

Report of the Committee on the Police Service of England, Wales and Scotland [Desborough Committee], 1919, London: HMSO 1947.

Devitt, Daniel, *Never Bet: A Garda Remembers and Reflects*, Dublin: Premier Publications 1997.

Donohue, James, 'Depot days at Kildare', *Garda Review*, July 1948.

Doyle, Tim, *Peaks and Valleys: The Ups and Downs of a Young Garda*, Dublin: TJD Publications 1997.

Dublin Metropolitan Police, collection of nineteenth and early twentieth-century instruction books and manuals, Garda archives.

Duggan, John P., *A History of the Irish Army*, Dublin: Gill and Macmillan 1991.

Dunne, John, *The Pioneers*, Dublin: Pioneer Total Abstinence Association 1981.

Evans, Peter, *The Police Revolution*, London: George Allen and Unwin 1974.

Fanning, Ronan, *The Irish Department of Finance, 1922–58*, Dublin: Institute of Public Administration 1978.

Fedorowich, Kent, 'The problems of disbandment of the Royal Irish Constabulary and imperial migration, 1919–1929', *Irish Historical Studies*, vol. 30 (1996).

Finnan, Frank, 'The garda as a Christian', *The Furrow*, July 1979.

Fisk, Robert, *In Time of War*, London: André Deutsch 1983.

FitzGerald, Garret, *All in a Life: An Autobiography*, Dublin: Gill and Macmillan 1991.

Forester, Margery, *Michael Collins: The Lost Leader*, London: Sidgwick and Jackson 1971.

Garda Representative Association, *Directory of Rules, Regulations and Procedures of the GRA and to the Rights and Obligations of its Members*, Dublin: GRA 1987.

Garda Síochána, *Aonach an Gharda Souvenir Programme*, 1926 and 1927.

Garda Síochána, *Na Caomhnóirí Áitiúla* [Local Security Force], Dublin: Garda Síochána 1940.

Garda Síochána, *The Handbook of the Local Security Force*, Dublin: Garda Síochána 1940.

Garda Síochána, *ABC of Police Duties for the Local Security Force*, Dublin: Garda Síochána n.d. [c. 1940].

Garda Síochána, Coiste Siamsa, *50 Historic Years of Sport in the Garda*, Dublin: Coiste Siamsa 1972.

Garda Síochána, collection of publications, Garda Archives, including: *Directory* (annual, beginning 1925); General Orders, Gnáth-Rialacha and Dualgaisí Airgid (1922); Dualgaisí Airgid (1923); Standing Orders for Guidance of All Members, foreword by Eoin O'Duffy (1924); Routine Orders (quarterly, 1925–1962); Code (1928) and Finance Code (1944): amendments in Routine Orders; Reed's *Irish Constable's Guide,* published as *Irish Police Guide* by Rice (1923); *Garda Síochána Guide* by Horgan and Carroll (1934 and later editions); *Manual of Law and Police Duties* (1942; Irish edition 1946); *Manual of Criminal Investigation* by Murphy (1946); *Manual, Orders and Instructions, Dublin Metropolitan Division* (1954); Benevolent Society Rules (1936), foreword by E. Broy.

Gaughan, J. Anthony, *Memoirs of Constable Jeremiah Mee,* Tralee: Anvil Books 1975.

Gaughan, J. Anthony, *Austin Stack: Portrait of a Separatist,* Tralee: Kingdom Books 1977.

Gaughan, J. Anthony, *Olivia Mary Taaffe, 1832–1918,* Tralee: Kingdom Books 1995.

Gorer, Geoffrey, *Exploring English Character,* London: Cresset Press 1955.

Gmelch, George, *The Urbanization of an Itinerant People,* Menlo (Calif.): Cummings 1977.

Gwynn, Denis, *The Irish Free State, 1922–1927,* London: Macmillan 1928.

Herlihy, Jim, *The Royal Irish Constabulary: Genealogical Guide,* Dublin: Four Courts Press 1997.

Hermon, John, *Holding the Line,* Dublin: Gill and Macmillan 1997.

Hogan, James, *Could Communism Come to Ireland?,* Dublin: Cahill 1935.

Horgan, John, *Seán Lemass: The Enigmatic Patriot,* Dublin: Gill and Macmillan 1997.

International Association of Chiefs of Police, 'Police employee organizations: report', *Police Chief* (New York), Dec. 1969.

Jackson, J., 'The Irish army and the development of the constabulary concept' in Jacques van Doorn (ed.), *Armed Forces and Society,* Den Haag: Mouton 1968.

Keogh, Dermot, *Ireland and the Vatican,* Cork: Cork University Press 1995.

Kotsonouris, Mary, *Retreat from Revolution: The Dáil Courts, 1920–24,* Dublin: Irish Academic Press 1994.

Leahy, Tim, *Memoirs of a Garda Superintendent,* Kilrush: Hero Press 1996.

Lecky, W. E. H. (ed. Curtis), *The History of Ireland in the Eighteenth Century,* Chicago: University of Chicago Press 1972.

Lee, Joseph J., *Ireland, 1912–1985,* Cambridge: Cambridge University Press 1989.

Liddy, Seán, 'Smothered history', *An Síothadóir,* no. 1–3 (Aug. 1962–June 1963).

Lowe, W., and Malcolm, E., 'The domestication of the Royal Irish Constabulary', *Irish Economic and Social History,* vol. 19 (1992).

Lynch, Patrick, 'The Irish economy since the war, 1946–51', in Kevin Nowlan and T. Desmond Williams (eds), *Ireland in the War Years and After, 1939–51,* Dublin: Gill and Macmillan 1969.

Lyons, F. S. L., *Ireland Since the Famine,* London: Weidenfeld and Nicolson 1971.

MacColl, René, *Roger Casement,* London: Hamish Hamilton 1956.

Mac Fhionnghaile, Niall, *Dr McGinley and His Times: Donegal, 1900–1950,* Letterkenny: An Crann 1985.

McGahern, John, *The Barracks*, London: Faber and Faber 1963.

McNiff, Liam, *A History of the Garda Síochána*, Dublin: Wolfhound Press 1997.

Macready, Nevil, *Annals of an Active Life* (2 vols.), London: Hutchinson 1924.

McRedmond, Louis (ed.), *Modern Irish Lives*, Dublin: Gill and Macmillan 1996.

Maguire, Conor A., 'The Republican courts', *Capuchin Annual*, 1969.

Manning, Maurice, *The Blueshirts*, Dublin: Gill and Macmillan 1971.

Mansergh, Nicholas, *The Unresolved Question: The Anglo-Irish Settlement and Its Undoing, 1912–72*, New Haven: Yale University Press 1991.

Martin, Patrick, 'O'Duffy: man with a mission', *Garda Review*, Sep. 1974.

Martin, Patrick, 'The General [W. R. E. Murphy]', *Garda Review*, Oct. 1974.

Martin, Patrick, 'The years of Ned Broy', *Garda Review*, Aug. 1974.

Neligan, David, *The Spy in the Castle*, London: MacGibbon and Kee 1968.

O'Brien, Edna, *Mother Ireland*, London: Weidenfeld and Nicolson 1976.

Ó Broin, León, *In Great Haste: Letters of Michael Collins and Kitty Kiernan*, Dublin: Gill and Macmillan 1983.

Ó Broin, León, *Protestant Nationalists in Ireland: The Stopford Connection*, Dublin: Gill and Macmillan 1985.

O'Connor, Frank, *The Big Fellow*, Dublin: Clonmore and Reynolds 1965.

O'Duffy, Eoin, 'History of the Garda Síochána', *Garda Review*, Mar. 1929–1930.

O'Duffy, Eoin, *Crusade in Spain*, London: Robert Hale, 1938.

O'Kelly, Denis, *Salute to the Gardaí, 1922–1958*, Dublin: Parkside Press 1959.

O'Mahony, Seán, *Frongoch: University of Revolution*, Dublin: FDR 1987.

O'Malley, Ernie, *The Singing Flame*, Tralee: Anvil Books 1978.

O'Rorke, Kevin, 'Dublin police', *Dublin Historical Record*, Sep. 1976.

O'Shiel, Kevin, *The Making of a Republic*, Dublin: Talbot Press n.d. [*c.* 1920].

O'Shiel, Kevin, 'Memories of my lifetime' (series), *Irish Times*, Nov. 1966.

O'Sullivan, Dónal, 'The disbandment of the Royal Irish Constabulary', *Síocháin*, Dec. 1997.

O'Sullivan, Dónal, 'The fate of John B. Kearney, district inspector of the RIC and superintendent of the Civic Guard', *Kerry Magazine*, no. 9 (1998).

O'Sullivan, Dónal, 'The murder of Superintendent John Curtin', *Síocháin*, Mar. 1998.

Pakenham, Frank, *Peace by Ordeal*, London: Sidgwick and Jackson 1972.

Palmer, Stanley, 'The Irish police experiment: the beginnings of modern police in the British Isles, 1785–1795', *Social Science Quarterly*, vol. 56 (1975).

Reddy, Tom, *Murder Will Out*, Dublin: Gill and Macmillan 1990.

Reddy, Tom, *The Murder File: An Irish Detective's Casebook*, Dublin: Gill and Macmillan 1991.

Reid, B., *The Lives of Roger Casement*, New Haven: Yale University Press 1976.

Reith, Charles, *A New Study of Police History*, London: Oliver and Boyd 1956.

Reynolds, Gerald, and Judge, Anthony, *The Night the Police Went on Strike*, London: Weidenfeld and Nicholson 1969.

Robinson, Sir Henry, *Memories: Wise and Otherwise,* London: Cassel 1924.

'Royal Irish Constabulary: a plea for reform', editorial, *Constabulary Gazette,* 1910.

Royal Irish Constabulary: *Royal Irish Constabulary Code,* several editions.

Royal Irish Constabulary, collection of nineteenth and early twentieth-century instruction books and manuals, Garda Archives.

Russell, Francis, *A City in Terror, 1919: Boston Police Strike,* New York: Viking 1975.

Ryan, Desmond, *The Rising,* Dublin: Golden Eagle Books 1949.

Shaw, John, 'In the beginning', *Garda Review,* Jan. 1976.

Shea, Patrick, *Voices and the Sound of Drums,* Belfast: Blackstaff Press 1981.

Stead, John Philip (ed.), Pioneers in Policing, Montclair (NJ): Patterson Smith 1977.

Taylor, Rex, *Michael Collins,* London: Hutchinson 1958.

Thompson, David, *England in the Nineteenth Century,* Harmondsworth (Middx): Penguin 1950.

Ua Maoileoin, Pádraig, *De Réir Uimhreacha,* Dublin: Muintir an Dúna 1969.

United States of America, President's Commission of Law Enforcement and Administration of Justice, *Task Force Report: The Police,* Washington 1967.

Viceregal Commission on the Irish Police Forces [Ross Commission], *Report, 1919,* London: HMSO 1920.

Walsh, Dermot, *The Irish Police,* Dublin: Round Hall, Sweet and Maxwell 1998.

Wardwell, William, 'Strike: Montreal police strike, 1969', *Police,* Nov. 1969.

Wilson, James, *Varieties of Police Behaviour,* Oxford: Oxford University Press 1969.

Wilson, O., and McLaren, Roy Clinton, *Police Administration* (third edition), New York: McGraw-Hill 1963.

Wright, Arnold, *Disturbed Dublin: The Story of the Great Strike, 1913–14,* London: Longmans Green 1914.

Younger, Calton, *Ireland's Civil War,* London: Frederick Muller 1968.

INDEX

Accounts Branch, 94
Administration
    interdepartmental, 145–6
    office procedures, 161
age limit, 77
Agriculture, Department of, 143
Aiken, Frank, 72
alcohol abuse, 84–5
Allen, Christina, 23
Allen, Sgt Patrick, 59–60
allowances, 124–5, 128–30
    special, 208
Almond, C.S., 142, 145
Ancient Order of Hibernians, 64
Anderson, Sir John, 64
Anglo-Irish Treaty, 1921, 7, 8, 13, 23, 33,
    106, 124
Aonach an Gharda, 99–100
appointment regulations, 77–8
arbitration. *see* conciliation and arbitration
armed crime, 194–5, 210–12
Army, 13, 26, 36, 48, 50, 77, 193, 196
    and armed crime, 70
    badge, 22
    ex-members in Garda, 78
    mutiny, 1924, 57, 102–3
    reserve, 117
    strength of, 50
Army Comrades' Association, 110–13
Army Ordnance Corps, 198
Artillery [McGee] Barracks, 26
Association of Garda Chief
    Superintendents. *see* Associations
Association of Garda Sergeants and
    Inspectors. see Associations
Association of Garda Superintendents. *see*
    Associations
Associations
    Association of Garda Chief
        Superintendents (Chief Supt W.
        O'Halloran), 182
    Association of Garda Sergeants and
        Inspectors (AGSI), 210, 212–13

Association of Garda Superintendents,
    204–5
Garda Representative Association (GRA),
    190, 204–5, 212, 216
Joint Representative Body (JRB), 6, 56, 75,
    84, 140, 151, 196, 208–9, 216
    accounting system, 94
    arbitration, 155–9, 163–5
    arming of force, 65
    barracks, 79–80, 81
    Coakley committee, 180
    differentials, 177–8
    health, 98
    hours of duty, 148–9, 181–2
    Macushla Ballroom affair, 173–4
    non-police duties, 142–3
    office staff, 161–2
    pay, 131–4, 138–9, 167–8, 175–6
    PRO, 215
    promotion, 86, 88
    regulations, 185
    role of, 121–30
    sub-committees, 98
    training, 166
    Representative Body for Guards (RBG),
        164, 191, 196
    Conroy Commission, 184, 187–90
    pay claims, 175–6, 179, 182–4
    Representative Body for Inspectors,
        Station Sergeants and Sergeants, 177
Auxiliary Police, 23, 27

badge, 20–22
Balbriggan, Co. Dublin, 14
Baldonnel Aerodrome, 26
Ballsbridge depot, 22–6, 44, 56, 89
Baltinglass, Co. Wicklow, 62–4, 126
barony police, 3
barrack accommodation, 22–3, 57, 73–4,
    137
    Coogan report, 81–3
    early years, 79–81
    housekeeping, 82

barrack accommodation *continued*
 poor conditions, 25–6, 145
Barry, Sgt Patrick, 124, 126–7
Barry, Gen Tom, 29, 41
Barton, Robert, 8, 106
beats and patrols, 116, 144, 148, 153, 189, 200, 209–10
 three-relief system, 207–8
Beggar's Bush Barracks, 23, 24, 37
Belfast (recruits), 78
Belfast Boycott, 8, 9, 49
Berry, Peter, 149, 150, 158, 170, 180–81, 185
 Conroy Commission, 187
Bewley, T.K., 125
bicycles, 89, 141, 147
 allowance, 126, 128–9
 protective clothing, 125
 thefts, 198
Black, Mr Justice, 38
Black and Tans, 14, 29, 32, 44, 47, 51, 92
Blueshirts, 67, 102, 112–13
Blythe, Ernest, 20, 51, 93, 129
Bohane, Edward, 23, 25
Boland, Gerald, 115, 146
boot allowance, 128, 132, 133
Bow Street Runners, 209
Brady, Conor, 102, 111, 112–13, 191
Branigan, Sgt J.J., 29
Breen, Dan, 113
Brennan, Dep Commr Garret, 163, 198 (as Chief Supt)
Brennan, Chief Supt James, Barrackmaster, 15, 30 (as Head Const); 27, 37, 57 (as Supt); 75 (as Chief Supt)
Brennan, Joseph, 125
Brennan, Asst Commr Patrick, 23, 28, 29, 31, 57
 arming of force, 18
 Civil War, 50, 51–2
 Garda costs, 89
 Kildare Mutiny, 32, 34, 35, 38–42, 49
 Kildare Mutiny inquiry, 44–5
 Police Organising Committee, 15, 27
Bridewell station, 214
Britain, 153, 167
British Ambassador (murdered), 192

British Army, 23, 26, 74
Britton, Dist Insp Frederick, 29, 30
Broy, Commr Éamonn, 19, 79, 109, 128, 148, 150
 Garda pay, 133–4
 pilgrimages, 102
 Police Organising Committee, 16
 and politics, 164
 recruitment, 110–13
 Special Branch head, 104
 War of Independence, 17
Broy Harriers, 110–13
Brunswick Street, 17
burial (obsequies) fund, 97
Burke, Supt Francis, 27, 37
Byrne, Alfie, 138
Byrne, Dr Edward, Archbishop of Dublin, 71
Byrne, Garda Henry, 194
Byrne, Supt John J., 28, 29 (as Sgt J.J.); 36, 37, 40

Cadden, Nurse Mamie, 198
cadet system, 18, 86–9, 92, 124–5, 205
Campion, Father, 71
car allowances, 152
Carlow, County, 65
Carroll, Commr Patrick, 83, 180, 181, 183
Carroll, Deputy Commr Patrick J., 83
Carter, Samuel, 3
Casement, Roger, 29–30
Catholic Guild of London Metropolitan Police, 100
Catholics, employment of, 4–5
cattle seizures, 112
Cavan, County, 47
Censorship of Publications Board, 143
Central Detective Unit, 153
Chamberlain, Insp Gen Sir Neville, 12, 87
chaplaincy, 71–2
Chiefs of Police, International Association of, 21, 57, 66
Chisholm, Thomas, 101, 102
Christian Brothers, 4
Churchill, Winston, 39, 49, 52
Civic Guard. *see* Garda Síochána
Civic Guard of 1795, 3, 19

Civic Guard Active Service Unit, 51
civil service, 21–2, 128, 130, 139, 146, 180
  allowances, 152
  conciliation and arbitration, 155
  interdepartmental inquiry, 142–9
  pay, 125, 156
Civil Service Commission, 77
Civil War, 15, 18, 41–3, 46–7, 71–2, 149, 193
  attacks on Garda, 58–64
  deployment of Garda, 57–61
  effects of, 80, 101, 116, 125, 126
  police unarmed, 64–8
  role of Garda, 9–10, 49–72
  siege of Limerick, 52–4
civilians, employment of, 75, 161–2, 182
  domestic servants, 82
  JRB complaints, 125
Clare, County, 59, 61, 78, 82, 85–6, 103
  recruits from, 32–5
Clerkin, Garda Michael, 194
Clonskeagh Castle, 89
Closing the Gap, 176
Coakley, Chief Supt John, 180–82
Coiste Siamsa, 98–9
Collins, Gerard, 191, 205, 206
Collins, Michael, 4, 7–8, 9, 19, 22, 23, 28, 33, 110
  barracks, military, as depot, 26
  Civil War, 49–53
  death of, 54
  Kildare Mutiny, 35, 37, 38–40, 43, 44, 45
  naming of force, 20
  and policing, 9–10, 13, 14–17
  and Staines, 34, 56
Collins, Chief Supt Tom, 157, 162, 175, 177, 185
Collinstown Aerodrome, 13, 71, 73
Collison, Guard Malachy, 50
Comhdháil Náisiúnta na Gaeilge, 96
Commission on the Garda Síochána, 1968, 176–7
Communist Party, 103
conciliation and arbitration, 139, 146, 148, 155–9, 160, 175, 182
  appointment of chairman, 183–4

draft scheme, 163–5
  hours of duty, 188–9
  overtime, 204–5
  pay and allowances, 167–8
  conditions of service, 6, 18, 105, 140–41, 145–9, 188–9, 215
  inquiry sought, 130
Connradh Gaolach an Gharda, 99
Conroy Report, 177, 184–90, 193, 197, 200–202, 205–6, 208, 215–16
Consultative Council, 188
Coogan, Dep Commr Éamonn, 20, 89, 90, 107, 109
  Civil War, 57, 59
  civilian labour, 75
  Code of Conduct, 24–5
  Corrofin hoax, 83
  Garda badge, 21–2
  inspection, 81–3
Coogan, Tim Pat, 83
Cook, Judith, 192
Cooney, Patrick, 191, 192–3, 196
Cope, Alfred, 23, 24, 26, 56, 64
Corish, Richard, 129
Cork, County, 53–4, 61, 66, 169
Cork city, 52, 112
Corrofin hoax, 81–3
Corry, Captain, 38
Cosgrave, W.T., 7, 45, 74, 99, 109, 169
  Civil War, 49, 52
  Emergency, 116
  and O'Duffy, 93, 105, 106, 142
  and policing, 10, 57
Costello, John A., 104, 140, 170
Costigan, Commr Daniel, 142, 145, 148, 185, 186, 187, 214
  appointment, 149–50
  crime statistics, 153–4
  and Dept of Justice, 158–9
  initiatives, 160–61, 166–7
  and JRB, 162–5
  Macushla Ballroom affair, 168–71
  resignation, 179
  uniforms, 151–2
County Constabulary, 4, 5
Courtney, Chief Supt James, 195–6
Courtney, Mary F., 13

Coy, Sgt Patrick, 29, 32, 36, 47
Coyne, T.J., 105, 141, 145, 150, 157, 214, 215
Craig, Sir James, 8
crime prevention, 153, 199–200
crime statistics, 152–4, 159, 181
crime and subversion, 193–6
Criminal Investigation Department, 70–71, 199
Criminal Law Jurisdiction Act 1976, 212–13
Cronin, Commdt, 53
Crozier, Brig-Gen E.F., 26–7
Crumlin, protest, 185–7
Cullen, Asst Commr Edward, 107, 109, 115
cultural revival, 5
Cumann na mBan, 23, 43
Cumann na nGael, 107, 110, 113
Curragh Camp, 26, 30, 36, 37, 51
Curtin, Supt John D., 104–5, 112
Cussen, Dist Justice George P., 25

Dáil Éireann, 5, 7, 11, 125
    Kildare Mutiny, 39–40
Dalton, C.F., 64
Dalton, Gen Emmet, 13, 52, 54
Daly, Father Clarence, 178
Daly, Guard Thomas P., 29, 30, 50
    Kildare Mutiny, 33, 36, 37, 39–41, 44, 47
Dawson, Insp Albert, 169
depot
    accommodation, 26
    organised on military lines, 74–6
de Valera, Éamon, 23, 39, 68, 70, 96, 113–14, 134, 174
    Civil War, 49
    Emergency, 116, 118
    and Garda, 109
    and O'Duffy, 102–3, 105–6
Deegan, Michael, 142, 146, 161
Defence, Department of, 13, 50, 67
Delahunty, Patrick, 17
Denmark Street station, 89
Derrig, Thomas, 134–5
Desborough Report, 121–2, 126, 136, 138, 142, 167, 183, 187
detection of crime, 199

Devitt, Asst Commr Daniel, 187, 196–7
Devlin Committee, 205
diamond jubilee, 178
discipline, 24, 83–4, 147, 209–10
    fatigues, 75–6
    military lines, 74–6
District Courts, 77
Doherty, Dep Commr E.J., 201
Donegal, County, 11, 12, 14, 61
Donegan, Insp Samuel, 194
Donlon, Garda John, 61, 64, 85
Donnelly, Simon, 9, 10
Donohue, James, 33, 34
Donovan, Dr James, 195, 199
double-jobbing, 213
Dowling, Garda Thomas, 85–6
Doyle, Garda Seán, 50
driving school, 160
drug abuse, 215
Drummond, Thomas, 4
Dublin, 3, 64, 78, 79
    Civil War, 61
    Crumlin protest, 184–7
    grievances, 163–5
    lockout, 1913, 124
    undermanning, 140, 141, 154
Dublin, County, 79
Dublin Castle, 4, 5, 14, 17, 23, 56, 111, 153
    handed over, 7–8
    headquarters, 73
Dublin Corporation, 3, 9
Dublin Institute of Adult Education, 163
Dublin Metropolitan Charge Court, 214–15
Dublin Metropolitan Division, 111, 138–9, 215
    allowances, 167–8
    discontent, 207–8
    divisional committee, 162–3
    reorganisation, 160
    undermanned, 141, 142, 180–81
Dublin Metropolitan Police (DMP), 5, 8, 46, 64, 78, 100, 116, 159, 197
    amalgamation, 70–71, 76, 106–7, 123–4
    ex-members in Garda, 11, 16, 17, 18, 19, 23
    forensic science, 198
    insignia, 20–21

office procedures, 161
promotion, 87
protests, 138–9
sports, 99
unarmed, 3
Duffy, Chief Supt Hugh, 77–8
Duggan, Éamonn, 7, 8, 26
Kildare Mutiny, 35–9, 41
name of force, 19–20
police organising committee, 14–17
police organisation, 9–11
and RIC, 29
Dun Emer Guild, 100
Dunlea, Fr Patrick, 71

Easter Rising, 1916, 4, 9, 19, 29–30, 64
Economic Affairs, Department of, 55
Economic War, 109–10, 193
Education, Department of, 134–5
educational standards, 77, 159–60, 176–7,
206–7
Electoral Acts, 163–4
electrification, 94–5
Ellis, Dr Vincent C., 154
Emergency, The, 116–18, 148, 149–50
bonus, 133, 136
Emergency Service Medal, 118
Ennis, Captain P., 10
Equitation School, 104
European Forensic Science Institute, 199
Evening Press, 213
Ewart-Biggs, Christopher, 192
examinations, 77
extradition laws, 212–13

Fahy, Frank, 113
Fallon, Garda Michael, 41
Fallon, Garda Richard, 193, 194
Fanning, Ronan, 146
Feakle, Co. Roscommon, 59
Fehily, Msgr Thomas, 188
Fenians, 5
Fianna Fáil, 11, 22, 67, 68, 102–4, 129,
130, 149, 212
and O'Duffy, 104–6
in power, 109–13
Finance, Department of, 65–6, 79, 92, 93,
94, 114, 128, 176

allowances, 128–30
barracks, 80
conciliation and arbitration, 156, 158
economy committee, 125, 130
Garda memorial, 174
Garda problems, 145–9
Medical Aid Fund, 98
pay, 132, 133–4, 136–7
recruitment, 111
uniforms, 151
fingerprint affair, 192
Fingleton, Sgt Daniel, 157, 158, 162
firemen, parity with, 183–4
First World War, 52
Firth, Garda Paul, 193
FitzAlan, Lord, 7–8
Fitzgerald, Desmond, 29
FitzGerald, Garret, 195, 196
Fitzgerald, Garda Jim, 182
Fitzgerald, J.J., 26
Fitzgerald, Chief Supt Michael, 112, 184–7,
191
Fitzgibbon Street station, 168
Fitzsimmons, Sgt James, 66, 97
flag, Garda parade, 100
Flood, Garda Tom, 71–2
Flynn, Supt Gerald, 113
Fógra Tóra, 20
Foley, Dr Patrick, Bishop of Kildare &
Leighlin, 71
Foley, Head Const J.P., 16, 17
Forde, Brig-Gen Liam, 52
forensic science, 195, 198–9
Forensic Science Laboratory, 195, 199
Fosdick, Raymond, 93
Four Courts siege, 41–2, 49, 55
franchise, 163–4
free association, 163–5
Freemasonry, 4, 18–19
fringe benefits, 189–90

Gaelic League, 8, 20, 21, 95
Gaelic revival, 5
Gaeltacht, Commission on the, 96
Gallagher, Sgt Patrick J., 6, 56, 98, 124,
132, 142, 157, 162
Galligan, Supt John, 15–16, 17, 27–8, 30,
33, 37

Galway, County, 60–61, 78, 82
  Corrofin hoax, 82–3
Garda Archives, 190, 201
Garda Band, 99, 193
Garda Benevolent Fund, 97, 107, 115, 162
Garda College, Templemore, 167, 175, 205, 214, 216
Garda Museum, 190, 201
Garda Representative Association. see Associations
Garda Review, 149, 150, 162–3, 213, 216
  arming of force, 210
  barracks, 79–80, 81
  bicycles, 128–9
  committee of inquiry, 142
  conciliation and arbitration, 137, 156, 157, 173
  Conroy Report, 190
  contributors, 6
  and Garvey, 191, 192
  Corrofin hoax, 83
  'heavy gang', 193
  Irish language, 95
  management consultants, 203
  name of force, 20
  O'Duffy, 74, 105
  pay, 131–3, 135–6, 138, 139, 167, 168
  regulations, 147
  selection of recruits, 206
Garda Síochána. see also pay; recruitment; training
  arming of, 18, 51, 64–8, 100, 110, 194, 210–12
  disarmed, 5, 46
  attacks on, 59–61, 66, 193–4
  blueprint for, 9–11, 14–17, 17–19
  and Blueshirts, 112–13
  changes sought, 1960s, 159–65
  committee of inquiry, 1950, 141–9
  commission of inquiry, 1969, 187–90
  deployment of, 57–61, 79–81
  diamond jubilee, 178
  DMP amalgamation, 70–71, 76, 106–7, 123–4
  established, 5–6, 8–9
  exemplary role, 213–15
  ex-RIC members, 15–18, 28–32, 44, 47, 57, 86, 92

  finances, 89–90, 92–4, 125
  General Order No. 1, 65–8
  golden jubilee, 215
  morale, 206–8, 209
  name of, 19–20
  non-police duties, 46, 142–4, 208
  philosophy for, 215–17
  and politics, 44–5, 163–4
  reconstituted, 45
  staff appointments, 26–8
  strength of, 28, 46, 76, 80, 142, 144
    recommended, 180–81
    undermanned, 140–41
Garda Síochána Bill 1961, 174
Garda Síochána Code, 25, 146–9
Garda Síochána (Discipline) Regulations 1926, 185
Garda Síochána Manual, 25
Garda Síochána (Temporary Provisions) Act 1923, 22, 122, 126
Garda Surgeon, 154
Garda Training Committee, 216
Gardiner, Sgt, 99
Garvey, Commr Edmund, 191–7, 208, 214
  crime prevention, 199–200
General Prisons Board, 106, 198
Geoghegan, James, 103
Gill, Garda Patrick, 113
Gleeson, Evelyn, 100
Gleeson, Fr William, 100
golden jubilee, 215
Gormanston Camp, 13
Gormley, Captain Augustine, 74
Government Information Bureau, 182
Grattan, Henry, 3, 19–20
Great Southern and Western Railway, 51
Greenwood, Sir Hamar, 17
Gresham Hotel conference, 14–17
Griffin, Laurence, 47
Griffith, Arthur, 7, 8, 19–20, 21, 23, 39, 41, 56, 110
Griffith [Wellington] Barracks, 22, 26
Gunn, Garda Patrick E., 157, 162, 164
Guthrie, A.P., 162

Habitual Criminals Registry, 198
Hallinan, Supt Daniel, 27, 43
Hamrogue, Garda John, 32

Hand, Garda Francis, 195
Handbook of General Instructions, 199
Hanna, Mr Justice, 112
Hanson, Sir Philip, 57, 80, 81
Harding, William, 128–9
Harrell, David, 139
Harrington, Dist Insp John H., 90–92
Harte, Supt Patrick, 16, 17, 27, 30, 33 (as Sgt), 37
Haugh, Supt P.J., 27, 32
    Kildare Mutiny, 33, 37, 40–41
    resignation, 47
Haughey, Charles J., 105, 169, 170, 174–5, 179, 188, 213–14
Haughton, Benjamin, 86
Hawthorne experiments, 207
Health, Department of, 159
'heavy gang', 193, 196
height regulation, 77
helmets, 151
Henderson, Leo, 49
Hennessy, Sgt M., 29
Henry, Sgt William, 198
Herrema, Tiede, 195
Hogan, Professor James, 103
Hogan, Col Michael, 103, 104
Hogan, Patrick, 7, 50, 103
Home Affairs, Department of, 46, 51, 54, 55–6, 75–6, 93
    badge, 21–2
    barracks, 26
    barracks attacks, 60
    bicycles, 89
    Code of Conduct, 24–5
    discipline, 84–5
    Garda appointments, 90–92
    Kildare Mutiny, 33
    and O'Duffy, 61–4, 78
    pay cuts, 126
    representative bodies, 122–3
Horizon, 212
hours of duty, 148–9, 180, 181–2, 188, 207–8, 213
Hue and Cry, 20, 106
Hughes, Garda J.J., 20
Hughes, Séamus, 10
Hunt, Insp James, 81
Hurley, Jeremiah, 135

hygiene, 75–6

Industry and Commerce, Department of, 105
insignia, 5, 20–22
intelligence work, 17, 28
interrogation
    allegations of Garda 'brutality' 193, 196
Iris an Gharda, 46, 62, 72, 85, 99, 125
Irish College, Rome, 101
Irish Constabulary, 4
Irish Free State, 55
Irish Independent, 10, 18, 201–2, 212
    arming of force, 210
    badge, 21
    Baltinglass attack, 63
    regulations, 185
    trade unionism, 173, 184
    Patrick Walsh tribute by Dr J.P. McGinley, 14
Irish language, 95–6
Irish Management Institute, 166
Irish National Teachers' Organisation, 134–6
Irish Press, 172–3, 186, 189–90
Irish Republican Army (IRA), 11, 195
    barracks attacked, 80
    and Fianna Fáil, 110
    and RIC, 32
Irish Republican Brotherhood (IRB), 9, 19
Irish Republican Police, 9–11, 13, 18, 23, 30, 32, 70
Irish Times, 11, 112, 116, 175, 190, 194, 204
    arming of force, 210–11, 212
    crime statistics, 152
    Crumlin protest, 186
    Macushla Ballroom affair, 170, 172
Irish Travel Agency, 101, 102
Irish Volunteers, 9, 50, 79
    Civil War, 52, 53
    ex-members in Garda, 18, 23, 28–9, 35, 42–4, 46, 76, 86
    and RIC, 13, 31
Irish Worker, 124
Irregulars, 41, 57–8
Irwin, Garda Tom, 71–2

Jesuit Order, 71
John Paul II, Pope, 178
Johnson, President Lyndon, 183
Johnson, Tom, 23
Johnstone, Sir Walter Edgeworth, 17
Joint Representative Body. *see* Associations
Joseph Magdalen, Mother, 14
Justice, Department of, 62, 70, 79, 105–6,
    113, 114, 124, 146, 161, 191–3
  Accounts Branch, 94
  administration, 201
  allowances, 128–30
  appointment regulations, 115, 176–7
  arming of force, 66, 67
  Broy Harriers, 111–12
  civilian clerks, 182
  conciliation and arbitration, 156, 157–8,
    160, 183–4
  and Costigan, 149–50
  crime prevention, 200
  'heavy gang', 196
  and JRB, 125, 128
  Macushla Ballroom affair, 169–72
  management consultants, 202–3
  Medical Aid Fund, 98
  pay, 132–3, 176, 180, 182–3
  pilgrimages, 100–101, 102
  and politics, 163–4
  promotion, 88
  public relations, 213–15
  regulations, 185–6
  relations with Garda, 86, 189–90, 215–16
  staff associations, 208–9
  undermanning, 141
  uniforms, 151–2

Kavanagh, Lt-Commdt Seán, 51
Keane, Supt John, 27, 37–8
Kearney, Dist Insp John, 15, 16, 17, 27, 44,
    56
  resignation, 28–30
Kearney, Thomas Moran, 29
Kelleher, Supt Patrick, 27, 36, 42–3
Kelly, Insp Michael, 16, 17, 19
Kelly, Lieutenant, 54
Kelly, Private P.J., 195
Kemmy, Jim, 213
Kennedy, Mr, 43

Kenny, J. Fitzgerald, 100–101, 113, 129
Kerry, County, 12, 29–30, 53, 62
Kevin Street station, 138
Kildare, County, 17, 26, 51, 61
Kildare depot, 50, 51, 71, 73, 89, 90
Kildare Mutiny, 16, 27, 29, 31–48, 78, 109
  armoury raided, 35–7
  Clare cabal, 32–5
  commission of inquiry, 43–6, 50
  inquiry report, 55–6
  Irregulars seize arms, 41
  men unpaid, 42–3
  Staines resigns, 36–7
  Staines resumes command, 42
Kilkenny, County, 59–60, 61, 71–2, 85
Kilroy, Sgt Thomas, 32
Kinnane, Commr Michael J., 77, 81, 88,
    92, 102, 127, 134, 150, 151, 162
  appointment, 113–15
  Code revision, 147–8
  death of, 149
  Emergency, 116, 117
  Garda pay, 136–8
  Irish language, 96
  Medical Aid fund, 98
  recruitment, 140
  strength of force, 144

Labour, Department of, 38
Labour Court, 183
Labour Party, 23, 105, 129, 213
Lally, Garda Patrick, 177
land annuities, 109–10, 112
Land Commission, 142
Land League, 138
Larkin, James, 124
Lawlor, Det-Sgt George, 25–6, 198
Lawrence, Lord Justice, 142
League of Nations, 134
Leahy, Chief Supt Michael, 70
leave of absence, 147
Lemass, Seán, 10, 159, 161, 173
Lenihan, Brian, 179
Leveson Gower, Lord Francis, 4
licensing laws, 75, 84–6
Liddy, Supt Seán, 27, 32, 44–5, 47
  Kildare Mutiny, 34–5, 37, 38–9, 41
Lillis (Black and Tan), 29

Limerick, County, 61, 78, 79, 169
Limerick city, 66, 213
  siege of, 52–4
Liston, T.K., 167
Lloyd George, David, 121
Local Defence Force (LDF), 117, 118
Local Government, Department of, 57
Local Security Force (LSF), 116, 118
Loftus, Seán, 169
London Metropolitan Police, 100, 121, 199
  National Union of Police and Prison
    Officers, 121, 122
Longford, County, 61–2, 81
Lynch, Daniel, 112
Lynch, Fionán, 7, 17
Lynch, Liam, 52–4
Lynch, Supt Martin, 15, 27, 34, 47
  Kildare Mutiny, 37, 40–41
Lynch, Michael, 112

McAleenan, Chief Supt John, 188, 197, 201, 214
McAuliffe, Michael, 35, 38, 44, 45, 46, 55
  arming of force, 65, 66
McAuliffe, Fr Patrick, 71, 72
McAvinia, Sgt Patrick, 23, 30, 40
McCague, Sgt Francis, 61
McCann Barracks, 175
McCarthy, Chief Supt Mathias, 16, 24, 27, 30, 56, 75
  Kildare Mutiny, 33, 35, 36, 37
  name of force, 20
  Police Organising Committee, 17
  sports, 25, 99
McCarthy, Chief Supt Thomas, 163, 164–5
MacColl, Rene, 29
McCormack, Chief Supt Michael, 14, 15, 16, 27, 30, 33 (as Sgt), 37, 89
McCrudden, Chief Insp Robert, 27, 29, 47
McDonagh, Asst Commr, 187
McElligott, J.J. (Dept of Finance), 111, 114, 145, 146
McElligott, Sgt Thomas J., 16–17, 28
McEntee, Patrick, 196
MacEntee, Seán, 79, 133–4, 146, 159–60
Mac Eoin, Seán, 92, 138, 142
Mac Fhionnghaile, Niall, 14
McGee [Artillery] Barracks, 26

McGinley, Dr Joseph P., 11, 13–14
McGowan, Garda Michael, 60
McGrath, Joe, 7
McKee [Marlborough] Barracks, 26, 65, 74
McKenna, Lt-Gen Daniel, 117
Mackin, Chief Supt John, 95
McLaughlin, Commr Patrick, 178, 197, 198 (as Chief Supt), 204, 213
McLoughlin, Sgt Patrick, 195
McManus, Chief Supt Seán, 73, 87–8, 124, 126
McManus, Commdt-Gen, 54
McNamara, Sgt Patrick, 32, 40, 44, 47, 50
MacNeill, Eoin, 7, 19–20
McNulty, Cadet John, 99
McQuaid, Dr J.C., Archbishop of Dublin, 172, 173, 188
McQuillan, John, 174
Macready, Gen Sir Nevil, 22, 26, 74, 121–2
Macushla Ballroom affair, 128, 138, 166–78, 179, 183, 188, 208, 214
Madden, Surgeon, 41
magistrates, 4
Maguire, Conor, 110
Maguire, Dist Insp Francis J., 90–92
Maher, Supt Jeremiah, 15, 17, 27, 30, 33 (as Sgt), 36, 37, 44
Maher, Supt Leo, 197
Mallon, Asst Commr John, 97, 99
Malone, Commr Patrick, 190
management surveys, 161–2, 201–3
Mangan, Dist Justice Frederick, 176, 179, 180
Marlborough [McKee] Barracks, 26, 65, 74
marriage, 147
Marrinan, Garda John, 169–70, 172, 175, 182, 184, 189, 194, 204, 212
Mathew, Father Theobald, 84
Maxwell, John F., 21
Mayne, Commr Richard, 199, 215
Mayo, County, 16, 61, 113
Mayo, George Elton, 207
Meath, County, 16, 81
medals, 61, 99, 118, 193, 194
Medical Aid Fund, 98, 115, 161
medical care, 154
medical fitness, 76–7
Meehan, Insp Patrick, 28

Mellows, Liam, 49
'memorandum of understanding', 209
memorial plaque, 174
mess committee, 27
M'Gettrick, Dist Insp Thomas, 16
Military College, 205
Military Intelligence, 102–3
Ministers and Secretaries Act 1924, 21, 86, 92, 125
Monaghan, County, 169
Mordant, Det-Garda George, 193
Morley, Garda John, 194
Morley, John, 87
Morrissey, Sgt Patrick, 195
motorcycles, 160
Mountbatten, Lord, 195
Moynihan, Maurice, 114, 118, 159
Mulcahy, Gen Richard, 9, 26, 79, 83, 84, 106, 126
    arming of DMP, 64
    Civil War, 49
    Commander-in-Chief, 54–6
    Police Organising Committee, 15
    recommendation of army officers, 86
    and Staines, 56
Mulcahy, Mrs Min, 106
Mulroy, Garda James, 61, 85, 99
Mulvey, Sgt John, 61
Murder Squad, 195–6
Murphy, Brig A., 57–8
Murphy, Dep Commr William R.E., 52, 54, 70–71, 99, 107, 109, 124, 141
    Emergency, 116–17
Murray, Supt Joseph, 113
Mussolini, Benito, 101

Naas Barracks, 51
Nally, Sgt Derek, 210
naming (title) of new police, 19–20
National Cycling and Athletic Association, 113
National Guard, 110–13
National Science Council, 199
National Union of Police and Prison Officers, 16, 121–2
Neary, Supt Thomas, 16, 19, 28, 37
Neighbourhood Watch, 200

Neligan, Chief Supt David, 17, 70–71, 102–4
Newbridge Barracks, 26, 36, 42–3, 50, 89
    Civil War, 51
Niemba ambush, 193
night watchmen, 3
Northern Ireland (NI), 193–4, 198–9, 201

Oaksey Report, 142, 155, 156
oath of allegiance, 18–19
O'Brien, Seán, 50
O'Brien, Supt Timothy, 169, 170
Observer, 155
Ó Colmáin, Stn Sgt Seán, 162, 163, 164, 175
O'Connell, Insp Edward M. ('Billy'), 102–4, 113–14
O'Connell, Lt-Gen J.J., 36, 49
O'Connell, Garda John Aloysius, 31, 34, 38, 45, 50
O'Connor, Chief Supt Bernard, 27, 37, 45, 47
O'Connor, Garda Cornelius, 185–6
O'Connor, Rory, 13, 29, 30, 33, 41, 49
    Kildare Mutiny, 36, 37
O'Donoghue, P.P., 142
O'Duffy, Supt Éamonn, 59, 61
O'Duffy, Commr Eoin, 19, 45, 47, 48, 97–108, 109, 150, 215
    allowances, 128–30
    on arming the force, 64–8, 68–70
    Baltinglass attacked, 62–4
    barracks, 80, 81
    and civil service, 21–2, 86, 90–94
    Civil War, 49, 52–4, 58–9
    clashes with government, 104–6
    conspiracy suspected, 102–3
    discipline, 73–6, 84–5, 157
    franchise, 163–4
    hours of duty, 148
    headquarters, 94–5
    inquiry called for, 142, 187
    Irish language, 95
    and JRB, 122–3, 125–7
    Kildare Mutiny, 37, 43
    monthly confidential reports, 61–2
    non-police duties, 142–3

offered army command, 54–6
parades, 72
pilgrimages, 100–102, 178
Police Organising Committee, 15, 16–17
political career, 106–8, 110–13
promotion, 88
recruitment, 76–9
training, 166
O'Dwyer, Angela, 43
O'Dwyer, Brigadier George, 42–3
Offaly, County, 51, 194
Offences Against the State Act, 192
office procedures, 161–2
Office of Public Works, 57, 81, 94–5, 145, 188
  barracks, 73, 80–81
Official Secrets Act, 104, 113
Ó Fiacháin, Éamonn, 151
O'Flaherty, Justice Hugh, 197
O'Friel, Henry, 57, 59, 89, 127, 217
  accounting officer, 93
  on arming the force, 65–6
  badge, 21–2
  barracks, 80, 81
  and DMP, 70
  economy committee, 125
  Garda as exemplars, 84–5
  Garda Code, 25
  and O'Duffy, 90–92
  pilgrimages, 100–101
  promotion, 86, 88
  representative bodies, 122–4
  training, 22–3
O'Halloran, Garda Patrick J., 62–3, 126
O'Halloran, Chief Supt William, 182
O'Higgins, Kevin, 7, 8, 39, 46, 107, 110, 113, 174
  accounting, 93
  arming of force, 66, 68
  assassination, 70, 97, 101
  barracks, 74, 80, 95
  blueprint for Garda, 11, 19–20, 28
  chaplaincy, 71
  Civil War, 79
  and JRB, 128
  and O'Duffy, 69–70
  pay, 126

recruitment, 78
  and Walsh, 13–14
O'Kelly, Captain Denis, 99
Olympic Council of Ireland, 113
O'Malley, Ernie, 41, 106
Ó Muirthile, Commdt Seán, 55
O'Neill, Sgt James, 82–3
Orange Order, 4
Ordnance Survey, 102–4
organised crime, 194
Oriel House, 70
O'Shea, Supt Jeremiah, 20, 99
O'Sheil, Kevin, 9, 35, 38, 44–7, 50, 55
  on arming police, 65, 66
Ó Súilleabháin, Gearóid, 26, 64
O'Sullivan, Garda (Baltinglass), 62–3
overtime, 148, 188–9
  senior officers, 204–5

Palestine Police, 13
papal encyclicals, 162–3, 164
parish constables, 3
Passionists, 71, 97, 178
patrol cars, 144, 152, 153, 160, 189, 209
patrols. *see* beats and patrols
pay, 18, 105, 128, 136–9
  allowances cut, 128–30
  claims, 167, 175–6, 182–3, 204–5
  complaints, 124–5, 131–9, 169–72
  cuts, 124
  differentials, 177–8
  equation with firemen, 183–4
  Mangan Tribunal, 179
  'rate for the job', 176–7, 207
  recruits' pay cut, 126
  supplementary payments, 179
Pay and Allowances Order, 188–9
pay order, 1947, 137
Peace Preservation Force, 4
Pearse, Patrick, 9
Peel, Sir Robert, 3, 4
pension books, 144
pensions, 168
Phelan, Garda Henry, 71–2
Phoblacht, An, 103
Phoenix Park depot, 64, 67, 71, 86, 89, 101

Phoenix Park depot *continued*
  chaplaincy, 71–2
  handed over, 74, 94–5
  library, 99
  RIC, 13, 26
  training moved from, 175
pilgrimages, 100–102, 178
Pioneer Total Abstinence Association, 71, 85
Pius XI, Pope, 100, 101–2, 178, 211
poitín trade, 61–2, 85–6
Police College, Bramshill, 161
police duty class, 182
Police Duty Manual, 167
Police Federation, 122
Police Organising Committee, 5, 14–17, 54, 90, 92, 126
  report of, 17–19, 20
Police Powers, Royal Commission on, 155
police stations, 181–2, 207–8
  closures, 153
  heating and lighting, 152
  indoor duty, 148
  inspections, 188
Policeman's Manual, 25
Post Office Stores, Controller of, 151
Posts and Telegraphs, Department of, 201
Prendeville, Supt Edmund, 16, 17, 24, 27, 30, 33, 37
  Kildare Mutiny, 36
prisons, 106, 199, 209
Prisons Board, 106, 198
Probationer Training, Report on, 216
promotion, 18, 96, 137, 174, 179, 205
  examinations, 161
  procedural changes, 150
  from ranks, 86–9
  system changes, 154
Provisional Government, 5, 7–8, 41, 89, 107, 125
  arming police, 65–6
  and Civic Guard, 9–11, 13, 19–20
  Garda training, 22–3
Public Accounts Committee, 90
public expenditure, 125, 126, 128, 130, 146, 176
public relations, 213–15
Public Works, Commissioners of, 57

Quaid, Garda James, 194
Quigley, Dr T.A.J., 154
Quinn, Commr William P., 148, 172, 175, 179, 215
Quinn, Gerald, 177
Quinn Tribunal, 176, 177, 207

Radio Advisory Committee, 201
radio service, 160, 201
railway protection, 51–2
recruiting officers, 23
recruitment, 18, 23, 129
  advice on training recruit gardaí, 166
  Belfast candidates, 78
  Broy Harriers, 110–13
  discipline, 74–6, 84
  discontinued, 140–41
  family links, 79
  JRB complaints, 124–5
  pay cuts, 132
  qualifications, 76–7, 206–7
  resumed, 78–9, 166
regulations, 125
  Crumlin protest, 185–7
  exemplary role, 213–15
  outdated, 146–9, 185–6
religious practice, 178
rent allowances, 129, 167–8
Representative Body for Guards. *see* Associations
Representative Body for Inspectors, Station Sergeants and Sergeants. *see* Associations
Republican Police. *see* Irish Republican Police
Research and Planning Unit, 200–203
resignations, 172
rest days, 180
retirement, 150, 159, 168, 174
  office employment, 161–2
Reward Fund, 98
Reynolds, Garda Michael, 194
Reynolds, Garda Patrick, 195, 196, 211–12
Rice, Sgt Richard, 162
Ring, Chief Supt Michael J., 15, 20, 27, 28
Ring, Chief Supt M.J. (Joe), 23, 46–7, 62
  Kildare Mutiny, 34–8, 41
Riordan, Dist Insp Patrick, 16, 24

Roche, Stephen, 111, 114, 133
  Emergency, 117–18
Rochford, Sgt Joseph, 34
Roscommon, County, 17, 59, 194
Ross, Lord Justice Sir John, 18, 126, 138
Rowan, Commr Charles, 199, 215
Royal Dublin Society. *see* Ballsbridge depot
Royal Hospital, Kilmainham, 95
Royal Irish Constabulary (RIC), 4, 56, 58,
    82, 98, 109, 124, 159
  accounts system, 93
  armed, 5, 67, 211
  barracks, 145
  burial (obsequies) fund, 97
  cadet system, 87
  chaplaincy, 71
  Code, 25, 147
  disbanded, 7, 11, 13, 23–4
  ex-members in Garda, 11, 15–18, 28–30,
    31–2, 44, 45–6, 47, 57, 86, 92
  family links, 79
  forensic science, 198
  hierarchy, 12
  history of, 4–6
  insignia, 22
  National Union of Police and Prison
    Officers, 121, 122
  office procedures, 161
  pay rates, 126
  records destroyed, 5, 18
  regulations, 185
  strength of, 17
Royal Ulster Constabulary (RUC), 6, 22,
    93, 167, 212
Ruttledge, P.J., 98, 104, 110, 111, 112,
    131, 132, 133
Ryan, Garda E.J., 50
Ryan, Dr Jim, 106
Ryan, Dr Louden, 205
Ryan Report, 205

Sacred Heart, devotion to, 72
St Joseph's Young Priests' Society, 98
Sandys, William, 177–8
sanitation, 75–6
Scanlan, Prof John, 201
Scanlon, Insp Seán, 32, 34
School Attendance Act, 143

Scotland Yard, 199
Scott Medal, 61, 64, 99, 193, 194
Second World War, 116–18
secret societies, 4, 19
security, 199–200
Sellars, Garda Patrick (Sonny), 33, 38, 39,
    47–8
sergeants, role of, 177–8, 182–3, 188
Serious Crime Squad, 195–6, 197
Severs, Sgt C.G., 81
Shanaghan, Dr Michael, 29–30
Shea, P., 16
Sheahan, Sgt, 99
Sheehan, Patrick, 75–6
Sheehan, Recruit-Garda Peter, 195
Sheehan, Asst Commr Seán, 201
Ship Street depot, 13, 66, 73, 89
Sinn Féin, 9, 11, 20, 23, 56, 68
  Courts, 23
Smith, David, 210–11
Spanish Civil War, 102, 106, 134
Special Armed Unit, 110, 112
Special Branch, 102, 110
sports, 98–9, 113, 161
Stack, Austin, 10, 11, 13, 30, 49
Staines, Garda Jim, 37
Staines, Commr Michael J., 15, 27, 47, 55,
    72, 210–11
  badge, 21
  barracks, 23, 73
  Civil War, 50, 51
  commander, 8–9
  costs of force, 89
  depot, 26
  Dáil election, 1922, 41
  Kildare Mutiny, 32–40
  Kildare Mutiny inquiry, 44–5
  name of force, 19–20, 20
  'People's Guard,' 17–19
  resignation, 36–7, 45, 56–7
  resumes command, 42
  on RIC, 29
  training, 24, 25
Stapleton, Supt Daniel, 198
Stokes Kennedy Crowley, 202–3
store accounting, 90
Store Street station, 169
stress, 154

strikes, 121–2, 138, 190
Sturgis, Sir Mark B., 64
subversion, special crime, 193–6
Sullivan, A.M., 30
Sunday Independent, 186
Sunday Tribune, 211–12
Superintendents' Association. *see* Associations

Taoiseach, Department of the, 114, 159
Tarpey, Edward, 16
Tavistock Institute of Human Relations, 94
teachers, 125, 130, 134–6
Technical Bureau, 25, 160, 198–9
technological change, 207
temperance movement, 85
Tidey, Donald, 195
Tierney, Fr Austin, 101
Tierney, Prof Michael, 107
Tipperary, County, 4, 65, 66
Tobin, Insp Edmund, 60–61
trade unions, 121, 127, 137, 173, 184, 207
traffic laws, 75
training, 25, 35, 216
    conditions of, 25–6
    in England, 161
    initiatives, 166–7
    RDS depot, 22–4
    reorganised, 160–61
    sub-committee report, 24–6
    Templemore, 175
    Walsh Report, 214
Training Centre, Templemore, 184, 187, 192–3, 216
transport, 91
Traynor, Oscar, 110, 113, 146, 153, 155–6, 157
Treacy, Seán, 174
tuberculosis, 98

uniforms, 17–18, 35, 81, 91, 102, 128, 151–2, 214
    Civil War, 51
    RIC, 5

United States of America, 183
Urwick Orr, 176, 180–81, 202

Volunteer Reserve, 116

Wallace, Michael, 163
Walsh, Asst Commr Patrick, 11–14, 17, 27, 66, 107, 166
    declines Commissionership, 134
    deputy to Staines, 15
    Kildare Mutiny, 33, 35, 36, 37, 39, 47, 109
    Kildare Mutiny inquiry, 44, 45–6, 50
    promotion, 86–7
    resented, 28, 32
    resignation, 37
Walsh, Sgt Thomas, 114–15
Walsh, Dr Tom, 216
Walsh, Una, 14
Walsh Report, 214
War of Independence, 15, 18, 34, 46, 52, 53, 80
    and Auxiliaries, 26–7
    disrespect for law, 84
    role of RIC, 5, 28, 31, 32, 92, 106
    spies, 17
Ward, Andrew, 191
Ward, Garda Hugh, 66, 97
Watch Committees, 121
Watchword, 105
Waterford, County, 47, 69–70
Wellington [Griffith] Barracks, 22, 26
Westmeath, County, 13
Wexford, County, 61, 180, 194
Wickham, Colonel, 93
Wicklow, County, 61
Wilson, Sir Henry, 49
women, recruitment of, 160
Wymes, Commr M.J., 185–90, 201

Yeats family, 100